Self-Help
Organizations
and Professional
Practice

Self-Help Organizations and Professional Practice

THOMAS J. POWELL

NATIONAL ASSOCIATION OF SOCIAL WORKERS
Silver Spring, Maryland

Cover and Title Page Design: Janet Koenig
Book Design: Margo Dittmer

Copyright © 1987, National Association of Social Workers, Inc.

Library of Congress Cataloging-in-Publication Data

Powell, Thomas J.
   Self-help organizations and professional practice.

   Bibliography: p.
   Includes index.
   1. Self-help groups—United States.   2. Self-help techniques—United States.   3. Social group work— United States.   I. Title.
HV547.P68   1986   361.7   86-21761
ISBN 0-87101-133-6

Printed in U.S.A.   3

Contents

Foreword

With the publication of Thomas Powell's *Self-Help Organizations and Professional Practice*, the self-help movement arrives at a new stage of development. The book offers a systematic, up-to-date, analytical review of the burgeoning literature in the self-help field, with particularly relevant chapters addressed to the effectiveness of self-help organizations and the relationship between the professional and the self-help unit.

Powell introduces a useful conceptual comparison of the three helping systems: professional, informal helping, and self-help, and offers important suggestions for their greater integration. A basic theme threaded throughout the book is the dialectic interpenetration of the professional and the self-help modes. A dialectic analysis includes both the unity and struggle of opposites. Thus, professional approaches and aprofessional interventions such as self-help and informal help have complementary and antagonistic potential. The rapidly improving cooperative relationship between the professional and the self-help systems should not obscure the contradictions and opposed emphases of the two interventions.

HELP VS. PRACTICE

Understanding the nature of help from a self-help perspective can be contrasted with the professional theory of practice. Professional practice, which is based on systematic knowledge ("objective" and external to the phenomenon), exists in a context in which the help provided is a commodity to be bought, sold, promoted, and marketed. This dimension affects every phase of professional practice—sometimes in the most overt manner and at other times in a highly subtle fashion. But the commercial content of professional practice is something that is always there and is typically ignored.

The help provided by mutual aid groups, in contrast, is free (with *vii* a few exceptions like Weight Watchers), and is generally based on less systematic knowledge and conscious use of methodology. Rather, it is based on indigenous experience, codified experience (like the Twelve Steps of Alcoholics Anonymous [AA]), and wisdom. Furthermore, it is rooted in the experience of people who have the problem and have found methods of giving each other help.

I believe there is a highly useful creative tension (or positive dialectic) between professional practice and mutual help, but this creative tension should not hide the differences or obscure the useful conflict and mutual questioning and criticism. Both systems can benefit most fully from their interactions if they recognize their oppositional and complementary dimensions.

Powell provides a magnificent overview of the data and issues involved in the interaction of the two systems. He observes that professionals frequently have played a major role in establishing voluntary self-help associations. Citing Borman, he notes that professionals were significant in the formative years of ten of the most important self-help organizations.[1] In six of these groups (Recovery, Inc., Integrity, GROW, Compassionate Friends, Parents Anonymous, and Epilepsy Self-Help), they played a key role in the founding.

Powell surveys the findings of other important studies to highlight the perceptions professionals and self-helpers have about each other. It is important to note that self-helpers often express significant dissatisfaction regarding professional practices and attitudes, while still desiring cooperation and cross-referral. And even the most militantly antiprofessional self-help organizations have developed effective relationships with carefully selected professionals.

There is no question that in the last decade, professionals have been far more open to the self-help model, and many local self-help clearinghouses (see Appendix Two) report that professionals make an increasing number of referrals to self-help units. One of the dangers that needs to be carefully considered, however, is the possibility that self-help groups may sometimes serve as dumping grounds for patients and problems less attractive to the professionals who prefer articulate middle-class patients.

Of course, the self-help movement, too, is essentially middle-class and white. Powell is appropriately sensitive to this issue, and among other proposals, he suggests the need for specific minority chapters of groups such as AA.

There are, in fact, a number of self-help groups that have effectively involved low-income and minority populations. The Sisterhood of Black Single Mothers, for example, was initiated in New York City by Daphne Busby, a black single mother. She had attended several meetings of the Mama's group of predominantly white single mothers and concluded that it did not meet black women's diverse needs, which more often are

---

[1] L. D. Borman, "Characteristics of Development and Growth," in M. A. Lieberman and Borman, eds., *Self-Help Groups for Coping with Crisis: Origins, Members, Processes, and Impact* (San Francisco: Jossey-Bass, 1979).

related to basic questions of survival. One of the main goals of the Sisterhood is to remove the stigma of being a single mother. Debtors Anonymous, organized by the National Council of Negro Women, is another self-help group that, while appealing to all classes and groups, has been strongly inclusive of low-income members.

Recently, groups for the unemployed have been developed by the New Jersey and the Minnesota self-help clearinghouses. These groups have great potential, particularly in light of the enormous number of unemployed in this country (over 8 million), even in a period of economic recovery.[2] As these groups take on more of an advocacy orientation, they are likely to have broad appeal.

Powell recognizes the advancing trend in the self-help world toward an advocacy focus concerned with external social change, including legislative measures. Traditionally, self-help groups have not engaged in advocacy. AA has always seen the problem it deals with as residing solely in the alcoholic, not in social conditions. AA does not call for restricting the sale of alcoholic beverages or relieving the social conditions that affect drinkers. Many newer self-help groups, however, such as Disabled in Action, Self-Help for Hard of Hearing People, and the Center for Independent Living, advocate for social change, and some groups have been deeply involved in legislative action.

A prime example is the Association for Retarded Citizens (ARC). Chapters of ARC were started in the early 1950s as parents' self-help groups. At first, the parents shared mutual concerns: "Why did this happen to me?" "This is tearing my family apart." "I feel guilty." Then they started to look at the options for keeping their handicapped children at home. They created and paid for educational programs until the early 1970s, when their lobbying efforts resulted in legislation guaranteeing every child with a handicap a free, appropriate education in the least restrictive environment. While other legislative efforts continue, local ARC chapters keep up with a difficult situation, but the burden they carry has been made less onerous by their social action.

Mothers Against Drunk Drivers (MADD), which now has 400 chapters in 40 states and a mailing list of 600,000, is concerned not simply with mutual support of those who have lost children as a result of drunk drivers. It is also concerned with having impact on legislation and other forms of institutional change.

An advocacy orientation builds directly on the self-help ethos. The ethos includes the following dimensions:

- a noncompetitive, cooperative orientation;
- an anti-elite, antibureaucratic focus;
- an emphasis on the indigenous—people who have the problem and know a lot about it from the inside, from experiencing it;
- an attitude of do what you can, one day at a time. You can't solve everything at once.
- a shared, often revolving leadership;
- an attitude of being helped through helping (the helper-therapy

---

principle). There is no necessary antagonism between altruism and egoism.

- an understanding that helping is not a commodity to be bought and sold;
- a strong optimism regarding the ability to change;
- an understanding that although small may not necessarily be beautiful, it is the place to begin and the unit to build on;
- a critical stance toward professionalism, which is often seen as pretentious, purist, distant, and mystifying. Self-helpers like simplicity and informality.
- an emphasis on the consumer, or, in Alvin Toffler's term, the "prosumer." The consumer is a producer of help and services;
- an understanding that helping is at the center—knowing how to receive help, give help, and help yourself. Self-victimization is antithetical to the ethos;
- an emphasis on empowerment.

EMPOWERMENT

Empowerment, one of the most noteworthy trends of the 1970s and 1980s, is a critical aspect of self-help. When people help themselves—join together to deal with their similar problems, whether these concern mental health or the neighborhood—they feel empowered; they are able to control some aspects of their lives. The help is not given to them from the outside—from an expert, a professional, a politician. The latter forms of help have the danger of building dependence—the direct opposite effect of empowerment. Empowerment increases energy, motivation, and an ability to help that goes beyond helping oneself or receiving help.

In addition, this self-help–induced empowerment may have significant political relevance, because as people are enabled to deal with some aspects of their lives in a competent fashion, the skills and positive feelings they acquire may contagiously spread and empower them to deal with other aspects of their lives. Frequently, the competencies they develop at the smaller or more immediate level can be applied to larger political issues. Most of the significant movements that arose in the past decade are really movements *for* empowerment and *of* empowerment—the consumer movement, the environmental movement, the neighborhood movement, the self-help movement, the tenants' movement, and the movement for the nuclear freeze—all these have arisen from an empowerment constellation.

Overall, Powell's book provides a comprehensive social science conceptualization that pays particular attention to the behavioral processes in self-help. It also presents the issues and the data in a highly readable, down-to-earth style, eminently accessible to a wide audience in the helping professions.

Frank Riessman, *Director*
National Self-Help Clearinghouse
Graduate School and University Center
City University of New York

Acknowledgments

Without self-help organizations, there could be no book. Without the insight and commitment of their members, there would be no reason for one. Lastly, without their generous gifts of time and information, one could not have been written. For these reasons, the author is deeply grateful.

The author is also grateful for the kind assistance of colleagues and self-help leaders who reviewed portions of the book in draft form. The following persons critiqued individual chapters: Barry Checkoway, Robert Farwell, Benjamin Gottlieb, Agnes B. Hatfield, Srinika D. Jayaratne, Leonard L. Lieber, Lambert Maguire, Jeanette M. Powell, Norma L. Radin, David Robinson, Kristine A. Siefert, Donald M. Traunstein, Lynn Videka-Sherman, Paul Wilson, Charles S. Wolfson, and Richard Wollert.

Other colleagues commented on large portions of the manuscript. Major sections of this book reflect the wise comments of Thomasina Borkman, Edward J. Madara, Louis Medvene, Norma Radol Raiff, Frank Riessman, Rubin Todres, and Ronald W. Toseland. Borkman, in particular, made detailed and trenchant comments on the chapters dealing with social science explanations of self-help organizations.

Several persons provided extraordinary support throughout the entire writing period: Alfred H. Katz was warmly encouraging while challenging many of the author's interpretations. The helpfulness of Linda Farris-Kurtz's comments was enhanced by her early replies. Her detailed knowledge, especially of anonymous programs, saved many errors and brought a number of new sources of information to light. Eugene I. Bender gave the entire manuscript a close and critical reading. He noted what was good as well as what was bad; he pointed out where additional data or examples were needed. His many comments resulted in numerous clarifications and his rival hypotheses often led to more precise formulations. Naturally, none of these good people can be held responsible for the book's shortcomings; however, I do hope they will recognize some of their own contributions in the book.

PART ONE

Orientation and Significance

Part One deals with some of the popular misconceptions and misuses of self-help organizations. Self-help organizations are not the result of the bankruptcy of professional services. Professional services continue to play an indispensable role and now, with the upsurge of self-help organizations, are needed more than ever. Self-help organizations have educated their members to become discerning consumers and critics of professional services. In the absence of self-help organizations, professional services have been burdened by expectations that they were ill-equipped to fulfill. It is no criticism of either self-help or professional services to recognize that they can do certain things well and other things not so well or not at all.

What is bankrupt, however, is the policy to substitute self-help services for professional ones. Nothing in self-help implies the elimination or cutting back of professional services.

Yet to say these things is not to gainsay that self-help is an elusive concept. It is sorely in need of better definition. In the minds of some professionals, it sometimes seems perilously close to a variation of professionally facilitated group therapy. The use of the term self-help organization instead of self-help group is meant to signify the boundaries that set it off from professional organizations.[1] Organization also signifies a structure sufficient to maintain itself. The self-help organization does not depend on the professional organization. Now, to be sure, other social entities draw on elements of self-help, and it is important to recognize the gradations of self-help as well as to recognize what it is not.

A different kind of bandwagon effect may also be observed in the varying estimates of the size and coverage of self-help organizations. Many of these estimates may reflect wish as well as actuality. Most of them fail even to consider the serious underenrollment of minorities. In any case, it must be recognized that in the absence of hard data, existing estimates are surrounded by considerable uncertainty. Yet this situation need not be permanent. Already it is impressive that the California Self-Help Center has a database containing information about the 2,000 self-help groups operating in California.[2] Computers will become increasingly important in keeping tabs on the number and size of self-help units. Self-help clearinghouses have already made valuable use of computers in linking potential members with groups.

Part One also addresses the effectiveness question. For if self-help organizations were demonstrably ineffective, there would be little point in writing about them. As it stands and given the developing state of research designs in this area, they have demonstrated a level of effectiveness that is comparable to other social interventions such as psychotherapy. That is to say, they seem to help some members, but it is uncertain which ones will respond to which components of the self-help experience.

The encouraging results of summative evaluation have also stimulated formative evaluation and process research. These latter types of research focus attention on the whys and hows of self-help organizations. Studies aimed at identifying the effective ingredients of self-help are necessary for a balanced program of knowledge development. They will be the source of theories that can be used to mold self-help organizations into even more effective social interventions.

Notes

1. R. H. Hall, *Organizations: Structure and Process* (3rd ed.; Englewood Cliffs, N.J.: Prentice-Hall, 1982), p. 29.
2. E. Fabian and M. Jacobs, "Help Is Just Around the Corner—Self Help, That Is," *Self-Helper: The California Self-Help Quarterly,* 1 (Summer 1985), pp. 3–4.

Some Introductory Points of View

Self-help has arrived; indeed it has burst onto the cultural scene. In *Lost in the Cosmos: The Last Self-Help Book*, Walker Percy asks this ironic question: "How can you survive in the Cosmos about which you know more and more while knowing less and less about yourself, this despite 10,000 self-help books, 100,000 psychotherapists, and 100 million fundamentalist Christians?"[1] Self-help has arrived, but it is, alas, sometimes slightly high on itself and, like other proposed remedies for the human spirit, disposed to make excessive claims. It is sobering to consider that the evangelists of self-help may now do more harm than the doctrinaire human service professionals once did with their old-fashioned condemnations.

Exuberant testimonials need to give way to critical analyses and empirical evaluations. Both the lay and professional publics need to know what self-help methods are like and whether their results justify trying them. Less advantaged self-help programs, however, should not be subjected to standards more exacting than those met by advanced professional programs. It must be understood that few, if any, psychosocial interventions are supported by precise and comprehensive rationales and few, if any, interventions are free from major uncertainties about their efficacy. Like professional interventions, however, it should be possible to demonstrate that at least core members of self-help organizations benefit from their participation in these programs. It should also be possible to understand self-help operations in terms of sensible social science propositions. And last, it should be possible to identify the features of self-help that distinguish it from professional counseling and from the informal "natural" helping of community caregivers. Since self-help is a distinct third system of helping, it is important to know under what conditions the system complements or substitutes for other systems. And if self-help is complementary, it is important to consider how professionals or natural caregivers can collaborate with the system without compromising the integrity of their system or of self-help.

The aim of this book is to address these issues across self-help organizations, which involves analyzing their common structures and processes. Are similar social processes operating across self-help organizations? In what way are the goals of gay rights groups and Parents Without Partners (PWP) similar? In what sense can it be said that such dissimilar-appearing organizations as Recovery, Inc., and Parents Anonymous (PA) utilize similar methods of personal assistance? How do the organizations that are similar in some respects—such as Overeaters Anonymous (OA) and Take Off Pounds Sensibly (TOPS), or to give another example, Alcoholics Anonymous (AA) and Women for Sobriety—differ?

The aim is also to discuss such critical questions as When might it be inadvisable to join a self-help organization? What can be done to improve the poor performance of self-help organizations in serving members of ethnic minority groups? What can be done to avert co-optation by self-helpers or professionals, assuming collaboration is desirable? These questions should suggest the importance of recognizing the shortcomings of self-help organizations and of subjecting their approaches to rigorous analysis. In the end, this orientation is likely to prove most supportive of self-help approaches. The reader is encouraged to be on the alert for the author's lapses from this standard.

MISCONCEPTIONS AND
MISUSES OF SELF-HELP

Some misconceptions of self-help organizations seem purposeful. Self-help is not a solitary "pulling-up" activity. Although self-help members probably know a good deal about pulling up, they, like the rest of us, may have difficulty finding "bootstraps" on modern-day footwear. Basically self-help involves social transactions, the exchange of mutual aid, and the mobilization of outside community resources.

Thus, it is also a misconception that being for self-help means being against professional services. Indeed, the available evidence indicates just the opposite: Self-help organizations have stimulated the growth of professionally sponsored programs. One must expect, however, that this relationship will be beyond the grasp of certain politicians who ally themselves with self-help and who use "self-help" as a code word for dismantling social welfare programs. Their inability to understand is politically motivated. Unfortunately, this calculating use of the term self-help twists the truth. It directly opposes the strong sense of social responsibility and support for human services found among self-help organizations.

Others twist the truth in another direction, as if to suggest that personal deficiencies are the root causes of human problems. If the individual were sufficient cause of the problem, self-help organizations would have little interest in shaping public policy. Just the opposite is true, however, and the relationship is even clearer when the work of groups informally affiliated with self-help organizations is considered. For example, the National Council on Compulsive Gambling, which draws many of its members from Gamblers Anonymous (GA), has a vigorous program to educate the public about casino gambling.

SELF-HELP–PROFESSIONAL RELATIONSHIPS

Stimulating Professional Services Growth

Through self-help experiences, many people have become more aware of professional services and more inclined to seek them out. Simultaneously, many people have become involved in lobbying to increase the availability of services, as reflected in the growth of services for compulsive gamblers in states where GA is strong (New York, Connecticut, and Maryland). It is also reflected in the National Alliance for the Mentally Ill (NAMI), which has become a vigorous, effective lobbyist at state and federal levels for the development of services for the chronically mentally ill. Some idea of how self-help stimulates the development of professional services can be inferred from two studies with quite different methodologies. The first study, which involved intensive interviews of 30 members of several PA chapters, shows how self-help can foster favorable attitudes toward professionals. The second, a large-scale study of AA members, suggests that an enormous demand for professional services can be created by self-help organizations.

Members of PA felt that they were encouraged to use professional services.[2] And when they used these services, they found them complementary. According to these members, professional counseling contributed greatly to the resolution of their problems. Therapy, on the one hand, was primarily helpful in illuminating the dynamic factors contributing to their difficulties. Parents Anonymous, on the other hand, was better able to support them in such difficult decisions as voluntarily continuing a child in foster care. And PA was also especially effective in helping them maintain their "cool" under stress, for example, trying to get a meal ready with whiny children underfoot. These parents felt that PA helped improve their immediate performance as parents, but they also gave therapy high marks for helping them deal with more subtle problems related to their expectations and beliefs. Some also mentioned the advantages of the combination of self-help and professional services. Interestingly, they felt that PA compelled them to be more honest about their commitment (or lack thereof) to therapy. As a result of their PA experience, they were less likely to deceive themselves by "going through the motions." And even those parents who were not in concurrent, outside therapy said they were thinking about entering it. Many indicated they would start when they left PA. The generally positive attitudes toward professional therapy seemed less the result of exhortation and more the result of the example set by the professional PA sponsor and the other members.

The heavy traffic between self-help organizations and professional services can be seen in the results of the other study: the fourth triennial Survey of Alcoholics Anonymous.[3] Some 26 percent of the 25,000 respondents cited counseling or rehabilitation services as a factor in their joining AA; 53 percent had outside assistance before joining AA; and another 40 percent sought such assistance after joining. The latter percentage suggests that many individuals are led to professional services through self-help experiences. The dynamic is often reciprocal: As professionals send more referrals, they receive more—and so it goes in a beneficent cycle until a stable plateau is reached. It seems reasonable to suppose that this pattern may also obtain between other self-help organizations and professionals.[4]

The importance of the self-help constituency for professional services has not been lost on officialdom. The National Institute on Alcohol Abuse and Alcoholism (NIAAA) has noted the parallels between the growth of AA and public expenditures for the treatment of alcoholism. During a 12-year period in which AA grew some 350 percent, the number of professional treatment programs shot up by 4,600 percent.[5]

8   A similar pattern of mutually reinforcing growth can be seen

in the relationship between PA and the public child welfare sector. During the 1970s, PA received major funding from the Office of Human Development in the then Department of Health, Education and Welfare to expand its state and local chapter network. Throughout much of this period, PA also benefited from the promotional efforts of the National Committee for the Prevention of Child Abuse. Not surprisingly, these developments were paralleled by an enormous growth in tax-supported, professionally sponsored protective services.

Challenging Professional Services

Self-help organizations not only increase demand, they also call attention to the strengths and weaknesses of professional services. Based on her experiences with self-help groups for incest victims, Herman comments on their advantages:

> First of all, most self-help groups are free and therefore available to many more people than psychotherapy is. Second, such groups foster a sense of health and competence, because participants do not identify themselves as patients in need of treatment. Third, since incest victims run such a high risk of insensitive or destructive treatment in the traditional mental health system, a self-help group may offer a safer and more therapeutic environment than the available professional services. The victim may find more comfort, understanding, and emotional support with her peers than in a therapist's office. Finally, self-help groups, in contrast to psychotherapy, develop a social analysis of personal problems, and sometimes offer the opportunity of collective action. Self-help groups have campaigned actively to increase public awareness of sexual abuse and to reform public institutions.[6]

Herman later notes that professional help is needed when complications (threats of suicide, substance abuse, and extreme distress) are present. Had she not added this, she might have gone over to the ranks of those overly zealous human service professionals, who, in their attempts to be "supportive," end up depreciating professional services. Often such professionals end up discrediting self-help, as well. Even the casual observer can see the problems of self-help: the desultory and eccentric activities; the leadership struggles; and the lack of resources that, in varying degrees, beset such organizations. Under these circumstances, the fair-minded observer will conclude that self-help services are not always superior to professional services.[7] Yet the larger dangers, which Gartner and Riessman enumerate, need not become realities if the advice of these two professionals is also followed: *9*

It may substitute self-help for system change—that is, it may reduce the responsibility of the system; it may fragment the forces working toward change; it may foster privatism—turning people inward, diverting them from social causation and social action; it may impose a middle-class self-help mode on low income populations; it may be co-opted by professionals and their agencies; it may foster dependence, it may impose new authoritarian orthodoxies; it may constrain against systematic evaluation; it may provoke strong anti-professional biases preventing a useful integration of the aprofessional and professional approaches; and it may stigmatize and blame the victim. Moreover, it may enhance the romantic belief that small group approaches are the essence of social change, that small alone is beautiful, and decentralization is the only way to change society. These dangers need not become realities, provided the self-help approach is not viewed as a cure-all for our deep societal problems, but rather one element in a strategy directed toward large-scale—ideologically based structural change.[8]

Misusing Self-Help

Well-intentioned, naïve professionals often threaten the integrity of self-help by embracing it too quickly and too fully. Sometimes they are too eager to start a "self-help group." They would, however, be better advised to consider whether existing self-help approaches could meet or could be adapted to meet the present need. Frequently professionals could make a more significant contribution if they encouraged the formation of a new chapter of an existing self-help organization rather than starting "one of their own." Existing self-help organizations often can facilitate their efforts with a chapter development packet. These packet guidelines distill the experience of many years in many communities. In addition, the national coordinating office or the central service office often will be regarded as a continuing resource. Professionals who rush to become involved with self-help without taking advantage of these resources are often either naïve or presumptuous.

But the misuse and misinterpretation of self-help is not a monopoly of professionals. Self-help leaders have misused their organizations to excoriate professionals. Their lashing out may have some value in deflecting attention from the internal problems of self-help organizations. But in the end, the maneuver is counterproductive, especially when it blocks the use of professional services by members. Moreover, the self-help organization does not escape unscathed when disturbed individuals are in distress.

Contributions of Professionals

Apart from their good or bad effects, diatribes against professionals are simply diatribes. They are contradicted by verified findings that professionals have been instrumental, though often behind the scenes, in the formative periods of self-help organizations. Independent studies by Borman and by Toseland and Hacker found that professionals contributed to the design and the early development of many self-help organizations.[9] Moreover, professionals were available when the founders needed support and technical assistance. The early leadership by professionals gave way to a more informal linking as the various organizations matured.[10]

Leonard Lieber, a social worker who initiated PA with its founder, Jolly K., is one of a significant number of professionals who have helped develop autonomous self-help organizations. Lieber, until his resignation in 1986, was a major factor in PA's impressive growth. The late psychologist O. Hobart Mowrer started Integrity Groups. He held, counter to the prevailing professional belief, that guilt usually signified a wrongdoing for which one should make amends. Besides nurturing Integrity, Mowrer strongly supported GROW in its early days in Illinois. In the 1930s, the much-revered psychiatrist Abraham Low founded and directed Recovery, Inc. About the same time, the beloved founder of AA, Bill W., sought frequent counsel from two physician friends, Harry Tiebout and William Silkworth, about the development of AA.[11] In their day, these pioneers were mavericks in their professions, but the climate has changed a great deal since those times.

In an earlier day, it was necessary to take on the biased professionals who belittled self-help, but now it may also be necessary to take on those persons who are too eager to blur the lines between professional and self-help services. It is not a proposition that holds equally for all organizations, however. Some organizations, such as consumer and liberation groups in the mental health area, allow very little professional participation, whereas other organizations, such as those dealing with physical conditions, welcome the regular participation of professionals. Thus, all generalizations must be adjusted to the circumstances of particular organizations. The category *self-help organization* is heterogeneous, and most generalizations are subject to numerous exceptions, given the great diversity among these organizations. This may be a good place to spell out what is included (and what is not included) in the term self-help organizations as used in this book.

CONSIDERATIONS IN DEFINING SELF-HELP

It is up to self-help organization members, not to outsiders, to decide what is to be called "self-help" and what is not. Only the members of Weight Watchers, for example, can decide whether their organization is a self-help organization. This suggests that a definition should evolve only after much inductive study. The primary approach should be to ask people affiliated with all kinds of organizations whether they consider them self-help organizations. Even this approach is insufficient, since such organizations as Welfare Rights may have significant latent self-help functions. Nonetheless, the decision about whether an organization is a self-help one should be based on input from those who have experienced it. The data should be carefully studied to determine the criteria these "experts" or experienced respondents use to define the term self-help.

One can also proceed from the opposite direction, but deductive definitions risk leaving out organizations that would be included by more valid criteria, that is, criteria based on experience. The deductive approach not only prematurely forces an answer to the definitional question by determining who is in or out, it also introduces a circularity into the analysis: Organizations are chosen by certain criteria—for example, they locate the problem in the individual rather than in society—and then it is "discovered" that self-help procedures rely heavily on personal assessment and control strategies. The inductive approach allows for a more independent assessment of the correlates of what is being defined. For example, if a participant defines an organization as self-help, it can be independently observed if this definition is related to a perception of the problem as residing within the individual or within society. The inductive approach, moreover, facilitates the refinement of definitional criteria after each wave of data collection. Then the definition should be based on empirical investigations of the criteria used by the participants to define self-help. In the process, these studies should shed light on the relative importance of the factors defining self-help.

These considerations notwithstanding, it is necessary to explicate what is being referred to by the term self-help organization. But this is not simple, and hence, over the next several pages, what is included, what is not, and what is somewhere in between are discussed. To begin with, the self-help organization must address people with personal difficulties. A large variety of difficulties are covered, as self-help members may be troubled by (1) problems (excessive anxiety, abusive tendencies), (2) conditions (obesity, deafness), (3) discrimination (homosexuality, advanced age). (4) difficult situations (single parenthood, loss of a child), and (5) physical illness (emphysema, sickle cell anemia). Not every organization calling itself self-help meets these criteria, however.

What Self-Help Is Not

The term self-help is often used in conjunction with a number of social organizations that, at most, are peripheral to this discussion. Some cooperatives designed to produce or distribute such commodities as food, housing, or child care have been designated self-help. Though this usage has a rich tradition, it differs from what is being referred to here, primarily because their concern is with economic reform and community development.

Foundations engaged in research and public policy work in relation to certain diseases [e.g., the Muscular Dystrophy Association and the National Foundation to Combat Birth Defects (The March of Dimes)] sometimes call themselves self-help organizations. Though many of them had their origins in mutual aid and direct specialized assistance, these foundations now serve their constituencies primarily through their involvement with research scientists, legislators, scientific policymakers, health care executives, and the like.[12] Any remaining direct assistance and mutual aid activities are decidedly secondary. In self-help organizations, the priorities are reversed.

Books aiming to help people cope with difficulties constitute a rather formidable self-help literature. Their popularity—and they are the largest single category on best-seller lists—suggests that they deal with less serious difficulties than those addressed by self-help organizations. In any case, these books are not considered as part of the phenomenon studied here because they are used in a solitary manner rather than as part of a larger social activity.[13] Social interaction, especially in the form of personal disclosure and the exchange of mutual aid with others, is an indispensable component of self-help organizations. When the social interaction criterion is applied to the health field, *self-care* is *self-help* only insofar as it involves other people in the mutual exchange of care. Notwithstanding these limitations, self-care and books often play an important role in self-help organizations. The literature of self-help organizations, in particular, serves to develop and maintain the self-help culture. The production of brochures, newsletters, manuals, and inspirational essays creates valuable opportunities for members to work together. These products enrich the self-help experience when they are incorporated into organizational ritual and used for group and private study. Many are attractive emblems of the detailed programs.   *13*

Degrees of Self-Help

Agency-sponsored support groups are sometimes called self-help groups. Their range of activities, however, is narrower than that of self-help organizations, and their members are active for shorter periods because of their dependence and marginality with respect to the professional agency.[14] Also, agency support groups are more apt to employ professionals as leaders or facilitators, which truncates the self-help experience. Thus, the practice of calling agency support groups self-help groups contributes to terminological confusion and fails to distinguish among degrees of self-help. Under some circumstances, of course, agency hybrid forms can be exceptionally effective. They will be discussed in the next chapter, but under typical circumstances, support groups within agencies are a weak form of self-help.

Groups that stand free of agencies tend to be higher in the scale of potential autonomy and integrity as self-help forms, even though they are not connected with other self-help groups—mainly because their activities are neither compromised by, nor dependent on, professionals and their organizations. But still these groups, on average, tend to be less robust than the local chapters of national organizations, which receive regular support (including printed materials) from their national office and other chapters. Consequently, the helping methods of the freestanding group tend to be more ad hoc than those of the organization. The lower level of standardization also makes it more difficult to generalize.

Self-Help by Different Names

Some organizations do not use—and may even disavow—the label self-help, even though they perform important self-help functions. These organizations include those that combine political and personal assistance interests. The National Welfare Rights Organization, for example, combines direct assistance with a vigorous social action program. The Association of Retarded Citizens, the National Organization for Women (NOW), and the Gray Panthers have also combined personal development and social action in various ways, depending on time and place. Notwithstanding the earlier comments about having participants decide what is self-help, organizations should be judged not on the basis of what they say but rather on what they do; thus latent functions must be considered along with manifest ones. By these lights, Fathers for Equal Rights and the affiliates of the National Gay and Lesbian Task Force have significant personal assistance functions in conjunction with their social change activities.

Nor does eligibility depend on whether organizations use the term *self-help* or the term *mutual aid*. These terms are often used synonymously, though they may have somewhat different shades of meaning. Mutual aid stresses the exchange of assistance, whereas self-help stresses its role as an alternative or a distinct complement to professionally sponsored assistance programs. Some support for this assertion lies in the apparent tendency of groups using the label mutual aid to admit professionals as participants. Some prefer the more exact term mutual aid and self-help organizations or groups, but this mouthful will not be accepted in everyday use, and the acronym—MASH—is not very appealing.[15] This writer prefers the term self-help because it highlights what is arguably its most distinctive property and presumably its most powerful dynamic. The term mutual aid, however, may admit more backsliding toward conventional, professionally led groups, for mutual aid is not always seen as operating in self-help groups.

Necessity of Face-to-Face Interaction

Self-help organizations, no less than agency support groups and freestanding self-help groups, are social forms within which primary social interaction takes place. Self-help organizations differ only in that the face-to-face interaction is more formally structured because it is more highly developed. Other things being equal, its more formal norms and procedures should enhance rather than diminish such interactions. And even if this point were arguable, it must be remembered that the formal design regulates only some, not all, of the organization's activities, and then only to a degree. There should be no doubt: Ad hoc personal and situational factors are major influences in most of what local chapters do. It also must be remembered that organization does not imply steep leadership hierarchies or professionalization. Borman's study of major self-help organizations showed that organizational forms are compatible with decentralized decision making and member control:

> None of the ten groups discussed here has followed the path of the handicapped groups described in an early work by Katz (1970)—that is to say, they did not evolve into professionally run associations with founding members relieved of most responsibilities. In a later publication, Katz (1976, p. 122) also found the latter stages of his original model—the emergence of leadership, the beginnings of formal organization, and the beginnings of professionalism—do not universally occur among self-help groups.[16]

The local chapter is strong because it is one of a series of units linked to the regional or national coordinating office of the organization. Through this linking, the local chapter can enhance its stability and vitality. Policies and procedures are available to deal with such recurrent concerns as eligibility for membership, qualifications for leadership, the appropriateness of problem-solving methods, and the resolution of conflicts. These linkages enhance the identity of the local chapters and protect them from the encroachment of other organizations, especially those providing professional assistance, which could limit their independence and curtail opportunities for development

Illustrative Organizations

Some examples of self-help organizations are Alcoholics Anonymous, Women for Sobriety, Parents Anonymous, Overeaters Anonymous, Parents Without Partners, Recovery, Inc., National Gay and Lesbian Task Force, National Alliance for the Mentally Ill, Network Against Psychiatric Assault, Gamblers Anonymous, Mended Hearts, Stroke Clubs, Reach to Recovery, Take Off Pounds Sensibly, Emotions Anonymous, Toughlove, Families Anonymous, Al-Anon, The Compassionate Friends, Candlelighters, Narcotics Anonymous, and Make Today Count. The brochures of many of these organizations are reproduced in a useful monograph by Gartner and Riessman.[17] From it, one can obtain more information about self-help organizations that may be available in local communities. And if they are not available, it is a good time to begin thinking about the self-help organizations that should be available.

SIZE AND SCOPE OF SELF-HELP ORGANIZATIONS

Flaws of Global Estimates

In an ideal world, estimates of the magnitude of self-help organizations would be deferred until data were available to support them. But in the real world, promotional interests will not be restrained by unresolved problems of definition and missing data. The result is that estimates are based on vague, all-encompassing definitions and "best case" interpretations of scant data. Consequently, the figures are crude and probably inflated estimates of the magnitude of self-help. These problems are compounded when early estimates are used as the base for the next, ostensibly independent estimate. Nor can the fundamental problems of definition and data be eliminated by the gloss of scientific methodology. Mind, too, that similar estimates do not assure validity; in fact, they assure just the opposite unless the estimators state that they are using the same criteria.

These problems cannot be eliminated by even the most objective estimator. Thus, the estimates below raise a number of questions. The questions should also lessen the desire to boast about numbers, lest these conjectures come back to embarrass self-help. In 1976, Katz and Bender estimated that some 500,000 local self-help chapters had ten million enrolled members.[18] In 1981, Katz called these figures "outmoded" and listed other organizations previously not included, such as Weight Watchers, with over two million members.[19] In 1982, he updated the original estimate to 15 million members said to be enrolled in 750,000 self-help groups throughout the United States and Canada.[20] These figures, however, are extrapolations from the still unsubstantiated earlier figures. The Task Panel of the President's Commission on Mental Health (1978) pegged the total number at ten million, noting some 1,300 chapters of the Association for Retarded Citizens alone, an organization that might not have been included in other estimates.[21] Looking for additional support, the Task Panel cited a study that found 180 self-help groups in a two-county New York State area. However, how this finding and the global estimate were related was not discussed. Another source, estimating the narrower category of psychological and physical self-help groups, put the figure at more than ten million members but offered no evidence.[22]

These estimates are obviously not independent and are kept alive by repeated assertion. Nonetheless, the substantial size of many of the individual organizations (e.g., AA and PWP) is sufficient to address any doubts about the magnitude of the self-help movement. All this suggests that any inclination to produce another set of inadequately supported estimates quickly should be discouraged. What is needed, rather, is a painstaking effort to collect information from participants about which organizations function as self-help organizations. With this information, it would then be possible to mark the boundaries that separate self-help from such other phenomena as self-care or foundation-related activities. This presupposes that the organizations within the self-help boundaries could be enumerated. The next step would be to count the members within a sample of these organizations. If sound sampling and statistical estimation procedures were employed, the resulting estimate would be one that people could stand behind. The bottom line, however, is that well- *17* trained personnel with adequate time must be paid to verify membership, to eliminate duplicate counts, and to estimate values for missing data. These requisites cannot be met as part of a "quick and dirty" global estimate. Thus, a moratorium should be declared on further "estimates" until some granter can be persuaded to provide the funds necessary to collect the data. In the meantime, there is no great shame in acknowledging that political interests have influenced current global estimates.

Political points may still be made with these estimates, provided they are recognized as estimates. For example, it is interesting to compare the number of service episodes offered by the organized mental health system with the admittedly rough estimates of self-help activity. The National Institute of Mental Health's Office of Biometry reported that 6.5 million episodes of service were offered in the public sector (excluding services of private practitioners) in the peak service year of 1977. Thus, if self-help members (using the ten million figure for this purpose) attended only one meeting a year, the number of self-help service episodes would have exceeded the total number of services offered by the public specialty delivery system.[23] For a number of reasons, however, including the absence of information about the similarity or dissimilarity of self-help members and clients, the comparison must not be pushed too far. Nonetheless, it could indicate that this is an important area to look into.

Usefulness of Specific Estimates

Some of the concerns about the validity of global estimates either do not apply or are of less importance in the membership estimates of particular self-help organizations. The figures for individual organizations are often based on a partial count of members or chapters and only sometimes on a complete census. Unlike the global estimators, many of whom are not members of individual self-help organizations, the leaders of specific organizations tend to be quite cautious about how they collect and interpret data on their organizations. Witness this excerpt from a letter from Emotions Anonymous:

> Because we are an Anonymous program, we do not gather information from our members. I *can* tell you that, at the moment, we offer over 1,000 active chapters worldwide, in 18 countries.[24]

Hence, a few figures should be sufficient to eliminate any doubt about the significance of self-help organizations. For example, AA counts over 585,823 members in the United States and 69,931 in Canada as of 1984.[25] The worldwide figure exceeds 1.1 million.

Other organizations, such as PWP and OA, report over 100,000 members. The NAMI has more than 645 affiliate groups, with more than 35,000 members. Numerous organizations estimate their memberships in the thousands, based on partial counts of chapters and members. Some of them are Parents Anonymous, Recovery, Inc., Emotions Anonymous, GROW, United Ostomy Association, The Compassionate Friends, and La Leche League. Because of their size, stability, and maturity, these middle-sized organizations have developed detailed, comprehensive programs. Yet the market for these organizations has scarcely been tapped. They only await people to seed them in other communities.

Scope

The broad range of problems, conditions, situations, and diseases covered is one of the great strengths of the self-help movement. The movement's comprehensiveness is also evident in particular sectors, such as health. The major chronic diseases, as defined by the World Health Organization, are represented by rapidly growing self-help organizations, including Emphysema Anonymous, Mended Hearts (heart surgery), Stroke Clubs, Ostomy Clubs, the International Association of Laryngectomees, and the Reach to Recovery program (mastectomy).[26] Apart from its extent, the self-help model created by the chronically physically ill and related health care professionals should be studied by workers in other fields. Its routine use of experiential wisdom and pragmatic assistance in rehabilitation programs could well be emulated by other human service sectors.[27]

Self-help organizations are also organized according to the stages of human development. The young are served by Alateen and PA; the elderly are served by the Gray Panthers. At key transition times (birth, breast feeding, divorce, and death), support is available from such organizations as Lamaze, La Leche League, Parents Without Partners, and Widow to Widow programs.

Other distressful conditions addressed by self-help organizations include chemical dependency (Pills Anonymous), disturbing emotions (Emotions Anonymous), organized prejudice (National Gay and Lesbian Task Force), and troubling relations with people who have difficulties (NAMI). Thus, most individuals have a number of self-help organizations they could join. For example, a particular individual might define his or her difficulty as a personal problem (PA), a developmental stage (PWP), a personal characteristic that evokes bias (National Gay and Lesbian Task Force), a disturbing habit (TOPS), a health condition (Diabetic Self-Help), or a relationship with a troubled significant *19* other (Al-Anon, Alateen). Moreover, within specific self-help organizations, additional services are available to fit particular circumstances. In GA, for example, some members may be working on "compulsive" personality tendencies, whereas others may be primarily concerned with resisting the urge to gamble. In a middle range, a large number may be thinking about how to repair relations injured by gambling.

How, then, are the magnitude and the scope of self-help organizations summed up? Is the glass half full or half empty? On the one hand, it is encouraging that there are self-help organizations for nearly every conceivable personal problem or problematic life situation somewhere in North America, and in many places overseas. On the other hand, it is discouraging that most organizations, except for a few, such as AA, do not have local chapters in many moderately sized communities and have too few chapters in most urban areas. This is true despite a population base large enough to support additional chapters. All that is needed (and this is not to say that they are easy to obtain) are enough residents to develop and sustain chapters.

Advantages of Organizations

When there is a choice, well-developed organizational forms should be given preference over agency-dependent support groups and one-of-a-kind, underdeveloped self-help groups. This is because the fledgling forms, the support group and the isolated self-help group, on average, offer fewer opportunities for social support. Fledgling groups are less well known and therefore less accessible to the general population. These once-a-week or once-a-month groups also provide fewer opportunities between meetings for members to participate in the meetings of other chapters. The size and composition of the mutual aid network are more limited; bibliographical materials are rudimentary or nonexistent. Compared with full-fledged self-help organizations, they have fewer resources and are less developed, though some day they may become self-help organizations. Self-help organizations are also likely to prove more durable. For though some chapters of an organization may be discontinued, the percentage is likely to be smaller than in groups started without a tested design to build on. The vulnerability of newly formed groups can be compared to the 50 percent failure rate for new businesses in one year: After four years, only 30 percent of such groups are in operation.[28] Some of the organizations are featured in this book because their names are well known and their approaches more widely understood. Thus, discussions of some of the more popular self-help organizations refer to widely shared concrete images. This option is not available in a discussion of one-of-a-kind local groups. It is the difference between talking about McDonald's and about neighborhood hamburger stands. But it is also talking about self-help franchises in which the quality is also apt to be superior.

Similarly, if there is a choice of which group to interact with, preference should be given to more robust affiliates of national organizations rather than to less well-developed local groups. When neither is available, it is better to begin a local chapter of an existing self-help organization than to start a support group. If a new *support or self-help group* is the only option, development along the lines of an organizational model rather than a support-group model should be encouraged.

MINORITIES AND SELF-HELP ORGANIZATIONS

Self-help organizations have an abysmal track record with members of minority groups. In the main, their programs reflect the cultural symbols and practices of the majority. Not surprisingly, they underenroll minorities. The problem is a serious one, and it may become worse with the growing number of minority group members in society. Thus, the ability to resolve this problem may well indicate the future vitality of self-help organizations. It can be argued that minorities per se are not a concern of self-help organizations or, at any rate, a concern they can do much about. Since self-help organizations are fellowships of individuals, there are no corporate boards to issue directives about minorities. Individuals, however, can be encouraged to raise their own consciousness about minority issues. Positive initiatives concerning minority groups can be featured in house publications. Individuals and informal subgroups can be encouraged to take action. But as an introduction to some of the actions that might be taken, it is useful to examine some of the explanations given for the low rates of participation by minority groups in self-help organizations.

The extensive use of informal help in the black and the Hispanic communities has been cited as a reason for lower participation in professional service programs as well as in self-help organizations. Natural neighborhood or community caregivers are said to provide the equivalent of, or better assistance than, the more formal self-help and professional-help systems. No doubt valuable informal help is available from caregivers based in such indigenous institutions as the church and the neighborhood. These resources should be cultivated even more in the minority com- *21* munity. They can complement the use of self-help and professional services. However, it is no slight to these resources to assert that, even under the best of circumstances, they are unlikely to compensate minority group members for their underuse of formal self-help and professional-help systems. Minorities must not be restricted to fewer helping systems. Self-help organizations and professional human service organizations must face this issue.

Some observers have been inclined to attribute the low rate of minority group participation to the fact that their members are not "joiners."[29] This indicates, however, that the problem is a personal disinclination to participate, not the structure of the available organizations. It would be more productive to balance this hypothesis with one based on such criteria as relevance and welcome. When organizations, such as the black church, have met these criteria, minorities have shown a strong inclination to join. The problem is that minorities do not feel welcomed by many self-help organizations. To change this feeling, self-help organizations must respond more adequately to the cultural distinctiveness of minority groups.

One approach might be to dedicate particular chapters of such organizations as AA to minority groups. This is consonant with the practice of dedicating chapters to other culturally homogeneous but privileged and largely white groups, such as businessmen and health care professionals. Some promising initiatives along these lines have been taken, though they have been small and are not sufficiently noticed. Black and gay chapters have existed within AA for some time, but they enroll only a fraction of the minority persons who could benefit from them.

In dealing with the parallel problem of a lack of sensitivity to women alcoholics Jean Kirkpatrick took a more radical approach. She founded Women for Sobriety, with the express intent of making it more responsive than AA to the needs of women. With admirable candor, however, she happily acknowledges that many members of this rapidly growing self-help organization continue to participate in AA and find the combination helpful.[30] Others have modified the format of meetings to decrease AA's emphasis on middle-class verbal skills.[31] In her studies of special AA chapters for the elderly, Borkman observed that special meetings supplemented but did not substitute for general meetings.[32] Like many of the members of Women for Sobriety, the elderly did not drop their general AA meetings. Perhaps these modest experiments point to the possibility of combining the relevance of a homogeneous chapter with the advantages of a broadly inclusive organization.

22   Other experiences also support the idea of creating culturally

distinct chapters within self-help organizations. In their study of AA chapters in the New York area, Lofland and LeJeune found considerable heterogeneity across chapters but considerable homogeneity within individual chapters.[33] A number of observers have described viable chapters dedicated to particular ethnic groups. Gordon described how AA chapters were developed for three Hispanic groups: Dominican, Guatemalan, and Puerto Rican.[34] Several AA chapters have operated successfully among American Indians. Maguire, a social worker, participated in the development of an AA meeting on the Pine Ridge Indian Reservation by helping secure a meeting place, by referring potential members, and by supporting them in the community.[35] The Coast Salish Indians[36] and the Passamaquoddy Indians[37] have also established successful AA chapters, despite the questions that have been raised about the viability of this strategy. Levy and Kunitz, for example, have questioned whether the AA conception of alcoholism as a disease is compatible with the Navajo world view.[38] Whitely goes further in questioning the generalizability of the AA program, since, in his view, its basic paradigm is that of a Methodist Class Meeting.[39] Most of these important questions, however, fail to consider the flexibility of the AA format, specifically, the potential of the group to accommodate the diversity of barrio and Baptist meeting styles.

In short, the establishment of culturally homogeneous local chapters could be pursued more vigorously. Minority members in currently mixed or majority-oriented groups could be encouraged to form minority-oriented groups.[40] And a higher priority could be attached to forming culturally distinctive, homogeneous chapters. This strategy may be necessary to achieve an organization representative of the great variety of people who could benefit from participation in it. The experience of another minority group supports the move in this direction. Humm has observed that the gay movement seems to thrive on separate groups for blacks, fathers, mothers, teachers, and Catholics, as well as for people with a variety of political affiliations.[41] Another approach might be to develop forums on ethnic self-help groups as did the New Jersey Self-Help Clearinghouse in June 1986. The forum conducted in Spanish had self-help leaders talking about their experiences in Hispanic communities. At the same time, it must be understood that changes in self-help organizations alone will not resolve these problems, since self-help organizations are, after all, only a microcosm of the larger society. Minorities will "join" general voluntary organizations as the organizations and the larger society become less racist and more sensitive to the special needs of these members.

PLAN OF THIS BOOK

Part One defines and assesses the field of self-help organizations. This first chapter of Part One establishes a context for the examination of self-help organizations. This context will be elaborated in the second chapter, as empirical assessments of the effectiveness of self-help organizations are reviewed.

Part Two conceptualizes the basic processes of self-help organizations in social science terms. Each chapter in Part Two explains how self-help organizations work from a particular social science point of view. Self-help organizations will be considered (1) as complex organizations that elicit commitment and develop social skills, (2) as reference groups that inculcate new values and standards of self-evaluation, (3) as social networks that increase resources, and (4) as vehicles that promote social learning and reinforce more effective, more satisfying behaviors.

Part Three compares the framework of such organizations with the framework of other help-giving systems. In Part Three, the other two major systems available to help seekers are examined. Chapter Seven compares the benefits available from self-help organizations with those available from informal caregivers in natural community settings. Chapter Eight contrasts self-help with psychotherapy and counseling systems. In both chapters, the similarities and differences between the assistance available from these systems and the assistance available from the self-help system are analyzed. These chapters set the stage for thinking about how the three systems might enhance one another or, when they are poorly articulated, counteract one another.

Part Four sets forth a typology of self-help organizations based in part on a differential use of the social science processes discussed in Part Three. Part Four is a taxonomy of the major types of self-help organizations. Chapter Nine analyzes habit disturbance organizations, organizations in which members have smoking, drinking, and eating problems. Chapter Ten examines general purpose organizations, so called because of their concern with the human problems that find expression in anxiety, hostility, grief, and depression. The overlapping coverage of problems by these organizations means that a particular individual may be able to have his or her needs met from such apparently diverse organizations as Recovery, Inc., Parents Anonymous, and Emotions Anonymous. Chapter Eleven deals with organizations that help support people in difficult situations, whether the situation is the result of transition, a variant lifestyle, or discrimination. This chapter points up, for example, the concerns single parents and gays have in common, as they strive to protect their rights and uphold the dignity of their lifestyles. Chapter Twelve examines organizations designed for parents, relatives, and significant others of those who are troubled by long-term substance abuse, mental disorder, or developmental disability. Members of these organizations often have two goals: improved services for their relatives and relief and protection for themselves. The fifth and last type of organization includes the numerous types—associated with physical conditions—that offer information and support to the growing numbers of people with chronic diseases.

Much of this work culminates in Part Five, which takes as its broad topic relations between human service professionals and self-help organizations. These relations can be divided into three categories. Chapter Fourteen discusses the development of a pattern of mutual referral between self-help organizations and professionals. Chapter Fifteen discusses consultations between professionals and self-help leaders. And Chapter Sixteen, the final chapter, highlights the opportunities for technical assistance exchanges between professionals and self-help organizations.

Forms of Exposition

The reader will find description, analysis, and prescription throughout the book. Each expository form calls for a different critical perspective. When description is primary, the question is whether it is reasonably complete and accurate. Since descriptions (or observations) are the data of the analysis, readers may disagree with the analysis because they are familiar with a different set of observations. To analyze is to explain how things work, and the value of analysis depends on the extent to which it enhances readers' understanding of their own knowledge of and interaction with self-help organizations. Analysis, it is hoped, will also help resolve some of the problems that emerge as readers become engaged with self-help. It is hoped that the concepts that have been chosen as the tools for this analysis will provide a meaningful framework for understanding self-help events and actions.

When possible problem-solving measures are discussed, the exposition tends to become prescriptive. Prescription involves recommending an action to resolve some self-help problem or to achieve some objective. Toward this end, a number of prescriptions will be recommended to self-help leaders, relevant professionals, and others with self-help interests. It should be understood, however, that the writer is not comfortable with the term prescription. Its use is tolerable only if it is qualified according to the following criteria: When a prescription is offered, it does not imply that other, more important changes could not be made. *25*

Recommendations, moreover, should be understood as qualified by the amount of confidence attached to them; some are merely hunches. Most recommendations should be understood as ideas to be explored or actions to be undertaken. Only once in a while should a recommendation be considered as something that definitely needs doing. But however much confidence is attached, it must always be assumed that the prescription should be adjusted, tested for applicability, and refined by actual practice with a particular self-help organization.

Summing Up

When possible, the writer has drawn on social science concepts and research findings. For readers who would like to expand the possibilities for this kind of analysis, the book can be thought of as a collection of testable social science propositions related to self-help organizations and professional practice. It is hoped that many of these propositions will become the focus of empirical investigation. With this in mind, the tables and boxed text throughout the book can be thought of as highlighting important propositions.

Notes

1. W. Percy, *Lost in the Cosmos: The Last Self-Help Book* (New York: Farrar, Straus & Giroux, 1983), p. 1.
2. T. J. Powell, "Comparisons Between Self-Help Groups and Professional Services," *Social Casework: The Journal of Contemporary Social Work*, 60 (November 1979), pp. 561–565.
3. Alcoholics Anonymous, *Analysis of the 1980 Survey of the Membership of A.A.* (New York: AA General Services Office, 1980).
4. L. H. Levy, "Self-Help Groups Viewed by Mental Health Professionals: A Survey and Comments," *American Journal of Community Psychology*, 3 (August 1978), pp. 305–313.
5. National Institute on Alcohol Abuse and Alcoholism, "Growth of AA, Treatment Cited Over Past 15 Years," *NIAAA Information and Feature Service*, IFS 104 (February 1, 1983), p. 15.
6. J. L. Herman, *Father-Daughter Incest* (Cambridge, Mass.: Harvard University Press, 1981), p. 197.
7. R. A. Lusky and S. R. Ingman, "The Pros, Cons and Pitfalls of 'Self-Help' Rehabilitation Programs," *Behavior Science and Medicine*, 13A (January 1979), pp. 113–121.
8. A. Gartner and F. Riessman, *Self-Help in the Human Services* (San Francisco: Jossey-Bass, 1977), p. 158.

9. L. D. Borman, "Characteristics of Development and Growth," in M. A. Lieberman and Borman, eds., *Self-Help Groups for Coping with Crisis: Origins, Members, Processes, and Impact* (San Francisco: Jossey-Bass, 1979); and R. W. Toseland and L. Hacker, "Self-Help Groups and Professional Involvement," *Social Work*, 27 (July 1982), pp. 341–347.

10. L. F. Kurtz, "Linking Treatment Centers with Alcoholics Anonymous," *Social Work in Health Care*, 9 (Spring 1984), pp. 85–94.

11. E. Kurtz, *Not-God: A History of Alcoholics Anonymous* (Center City, Minn.: Hazelden Foundation, 1979).

12. A. H. Katz, "Self-Help Organizations and Volunteer Participation in Social Welfare," *Social Work*, 15 (January 1970), pp. 51–60.

13. R. E. Glasgow and G. M. Rosen, "Self-Help Behavior Therapy Manuals: Recent Developments and Clinical Usage," *Clinical Behavior Therapy Review*, 1 (Spring 1979), pp. 1–20.

14. M. Yoak and M. Chesler, "Alternative Professional Roles in Health Care Delivery: Leadership Patterns in Self-Help Groups," *Journal of Applied Behavioral Science*, 21 (October–November–December 1985), p. 427.

15. D. M. Traunstein, "From Mutual-Aid Self-Help to Professional Service," *Social Casework: The Journal of Contemporary Social Work*, 65 (December 1984), pp. 622–627; and K. Larkin, A. Meese, and E. J. Madara, *The Self-Help Group Directory, 1984–85* (Denville: New Jersey Self-Help Clearinghouse, 1985).

16. Borman, "Characteristics of Development and Growth," p. 41.

17. A. Gartner and F. Riessman, *Help: A Working Guide to Self-Help Groups* (New York: New Viewpoints/Vision Books, 1980).

18. A. H. Katz and E. I. Bender, *The Strength in Us: Self-Help Groups in the Modern World* (New York: New Viewpoints, 1976), p. 36.

19. A. H. Katz, "Self-Help and Mutual Aid," *Annual Review of Sociology*, 7 (1981), pp. 129–155.

20. A. H. Katz, "Self-Help and Human Services," *Citizen Participation*, 3 (January–February 1982), pp. 18–19.

21. Task Panel on Community Support Systems, President's Commission on Mental Health, *Report to the President*, Vol. 2 (Appendix) (Washington, D.C.: U.S. Government Printing Office, 1978).

22. B. Stokes, "Self-Help in the Eighties," *Citizen Participation*, 3 (January–February 1982), pp. 5–6.

23. H. H. Goldman, N. H. Adams, and C. A. Taube, "Deinstitutionalization: The Data Demythologized," *Hospital and Community Psychiatry*, 34 (February 1983), pp. 129–134.

24. Personal correspondence from the Service Center Coordinator, Emotions Anonymous, St. Paul, Minn., December 5, 1985.

25. Alcoholics Anonymous, *Eastern U.S. Alcoholics Anonymous Directory* (New York: AA World Services, 1984).

26. Z. Gussow and G. S. Tracy, "The Role of Self-Help Clubs in Adaptation to Chronic Illness and Disability," *Social Science and Medicine*, 10 (July–August 1976), pp 407–414.

27. T. J. Powell and G. P. Miller, "Self-Help Groups as a Source of Support

for the Chronically Mentally Ill," in H. Fishman, ed., *Creativity and Innovation* (Davis, Calif.: Pyramid Systems, 1982), pp. 243–254.

28. J. H. Jackson and C. P. Morgan, *Organization Theory* (2nd ed.; Englewood Cliffs, N.J.: Prentice-Hall, 1982), p. 359.

29. M. Hausknecht, *The Joiners* (New York: Bedminster Press, 1962); and H. H. Hyman and C. R. Wright, "Trends in Voluntary Association Memberships of American Adults: Replication Based on Secondary Analysis of National Sample Surveys," *American Sociological Review*, 36 (April 1971), pp. 191–206.

30. J. Kirkpatrick, *Turnabout: Help for a New Life* (Garden City, N.Y.: Doubleday & Co., 1977).

31. J. F. Lofland and R. A. LeJeune, "Initial Interaction of Newcomers in Alcoholics Anonymous: A Field Experiment in Class Symbols and Socialization," *Social Problems*, 8 (Fall 1960), pp. 102–111.

32. T. S. Borkman, "Where Are Older Persons in Mutual Self-Help Groups?" in A. Kolker and P. Ahmed, eds., *Aging* (New York: Elsevier Biomedical, 1982), p. 269.

33. Lofland and LeJeune, "Initial Interaction of Newcomers in Alcoholics Anonymous."

34. A. J. Gordon, "The Cultural Context of Drinking and Indigenous Therapy for Alcohol Problems in Three Migrant Hispanic Cultures: An Ethnographic Report," *Journal of Studies on Alcohol*, 9, Supp. No. 9 (January 1981), pp. 217–240.

35. L. Maguire, *Understanding Social Networks* (Beverly Hills, Calif.: Sage Publications, 1983), pp. 93–96.

36. L. Jilek-Aall, "Acculturation, Alcoholism, and Indian-Style Alcoholics Anonymous," *Journal of Studies on Alcohol*, 9, Supp. No. 9 (January 1981), pp. 143–158.

37. S. M. Stevens, "Alcohol and World View: A Study of Passamaquoddy Alcohol Use," *Journal of Studies on Alcohol*, 9, Supp. No. 9 (January 1981), pp. 122–142.

38. J. E. Levy and S. J. Kunitz, *Indian Drinking: Navajo Practices and Anglo-American Theories* (New York: John Wiley & Sons, 1974).

39. O. R. Whitely, "Life with Alcoholics Anonymous: The Methodist Class Meeting as a Paradigm," *Journal of Studies on Alcohol*, 38 (May 1977), pp. 831–848.

40. L. Jones, "The Absence of the Black Professional and Semi-Professional in the Membership of Alcoholics Anonymous," in *Proceedings, Association of Labor-Management Administrators and Consultants on Alcoholism, Eighth Annual Meeting* (Arlington, Va.: Association of Labor-Management Administrators and Consultants on Alcoholism, 1980), pp. 416–431.

41. A. Humm, "The Changing Nature of Lesbian and Gay Self-Help Groups," in A. Gartner and F. Riessman, eds., *The Self-Help Revolution* (New York: Human Sciences Press, 1984), pp. 33–40.

2

Evaluating and Improving Effectiveness

Many of this book's broadest concerns about how self-help organizations work and about how professionals collaborate with them are predicated on the assumption that they do work at least some of the time.[1] This chapter examines the evidence for this assumption. Ideally it would be useful to know if self-help organizations are an effective resource for the people they serve. Do AA and PA, for example, help a representative sample of alcoholics and child abusers, or do they benefit only a subgroup of them, if they help at all? Then there is the question of how help is to be defined and how it is to be measured: Will some aspects of members' problems be improved but not others?[2] Answers to these broad questions would require probability sampling. This procedure would ensure that the data are representative of all alcoholics or all child abusers—not simply the individuals who join these organizations or not even the large number of individuals who fail to return after one or two meetings. But since the parameters of these populations are unknown, an appropriate sampling frame cannot be defined. This problem is similar to that facing those who would make inferences about the need for services from those who use the services (in, for example, psychotherapy). Psychotherapists, too, do not know whether those who come to them are representative of all those who need their services. Thus, for either self-help or psychotherapy, the broadest question, Can it work for all?, is unanswerable.

A more answerable question is, Does a particular self-help organization help those who participate in it? Here an appropriate sampling frame can be identified, but assigning participants randomly to experimental and control groups is difficult. To do this, the self-help condition must be withheld from the control group long enough to determine whether significant differences have developed between the groups. Such a random assignment makes it less likely that particular outcomes were caused by differences present before the intervention. Strictly speaking, no such presumption is possible when already established groups are compared, even though post hoc statistical analyses should be used to rule out such obvious confounding differences as age, sex, ethnicity, and education. Time-series designs, in which the sequential presentation of the "treatment(s)" is carefully noted, are an alternative control for outside events and unrelated changes in the subjects (historical-maturational variables) without randomized control groups.[3] But it is still possible that the outcomes will reflect some crucial unmeasured variable.

OUTCOME STUDIES OF TWO TYPES OF ORGANIZATIONS

A number of studies of open-membership, multi-chapter, autonomous self-help organizations have used probability samples, but few, if any, such studies have randomly assigned members to experimental and control groups. Studies of other less classic self-help forms have used both probability samples and randomization procedures. These studies of professionally sponsored hybrid self-help groups can estimate the effect of the experimental condition. Their weakness, however, is construct validity. It is not clear to what extent the experimental intervention represents "true" self-help interventions. The situation is reversed in studies of autonomous self-help organizations. The self-help intervention is clearly true, but the validity of the pretest comparison groups is open to question. The sampling procedure is a major threat to the validity of studies concerned with the outcome of autonomous types. Nonetheless, studies of both hybrid and autonomous types contribute by addressing different kinds of uncertainty about the effectiveness of self-help organizations. In this section, a representative, though not exhaustive, selection of these studies will be examined.

Hybrid Self-Help Groups

The hybrid self-help group, a professionally supported unit, may have been formed by professionals and usually is supervised by
30   a professional. It differs from autonomous self-help organizations

in that its members are usually specially selected from a sub-population. The construct validity question raised by hybrid groups asks whether they have the essential components, such as mutual aid and experiential knowledge, to warrant the label self-help.[4] Of course, apart from this question, these hybrid groups may be valuable in their own right. They offer services where otherwise there would be none. Furthermore, they may help specific populations, such as long-term consumers of mental health services, or enhance specific skills, such as those related to socialization and independent living.

The Florida Mental Health Institute used a hybrid approach in developing self-help and mutual aid groups for ex-mental patients.[5] The basic thrust of these groups was social and recreational. Selected consumers, called Client Area Managers, were paid to organize their peers. Together with their peer leaders, the consumers arranged outings, raised funds for projects, ate cookies, phoned their peers, organized covered-dish suppers, watched movies, planned transportation, participated in self-improvement classes, and engaged in recreational sports.

The evaluation design involved the random assignment of 80 ex-patients to self-help and control groups after they had received standard discharge planning services. Testing after assignment disclosed no background differences between the two groups. At follow-up, an average of ten months after discharge, only half as many of the self-help participants (17.5 percent) as compared with the control group participants (35 percent) required rehospitalization, and when they did, the average length of stay was only one-third as long as that for the controls (7 days versus 24.6 days). Moreover, the self-help group members depended less on the official mental health system for service. This finding was more than the simple shift in service patterns that characterizes so much deinstitutionalization; in this case, the absolute amount of service was reduced.

In another example of a hybrid self-help group, Vachon, Lyall, and Rogers randomly assigned widows to either an intervention or a control group.[6] Each widow in the intervention group was paired with "a widow contact," a woman who had resolved her own grief and had been trained in bereavement issues. The widow contacts reached out to the widows, provided information about resources, offered companionship, and provided supportive counseling. The widows were evaluated at 6, 12, and 24 months in terms of their interpersonal adaptation and overall disturbance. The investigators found that the intervention group adapted more quickly than the control group and were less preoccupied with their loss.

31

In a study of two groups of new mothers randomly assigned to experimental and control groups, Gordon, Kapostins, and Gordon found that participation in mutual support groups was a positive experience. Women who participated in mutual support groups made better postpartum adjustments than those who did not participate.[7] On follow-up four to six years later, the mothers had fewer marital problems and divorces, and their children were healthier.

Another study focused on mothers of premature infants who were randomly assigned to hospital-sponsored self-help groups. The experimental group adapted better than the control group.[8] "From three weeks onward the mothers of the experimental group visit their infants more frequently, interact more with them during visits and feel more competent about their general caretaking role than mothers who do not attend such meetings."

In a situation classically suited to self-help methods, Richardson evaluated the rehabilitative outcomes for 39 individuals who had undergone laryngectomies.[9] "Participation in self-help groups, such as Lost Chord Clubs, correlated positively with social functioning and improvements in communication ability, and negatively with post-surgical depressions and decreased social interaction."

Lieberman and Gourash assessed a health promotion group for seniors, Senior Actualization and Growth Explorations (SAGE).[10] They found that though the experimental group benefited from the experience, the benefits were not in areas targeted by the program designers. Following a series of weekly meetings that focused on home health care practices, the participants scored higher than the controls on life satisfaction and self-esteem scales, and they were better able to cope with marital strain. Compared to the control group, however, "no changes in health behavior were reported. Only slight reductions in fears about physical illness . . . were observed."

Even if the positive effects observed in these studies could be replicated with other problems and programs, certain questions remain, such as, What produced these effects and how should it be labeled? Are the interventions of these hybrid groups similar to those used by self-help organizations? Are the differences in eligibility criteria and the use of professionals of secondary importance?

These questions might be explored according to the following logic: Some problems, such as child abuse, and some conditions, such as single parenthood, widowhood, and being related to a chemically dependent person, are dealt with by both hybrid self-help groups and autonomous self-help organizations. The interventions and effects of the hybrid self-help groups could be compared with such autonomous organizations as PA, PWP, Widow to Widow programs, and Al-Anon. If similar measures and data analyses procedures were used, findings could be directly compared. The objective would be to design an experiment in which subjects would be randomly assigned into two experimental groups, one hybrid and one autonomous. This procedure would clarify the relationship between the factors that were presumed to be causal and their effects. Do such factors as active linkage, mutual aid, experiential wisdom, formal procedures, and organizational development activities operate similarly across both groups? If not, how do the hybrid and autonomous forms differ? Another benefit of this approach is that empirical findings could be used to define and classify self-help activities.

Autonomous Self-Help Organizations

Many of the construct validity concerns for hybrid groups are not relevant to studies of autonomous self-help organizations; in the latter, the concern centers on the internal validity of the quasi-experimental design. Without random assignment, the equivalence of the groups is unknown, though tests for differences in background variables, for example, age, sex, and ethnicity, or the use of elaborate covariance analysis strategies, can eliminate some questions. Moreover, if the internal validity of the autonomous study seems adequate, the external validity of the study will be greater since inferences can be made about other chapters of the *same* self-help organization. Then, too, it may even be plausible to make inferences about the relationship between these variables in other self-help organizations using similar approaches, for example, other organizations following a twelve-step model or making heavy use of mutual aid strategies. The long-range goal might be to evaluate the effectiveness of different types or "blocks" of self-help organizations in a series of combined and separate experiments.[11] For now, the less certain internal validity of autonomous self-help organization studies means that the findings may change as improved designs eliminate additional sources of error.

Videka-Sherman was very mindful of the problem of internal validity in her meticulous comparison-group study of an autonomous self-help organization. She studied 18 chapters of The Compassionate Friends, an organization for people faced with the untimely death of a child. She compared people who experienced the loss at approximately the same time, some of whom became Compassionate Friends members and some of whom did not. To minimize the threat to validity posed by the lack of random *33* assignment, she tested both groups and found no background differences between them. Thus, it is less likely that any posttest differences can be attributed to pretest differences, though it does not rule out such a possibility. Other unmeasured factors, a difference in initiative, for example, might account for both superior coping and the decision to affiliate with a self-help organization.

To illustrate the problems faced by the investigator, it might be asked if a different approach could have eliminated this a priori factor. What if Videka-Sherman had selected one group from a frame in which a high percentage of the eligible population participates in The Compassionate Friends and compared it with another group of bereaved individuals who had little or no opportunity to participate in this self-help organization. Though such an approach might control for initiative, it is readily apparent that it merely substitutes one doubt for another. If the communities are so different, the people may be different too. And so it goes. There is no satisfactory solution apart from random assignment.

On balance, however, considering her checks for background difference, her attention to the reliability of her measures, and her careful statistical analysis, Videka-Sherman's study seems to have had a high degree of internal validity. Her findings show that many people dropped out or participated for a short time only. These early-leavers seem unlikely to have been helped much. Measurable benefits were recorded only for the active participants, for they were the ones who were the least depressed and the best adapted after the loss.[12] But even these parents failed to reach the norms established by the general population on these measures of mental health and social functioning.[13] The self-help organization could not entirely expunge the effects of the loss of a child. Notwithstanding this ceiling on benefits, members who took an active role in the maintenance and development of the self-help organization, who helped with meeting arrangements, who planned publicity, who offered rides, who welcomed newcomers, and so on did fare better than those who simply sat in.

An outgoing, external orientation may have benefits at the organizational level as well. In her study of self-help units for stutterers, Borkman found that reaching out to other stutterers was the strongest predictor of which units survived over a ten-year period.[14] Another study, outside the formal domain of self-help, also found that an "other" orientation, labeled *altruism*, was an important factor in later adjustment. Chodoff et al. found that parents facing the death of their child from leukemia exhibited higher levels of adaptation at follow-up if they had earlier helped the nursing staff with the care of both their own and other children.[15] The mechanism by which altruism works seems to follow that of the helper-therapy principle.[16] Similar dynamics may be operating when self-help members proclaim the word about their organizations and minister to others in need.

Evidence from another study by Videka also supports the importance of the level and direction of member participation. In her comparison-group study of Mended Hearts, she found that relatively inactive members did not benefit from the experience.[17] But those members who had more involving roles as accredited visitors to prospective heart surgery patients did benefit.

Active participation also seemed to be the effective ingredient of a politically oriented self-help organization. It is referred to here as a self-help organization not because it claims to be one but because of the effect it has on its members. Levens compared a group of Aid to Families with Dependent Children (AFDC) mothers who joined a welfare rights organization with an AFDC group that did not. The welfare rights mothers had fewer and less intense feelings of powerlessness. Levens concluded:

> Analysis revealed that such characteristics as age, education, number of children and other organizational affiliations were not responsible for differences in powerlessness. It would appear that the impact of the league was greatest in effecting changes in political activism. Attitudes of powerlessness. . .were sizably reduced by membership.[18]

The diversity of the sample used to evaluate an intervention that included PA makes this study more generalizable than most.[19] Data were collected from 11 federally funded demonstration projects that treated child-abusing parents in various parts of the country. Two groups were compared, those with a "lay service component" and those without such a component. The component included a parent aide or PA or both. Unfortunately, the analysis did not separate the effects of PA from those of the parent aide; thus, it is impossible to assess the relative importance of PA and the parent aide.

The major finding was that the entire service package was more effective when it included a lay service component. Here, 53 percent of the parents improved with a lay service component, compared to 40 percent who improved with professional services alone. These statistics were based on the ratings of trained judges who did not know which parents received the lay service component. The judges also rated the clients who received PA–parent aide services as having more potential for growth with the aid of professionally sponsored services.

Though all the clients, both those with a lay service compo- *35* nent and those without one, were judged to have a significantly lower risk for the recurrence of moderately severe physical abuse and neglect, the difference was disappointing. Similarly, though the combination of lay and professional service was better than professional service alone, the difference was again disappointing. It is sobering to consider that 30 percent of the children were further abused while they were under the nominally protective wing of these federally funded demonstration projects.

Unlike PA, Recovery, Inc., the last organization of the comparison-group studies to be discussed, has no professional "sponsors" or other form of professional participation. Its claim to be a "professionally designed" program is based on the design contributions of its psychiatrist founder, Abraham Low, who was a dominant force in the program from 1937 to the 1950s.

Raiff collected data from Recovery "staff," that is, volunteers who were formally trained by the organization for their leadership positions. She compared them with "normals," a probability sample of American adults who were tested on the same scales by independent investigators.[20] Eighty percent of the Recovery sample had been treated for mental problems and fully half of them had been hospitalized for these problems. Using multiple scales, she found that the Recovery staff rated their "quality of life" higher than did the comparison group, the probability sample of American residents. The unanswered question is whether the "nonelite" general membership would show a similar pattern. A follow-up study to investigate this important question should be a high priority.

Another creative approach to the development of a comparison group is reflected in a study of the members of scoliosis clubs by Hinrichsen, Revenson, and Shinn.[21] They compared members of the Scoliosis Association with people who wrote to the association after an article appeared in a Sunday magazine supplement. Many of the potential biases of this procedure were addressed by careful statistical control of such background factors as religion, number of organizational memberships, and medical condition. The results showed a high degree of satisfaction with the clubs, but the psychosocial benefits tended to be restricted to adults who had undergone severe medical regimens. This study suggests that self-help organizations may help some members in certain ways but not in all ways.

Lieberman and Videka-Sherman's study of THEOS (They Help Each Other Spiritually), an organization for the newly widowed, is a rich and sophisticated comparison-group study.[22] Statistical procedures are used to control the possibly biasing effects of behavioral patterns (e.g., participation in other organizations and number of friends) as well as biographical factors (e.g., age, sex, education, and marital status). Several levels of the independent variable were studied. Nonmembers attended two or fewer meetings, a second subsample attended meetings "only," a third had "some" exchange with members outside meetings, and a fourth had a "high" level of exchange outside of meetings. The scores of the last three subsamples on outcome scales were compared with the nonattenders. The scales measured depression, anxiety, somatic symptoms, well-being, mastery, and self-esteem. The results showed no benefits were derived by those who only attended meetings. The gains made by those who had exchange relationships outside the formal sessions were statistically significant, though the "some" and "high" exchange subsamples were not distinguishable. Furthermore, when compared to those who had received professional therapy, the exchange subsamples experienced greater benefits.

Among the distinctive contributions of this study is the careful analysis of the mechanism of change. Change was associated with contact with other members outside the formal sessions, which the investigators in a detailed analysis show is not associated with preexisting background factors or behavioral patterns. The variable of outside contact, however, does not warrant the conclusion that other components of the intervention could not be responsible for the positive change. The benefits may also be associated with such component factors as stronger cognitive commitment to the assumptions of the organization, more intense participation, or closer adherence to the prescriptions of the program. This is not to discount the importance of outside contact but to suggest that it may also be a marker for other potent variables that should also be investigated. It is also compatible with the mounting evidence that the more active members, often those in leadership or outreach positions, benefit the most from self-help groups.

The attention to organizational variables is another distinctive contribution of this study. Lieberman and Videka-Sherman found that chapters varied in the development of their normative structure. Those with more highly developed norms encouraged more outside contact, which, in turn, was related to greater gains for the average member: "The number and type of norm-regulated behavior characteristics in the group [were] highly linked to the number of people who show[ed] positive outcome."[23]

The importance of organizational properties will be taken up in Chapter Three but before that it will be useful to consider what can be learned from negative findings. These are presented in the subsequent section.

Lessons of Negative Findings

Several studies produced negative findings, which identify some of the factors that account for the lack of benefit from self-help experiences. One factor is the lack of fit between the problem and the self-help organization. This is exemplified by a study that showed that the acutely bereaved did not benefit from NAIM.[24] NAIM is intended for widowed women who are ready to rebuild their social lives. Individuals with acute problems could hardly be expected to benefit from an organization with the primary purpose of increasing long-term social opportunities. But NAIM may provide valuable opportunities at a later time to resolve the lingering effects of acute grief. It illustrates the point that self-help organizations must be keyed to the participants' phase of development.

The study of SAGE, the health-promotion group discussed earlier, points up the consequences of targeting the wrong problems. The seniors did not change in the targeted health behaviors nor did their fears of physical illness diminish. They did, however, become more satisfied with life and increase their self-esteem. This raises a question based on the acuity of hindsight: Is it reasonable to expect elderly people to fear physical illness less? Which health behaviors are amenable to change, and are the hoped-for benefits sufficiently attractive to outweigh the costs of personal change? Even effective methods will fail when they are misapplied.

These concerns are analogous to Kiesler's "uniformity assumptions" that plagued psychotherapy research for such a long time.[25] Not all therapists, clients, and problems are alike. Research in psychotherapy made it possible to determine which therapists, using which methods, with which clients, are more likely to be helpful with which problems. Self-help research must similarly focus on which methods with which members will be helpful with which problems. The task will not be easy. The enormous variability in members and methods will limit the extent to which findings can be generalized from one study to another. And within particular studies, the wide variations within subsamples make it harder to demonstrate positive effects across subsamples.

To complicate matters further, different organizations will show different patterns of variability. The differences from chapter to chapter in Recovery, Inc., are likely to be smaller than those for PA. In PA there may be wide differences in the mix of behavioral and cognitive methods, and the problems of PA members may cover an even wider range than those of Recovery, Inc., members. Given this variability, systematic replication of single-case experimental designs holds considerable promise.[26] Treatment-reversal and multiple-baseline designs can identify which organizations using which methods are effective with which people who are under study.

Given the complexities, it is important not to use them to rationalize negative findings. Some self-help interventions may simply not work. Negative findings, particularly when they are cumulative, should not be rationalized away. The pattern of early positive findings giving way to negative findings as subsequent studies are better controlled may become an increasingly common one.

Take Off Pounds Sensibly has been one of the most carefully investigated self-help organizations. Based on an early study, Stunkard was optimistic about the results of the TOPS program.[27] Later studies, however, dissipated much of the initial optimism. When short-term members were followed up, it was discovered that many of the members who lost small amounts of weight regained it after leaving the organization, thus lowering the organization's success rate substantially. When the problem of sample attrition was recognized, the earlier conclusion was revised to read as follows: "Although a small percentage . . . lose a substantial amount of weight . . . and maintain the weight loss, the vast majority find TOPS a relatively ineffective method of weight control."[28]

When behavior modification was introduced into the TOPS groups, the rate of weight loss over traditional groups improved. And when the same behavioral program was administered by professionals, the results were even better.[29] Professionals proved more adept at using behavior modification techniques. To ease their disappointment, self-helpers may be tempted to declare that peers will be more adept at such other tasks as promoting acceptance of the self, but in the absence of supporting evidence, they must also admit doubt and encourage free inquiry of which source of help works.

Stunkard's work also illustrates the bias of cross-sectional studies. His early designs oversampled long-term members and undersampled short-term members, which led him to overestimate the benefits of the self-help organization. Yet the bias of cross-sectional studies can also operate in the opposite direction. Schachter pointed out that many people who try to quit smoking, though they fail in the short run, will eventually succeed.[30] Cross-sectional data from dropouts do not take into account the individuals who will eventually succeed after repeated trials. Habit-control self-help organizations, in particular, require longitudinal design studies.

Uncontrolled Single-Group Studies

The problems of sample attrition are compounded by the lack of a comparison group in uncontrolled single-group designs. This lack makes it impossible to infer causality, no matter how large the sample. This lack is found in studies of some of the best-known self-help organizations for reasons that can be readily understood. Consider how difficult it is to obtain a representative sample from a loosely federated, widely dispersed self-help organization. Investigators have little choice but to accept questionnaires or interviews no matter how they are obtained. Also, former members are difficult to follow up. Comparison groups are difficult to define and even more difficult to operationalize. How could a comparison group for AA or Recovery, Inc., be found? Who would be members of these organizations, if an opportunity were available? (One answer might be those who would later become members if the opportunity presented itself.) And after solving these problems conceptually, how could the solution be operationalized to secure the cooperation of subjects?

Collecting data from self-help organizations is not simple. Already convinced of or possibly threatened by an evaluation of their effectiveness, they are inclined to dismiss evaluation as a waste of time.[31] They can have minds that are as closed as the professionals who insist that evaluation is meaningless because self-help groups inevitably foster negative identities.[32] When such attitudes prevail, the research climate is inhospitable.

Notwithstanding the lack of control groups and the low response rates, the stable pattern of positive results is consistent with the proposition that individuals who actively participate in self-help organizations over extended periods are likely to improve. Note, however, what it does not say. It does not say that members, regardless of the length of their tenure or the quality of their participation, are likely to improve. Nor does it indicate how much of the improvement should be attributed to history or maturation or nonspecific spontaneous remission.

Widely cited studies of the AA's membership illustrate the problems but also the possibilities inherent in this genre for describing and generating hypotheses about the population. These triennial surveys, begun in 1968, show a pattern of increasing effectiveness. Thus, the 1980 survey found that a member with less than a year of sobriety has a 41 percent probability of going through the next year without drinking. After one year, the probability rises to 81 percent. Both these figures indicate a gain in effectiveness over the 1977 survey.[33] But the gain may be the result of sample mortality. As more high-risk members drop out, a larger proportion of successfully recovering members remains—the same people who would be less likely to relapse even without AA. If the difference between the mean days of membership in the two groups was higher in 1980 than in 1970, this interpretation would be supported. But unless one is willing to attribute all the difference to sample attrition and maturation, it would seem wise to encourage active involvement in AA. Aside from the issue of summative evaluation, the use of similar items over the four surveys provides an opportunity to track changes over time. In contemplating program development, for example, it might be useful to ponder the implications of the data-generated hypothesis that professionals are an increasingly common path to AA.

DEVELOPMENTAL QUESTIONS

Formative Evaluation

Formative evaluation focuses on developmental questions, the answers to which can become input to program improvement efforts (if the difficulties with outcome or summative evaluation of autonomous self-help organizations can be sidestepped).[34] It seeks to assess the effectiveness of various subsystems rather than the entire system. This means that multiple pragmatic appraisals of the organization are made. Though these separate appraisals cannot be added to give a grand total, they also are less apt to mislead. Grand totals may conceal substantial error, and in any case, they seldom yield much information about the effective components of an intervention. Formative evaluation, however, can isolate subsystem variables that tend to be more easily modified. Thus, the recruitment subsystem might be evaluated to determine if its operations are consistent with the professed goals of the self-help organization. Does it attract members who are representative of those eligible for it and presumably in need of it? An important question might be whether the organization enrolls a representative sample of eligible racial, ethnic, social class, age, handicapped, gender, and sexual orientation minorities.

Wechsler's insightful study of Recovery, Inc., exemplifies this kind of evaluation.[35] After close observation, he evaluated Recovery against the then-current standards of professional ideology. He criticized the emphasis on personal control (willpower) because it was incompatible with uncovering and working-through approaches. He was skeptical that willpower is sufficient to bring one's emo- *41* tional problems under control. He felt that managing symptoms, including "bearing their discomfort" rather than eliminating them, was overemphasized. Anticipating contemporary standards, however, he did question whether Recovery's predominantly white middle-class female membership was consistent with its claim of serving the "nervous and mental patient" population.

Levy's investigation of the boundary subsystem shows how formative evaluation can stimulate program development.[36] He reasoned that if the self-help and the professional services systems are to function optimally, they should recognize their interdependence and interact with one another. Consequently, he asked: Do community mental health professionals know about and make use of self-help organizations? The questionnaire data showed that professionals were fairly well informed and favorably inclined toward self-help organizations. And specifically, they indicated that self-help organizations were relevant to the mission of community mental health. Yet these positive attitudes were not translated into a significant collaboration. What little collaboration there was involved an exchange of referrals, and very little consultation and technical assistance were exchanged. This held true even when the analysis included only a few of the major self-help organizations, such as AA and Recovery, Inc.

In working with a chapter of Make Today Count, an organization dedicated to the terminally ill and their significant others, Wollert, Knight, and Levy found a deteriorating situation.[37] Faced with low morale, dwindling attendance, and either desultory or acrimonious meetings, the chapter asked the consultants to assess the situation and recommend solutions. The consultants observed how goals were formulated, members recruited, information disseminated, leadership developed, decisions made, and tasks completed. Believing that the difficulties reflected the lack of a well-established problem-solving process, the consultants set out to model one. They solicited information and suggestions from the membership, being careful to show how this feedback was incorporated in their thinking about alternative courses of action. After this systematic fact-finding, the consultants presented several alternatives to the chapter. Then they helped members make a series of decisions about the chapter. The effect was to resolve a number of issues related to the role of family and professionals. When the consultation terminated, the chapter members had a stronger sense of purpose and appreciated the organization more. This intervention highlights how consultation and formative evaluation can work together. Indeed, the latter can be viewed as a prerequisite for an organizationally oriented

consultation.

Another more extensive research collaboration is now under-way with GROW, an organization that works to prevent the hospitalization of mental patients through a comprehensive pro-gram of mutual aid. The preliminary summative evaluation find-ings on this organization, which has flourished in Australia for some time, are encouraging. Members who have been with the organization for nine months or more have a better chance of being employed and having fewer disturbing symptoms than those who have been with the organization for less than three months.[38] In addition to the summative findings, this study is likely to make a major contribution to mental health in the form of a detailed analysis of the structure and operations of this self-help organization as the researchers develop measures of highly intricate group processes. And because of their close ties to the organization, the researchers are able to collect data on highly relevant but elusive transactions. They are also well positioned to observe how the various components of the program relate to the program's overall effectiveness. Their approach shows how single-system designs that collect data on multiple baselines and interventions can be used to assess the differential effect of various program components.[39]

The propositions that can be derived from formative evalua-tion suggest their pragmatic value: Community mental health needs to make better use of complementary self-help resources; Recovery, Inc., needs to broaden its demographic base; NAIM needs to help acutely grieving members use outside resources; and Make Today Count needs to continue to clarify its goals and procedures. But these propositions also point up the need to know more about causal variables. More details on the relationships between key variables are needed to support effective interventions.

Value of Process Research

Process research focuses on basic factors and mechanisms unen-cumbered by the necessity to link them, at least immediately, with outcomes. Its role is analogous to the one it plays in psycho-therapy research. Borman's work articulating the important role a small group of creative professionals played in the history of some major self-help organizations marked an important begin-ning in learning more about the relations between professionals and self-help organizations.[40] Levy found favorable attitudes among contemporary professionals.[41] Todres added new information about the frequency of professional interaction and showed how it varied according to type of activity and the discipline of the pro-   *43* fessional.[42] Toseland and Hacker verified the existence of numerous relationships but noted that the relationships vary according to the length of time the self-help unit has been established.[43] Relationships that are harmonious in the early years tend to be more mixed later.

From a different standpoint, Powell found that members of PA who were clients of professionals had little difficulty using both systems.[44] Focusing on AA, Kurtz discovered that professionals tend to overstate the importance and cordiality of their relations with self-help leaders.[45] She also observed how self-help leaders are "put off." Professionals alienate self-help organizations by engaging in one-up linking activities, that is, by enacting consultant and advisory roles that are perceived as condescending. An interesting next step might be to see if the perception varies according to the developmental stage of the organization. Less well-developed organizations may not be offended by advice, provided the consultant can "back off" after the self-help organization becomes established. These studies are rich in implications for action, partly because the studies did not start off burdened by the obligation to specify the issues to be decided from the outset.

Levy's identification of the major behavioral and cognitive processes operating in self-help organizations offers interesting possibilities.[46] Since these basic behavioral and cognitive processes are found in different proportions in different organizations, they might be used to develop a classification system.[47] Thus, organizations could be classified by how much they rely on which processes. Such a scheme should have more interesting correlates than the obvious and trivial correlates involving names, espoused goals, and the manifest activities of self-help organizations. For example, it might be useful to correlate the different processes with such formative measures of the program as perceived satisfaction with discussion groups or recreational programs. Variations in these processes might be subsequently correlated with positive and negative outcomes. But as earlier intimated, progress can be slowed by a premature search for shortcuts.

The value of wide-ranging, basic work is exemplified by Politser and Pattison's comparative study of the similarities and differences among voluntary organizations.[48] Self-help organizations share many characteristics with other voluntary organizations, with the exception that social interactions in the former are guided by fewer rules. Perhaps the differences between more formal and less formal self-help structures should be investigated by future research.

CONCLUSION

The results of experimental studies of selective-membership, professionally supported, hybrid self-help organizations were positive. Their construct validity, however, did not match their internal validity, since it is unclear whether the results of these studies can be generalized to traditional, autonomous self-help organizations. The results of studies of autonomous self-help organizations also were positive, though less so than those for hybrid self-help organizations. Findings on autonomous organizations, however, were obtained through the use of less sensitive quasi-experimental, comparison-group designs; they may be replicated in more significant form, however, as more robust formal experiments and time-series designs are used to test for effectiveness. By delaying the self-help intervention with the comparison group, as in time-series designs, or by introducing the components of the intervention systematically, it may be possible to devise more sensitive tests of self-help organization effectiveness.

The current moderately positive evaluation of autonomous self-help organizations refers only to those members who participate actively over an extended period. Moreover, it is suggested that participation in outreach activities or in relationships outside the formal sessions may be especially beneficial. On the negative side, there seemed to be few benefits for occasional or passive participants. The evaluation is further qualified in that the positive results apply only to those who resemble the members of self-help organizations, not necessarily to all persons who are eligible to join such organizations.

Formative evaluation has yielded useful information about the membership, referral patterns, and structure of these organizations. Process research has generated hypotheses about the relationship between important variables, many of which will be discussed later. It has helped explicate relations between professionals and self-help organizations. It has also begun to illuminate the basic social and psychological processes operative in self-help organizations. Thus, most of the formulations discussed throughout the book should be regarded as proper subjects for process research and formative evaluation.

Notes

1. This chapter revises and updates an earlier version by T. J. Powell, which appeared, with NASW's permission, as "Improving the Effectiveness of Self-Help," *Social Policy,* 16 (Fall 1985), pp. 22–29.   45

2. H. H. Strupp and S. W. Hadley, "A Tripartite Model of Mental Health and Therapeutic Outcomes," *American Psychologist*, 32 (March 1977), pp. 187–196.

3. T. D. Cook and D. T. Campbell, *Quasi-Experimentation* (Chicago: Rand McNally & Co., 1979), pp. 207–292; and T. Tripodi and J. Harrington, "Uses of Time-Series Designs for Formative Program Evaluation," *Journal of Social Service Research*, 3 (Fall 1979), pp. 67–78.

4. T. S. Borkman, "Experiential Knowledge: A New Concept for the Analysis of Self-Help Groups," *Social Service Review*, 50 (September 1976), pp. 445–456.

5. E. Edmunson et al., "Integrating Skill Building and Peer Support in Mental Health Treatment," in A Yaeger and R. Slotkin, eds., *Community Mental Health and Behavioral Ecology* (New York: Plenum Publishing Corp., 1982), pp. 127–139.

6. M. L. S. Vachon et al., "A Controlled Study of Self-Help Intervention for Widows," *American Journal of Psychiatry*, 137 (November 1980), pp. 1380–1384.

7. R. D. Gordon, E. E. Kapostins, and K. K. Gordon, "Factors in Postpartum Emotional Adjustment," *Obstetrical Gynecology*, 25 (February 1965), pp. 156–166.

8. K. Minde et al., "Self-Help Groups in a Premature Nursery— Evaluation," *Journal of Pediatrics*, 96, No. 5 (1980), pp. 933–940.

9. A. H. Katz, "Self-Help and Mutual Aid," *Annual Review of Sociology*, 7 (1981), pp. 129–155.

10. M. A. Lieberman and N. Gourash, "Effects of Change Groups on the Elderly," in Lieberman and L. D. Borman, eds., *Self-Help Groups for Coping with Crisis: Origins, Members, Processes, and Impact* (San Francisco: Jossey-Bass, 1979), pp. 150–163.

11. D. T. Campbell and J. C. Stanley, *Experimental and Quasi-Experimental Designs for Research* (Chicago: Rand McNally & Co., 1963).

12. L. Videka-Sherman, "Coping with the Death of a Child: A Study Over Time," *American Journal of Orthopsychiatry*, 52 (October 1982), pp. 688–698.

13. L. Videka-Sherman and M. Lieberman, "The Effects of Self-Help and Psychotherapy Intervention on Child Loss: The Limits of Recovery," *American Journal of Orthopsychiatry*, 55 (January 1985), pp. 70–82.

14. T. S. Borkman et al., "The Survivability of Self-Help Groups for Persons Who Stutter: A Discriminant Analysis." Unpublished manuscript, George Mason University, Fairfax, Va., 1985.

15. P. Chodoff et al., "Stress, Defenses, and Coping Behavior: Observations on Parents of Children with Malignant Disease," *American Journal of Psychiatry*, 150 (August 1964), pp. 743–749.

16. F. Riessman, "The 'Helper' Therapy Principle," *Social Work*, 10 (April 1965), pp. 27–32.

17. L. Videka, "Psychosocial Adaptation in a Medical Self-Help Group," in Lieberman and Borman, eds., *Self-Help Groups for Coping with Crisis.*

18. H. Levens, "Organizational Affiliation and Powerlessness: A Case Study of the Welfare Poor," *Social Problems*, 16 (October 1968), pp. 18–32.

19. A. H. Cohn, "Effective Treatment of Child Abuse and Neglect," *Social Work*, 24 (November 1979), pp. 513–519.

20. N. R. Raiff, "Self-Help Participation and Quality of Life: A Study of the Staff of Recovery, Inc.," *Prevention in Human Services*, 1 (Spring 1982), pp. 79–89.

21. G. A. Hinrichsen, T. A. Revenson, and M. Shinn, "Does Self-Help Help? An Empirical Investigation of Scoliosis Peer Support Groups," *Journal of Social Issues*, 41, No. 1 (1985), pp. 65–87.

22. M. A. Lieberman and L. Videka-Sherman, "The Impact of Self-Help Groups on the Mental Health of Widows and Widowers," *American Journal of Orthopsychiatry*, 56 (July 1986), pp. 435–449.

23. Ibid., p. 446.

24. E. A. Bankoff, "Widow Groups as an Alternative to Informal Social Support," in Lieberman and Borman, eds., *Self-Help Group for Coping with Crisis*, pp. 189–193.

25. D. J. Kiesler, "Some Myths of Psychotherapy Research and the Search for a Paradigm," *Psychological Bulletin*, 65 (February 1966), pp. 110–136.

26. Cook and Campbell, *Quasi-Experimentation*, pp. 120–124; M. Hersen and D. H. Barlow, *Single Case Experimental Designs: Strategies for Studying Behavior Change* (New York: Pergamon Press, 1979); S. Jayaratne and R. L. Levy, eds., *Empirical Clinical Practice* (New York: Columbia University Press, 1979); E. J. Thomas, "Research and Service in Single-Case Experimentation: Conflicts and Choices," *Social Work Research and Abstracts*, 14 (Winter 1978), pp. 20–31; and E. D. Gambrill and R. P. Barth, "Single-Case Study Designs Revisited," *Social Work Research and Abstracts*, 16 (Fall 1980), pp. 15–20.

27. A. J. Stunkard, "The Success of TOPS, a Self-Help Group," *Postgraduate Medicine*, 18 (May 1972), pp. 143–147.

28. J. R. Garb and A. Stunkard, "Effectiveness of a Self-Help Group in Obesity Control—Further Assessment," *Archives of Internal Medicine*, 134 (October 1974), pp. 716–726.

29. L. S. Sevitz and A. Stunkard, "A Therapeutic Coalition for Obesity: Behavior Modification and Patient Self-Help," *American Journal of Psychiatry*, 131, No. 4 (1974), pp. 423–427.

30. S. Schachter, "Recidivism and Self-Care of Obesity and Smoking," *American Psychologist*, 37 (April 1982), pp. 436–444.

31. L. H. Levy, "Issues in Research and Evaluation," in A. Gartner and F. Riessman, eds., *The Self-Help Revolution* (New York: Human Sciences Press, 1984), pp. 155–172.

32. R. C. Omark, "The Dilemma of Membership in Recovery, Inc., A Self-Help Ex-Mental Patients' Organization," *Psychological Reports*, 44 (June 1979), pp. 1119–1125; and A. Rosen, "Psychotherapy and Alcoholics Anonymous: Can They Be Coordinated?" *Bulletin of the Menninger Clinic*, 45 (May 1981), pp. 229–246.

33. Alcoholics Anonymous, *Analysis of the 1980 Survey of the Membership of A. A.* (New York: AA General Services Office).

34. Levy, "Issues in Research and Evaluation"; and W. Edwards, M. Guttentag, and K. Snapper, "A Decision Theoretic Approach to Evaluation Research," in E. L. Struening and Guttentag, eds., *Handbook of Evaluation Research* (Beverly Hills, Calif.: Sage Publications, 1975), pp. 145–146.

35. H. Wechsler, "The Self-Help Organization in the Mental Health Field: Recovery, Inc., A Case Study," *Journal of Nervous and Mental Disease*, 130 (April 1960), pp. 297–314.

36. L. H. Levy, "Self-Help Groups Viewed by Mental Health Professionals: A Survey and Comments," *American Journal of Community Psychology*, 3 (August 1978), pp. 305–313.

37. R. W. Wollert, B. Knight, and L. H. Levy, "Make Today Count: A Collaborative Model for Professionals and Self-Help Groups," *Professional Psychology*, 1 (February 1980), pp. 130–138.

38. J. Rappoport et al., "Collaborative Research with a Mutual-Help Organization," *Social Policy*, 15 (Winter 1985), pp. 12–24.

39. Tripodi and Harrington, "Uses of Time-Series Designs for Formative Program Evaluation."

40. L. D. Borman, "Characteristics of Development and Growth," in Lieberman and Borman, eds., *Self-Help Groups for Coping with Crisis*, pp. 13–42.

41. Levy, "Self-Help Groups Viewed by Mental Health Professionals."

42. R. Todres, "Professional Attitudes, Awareness, and Use of Self-Help Groups," *Prevention in Human Services*, 1 (Spring 1982), pp. 91–98.

43. R. W. Toseland and L. Hacker, "Self-Help Groups and Professional Involvement," *Social Work*, 27 (July 1982), pp. 341–347.

44. T. J. Powell, "Comparisons Between Self-Help Groups and Professional Services," *Social Casework: The Journal of Contemporary Social Work*, 60 (November 1979), pp. 561–565; and Powell, "Impact of Social Networks on Help-Seeking Behavior," *Social Work*, 26 (July 1981), pp. 335–337.

45. L. F. Kurtz, "Cooperation and Rivalry Between Helping Professionals and Members of AA," *Health and Social Work*, 10 (Spring 1985), pp. 104–112.

46. L. H. Levy, "Self-Help Groups: Types and Psychological Processes," *Journal of Behavioral Science*, 12 (July–August–September 1976), pp. 310–322.

47. Levy, "Issues in Research and Evaluation."

48. P. E. Politser and E. M. Pattison, "Social Climates in Community Groups: Toward a Taxonomy," *Community Mental Health Journal*, 16 (Fall 1980), pp. 187–200.

PART TWO

Social Science
Conceptualizations

Part Two outlines four different approaches to understanding self-help organization operations. In each of four chapters, a different social science theory is used to conceptualize the operations of self-help organizations. *Organizational theory* highlights the diverse role and career opportunities available in self-help organizations. *Reference group theory* suggests how members come to adopt a new culture, one that offers a different way of evaluating the self and determining appropriate personal conduct. *Social network theory* illuminates the process by which expanded resources become available through new, richer relationships encouraged by participation in a self-help organization. And finally, *social learning theory* provides insight about how new behaviors are acquired and perfected.

AFTER EVALUATION WHAT?

The summative evaluation studies discussed in Chapter Two provide only a limited understanding of how active, involved members benefit from participation in a self-help organization. These studies provide only modest clarification of the basic mechanisms of self-help organizations. Formative evaluation, however, assesses the adequacy of various elements of the group and thus can identify the problematic components of a self-help organization. If a study shows, for example, that an organization is having difficulty enrolling its target population, holding the attention of its members in meetings, and informing its relevant publics, it has discovered what is not happening and what must be done to improve the organization's general effectiveness.

Process research contributes more to an explanation of *how* the self-help organization works. It has the advantage of being linked to theoretically relevant variables. This means that it has a greater potential to yield broadly applicable, as distinguished from ad hoc, explanations of how the organization works. However, since process research must, perforce, deal with small questions, it will be some time before its findings will lead to a more comprehensive understanding of self-help phenomena. Thus, it is necessary to fall back on theory to identify and organize the important factors of self-help into a meaningful framework. These theoretical formulations have a heuristic function: They sensitize the observer to what may be the important factors and relationships and provide comprehensive, albeit provisional, explanations of self-help phenomena.

As an example, Levy set out to understand the activities and methods of self-help groups; he wanted to discover the basic processes common to self-help organizations despite their varied expressions in particular organizations.[1] His research team observed many local chapter meetings   *51* of some of the better known self-help organizations (AA, OA, PA, Recovery, PWP, and Make Today Count) and noted the numerous procedures followed in these meetings. From these procedures, the team derived four behavioral and seven cognitive processes, though it is not clear how these processes were derived. The study was limited in that only those chapters that could be persuaded to cooperate were sampled; it was also limited by the lack of reliability information about the coding procedures. Yet the study made use of firsthand observations to produce tentative propositions about the basic processes that are operative in self-help organizations.

Levy's interpretations of the data parallel the theoretical formulations that are discussed in Part Two. For example, he discussed the official "rationale" for the problem, the "indoctrination" of authorized problem-solving methods, and the "range of alternative perceptions and actions" sanctioned by the self-help organization. These formulations are related to the organizational concept of the self-help organization in Chapter Three. The self-help organization uses formal methods to foster normative behavior through specific, approved helping procedures. In both Levy's conception and the one used here, the self-help organization is viewed as an intentional unit using a particular conception of the problem and certain coping strategies.

Chapter Four, on reference group processes, discusses what Levy called a "reduction in the sense of isolation," "the development of an alternative culture," and a system for "support[ing] . . . changes in attitudes . . . and behavior," which offer a way to achieve a successful, satisfying life.[2]

Chapter Five deals with the concept of social networks. It shows how resources are developed through relationships and how these relationships are fostered by participation in a self-help organization. The concept of the network traces changes in relationships that occur both within and outside the self-help organization.

The processes Levy labeled direct reinforcement and modeling are discussed in Chapter Six, on social learning.

SOCIAL SCIENCE VS. CLINICAL FORMULATIONS

Although social science formulations are based on empirical research only to some extent, they offer advantages over the typical unsystematic explanations of self-help processes scattered throughout the clinical literature. They can be related to other concepts and are cumulative. Clinical formulations, however, tend to be nonsystematic and noncumulative. Yet clinical observations often foreshadow systematic and detailed social science formulations, as exemplified by Caplan:

> Organizations that help their members break a noxious habit—alcoholism, drug abuse, smoking, or overeating—offer not only individual and group counseling in dealing with the problems involved, and particularly anticipatory guidance from old-timers in preparing for diffi-

culties, but they also extend individual ego strength by group sharing of the miseries and discomforts of withdrawal symptoms. In addition, they provide a community in which friendships can develop to provide a new meaning to life, and social and recreational activities can take place that offer a distraction from the unsatisfied cravings.[3]

Though remarkable for its acuity, this clinical formulation does not, like its social science counterpart, lend itself to systematic refinement and elaboration. Moreover, the explanatory power of social science conceptualizations gains by the images they evoke in explaining phenomena in such nonclinical spheres as education, business, and politics. And finally, social science theory provides a supportive framework for identifying and testing promising variables.

Usefulness of Theoretical Models

Theoretical explanations are useful at both the organizational and the individual levels. When it is "known" what accounts for the success of self-help organizations, they can be developed further. Similarly, at the individual level, when the components that are most helpful to a particular individual can be identified, the individual's participation can be modified to enhance these components..

POSSIBLE ORGANIZATIONAL IMPROVEMENTS: If social network theory suggests that a system of mutual aid outside the meetings would be helpful, booklets might be supplied in which telephone numbers could be recorded. After a trial period, guidelines might be established to enhance the acceptability and effectiveness of the telephone network. Formative evaluation of the effects of the system would then lead to further refinements in the system.

In another example, if the theory suggested that emblems and rituals might inspire and unify members of a self-help organization, that organization might wish to develop special awards to recognize significant periods of membership and unusual services rendered. Similarly, if the complex structure and multiple functions of a self-help organization suggested that it might be advantageous to diversify the membership, an effort could be made to recruit a more heterogeneous membership.

IMPROVEMENTS AT THE INDIVIDUAL LEVEL: If it were shown that a particular individual benefited more from the informal sharing that occurs in social-recreational situations than in more formal discussions, a case could be made for more emphasis on selective participation. Thus, specific efforts could be made to point out the availability of certain types of experiences. This also suggests that most new members would benefit from a structured introduction to the complexity of the particular self-help organization and its program components. Of course, the determining factor may be the situation in which the individual finds himself or herself, more than the individual's personality. For example, people in a vulnerable situation might value a telephone network, whereas people in a less vulnerable situation might find it annoying. New members decide for themselves whether they want to avail themselves of a particular component.

IMPROVEMENTS AT THE PROGRAM LEVEL: Organizational theory suggests that it is important to address the ambivalence of new or prospective members who may need the opportunity to observe before making self-disclosures. New members may also need to be protected from embarrassing situations. Too much disclosure, too early, may only increase their discomfort, and reaching out to new members may be necessary before they feel they are valued in the organization. Denial by others may also need to be confronted. Propositions such as these should be part of a conceptual plan to alleviate anxiety and minimize barriers to participation. Gatekeepers and mentors, whether they are inside or outside the organization, can use these conceptualizations to enhance their intuitive understanding of how to obtain the most benefit from the organization.

Relevance of Theoretical Models

The theoretical formulations in Part Two are relevant to certain dimensions of self-help organizations. These dimensions can be summed up in four questions: (1) What attracts new members and sustains the interest of older members? (2) What influences individuals to choose a self-help organization as a reference group, and what are the consequences of their choice? (3) How does a self-help organization make available expanded and specialized resources to its membership? (4) What conditions facilitate positive changes in the way members cope with their conditions and problems?

These questions are addressed in the next four chapters, which develop distinctive, though partially overlapping, explanations of the benefits of membership in a self-help organization. It should also be understood that any of the theories—especially reference group and social learning theories—might have been expanded to account for more of the operations and the benefits of participation in a self-help organization. Reference group theory, for example, might have been used to explain the initial appeal of these organizations (here explained in terms of organizational theory) as well as the influence that an organization eventually comes to have over its members. This overlap notwithstanding, the theories were selected because they seemed to offer more cogent explanations than alternative theories of these dimensions of self-help organizations.

In candor, however, it must be acknowledged that other observers might have, with equal justification, chosen differently. Some might have preferred theoretical formulations that would have conceptualized the changes as shifts in attitudes, social roles, and attributions to the self and others or as the effect of various group processes. Yet even this list could be easily lengthened. Under these conditions, it can be seen that personal preferences, as well as the nature of the phenomena, influence the selection of conceptual frameworks. Thus readers, after comparing these theories with the selections they would have made, may wish to tally the pluses and minuses associated with each selection. The task of developing theoretically oriented, explanatory formulations is something to be accomplished incrementally rather than in one fell swoop.

Notes

1. L. H. Levy, "Self-Help Groups: Types and Psychological Processes," *Journal of Behavioral Science,* 12 (July–August–September 1976), pp. 310–322.
2. Ibid.
3. G. Caplan, "Spontaneous or Natural Support Systems," in A. H. Katz and E. I. Bender, eds., *The Strength in Us: Self-Help Groups in the Modern World* (New York: New Viewpoints, 1976), pp. 134–135.

3

Participating in a Complex Organization

Self-help organizations are like churches. And like church members, self-help group members may object to the use of organizational terminology to explain the group's operations. But in a broad sense, both organizations ameliorate distress and give meaning to life. In one sense, churches are the largest of all self-help organizations. Both types of organization use doctrine (ideology) and ritual (procedures) to support their members. For the individual, church doctrine and ritual are fairly constant; yet they are continuously evolving in response to the changing needs of the faithful and the exigencies of the world. Various church functions preserve tradition; others accommodate change. And the church is subject to larger influences beyond its internal forces. Major changes in the role of women, for example, have led to many changes within church organizations.

These forces have their parallels in self-help organizations. Central norms and procedures have emerged from repeated experience with recurring issues and tasks. These expectations and practices become tradition, and yet they continue to be refined through constant use. They are also responsive to changes in the external environment, such as funding developments, demographic changes, and scientific findings. Like the church, one part of the organization may be responsible for innovation while another part preserves its uniformity, stability, and predictability. The term *maintenance subsystem* is an apt one for the structures responsible for many of these functions of uniformity, stability, and predictability.[1]

But some readers may be put off by this terminology. Self-help does not take place in "organizations"; it takes place in fellowships, groups, or meetings. For many people, an organization is a rigid, bureaucratic hierarchy, which favors the suppression rather than the expression of feelings. This misconception can sometimes be corrected by referring to the use of organizational concepts in the material produced by self-helpers. The ninth tradition of Emotions Anonymous states that "EA as such ought never be organized; but we may create service boards or committees directly responsible to those they serve."

Other structures and divisions of labor are mentioned in EA's *Guide for Forming and Conducting New and Existing Groups of Emotions Anonymous*. It refers to a "treasurer, person in charge of literature, persons in charge of coffee and any other offices." Even sponsorship is governed by formal norms despite its claim of informality:

> Sponsorship is an informal thing decided upon by two individuals who wish to sponsor or be sponsored. When a new person identifies with and feels close to a member, and if the member has the same interests and feels close to the newcomer they could enter the sponsorship situation. We encourage people to select a sponsor of the same sex.[2]

These illustrations of structure and formality are not atypical. Thus, in the Narcotics Anonymous pamphlet *Group*, there is a section, "Structure," and within this section reference is made to a "Steering Committee [consisting] of a Secretary, a Treasurer, and a General Service Representative."[3]

The writer's positive appraisal of formal guidelines and a complex structure does not apply to nonvoluntary organizations. It does recognize, however, that compared to other organizations, self-help organizations tend to be more informal and flexible and that there is an important difference in their purpose.[4] The self-help organization is not utilitarian, as is the workplace; people do not depend on it for their livelihood. Nor does it use coercion; people are not compelled to stay. People choose to join, and they choose to participate because the organization supports their values and aspirations. It is a mutual benefit organization; there are no stockholders or customers other than the members themselves. Etzioni calls such an organization a normative institution to indicate that its members make a moral commitment to its values and beliefs.[5] Given these conditions, the risks associated with overcomplexity and formality seem smaller than the risks associated with ad hoc, underdeveloped, and possibly erratic support and self-help groups.

Agency-maintained support groups and isolated self-help groups can be distinguished from self-help organizations by their lack of formal methods and a structure sufficient to their own maintenance. Because these dependent, isolated forms are more apt to be underdeveloped, fledgling units, their members are less likely to share strong values and beliefs.[6] Moreover, the infrastructure is likely to be underdeveloped and only generally related to the characteristic problems of its members.[7] And last, without a differentiated structure to coordinate its efforts, members may be importuned by well-meaning but inappropriate attempts to help; thus, they may find themselves in potentially conflictual situations. The organizational theorist Thompson seemed to have a similar idea in mind when he noted that ad hoc arrangements make the performance of an organization's tasks uncertain.[8]

STRUCTURE AND FORMALITY IN ORGANIZATIONS

"Formalization [italics added] is the organizational technique of prescribing how, when, and by whom tasks are to be performed."[9] It denotes an orderly approach to the accomplishment of objectives and the use of continuous feedback to improve its operations. *Complexity* involves the specialized subdivisions and specialty sectors within the organization but does not imply an extensive hierarchy. Indeed, more extensive horizontal elaboration has been associated with less vertical integration and decentralization of decision making.[10] In this sense, a university is more horizontally differentiated, with fewer verticals and less central control than a similarly sized factory.

Organizational structures have many functions. They coordinate day-to-day operations,[11] they allocate power and authority,[12] and they allow the organization to adapt to the external environment over the long term.[13] The concern here, however, is on how structures enhance the initial appeal and the long-term retention capability of the self-help organization. Complexity of structure is discussed insofar as it stimulates the organization to recruit people with diverse characteristics, skills, and interests, and how it increases the number of leadership roles, which encourages leaders to make long-term commitments to the organization. This activity then results in more models being available for members.

Formality in organizations facilitates other functions as well. It establishes universal rules that increase the effectiveness of the organization and coordinates the various elements. Formal   *59* organizations also have a greater unity of purpose. Especially important in the self-help sphere, formality creates an imperative to measure personal judgments and improvised interventions against those that are normative for the organization. This imperative, however, is not a particularly dangerous one within self-help organizations because of a built-in limit: Formality can go only so far in conjunction with human problems. It does not eliminate spontaneous intervention or even assign it a minor role. Instead, it tends to structure personal expression so that organizational stability is enhanced and the harmful effects of idiosyncratic action are minimized. A key advantage of such standardization is the feeling of belonging to a reliable organization that is sustained from meeting to meeting and from year to year. Formality also makes possible the evolution of more robust and comprehensive problem-solving approaches and procedures as the organization develops. The particular advantages of an orderly, consistent approach (that is, a formal one) in the induction and socialization of new members will be developed in the next section.

Induction and Socialization Phases

Induction procedures aim to encourage the newcomer to make a firm commitment to the self-help organization. But interest in eliciting an early commitment must be tempered by the possibility of threatening the newcomer's self-esteem. Both these ends can be served, however; early commitment and maintenance of self-esteem can be enhanced by procedures that gradually introduce new members to the formal part of the meeting. Indoctrination and socialization can be facilitated by observation and by unthreatening, one-to-one conversations with senior members after the formal part of the meeting. The need for time and space is recognized. New members are routinely advised that it will take a number of sessions (perhaps six) to become familiar with the self-help organization. Some organizations go further and issue the paradoxical challenge that newcomers are not expected to succeed. The intention, of course, is to produce the opposite effect. New members in GA, for example, are frequently told about the heavy odds against their becoming successful members. The emphasis on possible failure seems to have more to do with the desire to fire up the new member than with any knowledge of the actual failure rate.

FORMALITY IN ALCOHOLICS ANONYMOUS: Like other self-help organizations, AA has developed some disarmingly friendly but still formal methods for greeting newcomers: Newcomers are asked to identify themselves, which alerts specially designated members to make them feel welcome. During the conversation period following the formal part of the meeting, the newcomer will receive informative literature along with coffee and upbeat conversation. This approach has evolved from considerable experience with reducing newcomers' discomfort and strengthening the appeal of AA. The gatekeepers and mentors who perform these tasks become quite adept at them with repeated practice, and many senior members regard such tasks as among the most important in their social life.

Yet the competition among members that might well be a by-product of this approach is moderated by formal norms that have been codified in the "traditions" of AA. Failure to deal effectively with conflict has probably been one of the most common causes of the demise of fledgling self-help groups. A sure way to demoralize a group and to create conflict is to encourage boasts about one's accomplishments or self-aggrandizing displays in public. The formal tradition of anonymity was developed precisely to avert this difficulty. Bill W., cofounder of AA, squelched the beginnings of a personal cult and, concomitantly, facilitated the development of an organization when he decided that only first names would be used. And since Bill W., the preeminent member, chose not to be known by his last name, others could hardly choose to do otherwise. In addition, however, it was also recognized that anonymity would be an important protection against potentially harmful exposure. But anonymity is just one of the many formal policies. Formal policies that govern assumption of responsibility and the manner in which leadership is exercised also contribute to the effectiveness of the induction and socialization process. Formal, systematic efforts are made to identify, promote, and retain experienced and effective members in leadership positions.

FORMALITY IN RECOVERY, INC.: Although sometimes criticized as having taken formality too far, that is, as having become "rigid," Recovery, Inc., uses a similar format.[14] Newcomers are asked to observe a panel for several sessions before they participate. In effect, they, as members of the audience, are being indoctrinated as to their future roles as panel members. This approach has a number of functions: Newcomers are not pressured to perform, experienced members model appropriate participation, and potentially disruptive activities are minimized. Yet the newcomer is warmly engaged by senior members during the informal conversation and refreshment period that follows the panel discussion. This allows the senior members the opportunity to   *61* recount how others with problems similar to those of the new-comer have found Recovery useful.

Complexity in Self-Help Organizations

The question of initial appeal has been discussed in terms of the formal procedures or technology used to recruit and orient new members. Technology, in this context, is not a series of mechanical actions, but rather an effort to adapt standardized methods to particular problem situations. It is important to remember, however, that these methods are not fully determined; moreover, they are applied by diverse, spontaneous human beings who are prepared to adapt them to achieve recruitment goals.[15]

A similarly flexible use of structure accounts for much of the sustained appeal of the self-help organization. Many members find the opportunity to assume specialized roles and to pursue a satisfying career in the developmental and coordinating structure of the organization appealing. These opportunities are often incentive enough to induce seasoned members not just to stay on but also to increase their commitment to the organization. In moving toward such participation, members become less dependent and more interdependent. This is true even for newcomers. From the beginning, they are told that they must participate if other members are to achieve one of the most essential parts of their own recovery—helping newcomers. There is also a desire to "pay back" the organization. Giving makes accepting easier. And then there is the moral appeal: As one member put it, "There are two reasons to be a member, because you need it, or because it [the organization] needs you." Whatever the motive, the result is often the same—sustained work in the substructures of the organization. And in this specialized work, the member shapes the technology as well as being shaped by it. Organizationally oriented workers are especially aware of developing the organization for future members. And it is common to hear members speak of benefits that accrue to the producer as well as to the consumer. Indeed, the goal is for everyone to become a "prosumer," a producer as well as a consumer of self-help.[16] This is a radical transformation of the power and dependency features associated with conventional helping and being helped roles. This structural feature gives self-help programs a great advantage over professional programs.[17]

DIVERSE FUNCTIONS AND ROLES: The substructures of the organization disseminate information to the public, negotiate with related professional organizations and community institutions, contact potential members, orient newcomers, and promote the organization's values and norms. Many of these substructures involve the development, refinement, and coordination of the procedures to accomplish these tasks and thus contribute to the vitality of the self-help organization. And as the structure is elaborated, more and more roles, often at the entry level, become available. As these roles are filled, they, in turn, generate activities that further differentiate the structure. Thus, as the structure becomes more differentiated, it creates a need for people with diverse skills. And as the structure is successful in recruiting and retaining such people, they, in turn, build new substructures.

If the self-help organization is to flourish, means must be found to harness the energies of the doers and self-starters. Since these people are required to be more than "good patients," a definite tolerance—and more than that, an appreciation—must be developed for those who otherwise might be dismissed as odd or difficult. Consequently, the self-help organization is forced to create an environment in which differences are valued and even sought out. This orientation is sometimes manifest in the pride self-help leaders take in the range of occupations and education levels within their organizations. They seem particularly pleased when the external system of social rank is reversed within the organization. They take pride in the frequency with which people who have a very modest social status can assume important leadership roles in the organization. Diversity is also evident in the different views members have about what one can get out of the self-help organization and what one can put into it. In this regard, the ideology of these organizations is very flexible. The organization can be a way to deal with a narrowly circumscribed problem or it can be a way of life.

A NEW LIFESTYLE OR A NEW CAREER: Another function of structure is to loosen the ties of members to dysfunctional aspects of their environments by providing them with the opportunity to become involved in a new lifestyle. It is common for many members of self-help organizations to have to consider giving up the friends, associates, and leisure-time activities associated with their difficulties. Time previously given to dysfunctional pursuits can now be absorbed by activities within the social structure of self-help organizations. Activities that to the uninitiated may appear to be simply recreational or housekeeping in nature may function to facilitate the individual's development of an alternative lifestyle. Opportunities in these areas tend to be limited only by the talent and energy of the members.

One of the major substructural responsibilities of self-help   63 organizations is the development and maintenance of the mutual aid network. Guidelines for the appropriate use of extra-meeting contacts must be developed. Who is encouraged to use this outside-of-meeting form of assistance, for what purposes, and under what circumstances? Will the organization encourage the direct exchange of services, for example, child care, respite care, or companionship, or will the contact be limited to emotional support by telephone? Many leadership opportunities in these areas can lead to meaningful work outside the regular self-help sessions. Many members will think twice before abandoning such opportunities, recognizing that few people have opportunities as rewarding as these in any sphere of their lives.

Some of the most rewarding experiences are associated with activities in the external community. Special planning and careful preparation are involved in media relations; public education; arrangements with such community institutions as church, school, and police; and coordination with the organization's regional and national offices or service boards. The leadership skills necessary to perform these activities differ from those required to provide primary support in the more socioemotional aspects of the program. Although these skills can be found in the same person, the environmentally oriented substructures call for instrumental skills that differ from the social support skills necessary to carry out the organization's more nurturant functions. It may very well be difficult to turn one's back on such an attractive package.

Self-help organizations can be thought of as comprising a series of behavior settings through which members rotate and from which they learn new methods of successful living. Early in their careers, the new members may be in a primarily supportive setting; later they may serve on committees and gradually advance toward more significant roles, including those with outreach functions. Still later, as part of ordinary rotation and advancement, members may come to preside over some of these committees. The multidimensional program of the self-help organization makes it a versatile instrument for satisfying individual developmental interests. Many of these organizations are far too complex for any member to participate in all aspects of their programs. Thus, formal or informal guides help new members select what will most benefit them.

PARENTS WITHOUT PARTNERS: The complex structure of PWP requires that experienced members not just develop and maintain it, but also guide newcomers in their selective participation. New members differ in their need and readiness to benefit from particular program activities, and this must be kept in mind when they consider the unusually wide range of activities offered them. They might first concentrate on the substructure that organizes wide-ranging discussions of topics focused on single-parent concerns. Another set of activities centers on developing parent-child relationships; they involve various recreational games and outings in contrast to the adult-centered activities that are more likely to involve parties and commercial entertainment. And after or instead of adult-centered activities, members may become involved in managing and coordinating certain aspects of the organization. One aspect involves who the parent interacts with in PWP activities. Some activities involve children and parents together; parents with other parents, usually of the same sex; or in a still different mode, date-like encounters with adults of the opposite sex. The readiness, interest, and stress associated with each of these activities will, of course, depend on the individual. It may be safe to generalize that many newly separated members are less likely to be threatened by the child-oriented activities, and moreover, they may derive more benefit from them. As the threat abates, however, they may be increasingly interested in activities offering more interaction with adults of the opposite sex.

Based on such considerations as these, the leaders formulate ideas about how newcomers might sequence and distribute their participation, suggesting that PWP is really several mini-organizations, with activities that vary greatly in terms of potential interest, benefit, and risk. Thus, selectivity is advisable, and some activities might best be avoided altogether (for example, activities that could stimulate vindictiveness toward the former spouse), whereas others (for example, adult parties) might be deferred until the member is better prepared for them. In this complex environment, senior members can create gratifying long-term roles for themselves as informal mentors.

GAMBLERS ANONYMOUS: The complex structure of other self-help organizations encourages the advancement and retention of those with special program and leadership skills. Gamblers Anonymous, like many other self-help organizations, has a sponsorship program, which is a major instrument for tailoring the program to the individual. From the point of view of the individual who has very recently gambled, the sponsor's availability may be the difference between resisting the temptation and "getting even with just one last try." Sponsors can also help newly and tenuously recovering gamblers extricate themselves from the destructive entanglements left over from their life of gambling.   *65*

To be chosen as a sponsor is an honor. It cannot help but affect the sponsor's deliberations about his or her future in the organization. And the opportunity to help oneself that is inherent in these activities must never be discounted. In an earlier version of the helper-therapy principle, Ralph Waldo Emerson observed:

> It is one of the most beautiful compensations of this life that no man can seriously help another without helping himself.[18]

The Budget and Pressure Group, a substructure within GA, illustrates another way extremely valuable skills can be utilized. The Pressure Group helps members develop a plan to repay their legal and illegal debts. Since repayment usually takes a long time, the new member must be helped to negotiate with creditors, to budget available funds (after basic family needs are met), and to consider the pros and cons of a second job. Because of the rigorous demands made on those who use GA, senior members must decide whether the member is ready to use it appropriately and is not just interested in another doomed-to-failure "bail out." The members of this group, especially the chair, have prestigious roles that are open only to senior members. One of their obligations is to uphold the GA attitude toward bankruptcy. Restitution, they insist, is integral to the recovery process. But methods have been developed to help the new member cope with urgent pressure to repay overwhelming debts, and when they judge him or her to be ready, they will schedule a budget and pressure meeting to share their experiences. This tough, confrontational encounter usually includes a family member or spouse to encourage the maximum possible honesty. For if the temptation to conceal the most embarrassing obligations, such as those incurred through fraud at the workplace or theft from the family, are not resisted, the process is doomed to fail. The group scrutinizes the standard GA financial statement the new member had prepared earlier with a view toward developing some resolution for these unpleasant realities. The formal norms governing this process are as follows: All obligations, even if they involve fraud or are still undetected and involve family and friends, must be acknowledged and repaid. The only secure route to recovery is regular payments, even if the amount is small. The bookies and "the juice men" (illicit lenders) are much less apt to be angered by a small repayment than by no payment. To paraphrase a frequent comment: "Doing something is not only better than nothing, it is less risky. In the past bookies have been approached in this way."

Other senior members, or the same ones at different times, have applied their energies to different substructures—perhaps to interorganizational activities. The National Council on Compulsive Gambling, an organization closely related to GA, frequently involves GA members in developing public education activities, speaking before groups, meetings with law enforcement officials, and testifying before official bodies. The manifest benefits of these activities are evident in better public information, the recruitment of new members, and so forth. The latent benefits may not be so obvious, but they are no less important. These activities create attractive roles, strengthen commitment, and keep senior members in the organization.

PARENTS ANONYMOUS: Although the strong family orientation and distinctive domain of PA mandate a different program, its organizational structure nonetheless is similarly complex and allows many opportunities for leadership. Members of various substructures plan refreshments; provide child care; arrange transportation; screen and train potential sponsors; and negotiate with related human service, protective, and public safety agencies. There is a role for everyone: for the timid and for those with a bit of temerity, for those who can give and those who must receive.

Self-help organizations appeal to people with skills ranging from the simple and common to the sophisticated and uncommon. Although the point has been argued, on balance, it can be said that the skills required for participation in local meetings are possessed by virtually everyone. The appeal of self-help organizations is sustained by the opportunity to help others and to assume leadership positions. And most often, rather than solidifying negative self-images, these other-directed activities prove to be an effective antidote for feelings of ineptitude; furthermore, they foster a positive identity for the member as someone competent enough to help others. As members "repay" the organization, they can reward themselves for having lived up to their own personal code of justice and fair play.

FORMALITY AND COMPLEXITY GONE AWRY

Of course, one can have too much of a good thing. The thesis that formal procedures generate an effective technology has its limits. Systematic procedures, such as those used in the induction and socialization phase, can prove inflexible and unresponsive to the needs of particular individuals. Instead of centering on key issues, they may belabor nonexistent problems or distract members from more urgent problems. For some members, orientation may be like filling out forms before one is treated in the emergency room.   *67*

As for too much complexity in the organization, some individuals may find that the myriad offerings interfere with becoming attached to any one thing. The climate may be felt as a relentless demand rather than a comforting opportunity. Helping with a mailing, answering the telephone, joining others for coffee, serving on a committee, "buddying" with another member, and so forth, may seem like invasions of privacy rather than cherished opportunities to socialize with one's peers. Instead of building morale and improving social skills, these activities may lead to dejection and bewilderment.

Alternatively, the virtually unlimited opportunities to participate in the substructures of self-help organizations may reinforce an unhealthy preoccupation with a minor imperfection such as being somewhat overweight. Worse yet, the proselytizing orientation of some self-help organizations may unwittingly encourage inappropriate participants to join. One self-help leader noted, for example, that people with anorexia or bulimia sometimes try to affiliate with weight control organizations.[19] Few helping approaches can entirely eliminate the possibilities for self-condemnation and self-flagellation. Few organizations can eliminate the possibility of inappropriate participation, particularly when those so involved pose as energetic workers. Mrs. Jellyby, one of Dickens's humorous but incisive characters, illustrates this point in *Bleak House*. This zealous but fundamentally self-indulgent character is a tireless worker for the imaginary people of faraway Borriboola-Gha, while at home, her own children are severely neglected.

No doubt there are also nonfictional examples of an inappropriate "helping" of others, which is reinforced by the extensive structure of a self-help organization. Quite likely, some members of PWP or PA would do better for their children if they were less involved in these organizations. Occasionally, AA members are advised by fellow members to reduce their twelfth-step work and attend to personal and family issues. The vast capacity of these complex structures to absorb effort can lead to a confusion between means and ends. And beyond compromising one's own best interests, an entrenched pattern of masochistically exhausting oneself for others can sometimes be used to justify sadistic expressions toward others, over and above the very few who need no such excuses to exploit others.

The "horror stories," however, whether personal accounts or tabloid articles, must be put in perspective. Without disputing the fact that vulnerable people have been misled and exploited by those who pose as helpers, the highly sensationalistic reporting may reveal more about the circumstances of the reporter than about the actual event. Thus, though self-help, like professional help, has its risks, the horror stories should not be considered a measure of their risk. It is also important to know that the systematic, time-tested, formal approaches of the self-help organization offer a measure of protection to the vulnerable.

A CONCLUDING WORD

The foregoing analysis should not be interpreted as an argument for self-help organizations to become full-blown bureaucratic organizations. Leaving aside the negative connotations associated with the popular use of the term *bureaucracy* and keeping in mind the developing nature of many self-help organizations, it is, however, possible to argue that many such organizations could benefit from a more bureaucratic orientation. But if the argument were pursued, bureaucracy should be thought of as a constellation of properties, with the argument applying only to some of the properties. The major properties of bureaucracy are division of labor, rules, procedural specifications, impersonality, technical competence, and hierarchical organization.[20] The first three are alternate labels for much of what has been discussed in this chapter. The latter three require some interpretation and qualification.

Impersonality is not a synonym for unresponsive, indirect relations entangled with "red tape"; in fact, close face-to-face relations are encouraged in self-help organizations, provided they are governed by the values and norms of the organization (confidentiality, acceptance of differences in others, respect for the dignity of others, and so forth) as well as by the personal predilections of the members. Impersonality, in this sense, helps soften the eccentricity and rough edges of individuals.

As for *technical competence,* self-help organizations are concerned only with pragmatic, experientially acquired knowledge, much of which is codified in their policies and procedures. Self-help organizations themselves do not use the knowledge acquired through formal study in one of the professions or academic disciplines, though they may encourage their members to pursue this kind of outside help. Moreover, many such organizations take the position that experiential perspectives can be articulated, to great advantage, with the professional perspective.

The bureaucratic property least relevant to self-help organizations is that of *hierarchical organization.* Decisions are seldom made by "higher ups." Most often, they are made in the local group. The exceptions, however, would be those decisions that might jeopardize such established norms as those governing closed meetings or the role of professionals in the organization. These would have to involve higher ups since they would impinge on established norms that had been institutionalized in the printed communications of the regional or national coordinating office. But for the most part, there is no need for a hierarchy to enforce norms, since they are simply part of the freely chosen reference group. In short, they elicit voluntary assent. There are certain practical obstacles, in any case; most attempts to impose authority would be defeated by the reality of distance, the lack of sanctions, and the tradition of local program control.

The adoption of bureaucratic strategies, therefore, must be selective and consistent with modern conceptions of organizational theory. Some of the largest and oldest self-help organizations favor certain kinds of bureaucratic practices and eschew others. Some have become as organized as is desirable, whereas others have a long way to go to substitute stable, widely approved, effective interventions for erratic, idiosyncratic ones of dubious effectiveness.

Notes

1. D. Katz and R. L. Kahn, *The Social Psychology of Organizations* (2nd ed.; New York: John Wiley & Sons, 1978).
2. Emotions Anonymous, *Guide for Forming and Conducting New and Existing Groups of Emotions Anonymous* (St. Paul, Minn.: EA, 1984).
3. Narcotics Anonymous, *Group, I. P. No. 2* (Van Nuys, Calif.: NA World Service, 1976).
4. M. Pilisuk and S. H. Parks, "The Place of Network Analysis in the Study of Supportive Social Associations," *Basic and Applied Social Psychology*, 2 (April–May–June 1981), pp. 121–135.
5. A. Etzioni, *A Comparative Analysis of Complex Organizations* (rev. ed.; New York: Free Press, 1975), pp. 23–67.
6. G. H. Weber, "Self-Help and Beliefs," in Weber and L. M. Cohen, *Beliefs and Self-Help* (New York: Human Sciences Press, 1982).
7. L. J. Medvene, "An Organizational Theory of Self-Help Groups," *Social Policy*, 15 (Winter 1985), pp. 35–37.
8. J. D. Thompson, *Organizations in Action* (New York: McGraw-Hill Book Co., 1967), pp. 52–61.
9. R. H. Hall, *Organizations: Structure and Process* (2nd ed.; Englewood Cliffs, N.J.: Prentice-Hall, 1977), p. 178.
10. Ibid., p. 151.
11. C. Perrow, *Organizational Analysis: A Sociological View* (Belmont, Calif.: Wadsworth Publishing Co., 1970).
12. Y. Hasenfeld, *Human Service Organizations* (Englewood Cliffs, N.J.: Prentice-Hall, 1983).

13. Katz and Kahn, *The Social Psychology of Organizations.*
14. H. Wechsler, "The Self-Help Organization in the Mental Health Field: Recovery, Inc., A Case Study," *Journal of Nervous and Mental Disease,* 130 (April 1960), pp. 297–314.
15. J. Hage and M. Aiken, "Routine Technology, Social Structure and Organization Goals," *Administrative Science Quarterly,* 14 (September 1969), pp. 366–375.
16. A. Gartner and F. Riessman, *Self-Help in the Human Services* (San Francisco: Jossey-Bass, 1977).
17. Hasenfeld, *Human Service Organizations.*
18. Cited by K. Larkin and E. J. Madara in *The Self-Help Group Sourcebook 1983* (Denville: New Jersey Self-Help Clearinghouse, 1983).
19. D. Robinson and S. Henry, *Self-Help and Health: Mutual Aid for Modern Problems* (London, England: Martin Robinson, 1977), p. 68.
20. R. H. Hall, "The Concept of Bureaucracy: An Empirical Assessment," *American Journal of Sociology,* 69 (1983), pp. 32–40; and R. Dewar, D. Whetten, and D. Boje, "An Examination of the Reliability and Validity of the Aiken and Hage Scales of Centralization, Formalization, and Task Routineness," *Administrative Science Quarterly,* 25 (March 1980), pp. 120–128.

Reference Group Processes

Personal change is both the cause and the consequence of adopting a new culture. The new culture alters the values a person holds and the meaning a person attributes to various aspects of reality. The frame of reference acquired as part of the new culture is thought to be a major factor in changing self-assessments and long-standing behavior patterns. In the following passages, Maxwell outlines the far-reaching personal changes that accompany immersion in the AA culture and acceptance of AA as a reference group:

> To change is to accept a change in "facts" which are accepted as true, a change in values, and a change in the perception of self and others in a social field. . . . [Change] may also be seen as the acceptance of new norms, folkways and mores, new roles in a new role-status system, a new charter and new sanctions. These are all aspects of culture—of a group-shared way of life.
>
> Accordingly. . . recovery [involves] gradually learning that group's culture. The A. A. subculture, moreover, constitutes a way of life which is more realistic, which enables the member to get closer to people, which provides one with more emotional security, and which facilitates more productive living. Thus, the A. A. group becomes an important new reference group—a new point of orientation.[1]

These changes are the result of what has been labeled *reference power*, which is distinguished by its capacity to elicit a voluntary acceptance of values and norms, in contrast to the promise of some reward, a contractual obligation, or a threat of coercion to exact conformity.[2] Reference power differs from other types of power in that the individual feels bound to the group's norms regardless of whether compliance is monitored or reinforced. Like a placebo, the group is presumed to have the power to bring about change. There is the expectation that changes will occur and that they will be beneficial. These positive expectations are based on a perceived similarity between the individual and the frame of reference, so that there is a predilection for the individual to accept the framework's values, beliefs, and norms.

"Reference group theory aims to systematize the determinants and consequences of those processes of evaluation and self-appraisal in which the individual takes the values or standards of other individuals and groups as a comparative frame of reference."[3] Much of the scholarship in this field has endeavored to specify either the conditions under which new reference groups are adopted or the results of their adoption. The following questions indicate some of the issues scholars have raised concerning the adoption of reference groups: Why is one reference group perceived to be more appropriate or personally more relevant than another? What kinds of anticipatory rewards are likely to induce a person to accept a new reference group? How does the individual choose among multiple groups that have an apparently similar appeal? When there is conflict over which reference group to choose, such as between family members and peers, how is the choice made? In a self-help context, how does one choose when there is a conflict between the values of one's drinking or gambling buddies and AA or GA?

Many of the results of belonging to a reference group are discussed in a book of readings edited by Hyman and Singer,[4] and in a masterful critical review, Pettigrew discusses the complexities and unsolved problems of reference group theory.[5] One of the dangers he sees is a tendency to lapse into circular explanations: Behaviors x_1 through x_n are "explained" by affiliation with reference group X without an independent measurement of the affiliation. "So and so behaves that way because he or she gives precedence to the family over co-workers as the primary reference group." If this primary allegiance has not been independently verified, however, the "explanation" is circular and gratuitous. Feld and Radin have developed formulations that integrate more recent studies, and they discuss the application of reference group theory to important clinical problems.[6]

Thus, having acknowledged the complexity of the questions surrounding reference group theory and having disavowed any intent to use it as an all-purpose explanation, this author suggests that the theory offers useful explanations of how self-help organizations help their members feel better about themselves and develop new ideas about what behavior is right for them.

REFERENCE GROUP FORMATION AND FUNCTION

Reference group theorists posit a need for people to check out others or to compare themselves with others. This need becomes more pronounced when the person is uncertain about the proper course of action to take ("Should I or shouldn't I?"), the situation is ambiguous ("Is it this or that?"), or there is conflict about what should be done. Under these circumstances, there is a strong tendency to rely on the reference group's judgment. Other situations may also increase the relevance of the reference group. As anxiety mounts, the person is drawn toward others (assuming all hope has not been lost) who are in a similar situation. Sometimes direct contact may be sought with these others, and if this is not feasible, there may be more interest expressed in similar people discussed or portrayed in the media. This is another form of contact in that the person imagines what others who are similar are feeling and what they are likely to do. In all instances, the aim is to determine how others are experiencing and managing their anxiety.[7] In their review of comparison group theory and research, Feld and Radin concluded that pain and discomfort can be better tolerated in the presence of a reference group.[8] This, undoubtedly, is one of the most important dynamics behind the appeal of self-help organizations, and much of the time, a group is chosen because the person perceives a similarity and feels an attraction to the group members.[9] Once similarity is established, self-evaluation follows. Other times, the sequence is reversed in that the self is first evaluated and then the person searches for people who are similar and to whom he or she is attracted. But whatever the sequence, the perception of similar attributes and personal relevance is the grounds for the selection of a reference group.

Reference groups serve two basic functions: One is a comparative (self-evaluative) or "How do I measure up?" function; the other is a normative or "What should I do?" function. "What grade did you get?" illustrates the comparative function, whereas "How much did you study?" (searching for guidelines) illustrates the normative function. In a self-help context, the self-evaluative question might be "How did you feel about yourself when you joined?" And the normative question might be "What helped you turn your personal situation around?" Almost simultaneously, then, people learn how to evaluate themselves and how to behave according to the values and norms of certain groups. Repeatedly, they raise the question: "How would they [their reference group] behave in this situation?"

The stability of the reference group, that is, its consistency as a frame of reference across time and under different circumstances, depends on the degree of perceived similarity between the individual and the group. The greater the similarity, the more likely the reference group will be a comprehensive, durable influence. Under these conditions, self-assessments will continue to be altered to bring them into ever closer harmony with the group.[10] It is common, however, for the reigning reference group to shift from family to ethnic group, co-religionists, or an illness or problem group, depending on the task at hand. For some tasks, the family may be referred to; for others, it may be co-workers who subscribe to norms and values that conflict with those of the family. In such situations, the self-help organization may be referred to in order to reconcile the input from these conflicting, subordinate reference groups. This, of course, would mean that the self-help organization is an extraordinarily powerful reference group, and if it is comprehensive and stable, it can have a very profound effect on the individual's behavior. The single-mindedness of the "born again" Christian, or the "peace and justice" activist, comes to mind as illustrating the power of reference groups. The obviousness of these examples, however, should not allow us to overlook the less sensational but equally powerful reference groups of such well-acculturated people as the workaholic professional. It is all too easy to underestimate the power of certain reference groups because they conform to approved cultural patterns.

Selection of Self-Help Organizations

CONFLICTS AND CHOICES: The major changes in behavior once the individual chooses a reference group (for example, PA) may be less surprising than the choice of the self-help organization as a reference group. Why do individuals refer to groups so at odds with their previous lifestyle when they could select a membership group (family) or an imaginary group (other parents who interact with their children in a similar manner) to justify their lifestyle? With so many choices, how does a self-help organization become the arbiter of decisions about drinking, parenting, or gambling? How does it come to supplant family, co-workers, or neighbors who had been the primary reference? Why does the person adopt a new reference group when it almost certainly requires a reassessment of "How hard I've tried" or "What I should do?" What makes it possible to modify earlier positions so that change becomes possible?

The appeal of the organization depends on a number of factors. In some self-help organizations, age, sex, and ethnicity may be highly salient, whereas income is less so; in most such organizations, even these factors will be less important than the similarity of the problem. "The important thing is that we are all compulsive gamblers [or single parents] and not whether we are doctors, lawyers, or Indian chiefs—or door-to-door salesmen or factory workers." Often the similarity of the problem will be strong enough to unify a very mixed group, in which, for example, the members have different ethnic backgrounds. In such a group, however, differences in ethnicity will detract from the power of the self-help organization as a reference group. When the similarity of the problem is less clear, when the problems are inherently more vague (for example, worrisome emotions), the power of the reference group may be further attenuated by the different backgrounds of its members. This is to say, other things being equal, a heterogeneous membership may pose fewer difficulties to a stop-smoking group than it would to one dealing with more ambiguous emotional problems.

Supportive individuals outside, and mentors inside, the self-help organization may be able to downplay these influences by confirming the importance of some similarities and questioning the importance of the differences. For example, similarities of income or education are less important than similarities of problems. This is usually true in many "Anonymous" organizations. Such organizations discourage conversation about occupation, education, and residence, since it may prevent communication about the common problem.

REWARDS: Another basic tenet is that individuals are moved by the expectation of significant rewards. Some of these may take the form of gains in competence and upward mobility. It is easy to underestimate the appeal of these qualities to a person who feels that his or her family has been going downhill for several generations. But perhaps the greatest reward will be a new self-respect as progress is made in solving basic problems.

Some of these dynamics are evident in the replies (here paraphrased) of parents who were asked about their reasons for joining PA.[11] "Even though they were child-abusers like me, they were nice people, attractive people, people who had respect for themselves and had learned to cope with their difficulties." Relief about

the present and hope for the future were evident in such comments as "lots of others, even well-educated and well-off people,"
seem to have the same problem. Typically the parents reported
that these encounters left them feeling "there may still be hope."
Some parents went on to say that they were inspired by the competence of the seasoned PA members. The process was one in
which the perceived similarity between what they were like then
and what successful PA members had been like earlier meant
that participating in the group could have significant benefits.

DURABILITY AND POTENCY: Once a new reference group has
been selected, the questions become: How durable will the commitment to the newly adopted self-help organization be? And will
the commitment be strong enough to withstand the regressive
pulls of groups to whom one feels loyalty, especially if they happen to be family and close friends? Or to address effectiveness
from a different perspective, will the comparative standards and
behavioral norms of the self-help organization be seen as sufficiently relevant to the specific areas of the individual's difficulty
to supplant the standards and norms of the old reference group?
　All these questions can be answered "yes," provided certain
conditions are met. Supportive professionals, significant others,
and self-help leaders can contribute to meeting these conditions
by discussing possible payoffs. Fewer problems, less distress,
higher self-esteem, and less guilt might be mentioned. Judicious
questions might be asked about the relevance of other groups.
How helpful have close friends or family members been in the
past? Replies may be interpreted to mean that the individual
already seems inclined to adopt the self-help organization as a
reference group. To turn this inclination into regular participation is to do no more than to validate the person's intuition. Moreover, joining a self-help organization may be interpreted as just
another instance of the person's willingness to accept responsibility or as a manifestation of the person's delight in a challenge.
　Other suggestions or prescriptions self-help leaders and mentors might consider involve ensuring accessibility and acceptability. They will need to discuss basic arrangements of transportation, location, and meeting hours and the various options the
newcomer has to observe and try out the organization before
deciding to join. The mentors who function as gatekeepers—or
better, gate-openers—must also convey the idea that the supportive presence of others may be indispensable to a resolution of
the problem. The supportive presence of others is often necessary
to elicit the individual's best coping efforts.[12] Thus, the self-help
dictum: "Only you can do it, but you can't do it alone."　77

Benefits of a Self-Help Organization

Many of the benefits of self-help organizations can be conceptualized in terms of reference group theory. This approach was first used by Powell and Levy, and the discussion draws on their articles.[13]

FEELING BETTER ABOUT MYSELF: Many people have poor self-esteem as a result of their self-destructive habits, their impaired functioning, their stressful personal situations, or their poor health. But when they participate in a self-help organization, they are in close contact with established members who have recovered their self-esteem despite similar difficulties. These established members have achieved an enviable level of self-acceptance and have mastered their problems. And they have accomplished this despite the similarity of their problems with "mine." Thus—and to hedge it as the newcomer might—the possibility of similar success need not be ruled out. "Despite what these people claim, they seem pretty decent. They aren't so down on themselves— maybe I can feel that way too." "And besides, if they want me, I couldn't be that bad."

RATIONALE FOR THE PREDICAMENT: Self-help organizations provide their members with a rationale for their predicament. Ironically, even when organizations insist there is no explanation, or that explanations are irrelevant, established members facilitate understanding through the actions recommended to resolve or cope with the problem. Despite statements to the contrary, "explanations" of a sort are embedded in the action formulas prescribed for members. These "Steps," "Guides," "Tools for Personal Development," or, sometimes, lists of suggested activities demystify troubling experiences. Injunctions such as "Move the muscles," and "Pretend you like it" imply simple working explanations, though the struggle to succeed is also recognized. Furthermore, the priority assigned to action in these formulas may suggest that the etiology of the problem may be a good deal more complicated than the solution.[14]

Parents Anonymous has developed a rationale for understanding child abuse through its conceptualization of the world of abusive relationships (WAR) cycle. It asserts that abusive tendencies usually spring from abusive experiences in one's own childhood. People are brought up to it, since abuse and neglect have been an inseparable part of everyday life from an early age. Thus, the PA member's abusive tendencies were all too predictable and now are all too understandable, though not excusable. And this warm understanding of victim-abusers does not weaken the expectation that abusive tendencies can be curbed. In fact, the tendency is in the other direction, for in order to believe that one has been exonerated, it is also necessary to make a strong commitment to the remedial actions prescribed by PA. As in professional therapy, the value attached to capturing the nuances of truth in the rationale is less important than its value as a stimulus for constructive efforts to solve problems.

INFORMATION AND GUIDANCE: The self-help organization can be thought of as a resource for information about appropriate patterns or norms of thinking, feeling, and acting under various circumstances. These norms command attention because they emanate from a reference group, a group to which the individual voluntarily grants influence over his or her behavior. Detailed prescriptions are most easily visualized in the habit control organizations that aim to curb excessive eating or to cut off the use of alcohol or tobacco. Every organization, however, proclaims principles ("Symptoms are distressing but not dangerous") and behavioral norms ("The first bet is the wrong one") according to its requirements.

Specialized information is often needed to cope with many problematic conditions and situations. The single parent, for example, may need detailed information about the options for personal financial credit or the options for child care. The handicapped individual, about to choose which of several suggested prostheses would be the best for his or her needs, wants to know how other handicapped people feel about these prostheses or how one or the other has worked out in the past. It may also be helpful to find out how the nonhandicapped react to certain models. The vivid detail with which this information is transmitted renders it highly usable. And whether people are addicted to gambling, food, alcohol, or illegal substances, they can benefit from the pragmatic, close-to-experience norms that have been developed to resist the temptations associated with each of them.

ANTECEDENTS: On a different level, self-help organizations often know a good deal about the immediate antecedents of problematic behavior. This information about the triggering perceptions and external events will often be codified and communicated in the printed word and through the oral tradition of the organization. And because of its strong orientation, the self-help organization may be uniquely positioned to educate its members about how to prevent the problematic episodes or to control their worst consequences. Thus, various self-help organizations might ask   *79* their members to consider how high-risk situations might be better dealt with through anticipatory planning. Such high-risk situations might involve contact with an ex-spouse, a reminder of a lost close friend, or the agitation or aimlessness resulting from the lack of regularly scheduled external activities. In some instances, members will be able to reduce their exposure to such risk factors; in other instances, when exposure cannot be avoided, they may discover more personally effective ways of coping.

SETBACKS: As a reference group, the self-help organization can communicate realistic, acceptable information about setbacks. Any other group may have a hard time convincing the person he or she isn't always bad and that, certainly, all hope is not lost. Progress or recovery, other members may note, rarely follows a smooth, upward course. In fact, uninterrupted self-control may have some disadvantages. The goal, for example, for PA members must not simply be the teeth-gritting control of abuse, but a warm and pleasurable appreciation of the child. For those persons in AA, abstinence is not the goal; rather it is sobriety. The drawbacks of uninterrupted abstinence may be especially apparent among substance abusers and other compulsive people. If separated from the globally critical context in which it is sometimes used, the phrase *dry drunk* does make an important point. Simple abstinence can interfere with full emotional recovery. This point is made with powerful images in the *White Book* of Narcotics Anonymous:

> There may be times when a relapse lays the groundwork for complete freedom. At other times only by a grim and obstinate willfulness to hang on to abstinence come hell or high water until a crisis passes, can that freedom be achieved . . . .We need to recognize two of our seemingly inherent enemies, apathy and procrastination. Our resistance to change seems built in and only a nuclear blast of some kind will bring about any alteration or initiate another course of action. A relapse may provide the charge for the demolition process. A relapse and sometimes subsequent death of someone close to us can do the job of awakening us to the necessity for vigorous personal action.[15]

Some setbacks can, of course, be prevented by sponsors and other members who may have more intimate knowledge than most people about the signs of an impending relapse. But if it is not possible to prevent a relapse, it will usually be possible to limit its most damaging effects. The worst one, the despair of the backslider, can be challenged by the assertion that the concern of the senior successful members persists despite the likelihood of setbacks. It is well known that many of those who succeed do so only after many reverses. And a peer who was a former backslider may be the best person to get this fact across to one facing a setback.

STRENGTHENING MOTIVATION: Because it is a group that the individual has voluntarily agreed to refer to, the self-help organization may be effective in raising the level of sacrifice and effort. The revised norms accepted as part of membership may lead to a fresh assessment of what is to be judged—sacrifice and effort. The self-help frame of reference may make it possible for newer members to conclude that they have not tried hard enough or as hard as successful members. Redoubled efforts will be required before they can consider that they are truly following the program to which they, of their own accord, earlier committed themselves.

The tension generated by this deliberate switching from a hard-nosed approach to a manifestly empathic one helps maintain members in an optimal state of arousal. If complacency were to set in, many more members would find themselves falling by the wayside because of inattention or a lapse in vigilance. When toughness accompanies empathy and tolerance, the individual is more likely to be able to fend off distractions and stay on the prescribed track. Many organizations hold that their goals can never be fully realized, but that these same goals can always be pursued.

A TRANSCENDENT CULTURE: When the self-help organization becomes a reference group, it creates a new personal culture, one of new values and lifestyle practices. This cultural change transcends the many specific changes that were implemented to attain the narrower objectives that were originally sought. The new culture protects and elaborates the earlier gains by providing access to people, activities, and especially organizational opportunities (intergroup, professional relations committee, leadership training) that afford constructive employment of time that was formerly used to pursue destructive activities. Support for the old culture, the one that encouraged destructive activity, came from dysfunctional reference groups. A new culture had to be created to replace the dysfunctional old culture, which hereafter should be used primarily as a negative standard of reference. For this to be accomplished, the new culture must compete with the one it is replacing. Often the self-help organization can become the core of this new culture through its program. By participating in the self-help organization's manifold activities, the individual will have a rich opportunity to fashion a new, comprehensive, and satisfying personal culture.

Potential Dysfunctions of
Self-Help Organizations

Practically anything carried too far can lead to its own downfall. Too much self-acceptance, too much concern over one's health, too much pride in one's lifestyle can be counterproductive. Frames of reference can be overextended or unbalanced.

Single-issue lifestyles should be avoided. A fanatic is someone who is preoccupied with a single theme. And in some chapters of self-help organizations, single-mindedness is carried to an extreme. Their misguided actions may entrench a negative self-concept by ascribing too much importance to such matters as body weight or to occasional lapses in parenting. When this occurs, a distorted self-concept is reinforced and self-esteem is undermined.

Moreover, vigilant monitoring is necessary to guard against the misinterpretation of standards or the unwarranted extension of norms to other, inappropriate spheres of the members' lives. For even when the broad self-help program is embraced, it must be realized that the formulas and practices of self-help organizations are unlikely to be sufficiently discriminating to support an effective, satisfying social life.

It is important that individuals not lose their sense of proportion about their lives. In adapting to their surroundings, individuals must live by multiple and sometimes contradictory imperatives. They must refer to multiple groups to evaluate themselves and to look for norms to guide their behavior. If too few groups are chosen, an individual's frame of reference may become unbalanced and be extended to situations in which it does not apply. If individuals are not careful or if they are not properly guided, they can choose the wrong groups for evaluating themselves or deciding on a course of action.

Notes

1. M. A. Maxwell, "Alcoholics Anonymous: An Interpretation," in D. J. Pittman and C. R. Snyder, eds., *Society, Culture, and Drinking Patterns* (New York: John Wiley & Sons, 1962), p. 582.
2. J. R. P. French, Jr., and B. Raven, "The Bases of Social Power," in D. Cartwright, ed., *Studies in Social Power* (Ann Arbor: University of Michigan Press, 1959), pp. 150–167.
3. R. K. Merton and A. K. Rossi, "Contributions to the Theory of Reference Group Behavior," in H. H. Hyman and E. Singer, eds., *Readings in Reference Group Theory and Research* (New York: Free Press, 1968), p. 35.

4. Hyman and Singer, eds., *Readings in Reference Group Theory and Research*.

5. T. F. Pettigrew, "Social Evaluation Theory: Convergences and Applications," in D. Levine, ed., *Proceedings: Nebraska Symposium on Motivation*, Vol. 15 (Lincoln: University of Nebraska Press, 1967), pp. 241–318.

6. S. Feld and N. L. Radin, *Social Psychology for Social Work and the Mental Health Professions* (New York: Columbia University Press, 1982), pp. 110–133.

7. S. Schachter, *The Psychology of Affiliation* (Stanford, Calif.: Stanford University Press, 1959).

8. Feld and Radin, *Social Psychology for Social Work and the Mental Health Professions*, p. 117.

9. Pettigrew, "Social Evaluation Theory," pp. 244–249.

10. Feld and Radin, *Social Psychology for Social Work and the Mental Health Professions*, p. 111.

11. T. J. Powell, "Interpreting Parents Anonymous as a Source of Help for Those with Child Abuse Problems," *Child Welfare*, 58 (February 1979), pp. 105–114.

12. R. B. Zajonc, "Social Facilitation," in D. Cartwright and A. Zander, eds., *Group Dynamics* (3rd ed.; New York: Harper & Row, 1968), pp. 63–73.

13. T. J. Powell, "The Use of Self-Help Groups as Supportive Reference Communities," *American Journal of Orthopsychiatry*, 45 (October 1975), pp. 756–764; and L. H. Levy, "Self-Help Groups: Types and Psychological Processes," *Journal of Behavioral Science*, 12 (July–August–September 1976), pp. 310–322.

14. Levy, "Self-Help Groups."

15. Narcotics Anonymous, *White Book* (Van Nuys, Calif.: NA World Service, 1976), pp. 9–10.

Social Networks and the Acquisition of Resources

At this midpoint in using social science theory to explain how self-help organizations work, it is useful to take stock of what has been done thus far and to see what lies ahead. This chapter examines how self-help organizations enhance the individual's social network. Through the self-help organization, new ties are created and existing ones strengthened such that the individual has access to more adequate social support and, when necessary, specialized resources. Chapter Six examines how the self-help organization functions to promote social learning. Self-help organizations create an environment in which the contingencies facilitate learning to cope with problems more effectively.

This approach builds on the concept of the self-help organization (Chapter Three) as an intentional social unit designed to achieve explicit goals. Organizational theory offered some insight into how self-help procedures are developed and refined and how diverse opportunities encourage continued participation. The concept of formalization shows how induction procedures evolve into efficient instruments for eliciting the commitment of newcomers and for socializing them to the norms of the organization. The concept of complexity helps explain how the organization can accomplish such complicated tasks as gaining the recognition and support of the general community. The specialized public education substructures required for such tasks are usually designed and developed by veteran members. Because of the resulting attachments and because of the continuing challenges, experienced members are encouraged to stay on.

The reference group perspective developed in Chapter Four outlined a process by which newcomers come to see themselves as belonging to the self-help organization. Reference group theory also offered insights into how the standards and the norms of the self-help organization can become salient for the members. As a member might have put it, reference group theory explains how "I decided that these are my kind of people, and how I can do it, as long as they can."

Here, network theory will be used to examine the impact of the self-help organization on the individual's personal network. Networking begins in the first few meetings. The new relationships formed in the self-help organization help boost morale and help make the individual's problems seem more soluble. And as a result of the new internal relationships, the new member may be helped to initiate or to modify relationships outside the self-help organization. Once such outside relationships are established, they can be maintained and developed long after the person has left the self-help organization. Thus, beneficial effects may persist long after the period of active membership. For example, PWP members often form new relationships both within and outside the organization, and these relationships frequently decrease the need for the organization; thus comes the expression that PWP has a "stepping-stone" function.

Another feature of social network theory focuses on how one relationship changes another, just as marriage changes one's relationship with one's parents. A marriage, too, may be affected by the relationships associated with a new job or a membership, for example, in Al-Anon. Social network theory also makes it possible to trace the effects of relationships across institutional boundaries, for example, the effects of a relationship between self-helpers on their relationships with co-workers. Outside influences that arise from external club or neighborhood ties modify relationships in even the most formal of business organizations. Thus, network theory can elucidate how self-help organization relationships affect relationships in the neighborhood, the workplace, and the friendship and family sectors of the individual's social life.

The self-help organization and the person's network can interact in a number of ways: Existing relationships may be at cross purposes with the self-help organization. They may discourage participation or ridicule its purpose: "PA is just for 'women libbers'." The person may subsequently feel that it is necessary to modify these relationships or to form new ones, which may indicate that positive changes have been brought about by the self-help organization. New outside relationships may reinforce the *85* self-help orientation, but they also make it possible after a time to continue in a positive course without it. Initially, however, the questions asked are: "Whom do I know—or whom can I get to know—who can help me with my difficulties?" "How can new relationships, or changes in existing ones, improve my situation?"

NETWORK DEFICIENCIES

Appraising the Whole Network

Nearly everyone with a problem serious enough to take to a self-help organization or a human service organization can be said to have personal network problems. To begin with, there may be structural problems with the individual's entire network. Persistent feelings of loneliness and isolation may be the result of networks that are too small or networks in which there is too little interaction among those who make up the network. Some individuals lack linkages to some sectors; the long-term mentally ill may lack ties to noncompetitive housing or occupation sectors, sectors that themselves are underdeveloped. The distribution of relationships among kin, co-workers, neighbors, and friends may be unbalanced. Relationships may be terminated by divorce, and friends may have to be replaced; or more complex or closer relationships may have to be established with old friends. The newly single person may need to establish ties to people in the employment and credit sectors; relationships with singles may be necessary to compensate for losses in the area of married couple relationships.[1] Connections with one's relations may be few and tenuous. If there are too few connections with co-workers, neighbors, friends, and family members, the individual may feel isolated and without a sense of purpose. But too many connections can also be a problem. Ingrown or overly dense relationships, the kind where "everyone butts into everyone else's business," can be stifling. When too many paths lead to the same people, new ideas and experiences, as well as people, tend to be in short supply. Some network sectors (for example, leisure time activities) may be too small. These can often be increased by following the paths that lead to new contacts.

For more specialized problems, a searching out of resources little known to the general public may be necessary. For example, services for the long-term mentally ill or the developmentally disabled may be obtained from specialized rehabilitative agencies offering training activities for daily living or from lawyers who are experienced in designing trusts for impaired persons.

The self-help organization may also compensate for what Borkman has described as the selectively unsupportive behavior of lay or folk networks.[2] These networks, principally of family and friends, often provide insufficient or misguided support. Strategies to cope with these deficiencies may be of as much concern to self-help organizations as their concern with deficiencies in professional services networks. Self-help organizations know, for example, that it can be disastrous for family and friends to suggest that "An occasional slap is good for all children" or that "Beer is OK." The tragedies that can result from this "folk knowledge" can be prevented by the "experiential knowledge" of those who have intimate experience with the problem and its resolution. If left unchallenged, such commonly held assumptions as "Willpower is all that is needed" result in various forms of blaming the victim. If one uses Borkman's expression, one sees that family and friends do not have sufficient knowledge about the problem's "emotionscape."[3] They do not know how the person with the problem is affected by situations, places, interactions, and people associated with his or her problem. It is hardly surprising, then, that the general public will not be aware of the different kinds of anxiety going to a restaurant, for example, may evoke. Borkman suggests, by way of example, that the stutterer may be anxious about verbalizing the order, the alcoholic about avoiding embarrassment as the drink and wine order is taken, and the ostomate about whether the ingredients of the meal will cause gastrointestinal upset. Indeed, who could be expected to know the details of these emotionscapes, except those who have experienced them?

Individual Relationships

A number of other shortcomings may exist in the relationships that make up an individual's total network. Relationships with particular individuals may be distressing because their focus is too narrow. "All he ever talks about is work. . .or the children." Some relationships, however, may involve too many focuses. The entanglements of people who are both lovers and co-workers is a common dramatic theme imitating life. The distress caused by financial rivalry among members of a family with already complicated family relations is another such theme. A different problem is one-sidedness: too much going out and too little coming in. Too much or too little of other relational properties—frequency, intensity, or duration—will also be distressing when they run counter to expectations. The formal properties of social networks identify important foci for efforts to assess and ameli- *87* orate personal difficulties. For when the value of even one such property changes—a change, for example, in the number of significant relationships or in the mutuality level of one important relationship—ramifications are likely to be felt throughout all relationships.

ASSESSMENT AND REMEDIATION

Elements of the Theory

Mitchell defined *social network* as a "specific set of linkages among a defined set of persons with the additional property that the characteristics of these linkages as a whole may be used to interpret the social behaviour of the persons involved."[4] Some properties refer to the individual's entire set of linkages; others refer to each tie or relation making up the set. When these properties have different values, they will be associated with different consequences for the focal person.[5] The systematic assessment and modification of these properties distinguishes the analytic concept from the colloquial expression "networking," the latter being a fashionable, but much less powerful, reference to making and maintaining contact with supportive people. By going beyond popular usage, by using the conceptual properties of network theory to assess the adequacy of particular networks, it should be possible to develop some highly leveraged interventions. Self-help organizations can be instrumental in making important changes in such properties as the size and distribution of the entire network and the content and intensity of particular relationships.

Functions of the Theory

Since the theory traces causal forces across boundaries, it can be used to monitor the back-and-forth effects between the self-help sector and other sectors, such as family, job, and neighborhood. It can illuminate the workings of the mutual aid system, a function most self-help organizations fulfill by encouraging phone calls and extra-meeting contacts. It can provide insight into the antecedents of otherwise puzzling behavior in self-help meetings. The behavior will often be understood when it is traced to an earlier event, such as a sexual encounter or a dispute that occurred outside the formal self-help meeting. Or the puzzling behavior may precede an event, such as asking a favor or instigating a fight. Social network theory, unlike social role theory and small group theory, is not restricted to processes that occur in single settings. By cutting across settings, social network theory can be used to conceptualize how external forces affect the self-help experience.

Within the self-help organization, social network theory can be used to assess whether a relationship might benefit from additional content, more intensity, or greater mutuality. Should a broader variety of topics be discussed in a way to intensify the relationship or to encourage more mutual interaction? As far as encouraging more supportive relationships between meetings, would it be useful if leaders made more in-between meeting calls? Or alternatively, should more social events be scheduled or some "do's and don't's" be developed for the use of the telephone network? Beyond the self-help sector, would it be useful to identify the internal antecedents of supportive outside relationships with nonmembers? *What* is critical? Is it the example or the encouragement of senior members who have formed new ties beyond the self-help organization? These relationships, originally prompted by self-help experiences but now independent of them, should be studied to determine the extent of the effects of the self-help experience. A better understanding of these now-independent relationships might also yield more information about the benefits that are presumed to continue following active participation in the self-help organization.

Means of Transmittal

Whatever the effects of the self-help organization, they must be mediated through the primary network. The primary network consists of the people to whom the individual is directly related (sometimes called the star, after the image of ties radiating out from a central individual). These relationships also provide secondary access to other people with whom the primary person has ties. The concept of secondary and extended networks is especially useful to the understanding of how access to special resources occurs. These indirect "through a mutual friend" relations make "contacts" possible. These contacts, however, are of little use until they are activated, as facilitated by the self-help organization through intergroup meetings, workshops, newsletters, national coordinating activities, and, of course, contacts between members.

Importance of Interconnections

If the projection of ties into the secondary networks and beyond is thought of as a vertical elaboration of the network, the fre-   *89* quency of these interconnections can be thought of as a horizontal elaboration. Interconnections between members of the primary network may be particularly important to the operation of self-help organizations. A referral to AA is likely to be more effective when the contact person has a number of solid ties with other AA members. Astute linking agents have assumed that their ties will be more solid if members of both organizations know of their efforts. In ongoing assistance efforts, self-help participants, particularly isolated ones, will be better served when caregivers are coordinated. A caregiver (for example, a substance abuse counselor) will tend to relate differently to a client if other caregivers (for example, AA members) are helping to support the client.[6] Intuitive reviews of clients' networks often don't attend to whether these "others" know each other. Thus, the familiar vertically oriented aphorism needs to be extended horizontally: It's not just whom you know, and whom they know, but whether these "others" also know one another.

The impact of self-help organizations will vary depending on the value of the eight formal properties of social networks.[7] The first three—*size, reachability,* and *density*—refer to the entire set of ties. These properties focus on certain broad aspects of an individual's experience, for example, a need for more friends and for connectedness among existing friends, or the need for career opportunities. Since the next five formal properties concern each relationship within the total set, they can enhance understanding of the various dimensions of these relationships: In what ways could my relationship with X be improved? Insofar as there is a pattern to these individual relationships, however, the analysis can be applied to several relationships. Nonetheless, the distressing qualities of individual relationships may be pinpointed by assessing their (1) content, (2) durability, (3) directedness, (4) frequency, and (5) intensity.

PROPERTIES OF THE TOTAL NETWORK

Size

In the property of size, the qualities of simplicity and power coincide. It is simple to understand and easy to measure, and yet it is one of a network's most significant properties. A deficient base —too small a network—may cause significant problems in individual relations. This point was made by my secretary when she was transcribing tape-recorded interviews with members of PA.[8] "Their problem," she said, "is their lack of relief from the children; they neither have the money to buy child care nor the families that can provide it."

Too few relationships overburden available relationships. The strain will be evident in too high expectations, too much analysis, and too little flexibility. When the already-too-few relationships are strained, there is too little to fall back on and little opportunity to take refuge in other relationships. This might well be the situation of the recovering mental patient. Of perhaps less concern, but in the interests of symmetry, there is also the other side: One can almost always have too much of a good thing. Too large a network may crowd out opportunities for close relations, or extensive social obligations may cut into quality time with the family.

When one returns to the more common problem of adequate size, there must be enough relationships to cover the major social institutions, including family, workplace, and neighborhood. Typically, ties in each of these sectors form more or less separate clusters with interconnecting bridges. The ideal seems to be some, but not a complete, overlap among these sectors. Such an arrangement trades the support available from closely meshed relationships for the fresh inputs obtainable from less familiar ones. In the worst cases, the network is distressingly ingrown or skewed in the opposite direction by being composed of nearly all outwardly radiating, but superficial, relationships.

The self-help organization can make an obvious but far from trivial difference in the size of a person's social network. At the organization chapter level, there may be the potential for a few to several score relationships. The modal range for the number of members in local chapters is probably from 10 to 25 members. When there are more than 25 members, it may be difficult to maintain a close relationship with a substantial number of the members. This may stimulate the local chapter to divide so that it is small enough to allow members to participate more effectively. By dividing the chapter in two, meetings become accessible to potential new members who could not have come at the original time or to the original location. In any event, the relationships formed at the home-chapter level often become bridges to relationships with members in other chapters and coordinating bodies of the self-help organization. These relationships are the natural result of participation in fundraisers, workshops, leadership-training classes, social events, and regional and national conferences. Some members also encourage new contacts through distinctive pins and bumper stickers (for example, AA's "Easy Does It"). In general, however, forays into the larger self-help organization usually are prompted by increasing responsibility   *91* at the chapter level. "Having come this far, I thought I should get more involved."

Reachability

The ability to contact desired persons, the property of reachability, is of great importance when nonroutine needs must be met. The handicapped person may need a custom-made prosthesis. But special needs may be the norm rather than the exception; both the compulsive gambler and the PA member may require special assistance to manage their complicated entanglements with the legal system. In such situations, the reachability of people who can provide specialized information and informed support may be critical. Surprisingly, however, this expertise, which is difficult for the ordinary person to obtain, may be readily available to members of a self-help organization because the organization has been expressly designed for that purpose.

But reachability is important not just to those who have special needs. All people need satisfying and effective ties in the major sectors of their lives, and for many, this means family, workplace, neighborhood, social, and leisure-time sectors. Overly segmented[9] or inadequately composed[10] networks cause distress. Some people, for example, may feel trapped by the intensity of their family relationships. Many such people face the straightforward, but not to say easy, task of cultivating relationships in other sectors. They simultaneously face the task of reducing the intensity of family ties. These tasks were of concern to the female single parents studied by McLanahan et al.[11] These researchers identified three patterns of relationships, each with opportunities and limitations. Female single parents tended to cluster their relationships in one of three sectors: with their own parents, with a male companion, or with other single parents. Problems arise when the network does not correspond to the tasks that must be performed or when dependence on a particular sector is seen to be dictated by circumstances rather than free choice.

In such situations, a self-help organization may help fill in gaps and balance the network. Parents Without Partners, for example, can allow the single parent to learn how others have dealt with changes in family relationships or changes in social and recreational opportunities and interests. After a year or two, however, many members grow restive in PWP. The predominant themes—vicissitudes of single parenthood and concerns related to separation and new beginnings—may be too limiting for the person who has adapted to a new lifestyle. And it must be said that just as organizational forces may retain senior members, other forces, particularly network forces, may spin members out toward new interests. These centrifugal forces make "graduation" from the organization a viable and positively sanctioned option.

Density

The property of density focuses on interconnections in social networks. Density is the proportion of people who relate to a focal person and who also relate to each other. Another way to put it is that density is the proportion of actual to potential interconnections. If A and B, who both relate to C, also relate to each other, they are part of C's dense or closely knit network; if they do not relate to each other, they are part of C's low density, more open, loosely knit network.

A number of empirical studies support the interpretation that high density is advantageous for some purposes and disadvantageous for others. When emotional support is desirable, high density relationships are preferable. But when fresh input is desirable, low density relationships are preferable. These conclusions are based on the following findings:

Hammer's work highlighted the correlation between emotional support and tightly meshed, enduring relationships.[12] Her study and a similar one by Horowitz found that the pathway to the mental hospital varied depending on the density of patients' networks.[13] During the admissions phase, the relatives of patients with high density networks were more likely to be an integral part of the process, whereas patients with low density networks dealt with doctors and social workers on their own.

But dense networks can also be dysfunctional. McKinlay's study found that new mothers with high density networks underutilized maternal health services.[14] And though, in Hirsch's study, the college students suffering from anxiety acknowledged the value of support from their dense networks, they also felt ambivalent about their experience.[15] They seemed to regret the loss of privacy and confidentiality commonly experienced in dense networks. Thus, relationships in high density sectors can be potentially intrusive as well as supportive; this mixed bag may be too often overlooked by those who tend to idealize high density.

The review by Mitchell and Trickett highlighted the advantages of the alternative network, the relatively open or low-density network.[16] Relations unconnected to others in the network, and therefore more likely to radiate out to new people, are beneficial because they form paths or bridges to resources that are scarce or unavailable in the existing network. Hirsch's study of widows and other women returning to college after long absences showed *93* they fared better when significant numbers of their relationships were open and radial rather than closed and interlocking.[17] The openness contributed to the acceptance of new influences since they were less encumbered by old ones. Walker et al. pointed out in their discussion of the needs of the bereaved that the property of density must be balanced between high and low density.[18] Widows need to accept, and have others acknowledge, their loss, but they must also be able to get away from it and on to other business. A widow-to-widow program can help them with both tasks, and insofar as it opens up new vistas beyond their families, it facilitates the development of low density subnetworks.

The truth of Granovetter's phrase, the "strength of weak ties," refers to low density networks.[19] Their strength is most in evidence when a task such as finding a job is encountered. Numerous un-connected ties can provide pathways to pursue many different and distant options. The low density or loosely knit portion of the network is built up by adding ties to new people who are connected to few, if any, of those already in the network. These ties can then be used to develop new resources to deal with the inevitable new challenges or transitions. Unfortunately, it is not usually possible to determine the optimum balance between low and high density segments. It depends on the complex realities of each individual's situation and the priority of each function.

DENSITY BALANCE: Participation in programs of local chapters of self-help organizations creates a new sector of high density relationships: Everyone tends to know everyone else. The far-reaching interests of the self-help organization, however, also pro-vide opportunities to add a low density sector to the network. Many organizational activities require their members to be in contact with other chapters, regional or national coordinating bodies, the media, agents of relevant human service organiza-tions, and the general public. These externally oriented activities add to the local high density ties a sector of outwardly radiating, loosely knit ties. The low density network allows members a con-siderable freedom to choose a small number of people with whom they will form close ties. This is considerably more choice than may be available in such other sectors as family, workplace, and even local chapters.

The potential for choice may be especially important to minor-ities, since they can use the outwardly radiating paths to make contact with people who are sensitive to the minority situation. Taking advantage of this feature, black and Hispanic members in mostly white, Anglo organizations may be able to enhance their solidarity with others in their minority group. In parallel fashion, women may be able to meet other women in a setting where they are outnumbered by men and vice versa. Though this opportunity does not eliminate the racist and sexist features of self-help organizations, it can mitigate some of their effects. Joining other discriminated-against persons through the low density network may also be a way to form a group to push for structural reform. Thus, using the low density capability of self-help organizations to reach out to like-situated people can be the first step in reducing discrimination associated with race, ethnicity, sex, sexual orientation, age, or handicapped status.

PROPERTIES OF INDIVIDUAL RELATIONSHIPS

The experience and the functional adequacy of a particular relationship depend on the values associated with each of its five properties. The pattern of the values associated with self-help relationships frequently differs markedly from those found in outside relationships. The priority, for example, that is given to mutuality in self-help relationships may contrast with the new member's usual experience. The intent to compensate for deficiencies in existing relationships and to enhance self-esteem by this expression of faith in the individual member is emphasized by mutuality. The aim is also to encourage movement toward these values in outside relationships. The content of one tie, for example, may be altered to reduce conflict, whereas the frequency of another may be increased to obtain more satisfaction. Membership in a self-help organization can be a remarkably effective incentive to change outside relationships. The marriage relationship may never be the same after one spouse makes a commitment to Al-Anon or PA.

Content

The content of a relationship refers to its single or multiple themes. A theme can be something exchanged (material assistance, information, emotional support) or the context in which the exchange takes place (neighborhood, workplace, school). The idea behind combining the thing exchanged and the context of the exchange is that context, at least at a general level, determines content. The dominant content or theme of relationships in school or workplace contexts is fairly predictable as long as it is the only context in which the people know each other. If they also relate in other contexts, then the content will be modified by themes from the other context. Thus, a transaction that is nominally a business one may also be affected by norms emanating from friendship or neighborhood ties. Viewed differently, every transaction can be said to be affected by whether the relationship has carried other kinds of content in the past or is expected to do so in the future.

The content is multiplex, or multistranded, when the relationship carries more than one theme or when it cuts across different social contexts. Multistranded relations are thought to be more durable and more emotionally satisfying than single-stranded ones.[20] Since they have more fasteners, they are less likely to come apart, but should they do so, more would be lost. And when multistranded relations are strained, the resulting distress is likely to be in proportion to the complexity of their themes. This realization may lead some participants to restrict their self-help relationships to a single theme, the vicissitudes of their common problem or condition. Others, however, will introduce additional dimensions or strands into their relationships. Sometimes this is necessary to carry out the complex tasks of the self-help organization. As initiatives are undertaken to recruit and sponsor new members, to negotiate with agencies, and to raise funds, the relationships of those engaged in these tasks will become increasingly multidimensional. Still other facets of a relationship may emerge as members attempt to influence government policy or educate the public. Given their multiple interests, members of self-help organizations may very well meet one another coming and going in a variety of organizational and community settings.

VARIETY OF CONTENT: The following scenario portrays two highly committed members of GA working on several projects and engaged in multiple exchanges. With appropriate substitutions, this scenario might also portray a scenario in other self-help organizations. It opens with the two men "giving therapy" to one another, that is, recalling their compulsive gambling experiences, detailing how they harmed themselves and others, and describing how they have used the GA program to arrest their "disease." Therapy is organized according to the prescriptions set forth in the Twelve Steps of GA. These steps, which are part of GA's credo, are printed in the "Combo" book, from which a passage is read at each meeting.

After the meeting, they move to one member's apartment to work on plans for a regional GA conference. Planning, however, is interrupted by a series of crisis calls that include talking with several family members of a compulsive gambler as well as the gambler himself. A few days later, while driving to court to testify for another compulsive gambler, the protagonists discuss how to handle two educational sessions, one for counselors who want to learn about the role of compulsive gambling in family problems and the other for a Chamber of Commerce group investigating the implications of casino gambling. These heavy responsibilities would not be feasible without the opportunity to coordinate them in the context of their easy contact in the workplace and in the neighborhood. Thus it might be said their work is made possible by a highly complex relationship, one with many strands.

Although it has been stated that multiplexity is beneficial, it should also be noted that it involves certain risks for both the self-help organization and its members. Multiplexity quickens the pace. Some twelfth-step work may catapult people into high visibility or high stress situations. Moreover, the role overload they carry may lead to serious problems in other spheres of their lives, for example, at work and at home.

Frequency

The number of contacts, or frequency, may be a useful indicator of the importance of a relationship. The exceptions, such as one's mother and other highly cathected figures, remain important though they may be infrequently seen. But in general, frequency tends both to cause and to be a consequence of a high valuation of the relationship. This is why self-help organizations encourage frequent attendance at meetings—as many as are necessary to prevent backsliding. They take seriously the slogan, "Meetings Make It"; the GA Bulletin (July 1981) honored a member for attending more than 2,500 meetings in a ten-year period. Aside from the family, most other sectors do not offer such frequent contact. Certainly the typical human service organization cannot do so, considering the drain on staff resources that such frequency would represent.

Durability

The longevity of relationships within a self-help organization is the result of the organization's striving for the goals of maximum effectiveness and durability. These goals require recruiting new members, scheduling activities, refining procedures, and, what is most important, actively ensuring the viability of the organization for succeeding cohorts of members. "Giving back" some of the help received is a cherished value, and it often will be expressed in training roles. The leadership training program of Recovery, Inc., offers a series of steps to more responsibility. Most qualified and committed members feel that they will never run out of challenging roles.

Directedness

The qualities of mutuality and reciprocity in a relationship are combined in the property of directedness. Peer assistance and reciprocal relations among members are primary goals of self-help organizations. These goals rest on the belief that everyone, either now or just a short time ago, has suffered from the same problem. They joined not because they wanted to but because, desperate and alone, they could not cope with their problem. Since this common problem makes them essentially alike, no one is more qualified or more obligated than anyone else to take responsibility. Reaffirmations of this belief can be a powerful stimulus for self-help members who are struggling to increase their activity and initiative.

Intensity

An intuitive grasp of intensity can be obtained by imagining family members who, though infrequently seen, are greatly valued. Like family, members of self-help organizations often share intimate thoughts and feelings. The relationship that grows out of these experiences may be of an intensity that far exceeds the amount of time spent together. Studies of intense, confiding relationships have shown that these relationships have a number of important effects, particularly in the health area.[21] For example, Berkman and Syme's study found that the absence of a confiding tie whether to a marital partner, family member, or friend was associated with an earlier death.[22] The relationship between a confiding tie and longevity held up even after controls were introduced for the initial state of health. Sometimes the opportunity to invest in self-help relationships may result in diversifying an excessive investment, as in family members. This will be especially important for members whose networks are too small.

BENEFITS AND RISKS:
A NETWORK PERSPECTIVE

The positive changes in a person's social network resulting from participation in a self-help organization are summarized in Table 1.

Table 1. Probable Changes in Personal Network Properties Following Participation in a Self-Help Organization

Properties	Change after Participation
Total Network	
Size	Increases number of relationships
Reachability	Covers basic sectors more adequately
Density	Adds new outwardly radiating ties
Individual Relationships in Self-Help Network	
Content	Adds multistranded relationships
Frequency	Provides high-frequency contact
Duration	Offers enduring relations
Directedness	Provides reciprocal ties
Intensity	Adds strongly felt relationships

For the network as a whole, the probable consequences are an expansion of its size, an increase in its coverage of important sectors, and a greater access to specialized resources. For individual relationships formed as a result of participation in a self-help organization, the likelihood is that the organization will add permanent, reciprocal, multidimensional, frequent, and intense relationships to the individual's network. And considering relationships outside the self-help network, they also may be positively modified by generalizing from the self-help experience.

But like most interventions powerful enough to produce positive effects, there are certain risks. By design as well as necessity, members are encouraged to select their own helpers. (This may be especially reassuring to new members.) Aside from informal means of control, there are few formal means with which to intervene in misleading and exploitive relationships. Moreover, the ambiguity inherent in determining what is appropriate in human problem solving further heightens the risk. New members are of special concern here. The lack of outside accrediting and regulatory bodies may to some extent further increase the risks.

Some protection against these risks involves grievance and ethical concern committees and other substructures concerned with coordination and improvement of the organization. On a one-by-one basis, new members and other vulnerable individuals can be helped to use the organization selectively. They can be, and often are, informed about the nature of the exchanges (including dating and, sometimes, frankly sexual overtures) in certain subsectors of the organization. Newcomers need to be made aware of the risks in certain kinds of relationships. This need for guidance highlights the important role played by mentors from the ranks of senior members and by sensitive professionals. Although unfortunate experiences cannot be eliminated, their likelihood must be put in perspective. Harm can occur in professional services as well, and the data are simply not available to evaluate the conditions under which the risks are greater in conventional professional services or in self-help organizations.[23] These risks, however, can be lowered by a better understanding of organizational and network processes within self-help organizations.

Notes

1. S. S. McLanahan, N. V. Wedemeyer, and T. Adelberg, "Network Structure, Social Support, and Psychological Well-Being in the Single-Parent Family," *Journal of Marriage and the Family*, 43 (August 1981), pp. 601–612.

2. T. Borkman, "Mutual Self-Help Groups: Strengthening the Selectively Unsupportive Personal and Community Networks of Their Members," in A. Gartner and F. Riessman, eds., *The Self-Help Revolution* (New York: Human Sciences Press, 1984), pp. 206–211.

3. Ibid.

4. J. C. Mitchell, ed., *Social Networks in Urban Situations* (Manchester, England: University of Manchester Press, 1969), p. 2.

5. J. A. Barnes, *Social Networks*, Module 26 (Reading, Mass.: Addison-Wesley Publishing Co., 1972); J. Boissevain and J. C. Mitchell, eds., *Network Analysis: Studies in Human Interaction* (The Hague, Netherlands: Mouton, 1973); E. Bott, *Family and Social Network* (2nd ed.; New York: Free Press, 1971); D. J. Jonqinans, "Politics on the Village Level," in Boissevain and Mitchell, eds., *Network Analysis*; Mitchell, *Social Networks in Urban Situations*; and R. E. Mitchell and E. J. Trickett, "Task Force Report: Social Networks as Mediators of Social Support," *Community Mental Health Journal*, 16 (Spring 1980), pp. 27–44.

6. C. D. Erickson, "The Concept of Personal Network in Clinical Practice," *Family Process*, 14 (December 1975), pp. 487–498.

7. Mitchell and Trickett, "Task Force Report"; C. Swenson, "Social Networks, Mutual Aid, and the Life Model of Practice," in C. Germain, ed., *Social Work Practice: People and Environments* (New York: Columbia University Press, 1979); and D. Turkat, "Social Networks:

Theory and Practice," *Journal of Community Psychology,* 8 (April 1980), pp. 99–109.

8. T. J. Powell, "Interpreting Parents Anonymous as a Source of Help for Those with Child Abuse Problems," *Child Welfare,* 58 (February 1979), pp. 105–114; and Powell, "Comparisons Between Self-Help Groups and Professional Services," *Social Casework: The Journal of Contemporary Social Work,* 60 (November 1979), pp. 561–565.

9. Swenson, "Social Networks, Mutual Aid, and the Life Model of Practice."

10. M. Pilisuk and S. H. Parks, "The Place of Network Analysis in the Study of Supportive Social Associations," *Basic and Applied Social Psychology,* 2 (April–May–June 1981), pp. 121–135.

11. McLanahan, Wedemeyer, and Adelberg, "Network Structure, Social Support, and Psychological Well-Being in the Single-Parent Family," p. 612.

12. M. Hammer, "Social Supports, Social Networks, and Schizophrenia," *Schizophrenia Bulletin,* 7, No. 1 (1981), pp. 45–56; and Hammer "Predictability of Social Connections Over Time," *Social Networks,* 2 (1980), pp. 165–180.

13. M. Hammer, "Influence of Small Social Networks as Factors in Mental Hospital Admission," *Human Organization,* 22 (1963), pp. 243–251; and A. Horowitz, "Social Networks and Pathways to Psychiatric Treatment, *Social Forces,* 56 (1977), pp. 86–105.

14. J. B. McKinlay, "Social Networks, Lay Consultation, and Help-Seeking Behavior," *Social Forces,* 52 (December 1973), pp. 275–292.

15. B. J. Hirsch, "Psychological Dimensions of Social Networks: A Multimethod Analysis," *American Journal of Community Psychology,* 7 (June 1979), pp. 263–277.

16. Mitchell and Trickett, "Task Force Report."

17. B. J. Hirsch, "Social Networks and the Coping Process," in B. Gottlieb, ed., *Social Networks and Social Support* (Beverly Hills, Calif.: Sage Publications, 1981), pp. 149–170.

18. K. N. Walker, A. MacBride, and M. H. S. Vachon, "Social Support Networks and the Crisis of Bereavement," *Social Science and Medicine,* 11 (January 1977), pp. 35–41.

19. M. Granovetter, "The Strength of Weak Ties," *American Journal of Sociology,* 78 (May 1973), pp. 1360–1380; and Granovetter, "The Strength of Weak Ties: A Network Theory Revisited," in R. Collins, ed., *Sociological Theory 1983* (San Francisco: Jossey Bass, 1983).

20. J. A. Brim, "Social Network Correlates of Avowed Happiness," *Journal of Nervous and Mental Diseases,* 158 (June 1974), pp. 432–439.

21. K. Ell, "Social Networks, Social Support, and Health Status: A Review," *Social Service Review,* 58 (March 1984), pp. 133–149.

22. L. F. Berkman and S. L. Syme, "Social Networks, Host Resistance and Mortality: A Nine-Year Follow-Up Study of Alameda County Residents," *American Journal of Epidemiology,* 109 (February 1979).

23. A. E. Bergin and M. Lambert, "The Evaluation of Therapeutic Outcomes," in S. L. Garfield and Bergin, eds., *Handbook of Psychotherapy and Behavior Change: An Empirical Analysis* (2nd ed.; New York: John Wiley & Sons, 1978).

6

Behavioral Processes

Bored with AA?
Act enthusiastic.
Don't wait until you feel
enthusiastic.
Fake it till you make it.

That's how the *Grapevine* (June 1982) of AA put it. It's not what you think or feel; it's what you do. Recovery, Inc., says: "Move the muscles." Similar maxims are used by a variety of organizations: "Utilize, don't analyze." "Don't trouble yourself with the obstacles." "Try it even if you don't like it." "Pretend you like it and you may actually come to like it." All these expressions emphasize the primacy of behavior. Doing and results are what is important—not attitude. After behavior changes, expect changes in your thinking.

DOING

The emphasis on doing is a direct, and sometimes only, means of overcoming inertia. This emphasis also establishes that a change in behavior is the primary way to assess outcome. It may be the best way, at least initially, to change the attitudes that are presumed to be the basis of the behavior. Contrary to folk belief, action sometimes precedes attitude change rather than the reverse. But whichever is addressed first, behavior is the object of change. Beliefs and attitudes must not be allowed to interfere with action. If they interfere with socially adaptive and personally gratifying behavior, they must be overcome. Vigorous efforts may be necessary to accomplish this. Later, obstructing attitudes may yield to pressures to resolve the dissonance between action and attitude. Taking action, especially if it works, fosters favorable attitudes. But whether this happens, the primary emphasis and the ultimate objective, sought either directly by action or indirectly through attitude change, are a significant, stable alteration in cognition, affect, and motoric actions, that is, a behavioral change.

Specific Prescriptions

Another manifestation of the behavioral orientation of self-help organizations is a considerable knowledge of how to interpret and respond to specific situations. These organizations look at *what* is happening *how, where,* and *when,* that is, at the immediate antecedents and consequents of behavior. Because of their behavioral orientation, they are concerned with events that are closely related to changes in behavior. Self-help organizations are adept at isolating factors associated with the problem and its gradual resolution. Calling on this knowledge and using terms that their members will understand, they offer prescriptions for managing problematic everyday-life situations. Sustained use of these prescriptions often produces the desired changes. Yet this knowledge may not explain the problem or the personalities of those who have it. It is valuable not because it validates a larger theory but because it works; it is pragmatic. Participants are not hung up on explanations of why principles that work in one situation do not work in another. Foolish consistency is not one of the likely hobgoblins of self-help organizations.

Behavior Theory and Other Explanatory Frameworks

Behavioral change occurs in a context that can be understood using the terms of the theories discussed earlier. Organization theory explains how goals, structures, and formal procedures are involved in delivering reinforcement contingencies. Organizations determine which contingencies will be reinforced and how. Reference group theory can explain how a new culture and a value orientation are adopted and why the approval of other members of a group is a powerful reinforcer. And social network theory elucidates the grid that transmits reinforcement.

More than with the other theories, however, it is important   *103* that behavioral concepts and principles not be regarded as more than ideas to sensitize members. Since behavior theory can be overly deterministic, it is important to understand that self-help organizations are complicated, natural entities, not deliberate, formal instruments of behavioral learning. They become comprehensible and perhaps more accessible to program improvement only as their activities are conceptualized in learning terms. To describe what happens in a self-help organization as reinforcement is to deal with reality metaphorically and simplistically, though some incisive insights may be gained.

The principles of learning, such as those related to reinforcement, and their air of exactitude do not seem to suggest that self-help interactions are simple and invariant. In fact, the flexibility that allows them to cover a variety of interactions is an advantage, considering the complex differences among actual self-help organizations. The explanation, however, comes from learning theory. Diversity is typical of natural social interactions. Insofar as the self-help environment is diverse, members are more likely to learn how to distinguish among stimuli and to generalize responses to other natural settings. Thus, members learn to separate "the wheat from the chaff"; they learn which stimuli are more important. That is, they learn to recognize which specific stimuli in which contexts are consequential and to respond accordingly.[1]

The first, most fundamental way to facilitate learning is by external reinforcement. Since it requires the least amount of cooperation from the subject, it can be a disincentive if the subject is already inclined to the contingent behavior. Thus, it must not be used indiscriminately. The procedure involves immediate reinforcement following the contingent behavior. (Negative reinforcement procedures involve withholding the reinforcer if the response is maladaptive.) When, as often happens, the behavioral response is not the desired one but rather one that can be shaped toward that end, the reinforcer is presented. Thereafter the subject is reinforced as the behavior increasingly approximates the desired response. Through this successive approximation, the tendency to emit the desired terminal behavior is strengthened.

The second, higher, and less intrusive approach involves exposure to a model (person) with effective coping strategies. In a self-help organization, the newcomer observes the model's success. This exposure stimulates the newcomer to imitate the behavior of the model to achieve similarly reinforcing results.

The third approach, which uses self-regulation strategies, involves more use of cognitive processes and is compatible with a high level of user autonomy. Individuals reinforce themselves for the performance of contingent behaviors, often on their own schedule. "If I'm able to get through shopping without a scene with my daughter, I will treat myself to a . . . ." This approach has an additional advantage: It may modify the individual's perception of himself or herself as the locus that controls his or her behavior. Even more than modeling, however, self-regulation requires that the desired behavior be in the individual's repertoire.

SOCIAL REINFORCEMENT STRATEGIES

Many who come to self-help organizations are running away— from the miseries of alcoholism, family turmoil, or their own unremitting anxiety. Others want to escape from their shame and paralyzing depression. And the negative images associated with these feelings are kept alive by self-help organizations to use as negative reinforcers.

Negative Reinforcement

Organizations want members to remember how bad, how really wretched, it was. Recovery, Inc., is typical insofar as it reinforces the confessional tendencies of its members to recall "what it was like then, and what it is like now." Many of its speakers recall painful experiences that are negative reinforcers for both themselves and others. Negative reinforcers, however, are not unique to self-help organizations; they are commonplace in many social situations.[2] Consider, for example, the unflattering images of obesity that are posted on refrigerator doors to repulse "illegal" snackers. Within self-help organizations, however, the negative images can often be extremely vivid and compelling, thus reinforcing the commitment to work with the program. They evoke the torment of the child abuser, the strains felt by the single parent, the confining anxiety of the emotionally disabled, the agitated passivity of the chronically ill, and the despair of parents and other close relatives of persons with chronic mental disorders.

Positive Reinforcement

Self-help organizations work to reach those who need them. It does not matter whether they are thrashing about or just able to overcome their inertia. Distress can be ameliorated by active participation in the self-help program. Consequently, newcomers are reinforced for coming to the first meeting, whatever their reasons. They are reinforced for even elemental adaptive behaviors —anything to move them toward the terminal goal. The general approach involves extending warm greetings to them and appreciating their courage (or whatever it took) to come. Later they are told how important newcomers are to the progress of senior members. They will hear how skeptical newcomers remind senior members of how hard they must work just to maintain their own recovery and avert disaster. They hear talk of how senior members are benefited by helping others. In many ways, perhaps best symbolized by generous offers of rides to future meetings, newcomers learn that their participation is valued and that "Meetings Make It."

The warm, reinforcing responses continue as new people and old members participate in the program. As people get up to speak, they are applauded then—and later—as they tell how long it has been since they gambled, used drugs, or engaged in some other self-defeating behavior. These speaking-reporting arrangements not only reinforce the individual but also monitor his or her progress.

Operant Behavior and Its Function

Operant behavior is behavior that is affected by its consequences. Positive reinforcement increases its frequency; negative reinforcement decreases it. An operant class may include diverse behaviors, which, however, are related by function or the similar effect they have on the reinforcing environment. Many different behaviors, for example, must be included in the recovery operant for most members of PA. The same parents may be reinforced for firm but nonviolent discipline, whereas their children might respond in a reinforcing manner to the parents' flexible giving. Both behaviors indicate the parents' progress; both are from the same operant class since they affect the environment and the children the same way. Operant behavior explains why the self-help organization must be prepared to reinforce a complex package of behaviors selectively.

Operant behavior can be shaped by a series of successive approximations to match the desired terminal behavior. Members of Parents Anonymous, for example, will increasingly be reinforced only for more effective, less intrusive disciplinary actions. In other organizations, the operants differ, but the complexity is the same: Recovery, Inc., endorses thought-stopping behavior; PWP reinforces stress management procedures; Families Anonymous encourages its members to reframe their situations in a more workable context.[3] As these problem-solving strategies are established, less reinforcement on a variably intermittent basis is needed to maintain the response. Similarly, the prompts that once were necessary to stimulate performance can be eliminated. Paradoxically, when reinforcement becomes intermittent and discriminative stimuli are faded, the learned behavior is less likely to be extinguished. It depends less on the immediate environment. The less immediate the reinforcement and the less insistent the inducement, the less reactive the behavior is to the contingencies of the immediate environment. The behaviors may then be said to be strongly conditioned. When adaptive behaviors reinforced by the self-help organizations reach this level, it is gratifying for all concerned. This same resistance to extinction, however, can be very frustrating when it supports maintence of the maladaptive behaviors the self-help organization and others are attempting to change.

Positive vs. Negative Operant Behavior

Because of their detailed experiential knowledge of the problems and their resolution, self-help organizations are able to discriminate appropriately among the many possible behaviors available for reinforcement. Of the myriad possibilities, it is important to distinguish the constructive from the destructive without missing opportunities to shape low-level responses into more constructive higher level ones. The number and diversity of behaviors that members of self-help organizations reinforce can be surprising. Sometimes they seem to be reinforced for everything, even for their mistakes, whereas other apparently constructive behaviors will not be reinforced because experientially wise members suspect they head the individual in the wrong direction. For example, when the compulsive gambler is very optimistic over his or her prospects for "recovery," it may signal a return to "action."[4] Again, a PA mother's solicitousness for her child may indicate guilt related to a recent episode of neglect or abuse.

From another perspective, the self-help organization must assess which aspect of the new member's problem should be addressed. Members of PWP must respond differently, depending on whether the primary need is child care, adult companionship, or personal finance—all fairly common difficulties for single parents. Then, too, it is necessary to discriminate among behaviors that only faintly resemble the desired terminal behavior. Among addicts, for example, the outsider is almost certain to be impressed by the ability of members of Narcotics Anonymous to identify recovery operants in the behavior of recently relapsed addicts, *107* though sometimes they simply define certain behaviors as positive in order to establish a constructive sequence.

This ability can be quite astonishing: A group of "mental health consumers" displayed an almost unnerving ability to recognize the beginnings of what they called "spacy" behavior. When they noticed it in one of their members, they immediately attempted to "bring the individual down again." The person might be told firmly, for example, that "this is an important meeting and it is important to pay attention." It was hard not to be impressed with how remarkably helpful the interventions usually were: "Are you forgetting, we can't have that here?" On rare occasions, however, after the considerable patience of members had been exhausted, their harsh rejection was stunning: "There he goes again, f--- him, if he doesn't care why should we." At the risk of sounding judgmental, these frustrated expressions might have been toned down or channeled into a constructive response if the norms for such situations were better developed. Negative reactions may not be eliminated, but they can be softened if formal norms can be used to control the exciting situation. This particular self-help "group" was struggling without such norms partly because it had no links to other self-help groups. Nonetheless, it struggled mightily to establish rules to handle difficult situations.

Lapses aside, those "who have been there," the cultural insiders, tend to excel at reading signs of change. They can discriminate "play-acting" from "for-real," the impending relapse from normal ups and downs, and the about-to-begin recovery from another acting-out episode. Consequently, they can be uncannily effective as reinforcement agents.

Timing and Measuring Reinforcement

The self-help organization is a remarkable instrument for recognizing *what* should be reinforced and for determining *when* and *how much* it should be reinforced. If intermittent reinforcement can strengthen behavior, constant reinforcement can weaken it. Recognizing this dynamic, self-help organizations typically progress toward longer and more variable intervals between reinforcements. People work harder for larger, unpredictable rewards than they do for smaller, more predictable, and frequent rewards—up to a point. The reinforcements also become less contrived or more natural. This results in more stable adaptive behaviors and lowers the risk of a "slip" in discouraging circumtances. Many of the frequent and conspicuous "pats on the back" are replaced by pins and plaques marking less frequent anniversaries and by more spontaneous, quieter expressions of appreciation. For veteran members, these longer interval awards reinforce the intrinsic rewards of working with new members. The stream of new people, both visitors and potential members, challenges and gratifies the veteran. The new people encourage senior members to work harder to help others and to continue their own growth.

Members also prize the opportunity to regulate the rate and timing of their own reinforcement. They are encouraged to ask for support on an as-needed or as-desired basis. In Recovery, for example, panel members may begin with the phrase "I need help." Other self-help organizations provide parallel opportunities.

Cognitive Factors

The importance of cognitive factors is increasingly recognized by behaviorists. It is now generally accepted that behavior patterns are more effectively established when reinforcements involve cognitive factors.[5] Subjects, for example, who are given unexpectedly large rewards for performing certain behaviors are less likely to maintain the behaviors than if they are given more modest rewards. One interpretation of this result is that the subjects reasoned that large rewards were akin to a quasi-bribe for questionable behavior. If a large reward is required, the behavior must be counterattitudinal. A small reward, however, is an incentive to practice behaviors already in the person's hierarchy. In general, substantial external rewards are primarily effective when the behavior is not already high in the hierarchy. Thus, self-help organizations wisely restrain certain reinforcement practices; they try not to satiate their members with extrinsic reinforcement. Intuitively they understand that the injudicious use of external reinforcers can weaken intrinsically pleasurable behavior or behavior that has gained strength as the result of intermittent "natural" reinforcement. Pleasurable activity must not become work, and it might become that if it evolves into an activity for which one must be paid.[6] On the broadest level, recipients' discomfort is often dealt with by challenging them to pay back the self-help organization.

Self-help organizations are not alone in their integration of behavioral and cognitive perspectives. A similar integration has been manifest for some time in the practical eclecticism of many practitioners, and the professional literature is catching up with them. Rarely have practitioners been as doctrinaire as the writers of professional literature. Writing is seldom as free as doing. This freedom was strikingly evident as the slender member of Overeaters Anonymous recounted how she came to OA as a result of the suggestion of her former psychoanalyst. Because of her *109* leadership in OA and her splendid outcome, she was an effective model for many who were contemplating psychotherapy combined with a self-help organization.

MODELING

Slow, tedious shaping strategies are unnecessary and may be counterproductive when the components of the terminal behavior are already in the individual's repertoire. In such instances, it is actually more effective to model successful problem-solving styles.[7] The more variety evident in the model, the clearer it is that a wide range of behaviors can be incorporated in an effective operant. The prospective imitator usually will be encouraged by the differences among models. Variety increases the chance that he or she can match an effective pattern. The success experienced by models also encourages imitation. For even before imitation occurs, the prospective imitator-member shares vicariously in the success of the model. To the extent prospective imitators perceive important similarities to the model, they will be encouraged. Their shared characteristics makes it reasonable to think that similar success is within their reach if they imitate the model.

Facilitating Imitation

Modeling works best when exposure is frequent and at close range—the kind of exposure built into most self-help organizations. The self-doubting newcomer will be heartened to learn that the model has struggled to acquire and maintain the desired behavior. For most newcomers, success is thinkable only after a real struggle. Therefore, if success seemed to have been won easily by the model, newcomers to self-help would be offered no hope. The fantasy that others have achieved instant and complete success is dispelled through closely interacting with the model, as models assume their customary roles in weekly meetings and make their presence felt at various times of crises and celebration.

Imitation is further facilitated by models who are similar to the observer in some way. Similarities in age, sex, ethnicity, and socioeconomic status accelerate the rate and increase the amount of learned behavior.[8] Similarities also afford some protection against the potentially undermining reappearance of, for example, old cronies. Too much similarity, however, could dampen the challenge. If the model and the prospective imitator are too much alike at the start, the imitator may be uninspired; he or she may not be inclined to become like the model.

The opposite situation, however, is more serious. It has been shown that minorities, for example, are disadvantaged by the lack of models with their status characteristics. Thus, from another perspective, homogeneous local chapters of self-help organizations (discussed in Chapter Two) may be desirable. In general, modeling, and more broadly, cross-learning, are optimized when members are closely matched in terms of status. Ordinarily the natural heterogeneity of any two people is substantial enough to provide sufficient incentive for imitation.

Discriminative Imitation

Wholesale, uncritical imitation of a model's behavior must be discouraged as sometimes occurs in people who are so hungry for a solution, so in need of some rewarding experiences in their lives that they are excessively imitative. Such people need to discriminate more. Discrimination will be facilitated by exposing newcomers to diverse, but equally effective, coping patterns. The newcomer is reminded that many behaviors have the same effect and that it is important to imitate those behaviors most likely to be compatible with him or her in the long run. Behavior unsuited to the individual cannot serve its intended function. This orientation is strengthened by frequent paraphrases of the maxim that the program rests on principles, not personalities.

Link to Other Concepts

The concept of discrimination parallels the concepts of modeling and identification. The latter, which is frequently used to explain the benefits of service from professional counselors and informal community caregivers, is of special interest. *Modeling* stresses the desired terminal behavior and coordinates the component behaviors necessary for its achievement. *Identification* has somewhat different dimensions: It focuses on the disposition or trait responsible for the behavior, and it also focuses on the power of affection rather than of rewards, although the two substantially overlap. Selective and partial identifications parallel discriminating imitation. The indiscriminate incorporation of whole objects is maladaptive, and to prevent this, professional counselors and caregivers encourage partial identifications that are compatible with the existing personality.

Another aspect of the discriminative task is to consider when to set aside the values and norms of the self-help organization for those upheld by other social institutions. Under what conditions will the values and behavioral norms of Recovery, Inc., or *111* some other self-help organization be less relevant than the ones of the member's church, ethnic group, family, or workplace? This question raises issues of timing and balance—complex issues in the real world, in which few general prescriptions are possible. Here, the single-case thrust of behavioral tradition can contribute. An emphasis on the controlling conditions of a single case is compatible with a tradition of the heuristic use of theory. In this mode, theory is used to sensitize the member to key factors in a situation, without trying to predict how these factors are related. This makes helping people a process of conceptually guided discovery, of finding out what works and what does not work.

SELF-REGULATION

In this third and last application, learning theory is used to explain self-regulation in self-help organizations. Thus, in modeling, the selective reinforcement of numerous, closely similar responses is ignored, and in self-regulation, the need for others to reinforce the contingencies is eliminated. This is especially advantageous in solitary situations or in situations when those present cannot reasonably be expected to be discriminating agents of reinforcement. It is not appropriate to expect others to reinforce the smoker's decision not to smoke a cigarette or the gambler's act of changing the radio station when sports scores come on or even the "cool" maintained by the single parent who comes home to a sink full of dirty dishes and signs of snacking over half the house. It is, however, possible for these people to reward themselves. Sometimes a symbolic "pat on the back" may be reward enough, but frequently a more concrete primary reward may be necessary, depending on the strength of the competing responses (for example, flying into a rage). This strategy can be formalized by using the Premack principle,[9] which requires making a contingency contract with oneself. A more probable (desirable) behavior is used as a reinforcer for a less probable (difficult) behavior. A cup of coffee or an ice cream cone may be the reward for calling one's sponsor or for tucking the children into bed. Watching TV, or another pleasurable activity, can be made contingent on getting out of the house each day or attending the regular meeting of the self-help organization. A special dinner or a desired purchase may be contingent on being abstinent or maintaining some other behavioral standard for a specified period of time.

By shifting the locus of control from the environment to the self, self-regulation procedures underscore the role of cognitive processes and enhance self-help members' autonomy.[10] Where behavioral and cognitive approaches meet, there may well be benefits from synergy. The combination of the two may not be simply additive—the energy available for problem solving may be multiplied. It is not surprising that pragmatic self-help organizations have taken advantage of such beneficial interactions by combining self-regulation with modeling and direct social reinforcement approaches in their programs.

CONCLUSION

Social learning conceptualizations can be used to understand large and meaningful segments of behavior. The same concepts can be used to point up the dangers of uncritical imitation or preoccupation with very small units of behavior. These concepts, moreover, can enlarge the domain of corrective mental processes. Finally, they are used by self-help leaders and professional service providers to understand better how to transmit the values, norms, and problem-solving strategies of self-help organizations.[11]

Notes

1. G. Martin and J. Pear, *Behavior Modification: What It Is and How to Do It* (2nd ed.; Englewood Cliffs, N.J.: Prentice-Hall, 1983), provides a good introduction to reinforcement principles; see pp. 194–95 for a discussion of the overlap between stimulus and response.
2. Ibid., pp. 220–222.
3. These strategies are discussed in E. Gambrill, *Casework: A Competency-Based Approach* (Englewood Cliffs, N.J.: Prentice-Hall, 1983).
4. T. J. Powell, "Constructive 'Action' in the Treatment of Compulsive Gamblers," *National Council on Compulsive Gambling Newsletter,* 1 (December 1982), p. 5.
5. See D. Meichenbaum, *Cognitive Behavior Modification: An Integrative Approach* (New York: Plenum Publishing Corp., 1977); and P. L. Wachtel, *Psychoanalysis and Behavior Therapy* (New York: Basic Books, 1977).
6. For a more complete exposition of these ideas and a useful clinically oriented discussion of how cognition mediates behavioral processes, see S. Feld and N. L. Radin, *Social Psychology for Social Work and the Mental Health Professions* (New York: Columbia University Press, 1982), pp. 249–276.
7. A. Bandura, *Social Learning Theory* (Englewood Cliffs, N.J.: Prentice-Hall, 1977).
8. Feld and Radin, *Social Psychology for Social Work and the Mental Health Professions,* p. 254.

9. D. Premack, "Reinforcement Theory," in D. Levine, ed., *Proceedings: Nebraska Symposium on Motivation, 1965*, Vol. 13 (Lincoln: University of Nebraska Press, 1965), pp. 123–188.

10. E. K. Baker, "The Relationship Between Locus of Control and Psychotherapy: A Review of the Literature," *Psychotherapy: Theory, Research and Practice*, 16 (1979), pp. 351–362.

11. L. K. Miller, *Principles of Everyday Behavior Analysis* (2nd ed.; Monterey, Calif.: Brooks/Cole, 1979).

PART THREE

Professional Services, Informal Helping Systems, and Self-Help Organizations

The social science concepts discussed in Chapter Six were used to understand how self-help organizations work as sufficient systems. But the self-help system often operates in concert with the two other major systems of human service. The three systems—the self-help system, the professional-help system, and the informal, community caregiver system —will be compared according to the role of the provider, the role of the help-seeker, the basis of power, and the level of specificity. The analysis will show that the dominant value associated with these major properties differs in each system. By evaluating patterns in relation to the preferences of help-seekers, it should be possible to assess how well each system can meet the individual's needs. In most instances, it should be expected that the individual's needs will be best met by a combination of systems. Although it is possible to assess the properties of each system to determine the extent to which systems can substitute for one another, the major emphasis will be on how the systems complement one another.

Lest this discussion appear to minimize the most fundamental support system, it should be kept in mind that none of these systems is viewed as competing with the family. The systems should be viewed as specialized, extrafamilial helping systems that work best when they are articulated with the supportive features of the nuclear family and the extended family. Nonetheless, it is true that their use implies the need for additional support, either because the family is unavailable or because it needs to be supplemented. It may even be that the family influence must be opposed in some areas. This harks back to the discussion in Chapter Four of why dysfunctional beliefs held by lay people (for example, every child needs a spanking once in awhile) must be countered in self-help organizations.

Chapter Seven discusses the dominant value for each of the properties just mentioned in three different helping systems. Chapter Eight proposes that these properties be rated in terms of their *acceptability, availability, adequacy, cultural sensitivity,* and *equity.* The values for these properties will differ for each of the criteria in each of the systems. Occasionally, some individuals may clearly prefer one system over another. More likely, an individual may prefer the values associated with some of the properties in one system but not the others (for example, the individual may feel comfortable with the role of the consumer-participant but not with the basis of power). This is why a combination of systems often is preferred.

7

Basic Properties of the Systems

Four basic properties common to each of the three helping systems—professional, informal caregiver, and self-help—are analyzed. These properties, which show considerable variation across the systems, are (1) role of the provider, (2) basis of power, (3) specificity of function, and (4) role of the participant. Each helping system has a distinctive configuration of properties, as is discussed.

ROLE OF THE SERVICE PROVIDER

Professionals

Professional service providers differ from informal helpers and self-help leaders in terms of three attributes of their role. Their helping role is defined as an explicit, primary activity and they are paid for it. The role is often performed by counselors, physicians, nurses, social workers, psychologists, occupational therapists, and the like, whose express purpose is to develop or restore an individual's coping ability. Toward that end, they rely on professional training to sanction and guide their efforts.

Informal Caregivers

The help offered by informal "natural" caregivers is secondary and indirect. The primary role of these caregivers is to teach, minister, provide health care, maintain public safety or interact with people in the workplace. To meet these primary responsibilities, however, it may be necessary for informal caregivers to "help" those with whom they are involved. Without their help, many students, parishioners and workers would not be able to perform their roles adequately. Thus, help is an intrinsic or "natural" part of the caregivers' everyday activity. Although teachers, clergy, police, co-workers, and neighbors often have professional training, the training is almost always for their formal, primary responsibilities, not their informal, secondary ones. Even members of prestigious professional groups do not claim expertise in the mental health or the human service field. Thus, in this sense, physicians and nurses who are not practicing in the mental health field are informal caregivers. These informal helpers qualify as nonprofessionals because, even if they are paid, it is for their explicit primary duties, not for implied, secondary ones.

Self-Help

Self-help leaders are also unpaid "nonprofessionals" because their helping activities are not based on a systematic, theoretically oriented education program. Instead, their ability to help is based on their personal experience, modified by the ideology of the self-help organization. It is their problem, or predicament, and their indoctrination to the norms and procedures of the self-help organizations, rather than education, that forms the basis for their helping. Their helping also differs from professional helping in that it is not a primary activity in the sense of being an occupation, though some self-help leaders allow the organization and its work to make a greater claim on them than their paid jobs. They give in ways and amounts that cannot be paid for. Long and late hours and a willingness to be on call for difficult situations are common. Self-helpers operate a system that parallels the professional system. Their system's explicit goal is to provide direct personal assistance; self-help providers are specialists in their helping functions. This point is often lost on casual observers, who tend to confuse the specialized assistance of self-helpers with that of informal, community caregivers to whom assistance is a secondary consequence to the carrying out of their primary mission. Helping is explicit in the mission of self-helpers.

BASIS OF POWER

In a helping context, power is the ability to help and, to a considerable extent, it is an ability that is attributed to the helper by the help-seeker. Help-seekers are attracted to different kinds of helpers, depending on their perception of what kind of helping power is relevant to their situation. In the eyes of the help-seeker, each type of provider has a different kind of power, depending on his or her preparation for the role. The foundation for the unique character of each system involves such differences in preparation. Help-seekers, after making allowances for a considerable amount of random behavior, search out the most relevant system.

Technical Expertise

The patient or client seeking assistance in the professional system attributes technical expertise to the therapist. Such clients, whether disposed by lifestyle or by their perception of their problem, favor providers whose expertise is based on systematic technical studies. For some needs, however, even these people may perceive technical expertise to be either not relevant or not sufficient and come to see that technical expertise or expert power must be supplemented by other kinds of power.

Experientially Based Expertise

Some people believe that the most powerful helpers will be those who have successfully coped with a similar problem or predicament. Someone who was once like them will be the most powerful helper—someone who comes from a similar reference group. The help-seeker is attracted to these people because he or she attributes referent power to them. When referent power is perceived to be most relevant, the self-help organization will be chosen as the appropriate instrument for obtaining personal help.

Social Expertise

Still others prefer the help of such informal "natural" caregivers as teachers, physicians, and clergy. In gravitating toward such caretakers, they show a preference for helpers with social power, because people in these roles are assumed to have a responsibility to develop and maintain the quality of social life. One of the characteristics of social power is that beneficiaries need not be aware of it, or, if they are, they need not acknowledge it. The capacity to provide assistance through activities that are not explicitly labeled helping ones can be an important advantage. For example, this kind of indirect help may be the only help that is acceptable. (That is not to say that oblique strategies may not be misused.) When the individual has a strong personal preference, the informal system may be the only one that can exercise power over that individual. Preference, however, is not the only factor to be considered; the probable efficacy of the different types of power is also important when one is considering the task that needs to be done. Some problems—obtaining a job, for example—may be better served by the social power of a community leader than by the less relevant "expert" power of a therapist or the referent power of a self-help leader.

Other Power Bases

Two additional bases of power, which were conceptualized by French and Raven, are found, to a lesser degree, in all three helping systems.[1] Reward power involves the use of such reinforcers as money, food, praise, and awards to strengthen some behaviors and extinguish others. Legal power is utilized by those in the social authority structure. Compliance is based on the superordinate position of the person exercising power and ultimately rests on the power of the stronger person to exact compliance. In some instances, the legal and reward power available to functionaries in hospitals, courts, penal institutions, and welfare agencies may be an important factor for participation in AA or PA. On the whole, however, these types of power are secondary in all three helping systems.

SPECIFICITY OF FUNCTION

Functional specificity refers to the amount of specialization in each of the helping systems.

Informal Is Nonspecific

Because the informal system offers help indirectly through the primary activity, it is the least specialized of the three systems. Almost any problem that interferes with the efficient operation of the primary activity (education, health care, church participation, and the like) will attract attention and effect remedial action. Naturally, not every problem is equally likely to be expressed or recognized in every setting. Loneliness may be more evident in a church or neighborhood setting, whereas substance abuse may attract attention in the workplace. In either case, helpful initiatives may be taken without directly referring to the difficulty. The lonely person may be asked to join a church group or invited to a neighborhood social gathering. Substance abusers may be invited to special programs to deal with poor work performance.

The importance of interventions by community caregivers was rediscovered by community mental health programs in the 1960s and 1970s. Now they pay less attention to this resource, which is partly a reaction to their earlier idealization. But despite the seesaws of community mental health, the giving and receiving of help continues in the informal helping system. Much of the activity, however, may be perceived to be something other than giving help and receiving help. Though the transactions are not perceived as unhelpful, helpfulness is not seen as a primary characteristic. If recipients are asked directly if the transactions were helpful, most say yes. At the time of the interchange, however, "help" did not seem to be the most salient feature; it was simply what the person might have expected, or it was a nice thing to have in the work, neighborhood, or school setting.

Since help can be provided in natural settings obliquely, it is important to look beyond appearance and stated intention. It is necessary to look at the impact or the consequences of the activity. For despite the understandable reluctance to speak frankly of help, the operations of the primary systems would soon be slowed if this lubricant were not available. Contributions (for example, work productivity) of the beneficiaries of these actions would be lowered, and their overall social functioning would decline if this caregiver support were withdrawn.

Self-Help Is Specific

Self-help organizations, as distinguished from the informal caregiving system, have specific missions. To belong, an individual must have a specific "problem" in the area associated with the organization. Simple, specific criteria also govern not just those who can belong but what can be dealt with in a self-help organization.

Specificity may enhance the organization's appeal and its perceived effectiveness. Unambiguous objectives and methods are easier to understand and inspire greater confidence. This sharp focus was reflected in a reply to a question about the general suitability of Overeaters Anonymous. "No one is too dumb to follow the Twelve Steps, but many are too smart," replied the member. This maxim, which originated with AA, is typical of the treatment reserved for actions that distract from the major purpose. Concreteness (for example, living with widowhood, cancer, or herpes) is often linked with specificity. One can have little doubt about being in the right place.

The appeal and effect of specificity are reflected in the growth of organizations from shaky groups whose very survival was in doubt to organizations that are now major factors in American culture. Consider the many hundreds of thousands of parents whom PWP has helped through their transition to single parenthood. Or consider that, for 50 years, AA has been a major factor in helping people with drinking problems. And because of their knowledge of specific combinations of goals and members, these organizations have fine-tuned their ideology to the characteristics of the particular problem.[2] Take PA: Members are indoctrinated in the rationale that their own abuse as children explains their abusive tendencies as parents. This same idea, however, obligates the parents to make strenuous efforts to control the behavior "they have been brought up to."

Specificity also leads to an option to develop a program that is ethnic or gender relevant. Women for Sobriety, for example, addresses the special interests of women alcoholics—the ones who may be overlooked or given short shrift in the predominantly masculine AA or in a professional service program.

However, specificity does have certain disadvantages. For example, some critics feel that individual self-help organizations may oversimplify and overspecify the problems they purport to address. Understandably, the desire to instill confidence in new members may lead to some oversimplifications, which are often retained for the sake of tradition even if they begin to sound a bit quaint. In an attempt to concretize and simplify its approach, Recovery, Inc., explains that people experience symptoms because they indulge their "angry temper" or their "fearful temper." And Recovery, Inc., along with other self-help organizations, may pay too much attention to such physical symptoms as sweaty palms, headaches, palpitations, and nervous stomach. There are other disadvantages to specificity as well. Individuals may think they do not qualify for organizations that could be helpful to them; they may have to give up a support network, such as PWP, if they are no longer in the situation; or they may be reluctant to declare the problem resolved if the organization, for example, AA, assumes that one can only be recovering and never cured. The person may be reluctant to accept the recovering assumption even though it applies not simply to abstinence but to the much more difficult objective of sobriety.

To be sure, there are exceptions to this specificity. PA is accepting a wide range of people who "lose their cool" with children, and the names of such organizations as Recovery, Inc., and Emotions Anonymous seem purposefully ambiguous. On balance, however, self-help organizations favor specificity. As was noted, self-help organizations tend to define their interests narrowly, whereas informal helping systems can respond to a broad variety of problems. The two systems, in fact, are at opposite ends of the specificity continuum.

Professionals—Midway Between

Professional agencies are midway between the informal and self-help systems. They are not as broad as the informal system, since some requests (for example, finding a job) may be judged inappropriate or unprofessional. Yet the professional agency is not as specific as the self-help system, though there are some exceptions, such as substance abuse agencies. Despite the nominal specificity of agencies labeled vocational rehabilitation or mental health, such agencies encompass a diverse range of problems. In short, the tendency in the professional agency is not to limit its practice to certain classes of problems. Rather, such agencies emphasize their expertise in using general problem-solving methods that can be applied to a variety of human difficulties.

ROLE OF PARTICIPANT

The role of the help-seeker varies in the three helping systems. The level of perceived mutuality and perceived self-direction differ for the self-help member, the client of the professional system, and people who obtain support from the informal system. Mutuality, in its fullest sense, implies that everyone is working for similar benefits and has similar rights and responsibilities in the organization. Thus, the self-help system ranks higher than the other two in mutuality.

Self-direction or autonomy implies that help-seekers not only define their own goals but that they decide on the means to achieve them. Because of this emphasis on means, self-direction is different from what counselors and therapists understand by self-determination. According to professionals, clients, using self-determination, are free to choose goals but are not so free to determine the means used to obtain these goals. Therapists may judge that certain methods or means are inappropriate in light of the goals a client has chosen. Of course, this is the way help-providers see it; help-seekers may not see it in the same way.

Most clients will see the qualities of mutuality and self-direction as most fully developed in a self-help organization. This is not to criticize professional service but, rather, to recognize some of its limiting structural features. Nor does it imply *125* that therapists oppose mutuality and self-direction. In fact, many professionals work hard to foster these qualities in therapeutic relationships, short of denying their responsibility for structuring the means of therapy and their realization that different benefits accrue from therapy.

Professional Caregiving

The importance attached to developing mutuality and self-direction in counseling is reflected in the tradition of examining the vicissitudes of the therapeutic alliance. Therapists are urged to become partners with their clients, allied against the alien, unwanted parts of the clients' personalities. Therapists must ally themselves with the observing component of the client's ego and against the problematic experiencing component. But even these ideal statements reflect different benefits for both partners. The client is helped, and the therapist is paid and, it is hoped, has the pleasure of having been part of the client's growth.

Unless the professional has allowed countertransference to get out of control, the client cannot offer meaningful help to the therapist. Some might argue that group therapy offers an opportunity to give help, but, since this process is also controlled by the therapist, it should be considered, in varying degrees, an attenuated form of the reciprocal relationships offered by self-help organizations.

It is little wonder that it is difficult for the client to maintain feelings of mutuality and autonomy. It continues to be difficult, despite some rather insightful explanations and apparently ideal treatment circumstances. For example, Perlman sensitized many to the differences between clients and applicants.[3] Other distinctions have been made between clients and others, such as casual shoppers or people with hidden agendas. Yet many of the problems associated with these distinctions remain and affect helpers and help-seekers in apparently even the most favored circumstances. Greenson noted that many analyses have been terminated in failure, sometimes after hundreds of sessions, because of the lack of alliance.[4] Thus, although it is no longer surprising, continuing efforts need to be made to understand why professional relationships are sometimes experienced as more adversative than mutual. Numerous studies of premature discontinuance have documented the commonplace failure to dispel the prospective clients' feeling that professional relationships are deficient in mutuality and self-direction.[5] Ambivalence about adopting the client role all too easily becomes "we-they" and "I-you" perceptions. Here, the therapist seems to want to control everything about the client, not just the treatment methods. In other systems, the help-seeker is not so likely to perceive the same level of threat to self-direction and mutuality.

Informal Caregiving System

In the informal system, support seems more natural. The issue of getting help, as was noted, may not even be salient. Consequently, help for what (the goal) and how (the means) may not be issues. Because help-seeking is not a dominant issue, the lack of mutuality in caregiver relationships may never be an issue.

Self-Help System

The helping focus, in contrast, is fully explicit in the self-help system, and methods may be accepted with less difficulty because they have been designed and are being implemented by other members (past and present) with whom the help-seeker has much in common. Moreover, new members soon learn they are also helpers. From the beginning, for example, they are given to understand that listening to twelfth steppers helps twelfth steppers. Thus, helping and receiving help, to an important extent, are inseparable.

RATING DIMENSIONS

The properties of the systems summarized in Table 2 interact in different ways with the personal preferences of help-seekers. Individuals may like one property in a system but not another. And the summary rating given each property itself has many

Table 2. Properties of Three Helping Systems

Type of System	Role of Provider	Basis of Power	Specificity of Function	Role of Participant
Self-Help	Volunteer (explicit)	Referent	High	Mutual, self-directed
Professional	Paid (explicit)	Expert	Medium	Nonmutual, other directed
Informal	Indirectly paid (implicit)	Social	Low	Experience of mutuality and direction vary

127

components. Each property can be rated in terms of its acceptability, availability, adequacy, cultural sensitivity, and equity or fairness as it is found in each system. These ratings, furthermore, may be independent. That is, the type of power available in the self-help system, for example, may be seen as culturally sensitive but inadequate. To take another example, the availability of assistance in the self-help system might be rated high, but its acceptability may be low. The point is that even the best system, overall, may have certain properties that will get mixed ratings, depending on which criteria are used or which dimensions are salient. This point is the basic rationale for combining these systems to form a comprehensive service package in light of the individual's preferences and needs. Chapter Eight shows how these properties can be rated according to several criteria or along several different dimensions.

Notes

1. J. R. P. French, Jr., and B. Raven, "The Bases of Social Power," in D. Cartwright, ed., *Studies in Social Power* (Ann Arbor: University of Michigan Press, 1959), pp. 150–167.

2. P. Antze, "Role of Ideologies in Peer Psychotherapy Groups," in M. A. Lieberman and L. Borman, eds., *Self-Help Groups for Coping with Crisis: Origins, Members, Processes, and Impact* (San Francisco: Jossey-Bass, 1979), pp. 272–322.

3. H. H. Perlman, "Intake and Some Role Considerations," *Social Casework*, 41 (April 1960), pp. 171–177.

4. R. R. Greenson, "The Working Alliance and the Transference Neurosis," *Psychoanalytic Quarterly*, 34 (April 1965), pp. 155–181.

5. G. Peharik, "Follow-Up Adjustment of Outpatient Dropouts," *American Journal of Orthopsychiatry*, 53 (July 1983), pp. 501–511; S. L. Garfield, "Research on Client Variables in Psychotherapy," and A. E. Bergin and M. Lambert, "The Evaluation of Therapeutic Outcomes," in Garfield and Bergin, eds., *Handbook of Psychotherapy and Behavior Change: An Empirical Analysis* (2nd ed.; New York: John Wiley & Sons, 1978); and F. Baekeland and L. Lundwall, "Dropping Out of Treatment: A Critical Review," *Psychological Bulletin*, 82 (September 1975), pp. 738–783.

8

Assessing Components of
the Systems

As was mentioned previously, a comprehensive assessment should include a consideration of the dimensions of acceptability, availability, adequacy, equity, and cultural sensitivity. These dimensions can be assessed for the system as a whole or for each of its properties (role of provider, basis of power, specificity of function, and role of participant). Whether the assessment is at the property or system level, the dimensions of assessment frequently are independent of one another. The professional system, for example, may be perceived as adequate but not as culturally sensitive. At the property level, there may also be advantages and disadvantages. The participant's role may be viewed as equitable or fair for everyone but unacceptable to a particular individual. This idea, however, should not be pushed too far. With some properties, particular dimensions may not apply; it might be stretching a point to consider whether different levels of specificity have different values in terms of equity. Nonetheless, a form (Figure 1) has been developed to rate an individual's preferences along these dimensions for each applicable property in each system. Although the figure yields a summary score for each system, it should be used flexibly and adjusted to the relevance of the dimensions for different properties. (Figure 1 is presented on p. 130.)

The analysis, as structured by the form, will help assess the preferences of the consumer or the help-seeker. Ordinarily, this assessment will show that these systems fit into one another's   *129*

Figure 1. Help-Seeker's Assessment of Service Dimensions of the Three Systems[a]

System Property	Acceptability			Availability			Adequacy			Equity			Cultural Sensitivity		
	Prof	S-H	Inf	Prof	S-H	Inf	Prof	S-H	Inf	Prof	S-H	Inf	Prof	S-H	Inf
Role of Provider															
Basis of Power															
Specificity of Function															
Role of Participant															
Other Factors															
Subtotals (sum of +s and −s)															

Note: Users of this form should beware of false precision. The primary purpose is not to record all the elements that go into such decisions, but simply to identify some relevant considerations. Users are encouraged to add +s in the "other factors" row for factors the form does not address or simply because of their intuition in a particular situation.

[a]Prof = professional. S-H = self-help organization. and Inf = informal. + = high rating. o = neutral rating. and − = low rating.

strengths and weaknesses. Thus, generally, they should not be considered substitutes or alternatives for one another.

INTERSYSTEM COOPERATION

When about 17 to 23 percent of the population need care, cooperation among the systems would seem to be a reasonable norm.[1] When at least 35 million of the U.S. population need care, it would seem that the fear of losing one's market should be minor; even competition for the most prestigious or otherwise-prized clients and members seems insufficient to explain the level of threat that is sometimes felt. Furthermore, no one system aspires to cover all aspects of the problems it deals with. Psychotherapy may ameliorate anxiety, but a self-help organization may provide more supportive companionship. And no one would be foolish enough to claim that any one system could satisfy all or even most of the people who need services within its domain. Parents Without Partners cannot take care of all the problems of single parents any more than informal church-related helpers or psychotherapists can. Moreover, what evidence there is suggests that participation in one system, especially the self-help system, is positively associated with the use of other systems.

The small minority of those in need who actually receive assistance from the helping systems, and the incomplete way in which needs are often met, should spur cooperation among the systems. In a study undertaken earlier than but consistent with the catchment-area surveys cited in Note 1, Regier, Goldberg, and Taube described the de facto system of services in the United States.[2] Of the 15 percent, or 30 million, who needed help, one-fifth (21 percent) were receiving service from the specialty professional system. Even if this proportion is added to the liberal estimate of the percentage served by the self-help system, it still seems unlikely that more than 50 percent would be served by the combined human services system and the self-help system. Alternately, an enormous amount of unmet need is reflected in the statistic that over 50 percent of those with mental health needs receive services only from the general health system.

These figures should foster humility and cooperation, not the all-too-common arrogance and rivalry. More of everything—more professional services, more self-help organization opportunities, and more informal helping system experiences—are necessary. The professional system must make available more effective technical assistance. The self-help system must expand its programs of specific problem-solving strategies and disseminate information about its effective models. Community leaders in the informal system need to be more aware of, and make more deliberate use of, their power to offer companionship opportunities for the lonely and specialized job and housing opportunities for those whose needs are not met conventionally. These functions are not so easily performed by either self-help or professional services. A fast rate of growth in one system may, as suggested earlier, be the best way of developing the other systems. The wider use of self-help will stimulate a demand for professional services and the supportive assistance of community caregivers. More effective cooperation also requires the debunking of certain myths. One such myth is that self-help organizations owe their existence solely to the frustration of clients with the monopoly power of professional services. This vast oversimplification is more polemical than truthful. Another myth is that the growth of one system must come at the expense of another.

Narrow thinking about "hierarchies of service" or "alternatives to professional services" must be reformulated to assimilate the idea that the optimum helping relationship is not "either-or." It is necessary to explore how self-help opportunities can be combined with professional services or informal helping experiences or both. And when compatibility is questioned, the thinking of the naysayers—their assumptions and postulates—must be examined along with the characteristics of the systems, for obstacles will be found in the cognitions of partisans as well as in the objects themselves.

DIMENSIONS OF ASSESSMENT

This discussion of systems and their properties in terms of the dimensions of assessment is not necessarily comprehensive or systematic. The intent is not to preclude the application of other criteria, but, rather, to suggest how help-seekers might rate these systems.

Acceptability

Individuals socialized in the dominant culture may prefer psychotherapists over other providers. The straightforward, quasi-technical discussion of objectives may seem infinitely preferable to indirect communications with informal caregivers. The "up-front" discussion of fees fits in with their expectations and frees them from the amorphous, disquieting burden of helping others. These people, captioned YAVIS (young, attractive, verbal, intelligent, and single) clients by one wag, symbolize the values preferred by the dominant culture.[3]

Non-YAVIS persons, called HOUND (homely, old, unattractive, and dumb) by a later wag, may favor a different approach. Many of these people will find help more acceptable when it is offered by informal natural caregivers.[4] Their use of such helpers agrees with their beliefs about what is wrong and what kind of power needs to be evoked (such as talking to a teacher or advocating with unemployment personnel) to resolve it.

Other preferences are reflected in those who are attracted to self-help organizations. They stress the importance of the solidarity they feel with people in similar situations and find it heartening to discover that "others are telling my story." This opportunity to assimilate a new reference group is an essential part of the experience. They may also greatly value the reciprocal nature of participant relations: the opportunity to be helpful as well as to obtain help. "It makes me feel good to help and it also helps me to remember how close I am to them," they might say. Moreover, self-help may seem to symbolize freedom from the technical restrictions that are viewed as inevitable in professional service programs. This factor may be especially important to formerly institutionalized persons: "See how lively we are." Preferences, however, should not so much be analyzed or interpreted as recognized and built on. The negative connotation attached to the saying "There is no accounting for taste" should be abandoned. The idea, instead, should be that "Taste is not something to account for," since the esthetics of help-seeking cannot be defended. The way to attend to what people want is not to analyze why they want it or whether their choice is a good one.

Individual preferences can be accommodated only if all three systems flourish and only if people are encouraged to use combinations of helping systems. If a particular system, or a combination of systems, seems to have a theoretical advantage in certain situations, it must be recognized that these abstractions may ignore other factors that may be even more important to the individual. What does an abstraction matter if the individual finds the more "adequate" option unacceptable and won't go. This is the folly of attempting to make policies uniform. All things considered, it is better to ensure that information about options is available,and to help people take responsibility for their choices. The principle of "different strokes for different folks" should guide the operation of a suprasystem of all three vitally active helping systems.

Acceptability cannot be considered, however, apart from availability and adequacy, as demonstrated in a *New Yorker* cartoon that   *133* depicted a drowning man shouting: "Self-help—self-help."[5] But the excesses are not all on one side: Woody Allen, according to a tale that could be considered apocryphal only by those who are not fans, often mutters "Everyday life interferes with my analysis."

Availability

Universally available informal helping systems provide a significant amount of personal assistance. And the assistance is free, at least in two important ways in which this term can be understood. First, there is no direct charge to the user. And, second, it is difficult to detect or assign indirect costs to its provision, notwithstanding the sporadic arguments of those, such as teachers and health care personnel, who argue that the cost of in-house social service programs would be less than the costs of distracting these professions from their primary responsibilities. With proper support services, they argue, "We could do our jobs—cheaper and better." But since these arguments may also reflect feelings of discontent, it is hard to evaluate their overall importance.

Professional services, in contrast, are always costly and consequently may be available on a restricted basis, if at all. The amount and adequacy of professional services are ultimately limited by cost. In another sense, the monetary costs to the financially comfortable help-seeker may be less than the psychological costs of participating in either the informal or the self-help system.

On the whole, self-help organizations tend not to be so limited by financial considerations. Their "consumer intensive," not their "producer intensive," approach means that services are limited only by the number of participants and what they can give to the self-help organization.[6] Thus, in terms of the quantity of services, the availability of the self-help system resembles the informal helping system more than the professional services system. In terms of accessibility, the self-help system is often better able to respond during evenings and weekends or at other times outside normal business hours. This is not so much a failing of professionals or community caregivers, though it can be taken as that; rather, it is a comment on the radically different structures of their agencies or practices. The self-help organization, however, may have a different but parallel set of limitations in that many of its members may not be available during the day.

Adequacy

Specificity of function, type and strength of power, and duration of the intervention are key factors in how adequate service is.

Does the service focus on the problem or condition? Does it have sufficient power to change the problem or condition? Does it last long enough, but not so long or not in such a way that it prolongs dependence? The person's circumstances determine whether any of the three systems could be adequate. And occasionally one system will be superior, but usually within a context that would make it advantageous to use other secondary systems. The system's specificity needs to be judged in light of each situation. For some people, the phrase of Overeaters Anonymous "Thin is not necessarily well" may indicate an insightfully balanced specificity. Many people may wish to apply the "not necessarily well" standard to other areas of their life, and some people may feel that this can best be done through therapy with a professional. But other people may not agree, particularly if professional resources are limited to seeing people no more than ten or 12 times or no more than once a week. In such cases, self-help organizations have the advantages of strength and duration.

Although there are exceptions, the difference between the informal system and the other two systems is that the informal one may provide coverage for more of each day or week. However, it may sometimes need to be supplemented by more specifically focused or higher powered services. This means calling on the self-help or the professional services system.

Equity

The concept of equity raises a question about the level of social justice in the system. Will the individual feel he or she will be treated fairly by the system? The answer is likely to be related to a larger issue: the extent to which all categories of the population are provided service according to universal criteria. On this count, all the systems have shortcomings. The fee-for-service arrangements found in some professional service programs are discriminatory. After all, why should help be contingent on the ability to pay?

Self-help organizations may also be deficient, since many of them disproportionately involve members of the dominant culture. Thus, they may perpetuate the discriminatory tendencies of the larger society. Yet both the self-help and the professional systems can be more equitable, and some practices bring them closer to equity. Sliding-fee scales and public subsidies cancel some of the cost-related biases of professional service programs. On the self-help side, the outreach activity of members who follow the Twelve Steps and other self-help leaders can offset some of the ethnocentric, sexist, or class bias in their organizations. Of the three, the informal helping system, operating with indigenous helpers, probably is the least systematically biased, though this characteristic is not adequate compensation for the apparently discriminatory practices of the other two systems. Informal helpers, especially if they are overloaded, as they often are in minority communities, cannot make up for the lack of access to the other systems. Equity will be achieved only when all three helping systems are equally acceptable and available. The availability, acceptability, and adequacy of self-help and professional services are currently deficient from a social justice point of view in many minority communities.

Cultural Sensitivity

Sensitivity and equity often overlap, since without cultural sensitivity, the system is inequitable for many minorities. Improbable as it may seem, the apparent biases of the self-help and professional systems favor the majority culture even when minority clients outnumber nonminority clients. The large number of minorities who are the clientele of some big-city agencies often does not assure that the agencies are free of bias.

Since the informal system is locally based and is often managed by people who tend to identify with an ethnic group, it often has the best record of integrating elements of the indigenous culture into its helping activities. This surely is a large part of the reason why the church, a component of the informal system, is the most common source of extra-family help. In a mental health study, Veroff, Kulka, and Douvan found that 39.2 percent of those who went outside the family for personal assistance contacted their church.[7] General health personnel were sought next, whereas professional specialists in mental health or the human services were sought relatively infrequently. Within black and Hispanic communities, the pattern was even more pronounced; the church is a most important local institution, and blacks, in particular, seem to place great store in their ownership of this institution.

Support for the importance of churches among blacks has been reaffirmed by a major national survey of black people. James Jackson, the principal investigator of this survey, commented on the strength of this attachment:

> "We know black people have a history of being religious and oriented toward their kinship and friendship networks for buffering the stresses of life," Jackson says, "but we were surprised by the extent to which the data reveal family and church to be essential elements in the lives of our respondents."

An overwhelming 92 percent of the people interviewed in the national survey said they had attended a church since the age of 18, and 68 percent said they were official members of churches at the time of the interview. Eighty-two percent of the respondents felt that black religious institutions have helped black people. Some 78 percent of all blacks "prayed every day," 75 percent ranked going to church as a "very important activity in their lives," and 40 percent attended church at least once weekly.

Among the 63 percent of all respondents who had experienced "very serious personal problems," 87 percent had sought help from family or friends, 49 percent turned to professional helpers, and nearly 20 percent went to their pastors or ministers. . . .

Respondents said when they have needed help with money, advice, transportation, child care, and so forth, they often received it from family members (52 percent) and they often got help from fellow church members (63 percent). Jackson notes that families tended to help out by providing services and giving financial aid, while church members generally offered emotional support and advice.[8]

The professional service system and the self-help system, in contrast, do not enjoy the confidence of the black community or, for that matter, various Hispanic communities. These systems must make more of an effort to integrate minority cultural perspectives. And occasionally the special resources available to the professional system have been used for this purpose. Culturally sensitive staff might be hired or a staff development program might be implemented to enhance the cultural sensitivity of the existing staff. But the informal system, especially in minority communities, usually cannot take comparable initiatives since there are few surplus or discretionary resources to augment the informal helping system. The ratio of caregivers to population in minority communities often compares unfavorably with majority communities, and caregivers in minority communities are more likely to be overloaded. Unfortunately but understandably, overloaded caregivers will take protective action by defining their helping responsibilities more narrowly and by being more cautious about making commitments to those seeking help.

One approach to the problem of overloaded informal helping systems is to add components of the more formal professional and self-help organization systems. Fountain House, the formal successor to We Are Not Alone (WANA), has become a strong and stable hybrid agency that incorporates elements of both the self-help and the professional systems. Founded by a group of discharged mental patients and their Junior League informal helpers, WANA's first encounters (meetings?) took place on the steps of   *137* the main branch of the New York City Public Library. Later, after a period of substantial program development, a handsome residence was acquired with a fountain in the back, hence the name Fountain House. For many years, Fountain House has been a leading model of a club program for persons recovering from a mental illness.

In the self-help organization, cultural sensitivity is a key issue. It does not have the "natural" sensitivity of the indigenous informal system, but there are things it can do to improve its performance in this area. Some self-help organizations have established special chapters for black and Hispanic members, for gay people, and for people with a variety of religious and professional affiliations. In larger urban areas, there is even a tendency to combine two factors, resulting, for example, in chapters for "gay academic professionals."

Some professional agencies have improved their cultural sensitivity by using informal leaders and helpers from the broader community. The Urban League and various child welfare agencies dedicated to black children exemplify this approach. In the New York–New Jersey area, the Puerto Rican community sponsors Aspira, a grass-roots agency that promotes the education of community youths and nurtures their special talents through scholarships and guidance.

COMPLEMENTARITY, COOPERATION, AND LEADERSHIP

Obstacles

The partisan attitudes and defensiveness of the champions of the three systems embody a certain closed-mindedness about collaboration. The blind spots of these advocates make it difficult for them to see the similarities of the three systems beneath superficial differences in terminology and procedure. Some wait for someone to slip up so they can reject the entire approach, or, if their favorite explanations are not endorsed, they consider the lack of endorsement as further evidence that coooperation is impossible. Complementarity is, in some ways, even more difficult to accept because it implies that the championed system is not the complete answer, and the issue of leadership among collaborating systems is still more touchy. Coordination is another bugaboo since it implies that the systems share some functions. Thus, the would-be collaborator must be prepared for strong resistance. And the best way to counter resistance may be an emphatic reminder of how important the primary task is. In view of the usual scarcity and insufficiency of resources, it is imperative that pragmatic use be made of available resources, and the task of augmenting the assistance available from one system with that from another must be implemented.

It is axiomatic that the combined benefits of two or three helping systems are greater than the benefits of one system. Thus, arguments purporting to show that the methods of one system would be incompatible with those of another system should be viewed with skepticism. Sound theory, though it would not support the use of any one system over another, may provide guidance about how the systems would be best combined. Complementarity can be supported by demonstrating that all three systems are already involved in most of the problems. Then it is only a short step to show how they might be combined and coordinated more effectively.

Problems Extend Over Systems

No one system has a monopoly on effective approaches to the resolution of most problems. Although such self-help organizations as AA, Women for Sobriety, Weight Watchers, OA, and TOPS stand out as highly visible approaches to substance abuse problems, they operate alongside professional therapists and informal helpers. Ministers are often consulted about drinking problems, and co-workers may be an important source of support for a weight control program. Professional therapy is regularly used by people with habit control problems and, as a matter of fact, is often recommended by such organizations as OA and AA. Complementarity is supported by the quantitative findings of the 1980 AA survey, in which a majority of the respondents had consulted professionals before joining AA, and approximately half these users of counseling or rehabilitation services cited them as an important factor in their joining AA.[9]

The burden on the informal system is quite heavy when the great vulnerability of the help-seekers might seem to preclude their using this system. The informal system is often the primary, though not an adequate, caretaker of the chronically mentally ill. With many of these people, the professional system may be less active than either the self-help or the informal system. In this area of placement in the community rather than in institutions, the care of some of the most severely impaired people has been given over, by default, to informal community caregivers. And this is only one instance in which it might be argued that the professional system must be a more significant factor in the   *139* care of the mentally ill, lightening the burden of families and reducing the load on the informal system to a level more closely attuned to its capabilities. The public library should perhaps continue to function as an informal "drop-in center," but it should not be the only one. The specialty professional sector must also assume responsibility for providing services.

Coordination and Leadership

Given the overlap commonly found among the systems, some criteria are needed to identify the situations in which one system might be expected to take a lead role. In general, when accountability is a high priority, as it is when highly vulnerable persons, such as the very young or very old, must be protected, an auditable professional agency should take the lead. Accordingly, protective services might be designated the lead agency in joint efforts with PA. The lead or coordinating role, however, does not mean that the other systems are less valuable, but only that the professional agency is primarily accountable to mobilize and safeguard needed resources.

Similarly, when intensive, sustained interventions are required during a crisis period, the professional agency would ordinarily be expected to take the lead in providing round-the-clock technical resources. Furthermore, such an agency is also better able generally to position itself at an optimum emotional distance from the problem. This distance is often necessary to sustain constructive involvement and to minimize the caregivers' need to take flight or to respond in some inappropriate, anxiety-generated way.

Reality and the Ideal

But it is necessary to say a word about compromises and exceptions. Linking primary accountability to professional organizations must both bemuse and infuriate members of self-help organizations, since their very beginnings owe something to the shortcomings of professional agencies. Moreover, self-help organizations claim a better track record of service and accountability for such activities as detoxifying substance and alcohol abusers and coping with intense grief reactions or desperate panic situations. They have often been more perceptive than professionals in seeing that an individual was "bottoming out" and about to begin his or her recovery phase. With considerable cogency, such organizations can argue with the generalization that professional helping systems are superior in situations in which accountability and emotional objectivity are high priorities. In light of this, it is quite understandable that they are exasperated by discussions of the professional system as the lead system. Yet generalizations about lead agencies could be acceptable to self-helpers and informal caregivers if they were considered a starting point for the study of real-life patterns of behavior.

Special Contributions of the Systems

The self-help system has an advantage when access to resources is required intermittently, especially if these resources are needed outside normal business hours and over a prolonged period. Self-help organizations will often be able to help substantially, without advance notice, and thus complement the regularly scheduled assistance of human service professionals.

During in-between times—between therapy appointments or between self-help meetings (the other twenty-three hours of the other six days)—the informal helping system is an especially important resource, but there are exceptions here, too. The many functions of the mutual aid network, which is an integral part of most self-help organizations, sometimes plays an important role in meeting these needs. And the contributions of therapists also must not be overlooked; telephone calls or occasional extra sessions are often options with most therapists. Nonetheless, community caregivers usually have greater access to social resources (housing, medical care, jobs, child care, and the like) than do self-helpers or professional caregivers.

LINKING THE THREE SYSTEMS

When the relevant actors (self-help members, caregivers, and professionals) view their systems as complementary resources, not as competitive alternatives, more effective patterns of linkage can be seen. The term *linkage* is used, rather than cooperation or collaboration, because it does not imply loss of autonomy and because it leaves open the question of how much joint action is desirable. Protective services and PA or an official mental health agency and an activist group of mental health consumers should know enough about each other to plan their programs for maximum benefit, but they must be mindful of the disadvantages of too much contact, which can blur the differences among the systems. Some linkage among the systems can help consumers in one system who are participating in the other system. According to the Task Panel on Community Support Systems of the   *141*

President's Commission on Mental Health, respect for the autonomy of the self-help system was considered to be the single most important factor in enabling professionals to establish effective relations with self-help organizations.[10]

Additional ties will be forged with other systems when each system perceives itself, and is perceived by its counterparts, to be distinctive and self-directing or autonomous. These characteristics do not deny the interdependence among the systems, nor do they preclude mutual efforts to influence the systems that are part of a larger helping system. On the contrary, interdependence will be more readily acknowledged and openness to the constructive suggestions from external systems will be improved if each system is secure in its fundamental distinction, self-direction, and autonomy. These principles suggest that linkages will be most effective when they maintain and enhance the differences in the systems. Care must be taken, however, to ensure that self-help organizations do not begin to resemble professional agencies, and vice versa.

In extending their view of the simultaneous autonomy and complementarity of self-help and professional systems, the report of the Task Panel on Community Support Systems made two major recommendations. One was that individual community mental health centers develop and maintain directories of self-help organizations in their catchment areas.[11] Apart from its informational value, this sign of approval would facilitate referrals between the systems and might also include the exchange of consultation and technical assistance.

The other recommendation of the Task Panel called for clearinghouses to carry out a broader range of functions important to both systems, such as helping individuals connect with existing chapters and facilitating contact among people who are likely to establish a new chapter of an existing self-help organization, or even a new self-help organization if there were no national models. Clearinghouses, further, can provide a forum through which self-help organizations can present their distinctive perspectives to the professional system and obtain sanction, organizational development, and technical assistance from the professional system. In such a forum, professionals can help with such tasks as designing publicity campaigns, establishing community switchboards, and preparing an application for "tax exempt" status, whereas self-help leaders can provide professionals with an insider's view of the lifestyle and culture of the people served.

These mutually beneficial exchanges will be further discussed in Chapter Sixteen, but, for now, the significance of the
directory and clearinghouse recommendations of the Task Panel

is that they mark a high point in the recognition of the importance of the self-help and the informal systems, along with the specialty professional systems. The balance of these systems, however, will continue to be questioned. In the more than 20 clearinghouses now in place in the United States, the influence of professionals has been greater than that of self-help leaders, primarily because the professional system has greater access to the resources necessary to establish these clearinghouses. It would be better, of course, if self-help leaders could take a more active role in developing clearinghouses. But, apart from the usual disputes over turf, self-help leaders tend to be identified with their particular organizations rather than with the self-help system movement as a whole. Professionals, in contrast, are more likely to have significant attachments to the larger, professionally operated human services system.

AN APPROXIMATE GUIDE

Figure 1 (see p. 130) can be used to systematize decision making. If the user is limited to one system, that system would be the system with the largest number of pluses. But if more than one system can be used, the form is helpful in designing a multicomponent service package. Any of the three systems with several pluses on any of its five dimensions should be considered for inclusion in such a package. For example, the professional system might receive three or four pluses on its basis of power, whereas the specificity of the self-help organization might receive pluses on acceptability, adequacy, and equity. Thus, efforts should be made to design a package that includes both systems. But what kind of self-help organization? What features should it have, and what kind of linkage to the professional system? To address these complex questions, a typology of self-help organizations is developed in Part Four.

Notes

1. D. X. Freedman, "Psychiatric Epidemiology Counts," pp. 931–933; and W. W. Eaton et al., "The Design of the Epidemiologic Catchment Area Surveys: The Control and Measurement of Error," pp. 942–948, *Archives of General Psychiatry*, 41 (October 1984). Other articles in this issue of the *Archives* also report on this important research and are useful for understanding the magnitude of the need for human services.

2. D. A. Regier, I. D. Goldberg, and C. A. Taube, "The De Facto U.S. Mental Health Services System," *Archives of General Psychiatry,* 35 (1978), pp. 685–693.

3. W. Schofield, *Psychotherapy: The Purchase of Friendship* (Englewood Cliffs, N.J.: Prentice-Hall, 1964).

4. A. P. Goldstein and N. R. Simonson, "Social Psychological Approaches to Psychotherapy Research," in A. E. Bergin and S. L. Garfield, eds., *Handbook of Psychotherapy and Behavior Change: An Empirical Analysis* (New York: John Wiley & Sons, 1971), p. 161.

5. Cartoon drawing by D. Fradon, copyright © 1981, by *The New Yorker Magazine,* Inc.

6. A. Gartner and F. Riessman, *Self-Help in the Human Services* (San Francisco: Jossey-Bass, 1977).

7. J. Veroff, R. Kulka, and E. Douvan, *Mental Health in America: Patterns in Help Seeking from 1957 to 1966* (New York: Basic Books, 1981).

8. As quoted in "Black Americans Surveyed," *ISR Newsletter* (Institute for Social Research, The University of Michigan) (Spring–Summer 1983), pp. 3 and 7.

9. Alcoholics Anonymous, *Alcoholics Anonymous, Analysis of the 1980 Survey of the Membership of A.A.* (New York: A.A. General Services Office, 1980), pp. 2–3.

10. Task Panel on Community Support Systems, President's Commission on Mental Health. *Report to the President,* Vol. 2 (Appendix) (Washington, D.C.: U.S. Government Printing Office, 1978), p. 178.

11. Ibid.

PART FOUR

Typology of Self-Help Organizations

Up to now, self-help organizations have been compared with professional therapy and the help of informal caregivers, as if all self-help organizations were the same. Obviously, self-helpers would not agree with this. But the daunting reality is that unless a separate type is posited for each organization, objections will be registered, particularly by those with personal commitments to these organizations. To them, the focus on common properties seems to ignore the unique configuration of their organization. Thus, it is necessary to ask for their forbearance as this topic is broached. The tentativeness of much of Part Four is an effort to be sensitive to the concerns of the personally committed. A healthy dose of skepticism is appropriate, because any system of classification must select certain characteristics and ignore others. Self-helpers will recognize that even when typologies are based on important characteristics, other characteristics that also make the organization distinctive are ignored. Thus, abstracting a typology from the only partially understood arrangements of the "real world" risks antagonizing some people and misleading others.

Classification, however, offers a number of benefits. It is comparative and can lead to a deeper understanding of how similar problems and issues are managed in similarly classified organizations. It also points up the mismatches that result from inappropriate borrowing from dissimilar types of self-help organizations. The usefulness of a typology depends on selecting organizing concepts at an appropriate level. It seems to be impossible, for example, to classify self-help organizations by whether their primary strategy is behavioral or cognitive. The distinction is too abstract. But if too abstract a scheme is a problem, so is concreteness. Misleading typologies may be pegged to concrete but secondary characteristics that obscure fundamental differences as they focus on superficial similarities. Just because AA and PA share the anonymous name does not mean they are based on a similar model. Focusing attention on manifest content can also be misleading. Recovery, Inc., and the National Alliance for the Mentally Ill (NAMI) are both concerned with mental disorder, but this fact does not justify putting them in the same category. To do so would be to ignore important differences in the purposes and the type of people who become members. Yet the power of appropriate typological concepts is evident in their important, less obvious consequences. These concepts should illuminate how organizations follow different patterns in defining problems, using problem-solving methods, managing organizational structures, and relating to the general and professional community.

ORGANIZING CONCEPT

The present typology, which is still developing, is based on the different missions of self-help organizations and contains five categories. *Mission*   147 is a complex concept encompassing the purpose, the people, and the problem-solving approach (Powell's three Ps) of the organization. Although the purposes or goals have a high priority, they cannot be understood apart from the people who are involved and the particular problem-solving methods they use to pursue their goals.

In devising the typology, the structural properties of the missions were emphasized. To the extent structural rather than content properties are used, the typology will be more applicable. Since the typology builds on structural distinctions made by others, it will take on additional meaning as the reader refers to works of these others. Katz and Bender noted some important corollaries between "inner-" and "outer-" focused groups.[1] In a related formulation, Sagarin distinguished between those who manage deviance by attempting to change the norms of society and those who conform to these norms.[2] Similarly, Steinman and Traunstein made the colorful distinction between "ameliorators" and "redefiners."[3] Considered as a group, these distinctions parallel the distinction made between different targets of change in the present typology. Some organizations aim to change society; others, their members.

For example, the National Gay and Lesbian Task Force and Parents Without Partners are organizations with significant social change interests. The inclusion of PWP in this type is based on its more or less latent aim to reform, but not to revolutionize, society so that society is more supportive of single parents. If this seems to be too strong a way to describe its interest, however, this type of organization may be said to offer support for a particular kind of lifestyle or, in some cases, for a particular kind of transition. But to the extent that transition is emphasized, it may detract from one of the most powerful dynamics in these organizations—their opposition to traditional social arrangements. In passing over the manifest interests of these organizations (homosexuality and single parenthood), I do not deny their obvious and important differences but rather highlight their less obvious similarities. Each endeavors to sanction a different lifestyle and to protect it from a majority that is more often than not insensitive or antagonistic.

Those organizations with a mission to change the self rather than society can be broken down. Some missions encompass specific problems such as overeating, smoking, compulsive gambling or problem drinking; others encompass a wide range of problems related to such functions as managing distressing emotions and raising children. This distinction, though not an exact parallel, is related to Levy's distinction between groups designed to modify problem behaviors and those designed to alleviate stress.[4] The latter, stress-oriented self-help organizations may have a good deal in common. This is seen in two organizations, one dealing with child abuse, the other with distressing emotions (that is, PA and Recovery, Inc.). Despite their real differences, their intervention methods have much in common. Both depend on psychological approaches that they adapt to the broad range of problems of their members. In that this reveals some similarity in their tasks, these organizations should be able to learn much that is valuable from each other.

148

Almost certainly they will find that they can borrow and adapt more from each other than they can from organizations dedicated to changing such specific behaviors as eating habits. Similarly, organizations with missions to help people quit smoking or to curb compulsive overeating are likely to find much of value in each other's techniques and strategies.

The tie to structural properties is somewhat attenuated for the two remaining types of self-help organizations. One type is designed to meet the needs of relatives and significant others of troubled and troubling people—to ease their burden and to promote better care for their troubled and highly troubling relatives. The other type strives to maximize the adaptation of the physically handicapped by providing special resources and psychological support.

MISSIONS

The typology is organized by the five basic missions of self-help organizations. They are to change a highly specified behavior; to modify a broad range of difficulties and coping patterns; to reform society and/or validate a lifestyle; to relieve the burden of family caregivers; and to sustain the physically disabled. Habit disturbance organizations, especially as they may be perceived by newcomers or outsiders, pursue a specific behavior change, such as altering habits related to tobacco, food, and alcohol. Some members may object to the narrowness of this formulation. It should be acknowledged that, for the successfully recovering, more committed members, participation in these organizations is often a long-term means to a temperate way of life rather than mere abstinence from a habit. Nonetheless, in such organizations as Women for Sobriety, AA, Smokestoppers, and Overeaters Anonymous, the major concern of the new member is to eliminate narrowly defined habits.

To address a wider range of problems, such as anxiety states, abusive tendencies, and various forms of unresolved loss, it is necessary to use a more broadly applicable technology to improve general coping patterns. This type of organization includes Emotions Anonymous, Parents Anonymous, and The Compassionate Friends. A third type of self-help organization includes people who are intentionally or unintentionally discriminated against; these individuals are offered the opportunity to support one another as they seek to change the offending practices. Though some may question how much single parents are discriminated against, one can argue that it is interesting to consider how Parents Without Partners and the National Gay and Lesbian Task Force might be alike. The Federation of Parents and Friends of Lesbians and Gays (Parents/ FLAG) is similarly an advocacy organization, but like the next type of "significant other" organization, it advocates social reform and engages in mutual support. This fourth type is made up of last-resort caregivers, and especially family members, who find themselves in stressful situations because of the problems or conditions of relatives. The National Alliance for the Mentally Ill, a federation of local groups that arose in part because of the deficiencies in the community-based care   *149* movement, represents this important, fast-growing category. Others are Toughlove and Families Anonymous. The members of the fifth type of organization have diseases such as emphysema and stroke or have experienced a physical change such as an ostomy and laryngectomy.

DIMENSIONS OF SELF-HELP ORGANIZATIONS

To the extent that the organizations within each type have important themes in common, their profiles on six basic dimensions should be similar, whereas different profiles should form different types of self-help organizations. Like types of organizations should cluster; unlike types should separate themselves on public image, goals, technology, career patterns, normalization potential, and relationship to professionals.

Public Image

A discussion of public image must consider the extent to which an organization is known to its potential constituencies and the general public, followed by the extent to which its basic tenets are understood and approved of. Another aspect of the public image question is how the membership perceives its prestige, acceptability, and deviancy ratings. Some of these perceptions will be reflected in how members of these organizations are treated by the media, including the extent to which the organization has access to the media. Other important factors are the competence of the leadership and magnitude of the members' problem. Naturally the perception of these latter factors will be conditioned by the prevailing culture. To wit, consider that the American culture has only recently "discovered" child abuse or that it is more solicitous of people with physical rather than mental handicaps. Thus, public image is both objective—to the extent that it exists apart from its perception—and subjective.

Goals

Here it is only necessary to indicate the parallels between goals and the earlier discussion of differences in mission. In one type of self-help organization, advocacy and lifestyle-support goals are given primacy. In two others, the goals are frankly personal. In one, these goals are defined in terms of altering narrowly defined habits; in the other, these goals are defined broadly to include people with a range of problems. The goals of the fourth type address the concerns and problems of significant others, whereas those of the fifth type relate to the adaptions of people with physical illnesses and conditions.

Technology

As used here, the term *technology* should not evoke mechanistic connotations but rather the means, the activities, the methods, and the procedures by which goals are pursued, including the rationales that support these goals. These rationales are part of the methods and procedures. Thus, without a cognitive predisposition, procedures would have no meaning or positive expectancy; and without procedures, cognitions would not be expressed in confident action.

This discussion of technology will refer to the theoretical frameworks first encountered in Part Two, but the focus will be on whether the procedures used by particular types of self-help organizations adhere more closely to one theoretical framework than another. The question, then, is whether the dominant problem-solving approach of a particular type of self-help organization seems to be better conceptualized in terms of one set of psychosocial processes (reference groups, social networks, social learning, formal organization) than another. Are the dominant themes in social reform–lifestyle organizations best conceived of as the acceptance of a new reference group and a commitment to a new set of norms? Or is the emphasis on developing new resources through expanding and strengthening social networks the best explanation of what takes place in significant other organizations? Still another possibility is that the processes of social learning, especially reinforcement and modeling, explain why people improve in some habit disturbance organizations. In terms of organizational processes, most self-help programs encourage their members to participate in the organization by assuming specialized roles and leadership positions. But the number and quality of these opportunities vary across the different types of self-help organizations. This is not to suggest that a single, or even a multitheoretical, framework explains the technology of a particular self-help organization, but it is rather to suggest that certain images or metaphors may be especially suitable or insightful with particular organizations.

Career Pattern

If the typology is substantially valid, participants in different types of self-help organizations should have different careers. Members in lifestyle-advocacy groups, such as the gay-lesbian or Little People's organizations, may be more broadly involved in their organizations. The members of significant other organizations, however, may be less involved. The modal duration of membership is also likely to vary. Membership in weight control and stop smoking organizations tends to be relatively brief. Another aspect of participation has to do with the formality of the interactions among members, which will vary across types as will the discretion of leaders to interpret guidelines and improvise solutions. Lastly the types are likely to differ in terms of the leadership opportunities they offer, both internal and external to the organization.

Normalization Potential

Many people who come to self-help organizations have been stigmatized or discredited by society and perhaps by themselves. The critics of self-help warn that membership in the self-help organization will further   *151* solidify a negative identity. In their view, the self-help organization may cause

> an individual who might have been received easily in ordinary social intercourse . . . [to possess] a trait that can obtrude itself upon attention and turn those of us who [sic] he meets away from him, breaking the claim that his other attributes have on us. He possesses a stigma, an undesired differentness from what we had anticipated. We and those who do not depart negatively from the particular expectations at issue I shall call the *normals*.[5]

Thus, it is important to determine whether the self-help organization is likely to strengthen or diminish stimatizing traits. Insofar as it diminishes them, it will normalize the participant by bringing him or her into harmony with the larger society. As the individual is normalized, he or she assumes the same form as the rest of society. A self-help organization, however, may afford the individual another option for managing stigma. Although the objective stigma doesn't change, the self-help organization may insulate the individual from its consequences in the manner Goffman described:

> Also, it seems possible for an individual to fail to live up to what we effectively demand of him, and yet be relatively untouched by this failure; insulated by his alienation, protected by identity beliefs of his own, he feels that he is a full-fledged normal human being, and that we are the ones who are not quite human. He bears a stigma but does not seem to be impressed or repentant about doing so.[6]

How aptly this explains the cry "It's not us, but the homophobics that need to be cured."

But self-help organizations may also encourage negative forms of participation. Members can become compulsively preoccupied with a narrow aspect of the program or distort the program in line with their dysfunctional personal predilections. It can even be simpler than this: They may become so immersed in the program that they lose sight of the balance they need to maintain between the program and their other obligations and interests. These potential misuses will be considered in the discussion of how different types of self-help organizations can mark their members, thus causing them to feel and be perceived as different from the normal population. In more balanced terms, the self-help organization will be examined for its potential to amplify or mute deviance.

Relationship to Professionals

The last dimension determines how different types of self-help organizations relate to human service professionals, and how, and in what measure, professionals and self-help organizations cooperate. Are professionals encouraged to refer clients to local chapters? Is the relationship reciprocal; that is, do these organizations send people to professionals? After the referral is made, are the new members or clients encouraged to view the self-help experience and the professional counseling as complementary? Do self-help organizations and professionals consult with

Table 3.
Dimensions and Properties of Self-Help Organizations

Exemplar Organizations

  Public Image
      Level of recognition
      Degree of approval
      Understanding of purpose
      Prestige and conformity ratings

  Goals
      Specific personal changes
      Broad personal changes
      Advocacy and social reform objectives
      Physical vs. emotional objectives
      Focus on significant others vs. "deviants"
          or "problem bearers"

  Technology
      Acceptance of new reference group
      Reinforcement and modeling
      Expansion of resource network
      Development of competence through involvement in
          organizational tasks

  Career Pattern
      Average length and extent of involvement
      Diversity of roles and discretion in their enactment
      Opportunity for external relationships

  Normalization Potential
      Protection of rights and expansion of opportunities
      Stigmatization vs. destigmatization
      Positive and negative changes in functioning
      Functional and dysfunctional forms of participation

  Relationship to Professionals
      Overall:
        Amount of contact
        Dominant tone (positive or negative) of interaction
      Cooperation in relation to:
        Referrals
        Program consultation
        Policy development

one another? Is consultation reciprocal? Ascending the scale of collaboration, do exchanges of program consultation or technical assistance occur between professional organizations and self-help organizations, and, again, is the exchange reciprocal?

These dimensions and their component elements are summarized in Table 3 (p. 153). It is a template that will be employed again to display the dimensions of each of the five types of self-help organizations. In Appendix One, a composite table will be presented to facilitate comparative analysis of the five types of self-help organizations.

SUMMARY

In the chapters to follow, the reader should judge whether a particular self-help organization has a distinctive configuration or profile according to the five dimensions. Discussions of these configurations in the next five chapters will form the basis for discussions of the modes of collaboration open to self-help organizations and professionals, which are presented in Part Five.

Notes

1. A. H. Katz and E. I. Bender, *The Strength in Us: Self-Help Groups in the Modern World* (New York: New Viewpoints, 1976).
2. E. Sagarin, *Odd Man In: Societies of Deviants in America* (New York: Quadrangle, 1969).
3. R. Steinman and D. Traunstein, "Redefining Deviance: The Self-Help Challenge in the Human Services," *Journal of Applied Behavioral Sciences*, 12 (July–August–September 1976), pp. 410–418.
4. L. H. Levy, "Self-Help Groups: Types and Psychological Processes," *Journal of Behavioral Science*, 12 (July–August–September 1976), pp. 310–322.
5. E. Goffman, *Stigma* (Englewood Cliffs, N.J.: Prentice-Hall, 1963), p. 5.
6. Ibid., p. 6.

9

Habit Disturbance Organizations

Habit disturbance organizations include the following: Smoke-stoppers, I Can Quit, Alcoholics Anonymous, Overeaters Anonymous, Take Off Pounds Sensibly (TOPS), Weight Watchers, Narcotics Anonymous, Gamblers Anonymous, and Women for Sobriety. These organizations share a concern over a problem that is specific and concrete. The major dimensions of habit disturbance organizations are discussed in this chapter. In addition, Table 4, which can be found on p. 156, displays these dimensions by using the template described in the introductory comments to Part Four.

PUBLIC IMAGE—HEALTHY IS IN

Habit disturbance self-help organizations owe much of their astonishing growth to changes in social manners. In an era of nouvelle cuisine, aerobics, and Perrier, the values accounting for these preferences also account for the growth of habit control organizations. These organizations, focusing on what they conceive to be addictions, chemical dependencies, or compulsions, have become as popular as fruit-flavored yogurt. The growth of these organizations that address the compulsive use of alcohol, drugs, tobacco, food, and gambling is in part a response to changes in the values of the culture. Sophisticated lifestyles have become more sensible and less sybaritic. The standard-bearers

Table 4.
Properties of Habit Disturbance Organizations

Exemplar Organizations
Alcoholics Anonymous; Women for Sobriety; Gamblers Anonymous;
Narcotics Anonymous; TOPS (Take Off Pounds Sensibly); Overeaters
Anonymous; I Can Quit; Weight Watchers; Smokestoppers

Public Image
Widely recognized; large, well accepted
Easy to understand
Autonomous organizations
Some commercial forms

Goals
From a new member's point of view:
Single-minded in purpose
Specific, narrowly focused
Concrete

Technology
"Behavior" first
Standardized approaches
Reference group and fellowship processes
Additional resources available through expanded networks
Role development through leadership opportunities
Printed information available

Career Pattern
Slips common
Repeat members
Experience may be short and intensive for smoking
and overeating habits
Leadership roles formally structured

Normalization Potential[a]
Universalizes +
Accepts relapses
Preoccupation with recovering[o]

Relationship to Professionals
Mutual respect
Indirect, behind the scenes
Printed information often discussed
in professional journals

---

[a] +, positive; o, negative.

of the culture discourage smoking, excessive drinking, and the ample figure. "Personals" in the *New York Review of Books* or the *New Republic* proclaim the virtues of a slender figure and nonsmoking. A cartoon in the *New Yorker* made a similar point, showing a woman at a party rushing toward a man and exclaiming: "Oh good! I've been looking for someone who drinks and smokes." Related values are expressed by the importance attached to self-control and self-management as a means to personal fulfillment. One manifestation of these values is the proliferation of diet and other "self-help" books that show up on the best-seller lists.

The increased publicity given to the relation between lifestyle and general health has also boosted habit disturbance organizations. Few will claim that the benefits of even the most heralded medical advances can compensate for the damage of earlier excesses. Some parts may be replaceable, but they don't "meet or exceed original equipment standards."

New behavior paradigms have also insinuated themselves into the culture. Psychodynamic formulations now compete with more pragmatic conceptions of causality. It is no longer de rigueur to posit psychological conflict as the reason behind habit disturbances. And even if it were, it would not be considered primary, nor would psychoanalysis or intensive psychotherapy be automatically considered to be the best way to deal with such disturbances.

Whereas these cultural developments have energized all self-help organizations, their greatest impact has been on habit disturbance organizations. The impact, however, has not been uniform across all organizations of this type. Organizations concerned with smoking and overeating have been more responsive to these trends than organizations dealing with the more devastating substance abuse problems. Apparently people with less ominous habits have a greater potential to reach, or still respond to, cultural values. Other differences are also apparent within the category. Specificity, for example, takes on a special meaning relative to anonymous organizations. Though the problem is specific, the successfully recovering member may have to make sweeping changes in his or her life. But it should also be remembered that these views are not pressed vigorously on the newcomer, nor are they a prominent part of the public image of the mission of habit disturbance self-help organizations.

The point is that the enormous complexity of self-help must be oversimplified in any discussion. Notwithstanding this oversimplification, habit disturbance organizations, as a category, have responded to changes in the values of the culture. Romantic images of the generous tippler and the jovial fatty are scorned. And the image of the cool cocaine user is moving ever closer toward the image of the tragically ignorant heroin addict. The obverse is that the present climate favors simple, natural, holistic lifestyles, a climate within which habit disturbance organizations have flourished. Within the category, however, it is probably true that organizations concerned with dependencies on drugs other than alcohol have grown at a slower rate.

GOALS

Goal specificity is another factor in the widespread acceptance of these organizations, and it makes intervention in *some* areas of an individual's life possible, or so it seems to the newcomer. At a more advanced level, members experience a change of heart and conclude that they cannot recover from their addiction without making radical, long-term changes in their lives. At least initially, however, this is not part of the credo the newcomer feels he or she must accept. Indeed the focus on a narrow segment of the individual's life may be maintained indefinitely for smoking and eating disturbances, though it is harder to maintain for the abuse of alcohol and other more addictive substances. The devastation wrought by substance abuse affects the spheres of the individual's life quickly, and inevitably.

But the highly singular purpose should not be gainsaid, as this excerpt from an official brochure indicates: "*Narcotics Anonymous does not*. . .provide marriage, family or vocational counseling. . .provide welfare or other services."[1] Thus, even when the problem tends to spread into other areas, the organization strives to retain concrete, narrowly circumscribed goals. As a consequence, these organizations are less likely to rouse anxieties about "people messing around with my head." The avoidance of such anxieties may be harder when the organizations have broader goals.

But the narrow focus also has inherent risks. Preoccupation with a narrow problem may lead to other, larger problems being overlooked. A person with a chronic psychosis who also abuses alcohol needs a coordinated program addressed to both the alcoholism and the mental disorder. Similarly, the person who is "controlled" by demoniac plots to smoke more (beyond those openly pursued by tobacco companies) must be approached in a way that is sensitive to his or her overall mental condition as well as the smoking issue. For unless the possibility of primitive displacements is recognized, regression and destructive acting-out may inadvertently be encouraged. Also, reality testing may be eroded and needed psychiatric attention delayed.

As organizations have recognized the risks of their narrow focus, they have taken an important step to lower them. Weight control groups are alert to the need to direct people with anorexic or bulemic disturbances to appropriate sources of help. More generally, most self-help organizations declare they are not appropriate resources (implying perhaps they should not be considered the sole resource) for dealing with psychiatric disturbances. Most organizations handle the problems that do arise by making referrals. More complicated situations are individually considered, sometimes in special closed meetings.

This does not mean that the individual with a larger, more pervasive emotional problem must be excluded from the organization. One of the most salutary features of these organizations is that they encourage the person to isolate a problem, such as drinking or smoking, from a larger, less tractable condition, for if headway is made with the smaller problem, it may alter the individual's entire outlook, and no one can deny that there may even be hope for a better resolution of the larger problem.

In some cases, the apparently narrow goals may have to be reinterpreted to address a broader range of issues as a member faces up to the full import of his or her problem. Thus, in a sense, these organizations enjoy the benefits of specificity and breadth. For example, refraining from substance abuse may be just the start of a profound personal change, which is then viewed as essential to maintain the abstinence. Eventually these "narrow focused" programs can transform a person's life. Another slant on this theme of small beginnings highlights indirect benefits. For example, the small-group experience in a stopping smoking program may bolster the individual's morale. Or when weight loss leads to improved self-concept, the effects are likely to be seen in improved social functioning. The effects, however, can be in the reverse direction. If a stressful marriage seems to make achieving sobriety difficult, the AA fellowship may take an interest in the marriage. Practice in this regard is variable, according to local custom, but it is likely to be available in some form on an individualized basis.

Goals cannot be considered apart from the individuals who have access to the organization. Without access, goals are meaningless. Happily, access to the organization and widespread acceptance of its technology are among the most salutary features of these self-help organizations. The technology is relatively simple and frequently communicated in the idiom of the distinctive culture surrounding the substance abuse or the eating   *159* disorder problem. These organizations, relatively speaking, are highly accepted even among minority groups. And except for commercially run organizations, access does not depend on the ability to pay a fee.

TECHNOLOGY

The name *habit disturbance organization* was chosen because it implies a widely accessible, acceptable technology. It is probably less threatening to become a member of a habit disturbance organization than it is to become a member of an organization said to be for compulsive, addicted, or dependent people. The latter descriptors imply conflict, complicated motives, and ambivalent emotions from which relief is obtainable only through psychotherapy. A habit, however, is merely a learned tendency to act; it warrants concern not because habits are pathogenic but because a particular habit is disadvantageous. Moreover, the disadvantage can be removed by changing the habit. This more acceptable formulation relies to an important extent on terms associated with behavioral technology.

Behavior First

Not even the phrase "symptoms first" is accurate, since it is the behavior itself, not an underlying disorder, that is central. Behavior change is the thing sought, and fellowship is the supportive context within which change is encouraged. The behaviors to be changed are easily identified. Gradually, however, prompts can be faded and intervals between reinforcement for desired behaviors can be lengthened. These strategies thus render these behaviors more impervious to influences of the immediate environment. Yet they require no special arrangements; they will be implemented through customary activities and standard procedures of the organization's program. The program also spells out the nature of the rewards—praise and symbolic recognition (pins and plaques) that mark the achievement of a goal or the performance of a desired behavior. In Gamblers Anonymous, for example, disclosure of the self to one's peers, or "giving therapy" as it is called, elicits concrete applause. Telling one's story about "what it was like then and what it is like now" (a format commonly used by anonymous organizations) is reinforced by "Yeah," "That's for sure," "Yes," "Right on," and other verbal compliments. The recitation follows a standard format of how bad things were and how much better they are since the member began the program.

Earlier failures or relapses are attributed to insincere, half-hearted attempts to work the program. These lapses are often described to the entire meeting as a commentary on the "steps" of the anonymous programs. Reports of amends made to people who have been hurt and plans for others still to be made are enthusiastically commended by other members. The structure of the presentation highlights the discovery of personally effective ways to avoid or resist temptation. With similar ends in mind, members are commended for maintaining telephone contact with other members and for having a plan to deal with temptation before it arises.

Rules or slogans have also been formulated to help the members maintain control over these unwanted habits. "Only one drink away from being a drunk" is the AA expression. "No bets," says GA, "not even flipping for the coffee." Even Overeaters Anonymous, an organization that seems to attach special importance to emotional factors, says, "Three normal meals, and nothing in between."

Behavioral Technology Is Standardized

Habit disturbance organizations are in sharp contrast to other self-help organizations that employ general counseling procedures. Habit disturbance organizations, however, have a well-defined, consistent technology. Reliable accounts of their programs are often available in written form. Thus, the broad outline of the technology may be familiar to large elements of the population, and additional information is available to those who wish to know the details of the program. This feature may make it less difficult for some people to contact the organization and learn what the members do.

Detailed descriptions and explanations are often available in brochures and pamphlets. These organizations typically disseminate more printed material than other types of self-help organizations. The availability of these materials is a factor in the consistency from chapter to chapter and from region to region. This is in part why analyses of these organizations in the professional literature tend to be more useful than those of other organizations. Since the level of standardization is higher in these organizations, and since a good deal of it is described, and available, in print, analyses are less likely to pertain only to particular locales. Moreover, the tightly structured program of habit disturbance organizations tends to discourage professionals, who sometimes seem bent on fanciful interpretations of the reasons for people's behavior

Uses of Technological Information

The availability of reliable information makes possible a certain amount of imaginative, reassuring rehearsal before actual contact. For example, prospective members and their confidants can find out what is expected in the way of disclosures and participation in the first few meetings. This information helps ease newcomers' anxieties about first meetings and helps them know better what others are likely to think of them.

Prior information, whether oral or written, can also allow newcomers to formulate a plan to participate in the most relevant components of the program. Some may decide not to participate in the "social" aspect of the program (for example, the after- or between-meeting gatherings). For an initial period, at least, they may decide that these activities might be too intense and lead to confusing entanglements. But at the same time, the information can be used to assess whether it would be advantageous to participate in some important components of the program, such as choosing a sponsor or becoming part of the telephone network.

The brochures and official publications are also useful in helping newcomers place actions in their proper context. "Why do they do that (for example, hug each other in PA)?" "Are you expected to go out for coffee afterward (GA)?" In habit disturbance organizations, the rationales for important procedures usually are explained in official publications. The handbooks, sometimes called "big books," in part because they used to be printed on thick, cheap paper, usually discuss such matters. They are further discussed in newsletters and in occasional monographs.

Significant others, such as relatives or counselors, can use these publications to interpret the program independently. This may be important when relatives, for example, are in a position to reinforce the experience for the member or to avert a threatened discontinuation by the member. These written materials are valuable when the newcomer and the significant other want to understand the program as a whole. They may also be useful when certain practices seem questionable. If something is questioned, the first step is to use the organization's official publications to decide whether further inquiries should be made, and to whom. Publications can also be used to assess the member's fidelity to, and progress in, the program.

Modeling

But even detailed brochures or monographs can go only so far
162   in facilitating the newcomer's adoption of complex and subtle

behaviors. Sooner or later the strategy of specifying the desired behaviors, and appropriate reinforcements, reaches the point of diminishing returns, or it may even become counterproductive or tedious. And even if the tedium is accepted, it is increasingly difficult to define the many subtle, functionally equivalent behaviors precisely so as to direct reinforcement procedures (How is humility defined, and what are the different behavioral options for achieving it?). Shaping strategies will be hampered by the lack of detailed information about immediate relations between baseline behavior and the desired terminal behavior. It is inefficient or impractical to identify the myriad stimulus-response links controlling the habit. When this happens, modeling strategies are useful. Modeling does not require that the behaviors to be learned be specified. The newcomer is motivated to emulate the behavior of various models because of these models' obvious achievements and satisfactions. And even before emulation pays off, the junior member can take vicarious pleasure in the successes of the senior member.

Explaining Technology Nonbehaviorally

The explanatory power of the concept of modeling overlaps that of other conceptual frameworks. The model can also be considered a reference individual, that is, a member of a salient reference group. The model may also be involved in a key relationship in the learner's social network. Nonbehavioral explanations may be especially useful to understand the problems that occur in the lives of substance abusers and the changes that will lead to recovery. Chemically dependent people, people whose everyday activities have become inseparable from the acquisition and use of drugs, must abandon some, and expand other, parts of their social networks. Organizational concepts may be invoked to account for other processes and benefits. Members of GA, for example, find it beneficial to participate in the public education program of the closely related National Council on Compulsive Gambling. Though as participants they do not represent GA, they do learn from the council's efforts to change society's attitudes toward gambling. And even as GA members, provided they maintain their anonymity, they can participate in externally oriented programs that bring the word to other gamblers, court personnel, employers, clinicians, etc. The leadership roles assumed as a part of these activities fortify their resolve to control their own compulsive gambling impulses.

The fellowship experiences highly valued in anonymous programs can be appreciated by way of reference group concepts. *163*

The advantage is that it then becomes possible to use reference concepts to understand why self-help organizations are chosen, and the consequence of the choice. Reference group explanations may also be relevant in organizations that are sometimes not thought of as self-help organizations. Weight Watchers, despite its commercial nature, attaches considerable importance to interacting with reference individuals.

> We've helped millions of people of all ages and all starting weights keep their promises to slim down. In fact, everyone on our staff is a member of Weight Watchers, from the person who registers you to the lecturer who will guide and support you. They've all had a weight problem. And they've all kept the promises they made to themselves. So when you come to a Weight Watchers meeting, you'll be coming to people who understand your weight problem. And who want to help you.[2]

Thus, though behavioral concepts have primacy in explaining the workings of habit disturbance self-help organizations, they are not the only appropriate concepts, and, indeed, some practices may be better understood using other conceptual frameworks. The "fellowship" experience in anonymous organizations is an important example. Its importance would be underestimated if it were to be examined only through the conceptual lens of social learning theory.

Fellowship practices also illustrate the risk of considering various components of the self-help organization in isolation. Fellowship affects every aspect of the organization, including the technology, members' career patterns, normalization potential, and relationships with professionals. By examining fellowship practices separately, the interrelationships and their effects on the system may be underestimated. Thus, fellowship will be discussed again as each dimension of the self-help organization is considered, beginning with members' careers in the following section.

CAREER PATTERN

The nature of the habit disturbance, the desire to overcome it, and the technology used will affect members' careers. They also affect the duration of membership and the opportunities for leadership. However, for a person even to have a career, the organization must be accessible, and the huge numbers of people whose culture differs from that of the majority may never get this far.

Disadvantages of Minorities

It is widely conceded that racial and ethnic minorities and low-income people are underrepresented in self-help organizations, even if this is less true for habit disturbance organizations. Many self-help organizations do not accept responsibility for this situation or feel there is anything they can do about it. But if nothing is done about it, the negative cycle continues. When there are few minority group members, the programs tend to be insensitive to the cultural values and lifestyle practices of minorities and other disadvantaged groups. And because the programs are not congruent with minority group values and lifestyles, however unintentional this may be, minorities are less likely to think of self-help groups as a personally relevant option.

Some small but welcome initiatives to break this cycle, as discussed in Chapter One, take the form of AA chapters dedicated to Hispanic and black members. More recently a new appeal has been made to ethnic pride. The black weight loss group called ERASE (Eat Right and Slim Easily) illustrates this approach. This organization (predominantly female as well as black) was featured in a UPI story. ERASE, founded in Detroit by Mary Powell (no relation to the author), is based on the premise "that diets were all geared to the food white people eat. Most of the things we as blacks like to eat, we're taught, are fattening. That's not true. Mustard and collard greens. . . . Cornbread . . . ." According to the wire story, some 1,000 members in 32 weekly weigh-in meetings "receive food schedules, diet suggestions, menu sheets and recipes."[3]

A similar insensitivity to the needs of women within AA, which was equally unintended, stimulated the formation of Women for Sobriety, an organization that has been highly effective in attracting media attention. The Women for Sobriety program presumes that women alcoholics are disabled with guilt. Thus, instead of fostering humility, as AA does, Women for Sobriety strives to empower its members. For example, members begin their talks with: "Hi, I'm Jean and I'm a competent woman." The irony is that many women benefit from simultaneous participation in WFS and AA. WFS's emphasis on the positive is evident in the Thirteen Statements of Acceptance, a counterpart of AA's Twelve Steps. The second step suggests the predominant orientation:

> "Negative emotions destroy only myself." Negativism frequently precedes drinking bouts. A state of "what's the use," "who cares" is the initiator for an escape from reality. Overcoming these feelings of worthlessness is the object of this acceptance.[4]

There is less of a problem of underrepresentation and insensitivity to minorities in habit disturbance organizations because their specific goals and behaviorally oriented technology lead to less personalistic transactions. Nonetheless, it is still a serious problem, and such an organization is a good place for testing methods to interrupt the cycle. Accordingly, three initiatives, which up to now have been undertaken in very spotty fashion, might be pursued systematically. One strategy would involve imaginative recruitment programs to increase the number of minority members in existing organizations (AA). The second would involve more new organizations for minorities. And the third, which might be pursued by organizations such as Overeaters Anonymous, would involve dedicating particular chapters to specific minority groups, following the example of black and Hispanic AA chapters. However, all these initiatives would require the active participation of experienced minority members to implement them.

Duration

The length of membership in habit disturbance self-help organizations seems to depend on the extent to which the habit can be isolated from the rest of the person's life. Membership in smoking and weight control organizations tends to be short term (weeks or months) and intermittent rather than long term and continuous. These organizations are less likely to require the "total commitment" of AA, GA, NA, or Women for Sobriety. Participants in the latter, more completely involving organizations are apt to consider themselves long-term members, a view they retain even during periods of relapse.

A different pattern obtains for less threatening habits. In his "Don't Sell Habit Breakers Short," a report of people who tried to quit smoking or lose weight, Schachter noted that the reported success rate was usually below the true rate because people counted as failures eventually succeeded.[5] This several-trial pattern probably is typical whether individuals use a self-help organization, use professional therapy, or try to stop on their own. In each instance, the reported rates underestimate the true rates because the cross-sectional studies are limited to examining a single attempt to quit. But if the common pattern of repeated tries were studied longitudinally, the success rate would likely be higher. The pattern of multiple attempts also means that there will be more short-term and repeat members in these organizations than in other types of self-help organizations. The more devastating habits, which include gambling and the severe abuse of drugs and alcohol, tend to require longer periods of membership. This is important in creating leadership opportunities for members.

Leadership Patterns

Duration of membership also determines to a great extent how leadership is exercised in the organization. In organizations in which the duration of membership is short, the leader's behavior is structured by detailed manuals and the discretion of individual leaders is limited. The practice of paying leaders in Weight Watchers and Smokestoppers ensures further control.

Some observers, it might be interjected, argue that the commercial practices of these "for-profit" organizations disqualify them as true self-help organizations. Perhaps so. But it is an issue that should be resolved empirically. What do the members say? Do the members view these organizations as run by reference individuals, people like them, people who rely heavily on experientially developed knowledge? Alternatively, do they perceive them to be organizations run by professionals using knowledge from nonexperiential sources? Though the answers to such questions are not simple and will be influenced by commercialism, it may be misleading to exclude them. It might be speculated that many consider these for-profit organizations quasi–self-help organizations because they rely on peer leaders and on a pragmatic technology developed as a result of personal experience with the problem. But it is possible that this view may have been suggested by the desire to use these large, widely recognized organizations to illustrate various points in the text.

Notwithstanding the high degree of control in organizations such as Weight Watchers, the limits of formality, of protocols, and of leadership guides are eventually reached. And in less formal organizations, these limits are reached even sooner. This is especially true when the habit is an overwhelming one that quickly makes inroads into more and more of a person's life. The enormously complex situations that result limit the usefulness of rules and force leaders to exercise more judgment in interpreting the principles of the program. The amount of discretion increases with the complexity of the members' problems. Thus, leaders with tact and sound judgment are needed to respond to the widely varying circumstances found within AA, GA, NA, and Women for Sobriety. Leaders are forced to adapt steps and traditions to fit the circumstances of individual members. Moreover, they must tailor the public information and education programs offered by the central coordinating office to local circumstances. Delicate balances must be maintained. The local media must be enlisted while anonymity is protected and sensationalism is avoided. Efforts must also be made to cultivate and influence professional agencies. These tasks call for individuals with highly developed skills, and those who have them assume, quite appropriately, positions of leadership.

Yet there are risks in elevating people to leadership positions. Self-help organizations recognize that anything that spotlights models and sponsors creates situations in which hero worship can arise. And insofar as leaders allow themselves to be adulated rather than emulated, they compromise their ability to be effective models and servant-leaders. Bill W. set an enormously important precedent when he established the tradition of anonymity in AA. This tradition "place[s] principles before personalities." Where anonymity is not the norm, the program can easily be subverted by exhibitionistic preening in front of members and the media.

NORMALIZATION POTENTIAL

Amplifying or Muting Deviance

Nowadays it is hardly startling to learn that nominally helpful actions do not always turn out to be helpful. It is in this context, which is relevant to all interventions, that the risks of participation in a self-help organization need to be weighed against the possible benefits. This discussion does not impute a special potential on the part of self-help organizations to cause harm or to amplify deviance. Deviance is a state of being different, either in one's own eyes or in the eyes of others—and of being disadvantaged as a result of that difference. The extent to which one is different can be amplified or muted by participation in a self-help organization. Alternatively, the level of deviance may remain unchanged, but it may be managed so as to result in fewer or more disadvantages. The opposite, deviance amplification and deviance mismanagement, is an iatrogenic "illness." As in the medical area, interventions should be permitted only after the possibility of harm has been calculated and judged to be slight or worth the risk.

How does the effort to modify these habits possibly make a member more deviant? Does it require, as some charge, that the individual become permanently dependent on others? When does the zeal to alter or eradicate a single habit result in cementing and enlarging negative self-concepts? And to what extent does preoccupation with the habit, which may continue long after control or abstinence has been achieved, restrict the individual's possibilities for growth? The skepticism on which these questions is based is also the source of many of the negative attitudes held by clinicians.[6] Yet there is no denying the fact that the issues they raise should be addressed.

The Problem of Negative Identity

It is alleged that negative identities may be fostered, and an integrated self-concept be thwarted, by the common practice of sharpening the contrast between "what it was like then and what it is like now." And the risk of solidifying a negative identity may be even greater when the member fails to meet the standards of the organization with respect to eating or smoking behaviors. And perhaps worse yet, even when members resolve their problems, they may continue to be aware that they suffer from a chronic disease that can be arrested but not cured. In this scenario, the best that one can hope for is to be in an indefinite state of recovery from drinking, gambling, or drug abuse. To many, these seem like questionable assumptions. They are understandably concerned that the members' preoccupation with relapse, even after years of problem-free living, may encourage them to retain the habit as the central preoccupation of their lives. As such it may effectively restrict them from pursuing other interests and developing their personalities.[7]

Under what circumstances, then, is it permissible to encourage people to tell themselves that they have extraordinary problems and, thus, to make them permanently dependent on an organization for compulsive or addictive personalities? Such an action may be further impairing because it restricts their social life to other addicts. These are valid concerns and must be considered in a broader context. It may be just as hazardous, for example, to refer a person to a professional counselor without first considering the potential for stigmatization. These concerns must also be weighed against other concerns.

Some Questions from the Other Side

To begin with, there is the question of whose standards are being applied. This is not a trivial question, since judgments about such mental states as depression or such social conditions as dependency are known to hinge on who is doing the observing and the defining: The perspective of the member and that of the frowning professional may be miles apart. To the member, the opportunity to form interdependent relationships *169* with similar individuals, without being tied to a particular person and with the option to drop in and out of groups—no questions asked—may seem more than sufficient compensation for any theoretical loss of freedom. Such a user might also with some reason question the universality of the standard. Do therapists use the same standards relative to the risks of dependency, social isolation, and the possible reinforcement of a deviant self-image when they consider the possible consequences of psychotherapy? Or alternatively, do therapists overestimate—at least on paper—the possibilities of better living through psychotherapy, beyond even what is attainable for the tiny percentage of troubled people who complete a course of treatment with them? These questions are not intended to condemn therapy but rather to show the one-sidedness that sometimes characterizes the judgments of professionals when they discuss normalization versus stigmatization.

On a more upbeat note, a number of factors work against the development of a negative identity. Most members have a feeling of great accomplishment when they are able to control a compulsive habit. Long-term members are reminded of their success whenever they interact with beginners in the self-help organization. They see the difference in themselves, and this self-concept is reinforced by others. Thus, for many, continued participation will improve their self-concept and increase their self-esteem rather than the reverse.

Another positive factor is the salutary transfer of benefits from one area to another. It is commonplace to observe the lift people experience after losing weight. A similar feeling may be experienced even without the loss of weight, presumably because of the personal interactions that take place in the program. Insofar as this is empirically true for particular individuals, the weight control program can be considered an indirect treatment for a vague assortment of distressing moods and anxieties.

More speculatively, some chronic mentally ill may benefit from the regularly scheduled activities of the group and the companionship that comes from belonging to a self-help organization. As they are drawn into the organization, their attention, and that of others, may be deflected from a relatively intractable set of problems to a more manageable subset. This shift may help the person carve a small, soluble problem from the set. Such a strategy can be useful even when the relationship between the selected problem and the "core" problem is unclear. And yet this need not bar supportive interpretations. Persons with long-term, highly volatile symptoms may be able to view themselves as using weight control self-help organizations in the same way as the rest of humankind. In other words, they have a problem just like everyone else. Indeed, if they have successfully lost weight or are less heavy to begin with, they may be "better off" than the people to whom they, until now, have felt inferior. To be sure, not everyone will find consolation in the paradoxical distinction "of having a drinking (or other) problem, like everyone else." But neither should it be regarded as a dubious distinction without consolation. A variation of this "eye of the beholder" theme was observed among members of PA.[8] They felt they could accept a self-help organization because it was simply for "people who lose their cool with kids"; they were, however, unable to accept counseling because "that is for disturbed people." As might have been predicted, however, their attitudes toward self-help and professional services changed considerably as a result of their self-help participation. Many later opted to use professional services currently or planned to obtain them at a later time. This naturally occurring intersystem traffic validates the importance of considering relations between these two systems.

RELATIONSHIP TO PROFESSIONALS

Low Profile Cooperation

Relations with professionals need not be face to face, since they may be confined to such specific tasks as initial referral, and they need not be official or formal activities. There is a wide range of ways self-help and professional services can relate to each other. Self-help organizations and professional agencies, for example, may eschew public or official cooperation and yet maintain a significant relationship. Important relationships are often informally initiated and regulated, rather than determined by explicit policy. And though some forms of cooperation occur "in public," this alone does not guarantee significance. Some of the most important exchanges of consultation may in fact occur behind the scenes. Frequently this activity will be called by a less imposing term such as *linking* or *networking*. Professionals have been nonplussed at times to discover that a particular self-help organization that has been highly critical of them cooperates with selected professionals. This not uncommon pattern has much to recommend it and should not be thought of as something to be gotten beyond. It seems to work well as long as the self-help organization is assured that its participation will be confidential and will not compromise its public position.

The AA precept "cooperation but not affiliation," even when scrupulously honored, need not bar frequent informal exchanges   *171* between self-help organizations and professional agencies.[9] In fact, members of AA and other anonymous organizations, acting as private citizens, have considerable influence through their membership on the boards and advisory committees of professional agencies. At the staff level, many chemical dependency agencies employ, with great advantage, the recovering members of self-help organizations. But like anything else, it is possible to have too much of a good thing. Thus, the practice of requiring staff to be recovering can suppress innovation and foster a narrow conformity in professional programs to the extent that it bars nonrecovering individuals from employment.

Most professionals, however, will have an arm's-length relationship with habit disturbance self-help organizations. They seem to feel that the technology of habit self-help organizations is more or less adequate to the problems professionals define as being within organizations' scope. Yet professionals almost always welcome backup assistance for the occasional emergency and for suggestions about how to deal with unusual situations. This means that professionals flexible enough to respond to the rapidly changing needs of self-help organizations can develop important roles with them.

Cooperation is also encouraged by the partialization tendency that is an important potential of self-help organizations. Though partialization may help overcome inertia, maintain focus, and improve chances of success, problems do not always lend themselves to partialization or separation from the rest of the person's life, as the single-purpose nature of these organizations might seem to imply. Many members will need to deal with related problems as well. They may need to ponder the broad motivational patterns and internal conflicts that cannot be separated from their substance abuse. In short, the standard approach of the habit disturbance self-help organization may need to be complemented by an individualized, cognitively oriented form of counseling.

In a splendid exposition on the need for both, and indeed for a holistic conception of the person, an AA member, who is a Catholic and a veteran of several years of psychoanalysis, wrote:

> It seems to me that it always comes back to the Biblical injunction "There is a time and a place for all things." If tonight any of you would ask my help with your drinking problem I most certainly would not ask you, "Would you like to go to Mass with me next Sunday?" Nor would I ask whether you wanted an appointment with my former analyst. But I *would* unhesitatingly ask you, "Would you like to attend an AA meeting with me?". . .
> "There is a time and a place for all things." The real danger

lies in my opinion, in the recovered alcoholic's assumption that if he wishes to move to another time and another place he must perforce leave AA behind. Nothing could be more untrue; nothing could be more unnecessary.[10]

Cooperation Relative to Cases

Various forms of cooperation between self-help organizations and professionals will be discussed at some length in Chapters Fourteen through Sixteen. Here it may be useful to comment on specific considerations relevant to habit disturbance organizations. Though a beginning form of cooperation, making referrals to habit disturbance organizations is an important form of collaboration. Many clients can benefit from the experiential wisdom and the denial-challenging aspects of these organizations. Other clients can benefit from a source of support that is more continuously available than a therapist. However, still more may be gained if communication can continue between the self-help organization and the professional as long as the member participates in both systems.

Given a constant relationship, both parties may also be inclined to consult with each other about other people for whom they have responsibility but who may be unknown to the other party. These informal consultations can occur without the subject's being identified and thus not infringe on the confidentiality of the subject. And if it would help to enlarge the scope of activity, sometimes professionals and self-help organizations will be able to work together, formally or informally, to promote the interests of an entire class of individuals, for example, chemically dependent persons. Working on legislative and funding issues may also be a natural route to more immediately consequential joint program and policy development.

Cooperative Program and Policy Development

Leaders in both systems may not be aware of the advantages of exchanging technical assistance. The self-helpers, for example, tend to be intimately familiar with the culture; the professionals may know more about available services not specifically linked to the mission of the self-help organization.

Compared to other types of self-help organizations, habit disturbance organizations tend to be less threatening to professionals. But there are important differences within the type, and the subtypes parallel the distinction made earlier between more broadly involving and devastating problems and those less so. Organizations that address more circumscribed problems, such as smoking, seem to pose less of a threat to the professional, perhaps because they are perceived as dealing with a person's problem rather than with a person's dysfunctional personality. Moreover, the problem lends itself to the use of highly specialized, standardized techniques. The professional's identity, however, tends to be more closely linked to helping individuals with what the professional regards as more consequential problems, using methods intended to stimulate broad growth and development.

In view of the favorable attitudes of professionals, it is ironic that they are less apt to be regularly involved in the programs of habit disturbance self-help organizations than in other types of self-help organization. This is especially remarkable when habit disturbance organizations are compared with organizations focusing on significant others or on the physically disabled. Both professionals and habit disturbance self-helpers, it seems, agree that self-help organizations have become a competent, autonomous resource for people with habit disturbances.

Notes

1. Narcotics Anonymous, *Misconceptions* (Van Nuys, Calif.: NA World Service, undated), unpaged.
2. Weight Watchers International, *Promises* (Manhasset, N.Y.: Weight Watchers International, 1978), p. 2.
3. "Detroit Women Help Blacks Lose Pounds," *Milwaukee Sentinel,* February 28, 1983, p. 8.
4. J. Kirkpatrick, *Turnabout: Help for a New Life* (Garden City, N.Y.: Doubleday & Co., 1977).
5. S. Schachter, "Don't Sell Habit Breakers Short," *Psychology Today,* August 1982.
6. A. Rosen, "Psychotherapy and Alcoholics Anonymous: Can They Be Coordinated?" *Bulletin of the Menninger Clinic,* 45 (May 1981); pp. 229–246; D. L. Gerard et al. "The Abstinent Alcoholic," *Archives of General Psychiatry,* 6 (January 1962), pp. 83–95; J. L. Flaherty et al., "The Psychodynamics of the Dry Drunk," *American Journal of Psychiatry,* 112 (December 1955), pp. 460–464; and M. A. Maxwell, "Contemporary Utilization of Professional Help by Members of Alcoholics Anonymous," *Annals of the New York Academy of Sciences,* 273 (1976), pp. 436–441.
7. D. J. Pittman and C. R. Snyder, "Responsive Movements and Systems of Control," in Pittman and Snyder, eds., *Society, Culture and Drinking Patterns* (New York: John Wiley & Sons, 1962), pp. 547–552.
8. T. J. Powell, "Comparisons Between Self-Help Groups and Professional

Services," *Social Casework: The Journal of Contemporary Social Work*, 60 (November 1979), pp. 561–565.

9. T. S. Borkman, *A Social-Experiential Model in Programs for Alcoholism Recovery: A Research Report on a New Treatment Design*, DHHS Publication No. (ADM) 83-1259 (Washington, D.C.: U.S. Department of Health & Human Services, 1983).

10. Alcoholics Anonymous, *A Member's-Eye View of Alcoholics Anonymous* (New York: AA World Services, 1970).

10

General Purpose Organizations

Representative of general purpose organizations are GROW, Emotions Anonymous, Recovery, Inc., Parents Anonymous, and The Compassionate Friends. The first two (GROW and Emotions Anonymous) incorporate the Twelve Steps of the anonymous model. The latter three do not, despite the suggestion in the name *Parents Anonymous.* It is also noteworthy that the name *GROW* offers no clue to its anonymous character. Thus, organizations that use the twelve-step model may not indicate this by their names, nor do organizations with *Anonymous* in their names necessarily follow the twelve-step model. But even when they do, they are not a unitary group for many purposes. It will be remembered that AA and Overeaters Anonymous were classified as habit disturbance organizations in Chapter Nine. The main point, however, is that organizations may pursue a mission independent of the model they use. Table 5 provides a listing of the major dimensions of general purpose organizations as covered in this chapter.

PUBLIC IMAGE

The mission of the general purpose self-help organization is distinctive insofar as it addresses a wide range of problems or predicaments. Yet as in other categories, there is considerable diversity within the category.

Every person's problems are unique. No two drinking prob-

Table 5.
Properties of General Purpose Organizations

Exemplar Organizations
Parents Anonymous; GROW; Emotions Anonymous; Recovery, Inc.;
The Compassionate Friends

    Public Image
        Distinguished by distinctive methods and
            the charismatic personality of founder(s)
        Size of meetings small
        Number of meetings (chapters) may be large
        Remedial or problem-solving approach
            may have a quaint or marginal quality

    Goals
        General and abstract
        Require personal, concrete interpretation

    Technology
        Cognitive-expressive techniques
        Reference group processes
        Identification building
        Resembles psychotherapy; uses mentors
            and models

    Career Pattern
        Long term
        Intensity intermittent
        Involved in multiple life spheres

    Normalization Potential[a]
        "Graduate" groups +
        Open-ended
        Entrapping o

    Relationship to Professionals
        Professional founders
        Professional backup
        Susceptible to professional domination
        Potentially competitive

[a] +, positive; o, negative.

lems are alike. Still, within AA, everyone's problem does have something to do with drinking, whereas in Emotions Anonymous it is not possible to specify the problem except abstractly. The problem may have to do with anxiety, anger, or depression, and it may be felt in relation to a spouse, parents, or children; it may be external to the family, in relation to bosses, co-workers or friends; or it may involve the self primarily. By themselves, then, the problems brought to Emotions Anonymous and these other organizations contribute little to the organizations' unity. What does unify them are the methods used to deal with members' problems.

Emphasis on Method

Because these organizations must respond to a broad range of member concerns, their goals are loosely defined to accommodate this range. Methods rather than goals are thus emphasized. Unlike AA, for example, which evokes a primary association to its goal—recovery from alcoholism—Emotions Anonymous is more likely to evoke association to its method—a "self-help" or twelve-step program. Similarly, Recovery, Inc., and PA are better known by their "self-help" approaches than by their goals to aid "nervous and former mental patients" and "parents concerned about abuse and neglect," respectively. Yet the type—general purpose organization—should not be considered as constituting a crudè catchall category. Though the organizations do encompass a range of problems, each organization has a more or less formal technology for dealing with problems.

The effects of this open, inclusive orientation are observable in many aspects of the functioning of these organizations. How they define their goals, the technology used, the structure of members' careers, the potential for normalization, and relationships to professionals are also affected. An important task in general purpose organizations involves countering the centrifugal forces in a situation in which members typically work on very different problems; thus, these organizations must devise compensatory mechanisms. Oftentimes these mechanisms involve formal ways to recall the founder's philosophy and methods.

Unifying Function of Founders

Because the vague purposes of these organizations and their flexible methods are subject to interpretation, these organizations tend to unify their members following the traditions established by their founders. Some use the writings and the recorded memories of the founders directly to sanction present practice and orientation. It is not uncommon for meetings to include the reading of excerpts from the founder's work or the playing of a recorded message. At first, this may seem to be slightly quaint or even marginal. Yet conflicts can be resolved or averted by such references to the founders' views. The influence of founders may also be detected in the overall ambience of the program. Parents Anonymous, for example, still reflects some of the freewheeling spirit of Jolly K. and Leonard Lieber. This spirit was reinforced by Leonard's continuing supportive presence until he resigned in 1986. Historically, PA's spectacular development owes much to Jolly's charisma as founder and to Leonard's savvy as her professional partner. Following Jolly's death, the organization became more formal, as happens when organizations mature and as they respond to different times. In PA's case, moreover, this process was accelerated by a close cooperation with the National Committee for the Prevention of Child Abuse. Throughout this period, Leonard's "laid-back orientation" was still much in evidence. Now that the National Committee is no longer in the picture and Leonard has left PA, it will be interesting to see what new program styles develop.

The cofounder of GROW played a similarly important role for his organization. Father Con Keogh, who cofounded GROW in 1957 in Sydney, Australia, is now one of its inspirational forces in the United States. As a Roman Catholic priest, as well as the former mental patient who started GROW, Con attracts considerable attention from the media and is featured in the promotional literature of the organization. He is also featured in such mass-circulation publications as the *Reader's Digest.* An article in the October 1985 *Reader's Digest,* "How to Keep Cool in a Crisis," stimulated many calls and letters to GROW.

The founder of The Compassionate Friends was less involved in its program. He possessed the mix of genius and good fortune to recognize the potential of a not uncommon occurrence. As the Anglican chaplain in English hospitals in 1969, Simon Stephens observed the fortuitous help that two couples, each of whom had recently lost a child, gave to each other. Simon claims to have done little more than help them create an entity that could be of help to others. Despite this modest claim, his interest over the years has been a source of ongoing inspiration to the organization. Even though his present job as a military chaplain makes it difficult for him to maintain close connections, the organization makes a point of reporting his activities and communications in its newsletter.[1] His continuing influence may also be evident in the strong ties between The Compassionate Friends and churches.   *179*

At Recovery, Inc., its psychiatrist-founder, Dr. Abraham Low, closely supervised his creation in its early years. He attempted to create formal rules rather than a personality-centered program, and his orderly, no-nonsense approach is still very much in evidence. From its inception in 1937 until his death in 1954, Low carefully nurtured this self-help organization dedicated to preventing "chronicity in nervous patients" and "relapses in former mental patients." Part of its early impetus was related to its use as an aftercare program for his patients. Gradually, however, the membership became more diverse, and many new chapters were formed. At this time also, its tie to psychiatric hospitalization was loosened, and many individuals who had never been hospitalized became members. Ironically, despite the professional status of its founder, the organization historically has been either ignored or treated condescendingly by the professional community. This attitude is probably a consequence of the emphasis Low gave to his concept of "will" to counter what he saw as the excessive determinism of psychoanalysis. Recently, however, mental health professionals have become less doctrinaire, and Recovery, Inc., now seems to enjoy greater acceptance.[2]

Despite some people's grumbling about what is seen as a preoccupation with Low, the program is clearly centered in formal and explicit norms and procedures. Paradoxically, the program's emphasis on rules rather than personalities reflects Low's "move the muscles" approach. All things considered, however, Low achieved a kind of immortality through an elaborate program that makes good common sense to some[3] but seems slightly anachronistic to others. Nonetheless, it continues to flourish.[4] He also lives on through the public and private use of his writings, especially his major work on the Recovery method.[5] In light of these achievements in a vague, difficult area, Recovery, Inc., might well be scrutinized for what it may be able to teach other general purpose self-help organizations.

Advantages and Disadvantages of Flexibility

Flexible organizations are well suited to the fluctuating intensity and varied manifestations of real-life problems. Flexibility is also of help in situations in which people describe their problems in terms of the idiosyncrasies of their personal vocabulary and experience. And even where problem categories seem fairly fixed and concrete, it may help members to be flexible in interpreting them differently at various times in their self-help career. For example, though repeated hitting of a child will almost always be labeled child abuse, a constant "chewing out" may not be, at least initially. Later, however, it may come to be perceived as the more important form of child abuse. Similarly, a person's understanding of the causes of child abuse may change. Instead of its being the child's fault, it may come to be seen as a consequence of an abusive, conflictual marriage. Still later, however, the causes may be located in the initial decision to get married that, in turn, reflected fundamental problems with that person's self-concept. Flexibility allows the remedial approach to change to accommodate these changing perceptions of causality.

But flexibility has its disadvantages. Program style tends to mirror the personal predilections and styles of dominant members. In one locale, PA may be heavily influenced by transactional analysis; in another, the chairperson, or more likely the sponsor, may favor an ego psychology or behavioral approach. Though this is more variability than one is apt to see in Recovery or GROW, it is inescapable even in these organizations. And the variability that does exist, particularly in the less tightly structured PA, The Compassionate Friends, and Emotions Anonymous, indicates how difficult it is to utilize the charisma of founders in a standardized, transportable program. Along this line, it is also more difficult to franchise or reproduce chapters of these organizations in new areas. Consequently, such programs tend to be more heavily concentrated in the areas of their origin.

General purpose self-help organizations tend to have few members at meetings, compared to habit disturbance organizations, which is both an advantage and a disadvantage. With fewer members, the organization's or chapter's stability is more easily threatened as the membership changes. Moreover, as members leave, the approach of the chapter may change drastically, and sometimes the chapter may even disappear, which is especially disheartening to those who might wish to return after an absence. A corollary advantage, however, is that individual members are likely to receive more attention in these small chapters. Assuming, for instance, that a typical Recovery panel can handle only four or five examples, it is desirable to hold the chapter to a size that allows all members to have a regular turn on the panel. Twenty active members would afford each individual an opportunity to present an example once a month. With less frequent opportunities, individuals are more likely to become skeptical about the relevance of the program, because many of the problems presented by other members will not seem to be applicable to them.

This tendency to emphasize leadership style and deemphasize standard procedures is even more pronounced in smaller, less-well-known organizations. Thus, they are likely to have more interchapter variability than the larger organizations discussed here. The larger ones are discussed precisely because they are well-enough known to be widely recognized, though their broad national and international scope makes them less typical of the type. The more typical, smaller organizations are less uniform and thus show even more interchapter variability.

Problems of Fragmentation

Many general purpose organizations, unfortunately, cover only limited problems in their areas. Organizations dealing with human losses can be used to illustrate the problems of fragmentation, though it must be acknowledged that members do not share this view. There is a confusing proliferation of groups concerned with loss, at the expense of both their own vitality and of recognition by the public. A small sample of these groups would include Candlelighters (parents of children who have died from cancer), SIDS (parents who have experienced loss through the sudden infant death syndrome), and POMC (parents of murdered children). Though the distinctions represented are unquestionably important to certain members, this advantage should be weighed against the need for viable organizations that can help bereaved parents throughout the country, or even internationally. These organizations are currently handicapped by a too-small, unstable base to support the developmental work that would make them robust organizations. They may also not be recognized beyond their immediate locales. But even if their names are familiar, the public will still find it difficult to keep distinctions about the various kinds of loss in mind.

Fragmentation in the area of human loss is also a barrier to professionals who would make referrals to these groups. To the extent professionals share at least some of the public's confusion, they refrain from making referrals when it is a question of exposing their ignorance or possibly jeopardizing their client. Yet over the long term, the growth and stability of these organizations will depend on the understanding and approval of referral agents. Thus, many of these groups should consider recalculating the minimal size requirements for their organizations and the probable tradeoffs between a highly specific mission and the potential for organizational development and improved public understanding through a larger organization. However, given the fact that the organizational outlook may differ from the member outlook, these organizations might reconsider their relationships to other similar organizations. A new organization or an existing one, perhaps The Compassionate Friends, the largest of such organizations, might coordinate public information and referrals to all organizations serving people who have experienced a loss through death.

As general purpose organizations strive to increase the relevance of their mandate, they risk excessive fragmentation. Thus, they may splinter into ever-smaller, nonviable units. It is undeniable, however, that general purpose organizations may seem vague and lacking in relevance to many potential members.

What the self-help world may need are more Recoverys—not the Recovery that includes specific techniques and concepts of "spotting, endorsement, fearful temper, etc.," but rather new or revitalized organizations based on similarly sound organizational designs and similarly well-developed therapeutic approaches. One such promising organization is GROW.

Well-developed, autonomous organizational structures and systematic, standardized methods are needed to deal with a broad range of variously defined personal problems. It is likely that there are still better tradeoffs for relevance, size, and chapter standardization, taking into account the various considerations. Achieving an optimum balance among these qualities may be the most important challenge facing general purpose self-help organizations.

GOALS

Although the broad goal statements of general purpose self-help organizations can be applied to each individual's personal circumstances, the disparate nature of the members' problems also means that each member is apt to be working on a different personal agenda. Dissimilar problems mean that members will be more on their own in formulating problem-solving strategies. But too much independence threatens the organization, so the extent to which members deal with common problems may be overstated. The claim that members "hear their own stories in the stories of others" includes generous parts of wish and want.

Parents Anonymous illustrates how different the goals of individual members can be. Some members are not active abusers of their children—their nonmember partners are. A member may have joined the organization because she felt that her acquiescence made it possible for her partner to abuse their child. Other members may be striving to control their own abusive nagging of their children. Still others may be working on child neglect— their tendency to leave their children unsupervised for long   *183* periods. Others may recognize that they are overinvolved with their children, an involvement that, for some, carries over into sexual abuse. And lastly, there is the kind of abuse that is the first thought of the public: serious physical abuse. Given these diverse situations, each member must devise an individual plan that is both relevant to his or her situation and consistent with the PA approach. Plans often vary widely. Some parents may need to confront their partners; others may have to work on their own direct abuse. Neglectful parents must become more involved with their children; others who abuse their children through excessive criticism or sexual stimulation must become less involved. In all instances, however, the solutions must be consonant with PA values. The neglectful must offer care and discipline while refraining from abusive words and actions. The overinvolved must develop new outside interests and yet not abruptly withdraw from their children.

Though the similarities in the above scenarios should not be discounted, it may still be necessary to tailor one's story to fit with PA conceptions of the probable causes and resolutions of child abuse. At the least, it will be necessary not to mention some of the idiosyncratic factors to remain consistent with PA's more general statement of problems and solutions. The necessity to resort to higher level generalization will be seen to have important consequences for the technology, career patterns, and normalization potential of the members and the relationships to professionals of these organizations.

Thus, even after the cohesive forces of group have smoothed over some of the differences among members, significant differences must still be accommodated. Notwithstanding the subtle pressure to make "many different stories one story," the helping technology must accommodate a diverse set of goals among the members of these general purpose self-help organizations.

TECHNOLOGY

Procedures

General and cognitively oriented procedures are necessary to bridge differences in the nature and severity of member problems. Meetings feature discussions that have broad-ranging applications and that sometimes are inspirational-directive. More of the time, though this depends on the organization, the discussion will be expressive-reflective. Such discussions are remarkably similar to the discussions that occur in psychotherapy sessions. In the inspirational mode, testimonials are offered, not to self-congratulate but rather to remind the group of how good things are now compared to how bad things were then. Next, the speaker may launch into a series of reflections about what contributed to his or her recovery. Methods and principles of problem solving are apt to be emphasized, since detailed universal prescriptions are nearly impossible to formulate, given the different needs of the members.

An emphasis on cognitively oriented interventions carried out in a supportive group context is exemplified by GROW. This impressive organization has recently transported its highly developed technology from Australia to the United States.[6] The GROW training manual outlines five ingredients of a good meeting:

(1) An encounter of persons through personal testimonies, i.e., descriptions of a member's decline to maladjustment and growth to maturity.

(2) Friendly support and help through current problem solving.

(3) Adult education through reading and discussion of the GROW program.

(4) Mutual activation through the recommendation of practical tasks to be carried out in day-to-day living between meetings.

(5) Personal development through reports on the assessment of [a] member's progress.[7]

The process of "encounter," "mutual support," and "mutual activation" encourage the formation of a new reference group. As newcomers come to perceive their essential similarity with senior members, they are more willing to believe that they can also be successful.

The nonconfrontational style of general purpose meetings further facilitates the adoption of a new reference group. The emphasis in Emotions Anonymous is on solutions, not problems. The idea is to have members leave the meeting feeling optimistic and hopeful, as illustrated in the following excerpt from an Emotions Anonymous pamphlet.

WHY DON'T WE HAVE FEEDBACK OR CROSSTALK DURING THE MEETING?

Crosstalk and feedback can divert us from the Step of the meeting. Sometimes a dominating sort of person can take control of the meeting, denying other members the opportunity to speak. There is always time before or after the meeting to get feedback from other members.[8]

Emotions Anonymous elaborates on this point in another pamphlet:

We do not give advice on personal matters. We *do* give you feedback when you seek it or when it appears that you want it, but usually one-to-one after the meeting or by telephone.[9]

The desire to emphasize the positive and avoid conflict is nicely conveyed by the end-of-the-meeting ritual:

> CLOSING STATEMENT: In closing, we would like to say that the feelings expressed here were strictly those of the individual who related them. *Accept what you like and leave the rest.* [Emphasis added.][10]

Reference Group Benefits

In the context of the warm acceptance that characterizes these meetings, new members are urged to live the program and to allow it to guide their lives. The message may be summarized as follows: Work the program (accept the values and norms of the group) and you will reap the benefits. Let it change the way you think about yourself, and changes in your attitudes to other things and people will follow.

Senior members stress the similarity between their situations and that of the desperate newcomer—the only difference is that they have learned to work the program. Even the most competent and seemingly unflappable members are but a single step from turmoil. But without slighting the constant vigilance required to prevent relapse, nothing can gainsay that the senior members have been transformed from worried, indecisive individuals to confident and competent individuals. If newcomers adopt the reference group, they can avail themselves of the same healing processes. The self-help organization holds out a level of success that could not have been imagined at the beginning of the self-help experience. It can offer a spiritual, not to say a religious, rebirth. Having been accepted into the reference group, members can assume a new self, after ridding themselves of their earlier degrading, disabling preoccupations.

Reference Group Processes
and Psychotherapy

The process of engagement and socialization to the norms and standards of the reference group parallels the process of psychotherapy. As in psychotherapy, feelings are aroused, conflicts exposed, and disappointments highlighted. These affective expressions, many of which occur at the margins of the formal meetings, are then interpreted as a longing for or as implicit movement toward a new reference group. These emotional stirrings, the newcomer might be told, bespeak a wish to affiliate with the reference group and to become a new person.

As in psychotherapy, a particular course of action is not prescribed, but rather members are enjoined to use a method others have found successful in resolving their problems. The notion is that if the right methods such as "spotting" or "endorsing" are used, the right solution will follow. A secondary approach involves learning highly complex operant behaviors from members of this discriminating reference group. On a one-to-one basis, they can be exceedingly adept at distinguishing constructive efforts from destructive ones. They are particularly good at exposing and fostering recognition of bits of self-deception. Mostly, however, in true psychotherapeutic fashion, members are urged to overcome their resistance and discover their own solutions by honestly working the program. More than anything, they should not expect the solution to be bestowed on them from some mysterious source.

From both psychodynamic and behavioral points of view, the identificatory and modeling tendencies are encouraged by the warm ties cultivated among members of the reference group. Programs using formal sponsors operate within a structure that is explicitly responsive to the desires to become close to and to pattern oneself after admired senior members. Sponsors, like therapists, encourage newcomers to find their "own" solutions. Sponsors, however, have the added advantage that they demonstrate in their everyday actions an approach that, broadly conceived, can become a pattern for the newcomer. In another respect, too, sponsors function in a manner analogous to therapists, particularly group therapists, as they comment on the similarities among members and the natural ties they have to one another. The overall thrust is to strengthen links to others, though occasionally particular relationships may need to be attenuated.

CAREER PATTERN

Adopting a reference group is a matter of potentially great significance, since the organization may claim an interest or may intervene in many spheres of the person's life. The Compassionate Friends, for example, is interested in the bereaved individual's social life or lack thereof, in alcohol use, in anxieties, in feelings of guilt, and in moods, since all of these can be expressions of unresolved grief. Thus, where it leaves off, that is, what is not a concern of the organization is unclear. For some PA members, for example, the program may become a means to learn how "to give to myself." The parent-child problem is reinterpreted to be the consequence of this inability to give to the self. It is this inability that makes the parent behave in a harsh and impatient manner with his or her children. This illustrates the potentially *187* far-reaching influence of the general purpose self-help organization. The "problem" (anxiety, loss, fearful temper, emotional disturbance, etc.) may be expressed in a variety of family, friendship, and neighborhood settings. To the extent the organization becomes involved in all these spheres, membership in a self-help organization can greatly influence the member's outside life. This effect is reinforced by the inherently vague problems the organization deals with. Frequently the significance of a problem behavior will be hard to appraise. *Temper*, as used by Recovery, signifies a tendency to judge trivialities as right or wrong. This judgment is dysfunctional because it contributes to a nervous temperament. The vague, inclusive definition for *temper* may strengthen the rationale for continuing in a self-help organization.

With so many ambiguities, the organization might appear to claim an interest in the individual for an indefinite period. If the problem is difficult to detect or if it is manifested in different forms and then can reappear after being dormant for some time, its resolution may be difficult to determine. Will it surface again? Thus, it may be good "insurance" to remain in the organization. And besides, remaining has the virtue of providing an opportunity to pay back the organization for help received.

Ambiguity also creates a dissonance that favors long periods of membership. And the greater the dissonance initially overcome, the greater the resistance to abandoning this decision at a later point. "Staying in" involves dissonance considerations much as "staying out" did, before the individual resolved the dissonance and joined the organization. Membership that earlier was purchased at considerable emotional cost may be difficult to give up in light of the cognitive dissonance leaving might create. To leave something that was purchased so dearly, when all the problems have not been resolved, may raise questions about whether it was worthwhile in the first place. These considerations suggest that the career model in a general purpose self-help organization, leaving out individuals who attend one or two meetings, is likely to be long term. But it will also be intermittent as the ever-smoldering problems flare up and die down.

NORMALIZATION POTENTIAL

In Chapter Nine, it was noted that sustained membership in a self-help organization can continuously remind one of one's progress. The flip side of this proposition is that it may keep alive unnecessary concern about "how close I am" to relapse and disaster. The resolution of these dialectic propositions ultimately depends on the predilections of the particular individuals involved. And for those so inclined, the indefiniteness and open-endedness of the general purpose self-help organization may cement a deviant or disturbed self-concept. Given the vague definitions employed, almost any difficulty might seem sufficient to warrant becoming and remaining a member. It is a question of threshold: What level of discomfort or dysfunction should be exceeded to justify becoming involved in the self-help organization? And in reverse: What is the level below which the problems might be better interpreted as a normal part of the human condition rather than a matter of concern for a formal self-help organization? Distressing feelings (sadness, guilt, loneliness, etc.) are an inescapable part of life; some level of those feelings cannot be avoided. And if participation in a self-help organization would seem to deny this truism, then indeed matters can be made worse.

Aware that members can become bogged down in the help-seeker role, many self-help organizations have taken steps to prevent it. "Graduate groups" have been established in PA, for example, to recognize the accomplishment of successful members, to encourage their continued growth, and to provide an ongoing vehicle for their inputs to the organization. Not incidentally, it is also a vehicle that can respond to their occasional need for support. Other self-help organizations have designed means to recognize the progress of their members and to discourage acquiescence in the help-seeker role. Recovery, Inc., for example, maintains an elaborate leadership development program. As members complete various phases of training, they are moved to increasingly higher levels of responsibility within an elaborate district and area structure. But in Recovery and other organizations, there will have been many earlier opportunities for specialized roles and minor leadership positions. Right from the start newcomers will be asked to perform organizational maintenance tasks (coffee, cleanup, meeting arrangements, literature distribution, etc.), a routine which provides them with an opportunity to demonstrate an interest and reliability that eventually can help them qualify for positions of considerable responsibility. These latter positions often involve contacts with people outside the organization, such as professionals.

RELATIONSHIP TO PROFESSIONALS

Professionals and general purpose self-help organizations are closely related and, thus, more often engaged in rivalry. Sometimes they are like adolescent siblings who recognize their close *189* ties but rarely speak to one another. Both claim to be general purpose instruments for resolving problems. Both prefer broad, flexibly defined problems, which give them some flexibility to explore a range of possible causes and resolutions. And both prefer that the newcomer-client not assume that he or she is aware of all the possible causes and solutions of the problem at the start.

Rivalry also stems from the similarity of their methods. Both rely heavily on expressive-reflective techniques. This is partly out of necessity, in order to address a diverse range of problems. But it may also be viewed as a carryover from a time when professionals had an important role in the early development of these organizations. The danger is that professionals will draw the wrong conclusions about these early involvements and the similarities in their methods. They may assume that they are entitled to a cordial welcome and the opportunity to consult with self-help leaders. These feelings, however, are not apt to be reciprocated. Worse yet, professionals may be so parochial in their outlook as to presume they have a proprietary interest in expressive-reflective methods or that they know how to use them better than anyone else. Or they may act as if they should advise others about how to use these methods. The fact that some very unusual professionals once were, or even now are, involved does not mean that other professionals should be similarly involved. Having struggled mightily to attain their present level of autonomy and program integrity, self-help organizations are understandably wary of jeopardizing it by too much, or the wrong kind of, professional involvement.

A Little Goes a Long Way

But self-help organizations may believe that effective cooperation can be maintained without frequent contact with professionals or without allowing them to influence programs significantly. Like other kin, professionals and self-help organization leaders can be supportive of one another without being intrusive or infringing on their mutual autonomy.

In the present era, and as part of their everyday work, professionals as a matter of course address problems also addressed by existing self-help organizations. The present era differs greatly from the time when professionals founded Recovery, Parents Anonymous, and The Compassionate Friends. When Dr. Low was practicing, there were no consumer-run alternatives; Leonard Lieber found that abusing parents had no alternative to the system they perceived as harsh and punitive; and Reverend Stephens' initiative came in the early stages of society's rediscovery of grief and before peer mechanisms were developed to cope with it. Since these organizations and their self-help counterparts in other areas of difficulty now exist, it will often be sufficient for professionals to make clients aware of them, discuss how they might be used, and engage in supportive discussion about how they are being used. The last, and sometimes most important, thing is to support them in public.

More May Be Less

Some methods of involvement with self-help organizations should be reexamined. The establishment of a permanent role for professional consultants may be dysfunctional for some organizations. Even in situations where it might seem desirable, it seems to slow development. The growth of Recovery took a sharp upward turn after Dr. Low ceased his personal supervision. But it is not quite that simple. The present Recovery program prospers even though its executive director, Robert Farwell, was not a member of the organization when he was appointed to his post. But it should also be mentioned that throughout this period, the Board, which is made up of Recovery members, has been in firm control of the organization.

Leonard Lieber gained the support of professionals for PA, but the incorporation of professionals in the organizational structure does have some drawbacks. Parents Anonymous has a professional sponsor for each local chapter, for support and consultation; this person usually participates in each meeting. The professional sponsor is likened to the benevolent grandparent who is warmly supportive of the chairperson (parent) and other "family" members. But sometimes a less felicitous figure can capture the spirit of these relationships in some chapters; one such might be a stepmother nagging her eldest daughter. Since PA, unlike the twelve-step programs, does use professionals, perhaps the meaningfulness of the grandparent metaphor to the members should be investigated. Surely the power of self-help will be weakened if the professionals are seen as "running their groups."

The Compassionate Friends use a more traditional model in their relationships with professionals. They devote considerable effort to educating and linking with "local doctors, nurses, clergy, social workers, psychologists, funeral directors and others." Advisory committees function, and specifically designed brochures are distributed to these professionals. The Friends seem to have substantial relationships with professionals, but the professionals are not in a position to control the self-help organization.

If too much or the wrong kind of cooperation can be harmful, it may be preferable to flat rejection. Though some professionals may have eroded important distinctions by overinvolvement, hostile professionals may cause more harm by depriving people of an important resource. Because of the haughty attitude of some professionals toward the "inferior and dangerous" psychotherapy in self-help organizations, needy people are deprived of resources that are available nowhere else. Both extremes may ultimately be traced to unresolved competition. The difference is that one attempts to manage the threat by co-opting the movement, whereas the other attempts to destroy it by depriving it of new members and community approval. Fortunately, both extremes seem to be disappearing as the self-help movement is increasingly accepted by the great middle range of professionals and their clients.

Evoking images of strange bedfellows, the potential for a different problem needs to be careful monitored. There is also the possibility that self-help organizations and private practitioners on the hustle may cooperate. A survey of social workers in Michigan found that private practitioners had more interaction with self-help organizations than did agency practitioners.[11] It is hoped that most of these relationships did more than steer clients to private practitioners. On a more upbeat note, it is possible that these pioneers will come up with some innovative methods of collaboration.

Notes

1. *Compassionate Friends Newsletter* (Oak Brook, Ill.), 6 (Spring 1983).
2. C. Turkington, "Recovery, Inc., Joins the Mainstream," *APA Monitor* (March 1982).
3. D. M. Sheldon, "Self-Help in Mental Health?" *Journal of the Maine Medical Association,* 69 (July 1978).
4. H. Wechsler, "The Self-Help Organization in the Mental Health Field: Recovery, Inc., A Case Study," *Journal of Nervous and Mental Disease,* 130 (April 1960), pp. 297–314.
5. A. Low, *Mental Health Through Will Training* (Winnetka, Ill.: Willet Publishing Co., 1950).
6. J. Snowdon, "Self-Help Groups and Schizophrenia," *Australian and New Zealand Journal of Psychiatry,* 14 (1980), pp. 265–268.
7. J. Rappaport et al., "Collaborative Research with a Mutual-Help Organization" *Social Policy,* 15 (Winter 1985), pp. 12–24.
8. Emotions Anonymous, *Why Is This a Step Meeting?* (St. Paul, Minn.: EA, May 1985).

9. Emotions Anonymous, *Welcome! to this Meeting of: Emotions Anonymous,* Form No. 34 (St. Paul, Minn.: EA, January 1984).
10. Emotions Anonymous, *Suggested Format for EA Meetings,* Form No. 7 (St. Paul, Minn.: EA, March 1977; rev. March 1983).
11. G. P. Miller, "Professionals' Knowledge of, Referrals to, Utilization of, Linkages with, and Attitudes Toward Self-Help Groups." Unpublished Ph.D. thesis, University of Michigan, 1983.

11

Lifestyle Organizations

Lifestyle self-help organizations cluster in a number of sub-categories. Adult singles organizations include Parents Without Partners, Unitarian Singles, and the North American Conference for Separated and Divorced Catholics (NACSDC). Widow-to-widow programs, for some purposes, resemble specialized groups of singles; they include NAIM, THEOS, and the Widowed Persons Service of the American Association of Retired Persons.

Another subcategory pays less attention to social interaction and more attention to human and civil rights. Two organizations active in adoptions are CUB (Concerned United Birthparents) and ALMA (Adoptees' Liberty Movement Association). The Gray Panthers, which appeals not just to the elderly but also to supporters of all ages, has a huge potential constituency. They are engaged in a determined campaign against injustice, as the following shows:

> Gray Panthers believe it is long past time for change in society's view of the aging and the aged. In large part, *much of the attempted victimization of older people by politicians, bureaucrats, health care providers, landlords and unscrupulous promoters stems from the erroneous idea that people over 65 are powerless and unable to recognize their rights and fight for them.* [Emphasis in the original.]
>
> Yet citizens past 65 are consistently the largest and most active voting bloc in the United States. And the emergence of Gray Panthers as a vigorous, forceful organization with a broad national membership of young, old and middle-aged reaffirms

that older Americans are putting the country on notice that they will fight hard to keep all they worked toward and are entitled to receive.[1]

The National Organization for Women (NOW), an organization with a still larger constituency, may also be considered a self-help organization insofar as many of its members engage in face-to-face relationships as part of local chapter activities. Two additional examples involve much smaller organizations. And though their style is less confrontational, they are also fighting for greater social acceptance for their causes. La Leche League (an organization for the promotion of breastfeeding) and the Little People of America (for the small of stature) are engaged in campaigns to correct society's insensitivity to their needs.

Gays constitute one of the most important subcategories of different lifestyle organizations. Their organizations include the National Gay and Lesbian Task Force and Federation of Parents and Friends of Lesbians and Gays (Parents/FLAG). Many other local organizations, once a part of the impressive Gay Liberation Front, now operate independently in their communities.

Also active in numerous localities are organizations of mental health consumers. Some prefer the label patients' rights ("Do we have any?") organizations. In Michigan, for example, consumer organizations called Oasis, Dawntreader, and JIMHO (Justice in Mental Health Organizations) have been functioning for several years. These organizations have developed a statewide federation of consumers, Citizens for Action in Mental Health. In a 1983 book, *Politics of Schizophrenia*, some 32 consumer liberation organizations were listed in the United States, and ten were listed in Canada.[2] Though some of these organizations may no longer exist, the list was undoubtedly incomplete at that time, and many new organizations have been founded since then. Contact among the widely dispersed organizations in this volatile subcategory has always been difficult. Recently, however, Project Share (c/o the Philadelphia Mental Health Association) has been working to establish a communications network among local mental health consumer groups.

Table 6 (p. 196) lists the major dimensions of lifestyle self-help organizations discussed in this chapter.

THEMES AND DIFFERENCES

An important theme running through the organizations in each subcategory is that their members are different and that society is indifferent or hostile to that difference. In at least one respect,

195

Table 6.
Properties of Lifestyle Organizations

Exemplar Organizations
Widow-to-widow programs; Parents Without Partners and singles
groups; La Leche League; Little People; CUB (Concerned United
Birthparents); ALMA (Adoptees' Liberty Movement Association);
Parents/FLAG (Parents and Friends of Lesbians and Gays); National
Gay and Lesbian Task Force

Public Image
    Some may be viewed with suspicion,
        e.g., gay and patient liberation organizations
    Many larger ones, e.g., singles and
        widow organizations, pose fewer challenges
        to society and are better accepted

Goals
    Advocacy and social support
    Strengthen salience of reference group
    Obtain more support from reference group

Technology
    Companionship
    Network development
    Community mobilization
    Political campaigns
    Legal initiatives

Career Pattern
    Lifelong
    Affects broad sectors of members' lives

Normalization Potential[a]
    Society is abnormal [+]
    Exaggerates and exposes "deviancy" [o]

Relationship to Professionals
    Professionals are symbols of society's oppression
    Public relationships tend to be antagonistic
        but behind the scenes cooperation is
        not uncommon

---

[a] +, positive; o, negative.

members of these organizations do not fit the ideal cultural stereotype. And to differing degrees, these persons have chosen to deal with their predicaments through various combinations of companionship and social advocacy.

Connotations of "Different"

Though the name—'different lifestyle" organizations—seemed like a good fit for the category as a whole, some of its connotations might have been chosen as better fits for some subcategory organizations. Some might have been called "variant" because of their tendency to depart, and often to exult in their departure, from culturally approved norms. The term "variant" might better suit organizations, such as those formed by gays, whose members think of themselves as different. They would like to be seen as not better, not worse, but simply a "natural variation that develops from the same source as heterosexuality—our human capacity to love each other."[3] Variant, however, is farfetched for organizations for the widowed, some of whom might prefer the label "lifestyle support" organizations. "Counter lifestyle" organizations might have better suited the less conventional. But this label seemed too "far out" for some singles organizations, some of which might urge a reference to the transitional status of some members. Despite the need for a more general name, it will be useful to remember these connotations as they capture some of the "differences" felt by persons in subcategories.

Oppression of "Different" Persons

It may seem extreme to think that the dominant culture holds down the members of some of these organizations. It may seem farfetched to say that some organizations are aggrieved and protesting against the larger society and that a resolution of these grievances requires society to institute specific reforms. Consider that incredulity may have its source in society's insensitivity. Consider that these "differences" have been ignored, disparaged, and used to justify discrimination. Even the fastidiously polite La Leche League speaks of the "quiet revolution," "the legal rights of breastfeeding mothers," and "breastfeeding in a nonsupportive culture." These phrases arose in a culture that was perceived to be biased against breastfeeding, and they are the basis of a campaign to combat these "norms" and to encourage mothers to insist on their rights in a world that is inhospitable to mothers desiring to breastfeed. That they recognize the controversial *197* nature of their cause is also evident in this excerpt from a reprint sent by the International Office:

THE NAME—LA LECHE LEAGUE

Leche (lay-chay) means milk in Spanish. La Leche League is named after a shrine in St. Augustine, Florida, dedicated in 1598 to the Spanish Madonna, Nuestra Senora de la Leche y Buen Parto. La Leche League translates her title freely as "Our Lady of Happy Delivery and Plentiful Milk."

The name may seem obscure for an organization promoting a philosophy of breastfeeding and mothering. But remember that the League was founded in a more straight-laced time than the present. "In those days you didn't mention breast in print unless you were talking about Jean Harlow," says founding mother Edwina Froehlich.[4]

Happily, there have been some changes in the desired direction, as indicated in the following letter from the International Office of La Leche League:

In 1981, 57.6 percent of mothers breastfed their infants in the hospital. In 1971 the figure was only 24.7. At three to four months of age 35.2 percent of infants continued to breastfeed in 1981, compared with 8.2 in 1971. In five to six month olds, the breastfeeding rate increased from 5.5 percent in 1971 to 26.8 percent in 1981.[5]

Although the widowed and divorced differ in other ways from the cultural ideal, they also feel society is insensitive to their needs. Few escape what PWP describes in its brochure as the "society-imposed stigma of being divorced, separated or an unmarried parent."[6] The double load often carried by single parents is an injustice to them and their children. And instead of providing relief from their burden, their social life may only add to it. When their social life is not impoverished because of rigid couple-entertainment patterns, they may be treated like "fifth wheels." And a close cross-sex friendship may attract more curiosity than support.

Birthparents continue to be insulted by the common use of the term *biological parents*, which to them symbolizes a social structure that keeps them apart from their children, emotionally and physically. Parents, adoptive as well as birth, have been polarized by this structure, though the needs of the birthparents have almost always been viewed as less important. Their birthchildren, the adoptees, unlike everyone else, must not know the parents who gave birth to them. In a letter to the editor, a group of members of Concerned United Birthparents have indicated how society is involved in these arrangements.

Why aren't present and prospective adoptive parents encouraged to maintain contact with their child's birth family? How can contact be facilitated where desired?

Why do adoptive parents fear birthparents? What is this process of conditioning that has brought us as a society to this psychological place?[7]

The Little People are in a different situation, since many of their bruises are not caused deliberately. But how much does that matter when others are insensitive to their needs? Everything is too big, too tall, and too far away. Hope lies in corporate action to reform society and to help other people of small stature cope with the inhospitable climate.

The feeling of being different and unacceptable is perhaps most salient in the gay and lesbian communities. Lesbians and gays are under attack by many in the majority and often feel that they must create separate communities to thrive, or even to survive, in a homophobic culture. And though San Francisco is a spectacular exception, most communities have private networks of gay people. Through these countercultural specialized communities, gay people seek to escape from the demoralizing hostility of the cultural majority.

PUBLIC IMAGE

The differences represented by these organizations evoke reactions ranging from mild uneasiness to intense suspicion. Many of these organizations are suspected of wanting to subvert the established order. Actually they pose little real threat to the general order, and their modest aims are often misinterpreted. Their platforms simply call for equitable treatment and the end of injustice. But the public mistakes this desire to throw off the yoke of discrimination with a desire to overturn society's norms. The public tends to see nonconformism or an interest in reform as subversion. This view, however, may be changing, albeit begrudgingly. The salutary effect of the legal challenges initiated by these organizations has been a kind of forced education for the public. It has brought a reluctant awareness of the distinction between defending one's rights and subversion of the public order.

Degrees of Threat

Public suspicion varies directly with the threat different people are perceived to pose to conventional social arrangements. Widow organizations pose the least threat, and there is little reservation about accepting them. Even here, however, some people comment about widows' interest in dating and socializing. As additional evidence, consider that these organizations seem to have been named to anticipate criticisms. THEOS (They Help Each Other Spiritually), from the Greek word for God, focuses attention on a different matter and suggests a powerful patron; NAIM evokes the image of the pitiful biblical widow, as if to answer those people who might have an image of a liberated dating partner.

Members of PWP interpret the oft-heard questions and quizzical looks as expressions of the concern that they may be a "threat" to monogamous relationships. And experience has shown that such questions, if not asked, may only await a less inhibited setting. Parents Without Partners' defensive response may sometimes seem to give credence to these prejudices. The adult social and dating component of PWP seems to be deliberately underplayed; to some it may seem an attempt to hide something. The organization's statements seldom give the impression that adult parties and outings may be as important as activities with the children or as discussions about the loneliness, problematic finances, or burdensome child-care responsibilities of the single parent.[8] Their discussions on "how do we cope with loneliness?" or "sleep-in roommates" do not get equal billing, but they seem to attract at least as much interest.

Organizations that challenge traditional policies and practices relative to women, the elderly, and adoptees (including birthparents) are even more threatening. But gay and lesbian organizations are probably perceived to pose the greatest threat. At least this may be inferred from the harsh, unthinking reaction of the larger society. This reaction does nothing to belie the interpretation that it is unconsciously assumed that these organizations want to lure the unsuspecting into homosexuality. These reactions seem little affected by the gays' rightful insistence that the problem resides in the straight, not in the gay, community: It is homophobia and not homosexuality that must change. Society, however, is much more tolerant of those who want to change themselves than of those who want to change society. Yet as one parent responded when asked if she wished her child could be changed: "I'd prefer to change our homophobic society so my child could live his life without rejection and fear."[9]

GOALS

A major aim of these organizations is to make society more supportive and less oppressive through reform. In some instances, the term *reform* is an accurate representation of their activist orientation; in others, it may seem an exaggerated description of their modest goals. Yet even organizations at opposite ends of the continuum may have more in common than is usually recognized. Certainly, the public has a more polar perception of them than is warranted. On the left, few, if any, are as revolutionary as the public sometimes fears, and on the right, few are as acquiescent as the public might wish them to be.

Social Advocacy

If advocacy is salient even for the least conflict-oriented organizations, it must be even more salient for organizations whose members are most victimized by society. Recall that even apparently conforming widows have initiated legal suits. Despite their manners, they have challenged the sex-related actuarial policies of the social security system and the insurance industry. They have been successful in changing the formulas that resulted in lower annuities for females. These same organizations have worked to overturn "couple discounts" at movie houses, restaurants, and hotels. These objectives are intrinsically worthwhile. But as symbols for a host of other discriminations against singles, they take on additional appeal. Legal actions are an especially effective way to communicate the importance attached to otherwise easily dismissed aspects of the situation of widows. It might also give the public pause to consider that widows may also resent that they receive so few social invitations, that packaged items in the supermarket are too large for one person, and that home health care may be denied because a partner is not present.

The Little People find much of the tall people's world similarly disagreeable. They want to make it less hostile (sharp corners on furniture), less forbidding (unsafe traffic intersections), and better suited to their needs (lower cupboards). Mindful of their numbers, however, they realize that their strength lies in persuasion rather than contest. Yet their basic aim is to reduce the oppressiveness of their world.

Gay organizations deliberately sacrifice whatever social acceptability they might otherwise have in order to confront society's explicit oppression of gays. They engage in widely publicized community events. Legal action has been taken to protect their rights in the military service, in the civilian workplace, and in the world of education. In their readiness to stage marches against oppressive social institutions, including the arms of local government that have denied them their rights, they have proved themselves capable of forceful and dramatic demands for action. *201*

Personal Support

The publicly announced goals of these organizations for different people often do not mention the more private, personal goals of their members. Without questioning the integrity of their reform goals, gays (and members of other less militant organizations) simultaneously pursue more personal and private agendas to address the stress and constricted social opportunities they face. Most aim to develop a supportive network to counteract the oppression of the larger society. However, many will hesitate to acknowledge this aim publicly because it may make gays (and other discriminated-against persons) even more vulnerable. Some people will seize on these aims as "proof" that homosexuals are uniquely deficient, if not actually mentally disturbed. Lest this supposition seem improbable, remember that only in 1980 was homosexuality eliminated as an official diagnosis in the American Psychiatric Association's *Diagnostic and Statistical Manual of Mental Disorders* (3rd ed.). This change, long sought by gays, was one of the most abhorrent symbols of the hostility gays experience in this society. The fact that homosexuality was maintained as a mental disorder for so long suggests powerful cultural forces. These forces tend to continue unabated, and superficial changes in professional and legal nicety are hardly noticed. Thus, although gays may allude to the personally supportive aspects of their organizations among themselves, they are understandably reluctant to give their opponents ammunition.

Moreover, they want it clearly understood that the social support derived from these organizations should be considered an interim measure and not a permanent solution to oppression. Homosexuals have no intrinsic disability for which they must seek specialized support. Yet because they are stigmatized by society, they are forced to find a substitute for the everyday support that ordinary members of society receive from their primary social institutions. Thus, their specialized, secondary institutions have been created to compensate for the ordinary social provisions denied them.

TECHNOLOGY

Ironically, the ambivalence and outright hostility of the larger society not only unite the membership but are a major force behind the technology of these self-help organizations. Everyone is important; relationships are prized in beleaguered organizations. Though only the more activist members may be leaders pressing legal action, mobilizing public demonstrations, and managing political and social action campaigns, nearly everyone participates in the bake sales, the marches, and car washes that support these activities. These externally oriented activities also create relationship opportunities: "Everyone's meeting at _____ to go over to the Housing Commission Hearing." Additional relationship opportunities are part of the sessions to plan strategy and the postmortems to review results. Planning sessions are something to look forward to regularly. Further meetings to prepare for public celebrations, such as Single Parents Month or Gay Pride Week, or to respond to the public challenges of reactionary individuals and organizations, are often scheduled.

It has been assumed that social action leads to leisure-time and companionship opportunities, but the reverse may also be true. Social interaction may precede social action; the idea that only one or the other precedes is misleading. Everything is connected; consequently, it may be impossible to separate cause from effect or the personal from the political. But if a linear model is desired, it may be said that relationships that were initially a means to an end may become satisfying in themselves, though they remain instruments for accomplishing the original goal. The process may be even more subtle and slanted: Tasks or projects can encourage close relationships among participants because they afford the partners control over the intensity of their relationship. Thus, paradoxically, many will gain more support from task or action groups than from support groups.

Group environments, however, can compromise the otherwise sound judgment of individual members when there are strong group pressures. In their eagerness, members may compete to outdo each other or go along with "groupthink" actions.

This is not to imply that advocacy activities go on at a high pitch in all organizations. In the quieter organizations for widows and in the more frankly leisure-time-oriented singles organizations, the proportions of reform and support activities will be different. Widows and singles are more likely to pursue personal growth and relationship activities, and their community action will more often be described as public education and outreach. Nonetheless, the energy for these activities may have its source in individuals' real and fantasied grievances against the society that has made it harder for them to meet their needs.

CAREER PATTERN

Since the conditions addressed by these organizations tend to be long-term ones, the organizations strive to help the individual *203* adapt to his or her lifestyle. Though for some there may be a choice about how long they will remain in a particular lifestyle, others have no choice in the matter. Many singles and mental health consumers have some choice, but the elderly, adoptees, and birthparents have no choice. Even widows and single parents, who are in a potentially transitional status, must assume that it will be of indefinite duration. Otherwise the incentive to invest in these organizations would be insufficient. Furthermore, if all singles were assumed to desire marriage, the single status would be degraded for those who remain single, whether from choice or lack of opportunity. Prospective members must deal with the question of how much emphasis to give this side of their life. To what extent, for example, would it be better to network with married people and singles rather than to network with singles only? A member of PWP told of his amusement when his married friends did not even recognize an issue. When they asked him why he spent so much time with the singles crowd, he replied, "So there will be something there when you need it." The matter of emphasizing or acknowledging a difference is much more important when the difference is not so easily observed and when the consequences of the difference are negative ones for the individual.

Advertise, or Keep It to Yourself?

In an ideal society, people who are different would be able to form acceptable and enabling self-concepts. Since society is not ideal, the question is raised as to whether members of lifestyle organizations, for example, ex-mental patients or mental health consumers, should make their participation known. Are they placing themselves in unnecessary jeopardy even if it is conceded that participation need not involve advertising? Yet, no matter how circumspect the participation, it does increase the risk that people who otherwise would not know will find out that "so and so is a member of an organization for deviant people." However, some organizations contend that it is possible to be a committed participant in a consumer organization for a temporary period and then move on. Moreover, they argue that participation will facilitate the development of an empowering self-concept. Many leaders of consumer organizations, they point out, enjoy more rewarding careers as self-help leaders than they had as factory and office workers. In assessing the truth of this proposition, the actual alternatives open to consumers, and not some abstract alternative, must be considered. One thing, however, is clear: Uniform prescriptions cannot be made for everyone.

Broad Concerns and Frustrations

Lifestyle organizations' interest in a broad set of concerns is another important factor affecting the careers of their members. Unlike the more circumscribed interests of other types of self-help organizations, lifestyle organizations have agendas in nearly every sphere of social life. Discrimination occurs in residences, neighborhoods, workplaces, schools, and leisure-time organizations, that is, in public institutions. Thus, every social sector must be monitored for corrective action.

The scope of this mandate can be a major source of frustration. Each issue has the potential to absorb the organization's entire effort, and it is difficult to keep from feeling that members, having observed one fire, are rushing off to observe another. Are they onlookers, or do they have a meaningful role in resolving a problem or turning it in another direction? To avoid discouragement, vigorous support will be required from leaders. And where are the leaders to come from, and who is to prevent them from becoming discouraged? Obviously, it will be hard to mobilize and sustain enthusiasm especially if the experience of members would seem to justify more pessimism than optimism.

The low rate of participation in many of these organizations is another source of frustration. The number of their members is misleading if it is construed as indicating the commitment of the eligible population. The number of members is high because the conditions are common ones. Nonetheless, the majority of eligibles do not join; others come and go. Interest can be renewed, however, through the assumption of leadership positions within the organization. The challenge and recognition inherent can renew enthusiasm.

Loss of a Career

Like the loss of a valued job, a member who is required to resign from a self-help organization may experience it as a separation from familiar supports, even though his or her personal situation has changed for the better. The loss of companionship and support may result in less effective functioning. Cognizant of these possibilities, some former members of singles organizations attempt to compensate by meeting informally with others who have also changed their status. The arrangement is not as satisfactory as the "graduate" groups that enjoy the formal support of the antecedent organization. As with other career experiences, an unwanted or indeterminate separation from the lifestyle organization may affect how members feel about themselves.

NORMALIZATION POTENTIAL

"It's society, not me. People are abnormal; they're the cause of the problem," some different lifestyle organizations shout. To be sure, the shouting may subside as people later pursue more immediate interests. But the feeling is always there and can be activated and incorporated into an explanation of why the problem has been made worse, if it was not actually caused, by society. Even singles organizations cite defective arrangements for child support or the bias against the noncustodial parent as affecting their situation. Not surprisingly, gay organizations tend to shout the most: Homophobia not homosexuality hurts people. They attempt to enhance their normality by rejoicing in their deviance. In Goffman's terms, they reject repentance and use alienation to insulate themselves from stigma. The homophobics are the "ones who are not quite human."[10]

Abandoning Cover

Pursuing a career in a lifestyle self-help organization may involve a conflict of interest between the individual and the organization. "Coming out," for example, entails risks, and the values of the organization may not suit particular individuals. Such a possibility seems inherent in the initiative to develop a "Gay Pride" interest section within PWP as described in a brochure entitled *Pride in Parents Without Partners.* Affiliating with this interest within PWP may involve abandoning a near-perfect cover. Thus, these individuals may suffer negative consequences that far exceed the benefits derived from affiliation. Without discounting the guidance gay organizations give about the pros and cons of coming out, and without discounting their expert advice about where and when to come out, there is the possibility that the interests of the individual will be confused with the interests of the organization.[11]

A similar conflict threatens mental health consumers. Highly able consumers or ex-consumers are precisely the people who have the most choice about whether to incorporate the element of consumer in their public identity and also precisely the people who are needed to assume leadership positions in consumer organizations. There are no easy solutions to this dilemma, but sometimes satisfactory solutions for the individual are possible. A fully sanctioned, guilt-free means to "move on" when the member feels it is time is called for. Many organizations provide for this in their concept of a "way station," but the concept has only infrequently been translated into concrete steps.

RELATIONSHIP TO PROFESSIONALS

Single-Tool Mechanics

The relationship between professionals and members of lifestyle self-help organizations is often strained, and professionals must bear much of the responsibility for this. They frequently urge psychotherapy as the panacea, much as the very young feel they can fix anything with a hammer. They thus exhibit their naïvete and, not incidentally, a disregard for what the self-helpers know about the determinants of the problem. They disdain interest in other proven approaches to the problem. To consider how inappropriate this attitude may be, it is only necessary to call to mind some of the woefully misleading concepts some married counselors have about the singles culture. This lack of knowledge and the insensitivity that accompanies it sometimes rejects the possibility of other knowledge being relevant.

But even when professionals are knowledgeable and their therapy competent, results may still be disappointing. Therapy is not the answer to all the problems of the adult single or the widow. Some problems will defeat even the most skilled therapist and the most determined client. Thus, criticism of psychotherapy may sometimes be a criticism of a therapeutic intervention that promised too much rather than one that was improperly conducted. The root causes of the disappointment may have less to do with professional shortcomings and more with the limits of the method, and even more with the human condition and the nature of social arrangements. Against these odds, not even self-help organizations can offer adequate solace.

Agents of Oppression

Yet professionals are often criticized as one instrument of an oppressive society. As sanctioned agents, some professionals accept the values of the society uncritically. They fail to maintain their independence of the society and of the organization that employs them. Even though society must sometimes be held accountable for using professionals to control dissidents, society should not be considered the lone, or the only culpable, player in this morality play.

Self-help organizations may also have their own reasons for baiting professionals. Discomfited by internal strife, a leader may attempt to project its cause onto a source outside the organization. And again, some disaffected professionals make matters worse by allying themselves with particular self-help organizations. *207*

Eager to ingratiate themselves with potential clients, they may respond enthusiastically to the tacit invitation to criticize their colleagues. Naturally, the responding professional is exempt from criticism. And as one wag put it: "The distress of other people usually can be tolerated fairly well."

For his or her trouble, the professional, in this one-dimensional scenario, may be rewarded with an increased number of referrals. An understanding has evolved that these highly singular professionals are the only ones to be contacted when a "really" sensitive professional is needed. And is there ever a need for any other kind? However, some of the reasons behind conspicuous interactions between professionals and self-help organizations may be self-serving. This admittedly simplistic account may, nonetheless, highlight important dynamics in these relationships.

A Dilemma

But self-conscious playacting probably has little to do with the fierce criticism of such more openly antagonistic groups as gays and lesbians. Their antagonism, however, places them in an unfortunate bind. They must denounce psychotherapy because it perpetuates the myth that they are the sick rather than the victims. Yet psychotherapy can help relieve some of the strain caused by these very damaging cultural beliefs and practices. The mental health establishment can be both an instrument of the oppressive society and a source of support and comfort for the oppressed. Used properly, counseling can modify oppressive conditions, as well as work through internal conflicts, though many in the psychotherapy industry are preoccupied with the latter function. As a consequence, they effectively reduce the access of gays and other victims of discrimination to supportive counseling service. Their insensitivity inadvertently or deliberately tends to discourage such individuals from becoming clients. Moreover, a collective memory of being "messed over" by the professions is also a barrier to service. This memory is especially handicapping to the profession perceived to be incriminated by its association with hospitals, courts, and in general by its protection of the status quo: public psychiatry.

The Informal Solution

Self-help leaders have dealt with these predicaments by forming private informal relationships with a few carefully chosen psychotherapists while continuing to speak out against irrelevant or harmful psychotherapy. The professionals they consult often are deviant group members themselves. Gay counselors, for example, have shown that psychotherapy, sensitively administered, can be a liberating, growth-inducing force. These counselors, often "friends of a friend," are the major professional contacts for troubled members of the gay community. In addition, these trusted caregivers may have a role as informal consultants and ombudspersons in the gay community. Beyond this, the gay community, and other "different" communities, may confer on their trusted counselors significant leadership positions. To these leaders falls the continuing responsibility to criticize the negative effects of psychiatry and psychotherapy while making use of their benefits. Their ability to keep these opposites in mind and still function is the mark of first-rate leadership.

Notes

1. Gray Panthers, *Two Portraits of Old Age in America* (Philadelphia: Gray Panthers, undated), unpaged.
2. D. Hall, *The Politics of Schizophrenia: Psychiatric Oppression in the U.S.* (Lanham, Md.: University Press, 1983), pp. 547–548.
3. National Gay Task Force, *Twenty Questions About Homosexuality* (New York: National Gay Task Force, undated), p. 2.
4. V. Albert-Olson, "La Leche League at 25: The Quiet Revolution," *Family Journal* (July 1981), p. 24.
5. M. Lofton, personal communication, Franklin, Ill., September 8, 1983.
6. Parents Without Partners, *The Single Parent* (Washington, D.C.: PWP, 1967).
7. *Ann Arbor News*, April 9, 1984.
8. R. S. Weiss, "Parents Without Partners as a Supplementary Community," *Marital Separation* (New York: Basic Books, 1975), pp. 212–224.
9. T. Sauerman, *Coming Out to Your Parents* (Los Angeles, Calif.: Parents and Friends of Lesbians and Gays, 1984), p. 11.
10. E. Goffman, *Stigma* (Englewood Cliffs, N.J.: Prentice-Hall, 1963), p. 6.
11. Sauerman, *Coming Out to Your Parents*.

12

Significant Other Organizations

The members of self-help organizations for significant others are parents, spouses, and close relatives of troubled and troubling persons who have affiliated with such organizations as the National Alliance for the Mentally Ill, Families Anonymous, and Toughlove. The major dimensions of the organizations to which these significant others belong are listed on Table 7. These members have been described as "one step removed," since they are not the ones who behave in a troublesome manner or bear the primary burden.[1] The phrase, however, can be misleading if it suggests that these significant others escape the burdensome care of their relatives. Very often, in fact, they are last-resort caregivers. If things are going well, they may need only to supplement the care of official caregivers. But when needed services are not available, or if the relative absconds from a placement or refuses to accept a service, significant others become caregivers by default.

Significant others must contend with behavior that runs the gamut from the seemingly hedonistic acting-out of some delinquents to the obviously anguished, bizarre acting-out of some mentally disordered persons. What these others have in common are their disappointments, burdens, and—strange as it may seem— hopes for these people. In sharing their feelings, they obtain a measure of relief. In the course of sharing, they may also learn about new resources or new approaches. Most of all, perhaps, they discover other people who also ask the same question: "Why me?" They find they are not alone in their feelings that life has

Table 7.
Properties of Significant Other Organizations

Exemplar Organizations
National Alliance for the Mentally Ill; Families Anonymous;
Toughlove; Al-Anon; Gam-Anon

Public Image
Advocates for the mentally ill
Restores rights to families
Balances rights of family with deviants
Public is sympathetic with goals
Fits with the conservative 1980s
Growing fast

Goals
Provides relief to families
Protects and prevents problems in families
Reform-minded

Technology
Uses network and organizational
building strategies
Social support
Education
Advocacy
Policy development

Career Pattern
Medium-term memberships
Moderate commitment
Potential conflict between advocacy
and support interests

Normalization Potential[a]
Patient, not family [+]
Family vs. patient [o]
Professional, not family [o]
Professional vs. family [o]

Relationship to Professionals
Bargaining
Contractual

---

[a] +, positive; o, negative.

treated them unfairly. They deal with these feelings directly through affiliation. And sometimes they deal with them indirectly by involving themselves in organizational tasks. In some organizations, these tasks may involve social advocacy activities. This means pushing for more effective services for their troubled relatives and for more sensitive arrangements between themselves and public officials.

One subcategory of such organizations places a somewhat higher priority on members' modifying their own coping mechanisms as distinguished from working with others. Because of this orientation, which is also part of the twelve-step orientation, they are less likely to be, and sometimes are not, involved in social advocacy. Al-Anon, the forerunner of many of the significant other organizations, is the most prominent group in this subcategory. As the largest and oldest of the significant other organizations, it has inspired a number of close relations: Gam-Anon, Alateen, and the National Association of Children of Alcoholics (NACOA). These organizations are not discussed in this chapter because they are closely related to the twelve-step substance abuse organizations discussed in Chapter Nine (habit disturbance organizations). Also, these organizations generally maintain a less activist posture with their relatives and in the community. Interested readers are referred to a number of useful publications on Al-Anon for an in-depth study of this less activist significant other organization.[2]

A DIFFERENT APPROACH

The organizations that are discussed in this chapter are more activist. Toughlove, Families Anonymous, and the National Alliance for the Mentally Ill stress the importance of members' assertively approaching their relatives and various community caretakers as part of an overall strategy for problem resolution rather than members' managing themselves, as in organizations linked to habit disturbance. These distinctions, even if they seem to be somewhat vague, serve another purpose. They highlight a new brand of significant other organization that places more emphasis on an assertive approach to controlling behavior and managing heavy care responsibilities.

The Decision to Do Something

Families and others close to troublesome individuals frequently have endured harmful, degrading conditions over a period of years. It is not uncommon for them to have suffered for long periods before learning about these organizations, which tend to be of recent origin. Their own reluctance may have been implicated in their delay in finding these organizations. They may have found it emotionally necessary to reject any implication that only limited or very slow change might be possible for their relatives. When they come to feel that they cannot drift any longer, in a desperate effort to avert total despair, they are driven to think about the unthinkable. However reluctantly, they recognize it may be time to join an organization that forces them to face what may be a long-term, severely impairing problem.

Part of this reluctance may have stemmed from the realization that their behavior would have to change, too. This is not to imply that these families have been "enabling" the behavior, but rather to indicate that they now must take more forceful action to help their relatives control themselves or to allow others to do it for them. The squandering of money must stop. The obscenities and assaults must be curbed; the bizarre behavior must be controlled. Disruptive behavior patterns—banging around all night while sleeping all day—must cease.

Members must also overcome feelings of embarrassment and insist that community agents assume their mandated responsibilities in protecting troubled individuals from themselves and others—and the family and the rest of the community from troublesome individuals.

Initial Approach

New members of significant other organizations often start by getting help for their shame and guilt from the "been there" families. They have done things they thought they were incapable of. In their extremity, they have behaved monstrously. They soon learn from senior members that much of their monstrous behavior is, first, not so uncommon and, second, attributable to the extraordinary conditions they have had to endure. Increasingly, the newcomers will be comforted by a compassion offered by others who have been in similar circumstances. But right from the beginning, they may have to consider protecting themselves from the troubled family member; simultaneously, they must insist that public officials carry out their responsibilities. As these new members become more willing to try new approaches, senior families will offer them close guidance and support, which may be needed to stop the pleading and nagging and the overprotecting of the troublesome relative. Limits must be set, and reasonable standards must be enforced. A parallel approach must be taken   *213* with the socially sanctioned, behavior-regulating agents of the community. The particular approach, however, will depend on the extent to which the unacceptable behavior is viewed as a product of mental disorder or as an expression of willful acting-out.

VARIATIONS IN THE APPROACH: With the more "delinquent" person, the significant others must abandon their prime role as recipients of abuse. They must realize that positive reinforcement may not be enough; limits must be set and the offending person must be held accountable. Supportive but frank confrontations will be necessary to spell out the sanctions and then to apply them when unacceptable behavior is encountered. At the same time, such community caregivers and behavior regulators as teachers, social workers, doctors, hospital personnel, police, and court officials must be made to carry out their mandated functions.

With the more "disturbed" person, the emphasis will be somewhat different. Priority is given to securing the assistance of those charged with the protection and care of the disturbed person and his or her family. Disturbed individuals will need to be placed where they can be supervised to protect them from themselves while their families seek respite from the debilitating stress of such caregiving. The disturbed person needs more care and protection, whereas the delinquent needs more regulation from officially sanctioned agents; and these differences are reflected in the orientation of the different significant other self-help organizations. Affiliates of the National Alliance for the Mentally Ill, for example, emphasize mobilizing external resources on behalf of family members. Families Anonymous and Toughlove chapters, however, emphasize strategies to hold the offending family member responsible for his or her acting-out behavior. In the latter instance, community resources are used to reinforce parents and to inform delinquents about the consequences of their behavior.

THE GLUE: The bond between members of these organizations is their refusal to accept the continued abuse of their relatives and the unconscionable neglect of external caretaking and regulatory agents. A caregiving family will feel abused whether or not the relative is able to control his or her behavior. When the relative is out of control, caregivers and control agents are perceived as negligent in not assuming their role and relieving some of the family's burden. When the relative is capable of control, the family is apt to feel doubly abused because countless doctors, teachers, social workers, police, and other community agents excuse the offending individual and blame family members or their surrogates. Salt is rubbed into their wounds by an illogical assumption that if the troubled relative is not responsible for his or her behavior, the family is. This non sequitur, a common mistake of clinicians, causes much antipathy toward professionals. With hindsight, it seems a convenient rationalization for clinicians who have been unable to help troubled individuals and their families. But if this rationalization is allowed to persist, it can only lead to further deterioration in the families' ability to help relatives. In extreme circumstances, it may even be necessary to contemplate radical action. It may be necessary to detach from the relative—to "release with love." Should this be necessary, perhaps because harmful acting-out cannot be curtailed or because the relative's behavior is beyond human endurance, family members will be reminded of the distinction between "releasing" and "rejecting."

The Product of a Quiet Revolution

These changing views coincide with the appearance of a new type of significant other self-help organization. Families Anonymous was founded in 1972, Toughlove in 1978, and the National Alliance for the Mentally Ill in 1979. The rapid growth of these organizations correlates with certain changes in the prevailing zeitgeist. In the sixties and seventies, it was customary to presume that individuals were troubled because of pathological family processes. One member was the "bearer" of the pathology for the entire family. The term *identified patient* has become the most prominent symbol of what these families consider an abhorrent assumption.

But even when the family was not blamed, little was done to prevent its deterioration. Officials were seemingly blind to the burden on and abuse of family members; the concept of respite care was still largely unknown. For most of the sixties and seventies, public policy and caregiver ideology fostered a brutal insensitivity to the instrumental and emotional burdens carried by these families. It is not surprising that this attitude pushed families to abandon their troublesome members. The lack of "active" families, especially for long-term mentally ill, is, in part, the legacy of this era, in which public policy neglected the family while a small but influential group of family therapists claimed that a heroic reconstruction could cure the identified patient and his or her family. A survivor of this era, and a current board member of NAMI, remembers the following experience:

> During their son's second hospitalization, Harriet and her husband Charles took leaves of absence from their jobs and spent three weeks as inpatients in UW Hospital, at the doctor's urging.
> "Ward 2B, with its locked doors, was a pressure cooker. We   *215*

spent hours examining every aspect of our family dynamics. It took a long time afterwards to put back the pieces of our shattered egos. With AMI support groups now and with NAMI educational material, I hope that no family has to go through the 'Dark Ages' again," she explained.[3]

An Enlightenment

Even if the abject failure of this approach had not been enough to bring about change, the effects of deinstitutionalization and the community-based care movement of the eighties would have been. It led to the recognition of the contributions of families and significant others, even though it has not been accompanied by offers of concrete assistance. Specialized services, it was finally recognized, cannot replace basic community institutions, the most important of which is the family. It is also now recognized that if more than a fraction of those eligible for public services applied for them, funds would soon be exhausted. Enlightened public policy is now moving toward recognizing the caregiving contributions of families. It has begun to provide supplementary services to families to avert the enormous costs of providing total subsistence care even to a small percentage of the eligible population.[4]

Check the Bathwater

This recent swing must not preclude exploring the multiple, varyingly important causes of most problems that demand the service of caregivers. Neither the model of the family as the identified patient nor the model of the individual as an independently activated organism is realistic. It is important to acknowledge up-front that it is difficult to determine simple cause-effect relationships in caregiver/troubled-individual situations. Thus, it is important to keep an open mind and to explore all the possibilities for change. If this is not done, the countermovement may do little more than usher in another round of simplistic, dysfunctional "blaming the victim." Now, however, the place of the old victim, the family, will have been taken by the new one, the troubled individual.

PUBLIC IMAGE

The Family as Resource, Not as Patient

The more conservative social climate of the eighties has buttressed the growth of significant other self-help organizations, and more conservative views about the possibility of people changing have made it easier for caregiver families to come out. Instead of forcing intrusive, hazardous "help" on them, or heaping blame on them, their contributions have been more readily recognized. Nowadays, services are more likely to complement caregiving families rather than to compete with them. This goes hand in hand with a more realistic view of the potential of human relations experts to alter personal and social conditions. More attention is paid to the limits and possible unintended consequences of technical interventions. Reflecting this change, a move has been made to offer modest subsidies to families who care for disabled family members. In Michigan, for example, the Department of Mental Health began in 1984 to subsidize families of developmentally disabled persons for some of the extraordinary expenses they incur.

Accountable Professionals and Clients

Current trends are supportive of these families in another way: Professionals have been directed to give highest priority to the neediest individuals and their families. Since this policy by definition restricts the opportunity for professionals to use scarce resources for psychotherapy with clients who are able to use these services (because clients who can make use of psychotherapy are often not the neediest), it has already resulted in proportionately more services to seriously impaired clients. It also suggests that important changes in professional attitudes and behaviors may have already taken place. Another factor in changing attitudes may be found in changing care arrangements. Practically, professionals have been forced to hold clients more responsible for their deviant behaviors. As the excerpt below illustrates, it is now acceptable to argue that rehabilitation will be advanced if the chronically mentally ill must now face the legal consequences of their petty offenses rather than be excused, as was formerly the case.

> Another important clinical reason to treat patients as responsible is that many of them have learned that illness is an excuse for their behavior. We disabuse our patients of that notion. We tell them that indeed we believe that they are ill, otherwise we would not be prescribing medication, but that we do not believe their illness is an excuse for their behavior. . . . For example, we had one patient who would want to be rehospitalized whenever he became stressed and anxious. His way of doing that would be to go into a supermarket, take some soda and candy, and walk through the line without paying for it . . . .We had to work

very closely not only with the police but with the district attorney and the judges to see to it that this kind of minor crime was handled as it would be for any other citizen. The next time this patient shoplifted at a supermarket he indeed went before a judge. . . . For most patients that was enough, but a few patients had to find out if indeed the judge meant what he said. Thus after the second shoplifting event they went before the judge and they did get three days in the county jail. . . . We are not advocating using this approach for people who break the law who are in the midst of a psychotic episode. We must use good clinical judgment to determine when this approach should be used. We have little difficulty in determining when our patients are consciously breaking the law as a maladaptive coping strategy and when they are doing things because they are really out of touch with reality.[5]

Rethinking Responsibility

Significant other self-help organizations have also contributed to the new paradigm. They insist that the old cliches about parental pathology, guilt, and loss must go. The burden of care must be shared by the several parties: the individual, the significant others, and the human service and social control subsystems of society. Changes in assigning responsibility to each of these subsystems will reduce the alienation of family members, without whose cooperation troublesome relatives cannot be maintained in the community.

The Yorks, founders of Toughlove, an organization for the families of "actor-outers," speak to other necessary changes. Their comments also apply to the mentally ill:

> The pursuit of "causes" outside the individual person is our current cultural preoccupation. Fostered by the popularization of psychological notions, we are mired in finding reasons for unacceptable behavior instead of setting limits on what is acceptable and demanding that unacceptable behavior stop.
>
> That is not to say that therapists, rehabilitation centers, and counseling programs are useless. But without a clear focus on the real responsibility for problem behavior, by getting distracted in blaming parents or other "causes," we are largely wasting our resources.[6]

Members of significant other groups project an image of themselves as supportive—and above all—pragmatic individuals who reject condescending and phony explanations even if these explanations would absolve the family. They are tough on themselves, holding themselves accountable for their mistakes and their present and future obligations to the troubled individual. But they are

218

also tough-minded about the responsibility of the troubled individual and the caretaking system. Indeed, their savage criticism of popular and professional views has jarred more than a few professionals.

GOALS

The chaos that has enveloped these families means that, before all else, they must obtain some relief. Once some relief has been obtained, they will be ready to address their own dysfunctional guilt, the adequacy of their coping mechanisms, and such concerns as preventing problems among other family members. These preventive goals will become increasingly important as families obtain enough breathing space to consider how they might have been affected by their experiences. When they are ready to seek help for these concerns, they will rediscover that outside resources are unavailable or unresponsive. Many will turn their frustrations into a deep commitment to reform caretaking and regulating systems, to develop new and more sensitive resources. These goals and the experiences that give rise to them can now be taken up.

Relief

Many of these families have endured insults, thefts, and assaults, along with unremitting demands for care as long as they can recall. They have forgotten what it means to be treated with civility, with decency—to enjoy a measure of privacy and stability. Awakened by police, browbeaten by officials, and treated with disdain by their neighbors, friends, and other family members, they have sunk to a level of functioning they heretofore could not have imagined possible. Hence, the first goal that can be remotely meaningful is respite from further humiliation and degradation. They must be protected and, if need be, separated from the troubled individual for a time, so that they can work to regain their dignity and self-respect. These families know the truth of the saying that brutal conditions tend to brutalize individuals. Yet veteran members are proof that self-respect can be regained and that chaos can be reduced. Moreover, these veterans stand ready to help the newcomer mobilize the community's informal and formal systems. This mobilization includes reactivating networks of supportive friends and relations that have been allowed to become dormant and encouraging the newcomer to make use of these networks.

Alleviation of Guilt

Once some resolution of the focal person's situation is in sight, families often become concerned about their own "sanity." Some of the things they did or failed to do under severe stress now rise up to haunt them. The memory of some of these excesses is all the more vivid and disturbing now that they have time to ruminate about them. They are ashamed and embarrassed just to imagine what it would be like to tell others of their experiences. Before joining the organization, they felt that they were the only ones who had so humiliated themselves; now they are reassured when they hear that others in the organization have undergone the same experiences. This realization is brought out as newcomers disclose some of their own lapses and hear about the lapses of others. In fact, newcomers typically are astonished by the uncanny ability of veteran members to anticipate the plots of their stories even before they are finished. The astonishment dissolves into a blessed relief as the newcomer realizes how regrettably common these experiences are among their peers in the organization. Hope will also be aroused by the obvious success of the veterans' coping methods.

Better Coping Methods

Change in coping methods becomes a more salient issue with time and as the benefits of relief are experienced. Maladaptive coping methods, acquired over long years of stress, must be modified. Denial of the problem, according to the Yorks, may be the first to go and is replaced by a dependence on the group for advice and guidance.[7] In exceptional situations, and usually only for brief periods of time, this dependence can be very heavy. For a time, the family may relinquish responsibility for their troubled relation, which acts to disrupt dysfunctional patterns of interaction. Their fellow members may act as their proxies in negotiations with the acting-out person and the regulatory agents of the community. Usually after the situation has stabilized, authority will be returned to the family. The goodwill acquired through such services can later be used to persuade the member to move along prescribed paths in dealing with his or her own problems. This state of temporary dependence represents progress in the early stages of coping because it expands the options beyond what they were during the stage of initial denial. The dependence, in turn, usually evolves into a state of realistic interdependence with other members. Also, this development is usually marked by parallel changes in the nature of the dependency relationship between the significant other and the troubled family member.

Specific Questions

At this point, families may again worry about the causes of the troubled behavior. Is it inherited? Is it likely to show up in siblings, or perhaps in their offspring? Have members of the family, particularly siblings, been irrevocably harmed by the experience? Will the combination of the bad example and the stress to which they have been exposed have deleterious effects on other members of the family? To take one specific concern, has family life been so unpleasant as to discourage siblings from starting a family of their own? Here again, the newcomer will be surprised to learn how common these concerns are, how seriously they are considered, and finally how resilient most people prove to be.

Genetic Aspect

Many families will be concerned about the inheritability of the disorder. Relative to this concern, the significant other self-help organization is a repository of sound information. More often than not, members of the organization can dispel some of the patently false myths about the genetic transmission of certain traits. And to the extent there is the risk of inheritability, they can put it into a realistic context. They may explain, for example, that it is usually a matter of greater susceptibility rather than of definite inheritance. The idea is that environment can influence how and to what extent some traits will be expressed. This clarification naturally leads to a discussion of how the environment can be arranged to minimize qualities that are associated with the disorder. And, lastly, newcomers are reminded that such problems often are preceded by warning signals. Overall, then, the message is that it is realistic to be hopeful.

Though the organization may have up-to-date, detailed information about the genetics of specific disorders—which would not be surprising in light of their special interests—other sources may also need to be consulted. There may be the need to refer their members for genetic counseling. Considering the nature of the organization, veteran members are well positioned to appraise the competence of various professionals. They can also help members prepare their agendas for the professional consultation and later help them understand and cope with the results of the consultation.

Prevention

Nearly everyday, families struggle with how to interpret the behavior of the troubled person to other family members, especially to children, who are more impressionable. They want them to understand that it is the behavior, not the person, they disapprove of. Easy as this sounds, it can be very difficult when caregivers are worried about possible contagion. It is further complicated by the many different behaviors that can be worried about. One day it may seem that the other children are on the verge of imitating the self-indulgent behavior; another day it may seem they are acting bizarrely.

Beyond these specific concerns, significant others also realize that the family has been functioning in a stressful environment. Consequently, they need to reflect on how that stress might have affected their lives and how its worst effects can be minimized. As they are able to become increasingly proactive, they may also want to consider incorporating a variety of stress management techniques into their everyday lives. These can range from year-round support groups to residential camping experiences and separate summer vacations. Because of the help they have been given, they will be moved to help others, and as this shift occurs, they will further consolidate their gains. Over time, the privilege of serving their fellow members may come to be seen as increasingly essential to their own well-being.

Resource Development

Having experienced frustration in their own search for services and having become more conscious of how social arrangements have exacerbated their problems, the members of many of these organizations have set social reform goals. They want to reform the larger system—the social structure that has failed to ameliorate already-present problems or to eliminate the conditions that give rise to these problems. Most families have had personal experience with what they consider to be the imbalances of the caregiving-regulatory system (as in the lack of protection from continued assault), its inadequacies (as in aftercare), and its nonexistent services—public relations claims to the contrary. They bring strong motives and a detailed understanding of the systems' inadequacies to the reform task. They have suffered through the police's inept handling of domestic violence incidents. They have been victimized by ill-considered releases of their relatives from mental hospitals. But now, supported by the organizational base of the self-help program, they can make demands for the provision of services. In a more general way, they may be able to increase the sensitivity of the community to the plight of caregiving families. Individuals may be motivated to lobby for change because of what they have experienced in the self-help organization. This may happen, even if such organizations as Families Anonymous prohibit the use of their name in lobbying efforts. Personal spin-offs from community-oriented projects may be enormously empowering and gratifying. As members work toward better arrangements for others, they expand their own repertoire of methods to cope with problems, especially their guilt.

TECHNOLOGY

Building Confidence

Through small talk, as well as through directed conversation, members come to feel accepted and understood. They come to understand that excessive emotional reactions and ill-fated attempts to control the deviant relative are typical. They further learn that whatever the deficiencies in their present state of functioning, they are not a measure of how they might function under more normal conditions. These messages are transmitted in a number of ways: Informal talks frequently take place at break times or after the formal part of the meeting. They may be followed by telephone conversations. Regular sessions may be arranged to promote such interchanges. One such format involves beginning meetings in small discussion groups to catch up on recent concerns. Then the small groups become a large group for a special presentation. In the final part of the meeting, they may again break into small groups to discuss how to apply the content of the presentation. Supported by these group discussions, family members are less likely to persist in self-recrimination and projection of blame onto the deviant member. To the extent that these impulses are checked, families can begin to address the troubled member more realistically. They may now be ready to design a detailed, long-term plan that incorporates the ideas of veteran members who have made a peaceful, though still imperfect, accommodation to their difficult circumstances.

Developing Assertiveness

One of the first and most often repeated messages the family receives is that continuing to subject themselves to the deviant's abuse is not just harmful to them, but it is also contrary to the   *223* interests of the troubled person. Limits must be set. Toughlove calls these limits bottom lines. To implement increasingly realistic and enforceable bottom lines, family members will be given specific assistance. When they need to ventilate about the obstacles or need encouragement to carry out what they know they must do, other members will make themselves available to listen and encourage.

Developing Networks

"Dime therapy" (telephoning), as a member of Families Anonymous called it, can make all the difference in a difficult situation. Yet it is only one of several "buddying and sponsoring" mechanisms available to members of these organizations. Other possibilities include having fellow members accompany, and sometimes even substitute for, the significant other who may be too vulnerable or too distraught to deal with certain situations. If necessary, they can also intercede directly with the troubled individual or caretaking officials. This mechanism is one of the more potent ones available to link members with other less personally involved members who can help formulate plans to deal with troublesome situations and sometimes with the implementation of arrangements. Just knowing that these arrangements can be made is reassuring. And the comfort they provide far exceeds the number of times these extraordinary measures are used. Perhaps much of their value lies in what they imply about fellow members' worth. Should extraordinary measures be needed, it would be worth going to extraordinary lengths for them.

Helping Oneself Through Others

In the process of freeing themselves from excessive burdens, parents and significant others may find their attention focused on a "whole world that needs to be educated." The world includes not just the significant others, but also the legions of uninformed human service professionals and community regulating agents. Involvement in these outside activities can be tremendously important to members. The writer has observed this many times in the course of inviting members of self-help organizations to speak before groups of professional students and practitioners. Very often these members have made extraordinary efforts to be responsive, to the point of rearranging work schedules and sacrificing income. In the end, it has been common for more people to come than were asked for or than were necessary to do a perfectly creditable job of explaining the self-help program. The gratitude one feels in these situations slows the realization that the presenters are reaping important benefits. The benefits of this outreach work go beyond educating the audience and developing a constituency for the organization. It recharges the presenters and heightens their own enthusiasm for the organization. The camaraderie and support generated through these activities are of a different kind and often exceed those available through the more ordinary, internal, direct-helping activities. Indeed, the satisfaction derived from these activities often is an important factor in the retention of senior members. Many speak of the deep satisfaction they get in reaching out to others and "paying back" the organization for the help they received.

CAREER PATTERN

Length

The nature of the disorder and the commitment to outreach are two factors that affect the length of careers in these organizations. An extensive commitment to outreach requires a complex structure, and effective advocacy requires a strong supportive organization. These organizations have a virtually unlimited capacity to absorb the energies and talents of senior members in organizational and community-development activities, and the need to further this work is a strong incentive for many members to continue. They appreciate that there are no "theys" to whom they can pass on undone work.

Outreach work can also be challenging. Challenges include maintaining relations with representatives of the media, governmental officials, church leaders, human service professionals, police officers, and court officials. The opportunity to assume leadership in this outreach and to be a part of the development of the organization often provides meaningful social roles to members. Many say they obtain much more satisfaction from their self-help roles than from the roles associated with their outside jobs.

The Nature of Problems

The length and form of participation is also affected by the nature of the problem. When the condition or problem is short-lived, membership will be correspondingly brief. When it is longer, it tends to be associated with a more complex career, and one that may include advocacy. The typical career in significant *225* other self-help organizations is somewhere between the relatively brief tenure of some habit disturbance organizations and the long-term affiliations characteristic of members in physical disease-condition organizations. For whatever reasons, as long as troubled individuals are involved with their families, members will be strongly motivated to remain affiliated with significant other organizations. Within this category there will be variation as the nature of the problem differs. Delinquent individuals tend either to outgrow their problems or split from their families. This limits the amount of time their significant others will be interested in these organizations. A different pattern results from the often prolonged dependency of mentally ill and developmentally disabled individuals. They may be heavily dependent on their families for indefinite periods. Thus, their significant others are potentially long-term members of significant other organizations.

Members of the National Alliance for the Mentally Ill (NAMI), to take one example, tend to make long-term commitments to their organization. As a result, they have developed impressive state and national advocacy programs. At the state and national levels, they maintain a media watch program to root out stigmatizing references to the mentally ill. They also have successfully elicited the active support of state and national legislators. Still further, they have formed a sister research organization, The National Alliance for Research on Schizophrenia and Depression (NARSAD). All in all, with some 550 local affiliate organizations (as of March 1986), NAMI bids fair to become the mental illness counterpart of the Association for Retarded Citizens (ARC). It remains to be seen where the balance between support and advocacy activities will be set locally. Nonetheless, the foundation for much of this work is the continuing need of their relatives for assistance. They need help to obtain food, clothing, and housing; they need supervision and protection, as well as health care, legal services, and suitable employment. As long as these needs persist, significant others will also benefit from banding together to identify and exchange resources and to advocate for the more adequate provision of these resources.

Disadvantages of Minorities

Many organizations, such as NAMI and ARC, attract competent upper-middle-class persons. Unintentionally, the participation of these socially advantaged people may seem rather forbidding to low-income persons, particularly if they are also of color. The situation may be further complicated by the feeling, which a black member expressed: "We're also afraid to let 'the man' see that we have so many problems." This fear adds to the already existing obstacle of a culturally different, possibly biased group. A solution to this problem is, unfortunately, often not available. The formation of culturally homogeneous chapters is often not feasible, since there are so few minority members to "seed" dedicated chapters. This strategy, it will be remembered, worked best in attracting ethnic minorities in densely populated minority areas. The tragedy is that the needs of minorities are at least as great as the needs of members of the majority culture.

Recognizing this problem, NAMI took a survey and found the expected—too little participation by minorities. They also found some exceptions, and the following excerpt from the *NAMI Newsletter* indicates how the organization hopes to use these exceptions to achieve a higher level of minority participation:

> A small percentage of affiliates reporting moderate to good minority participation did respond positively to minorities assuming leadership roles in groups. Leadership roles ranged from being board members, committee members, speakers, and vice-presidents. In two cases, Threshold (Washington, DC) and Friends United to Help the Mentally Ill (Brooklyn, NY), the minority member served as president of the group. Positive outreach efforts were more likely from this small group of affiliates.
>
> The Ethnic Minority Concerns Committee of NAMI, formed in part to address the meager participation of minorities in AMI groups, will solicit support and input from affiliates reporting successful minority outreach efforts. A planned brochure by the Committee will become one vehicle to assist other affiliates in duplicating successful outreach efforts in their respective communities, such as New York City. The intent here is not to offer another high-pitched exhortation, but rather to suggest that the lack of minorities should not be dismissed as a matter of individual choice and responsibility. It needs to become part of the major agenda item for these organizations.[8]

NORMALIZATION POTENTIAL

It is customary nowadays to look for childhood causes when individuals behave in a troublesome manner. The assumption is they were "brought up to it." This reflex is reinforced by earnest, well-meaning professionals who become frustrated by the lack of progress of clients in therapy. When the therapeutic plan isn't working, a self-esteem-saving explanation is tempting. And the nearest one is the family, and thus the witch will be found. The pursuit of these villains may also comfort the troubled family member. It's always better to have the finger pointing in the other direction. However, it is dysfunctional when professionals lend credence to this simplistic lay bias and thereby add to the burden of significant other families. Professionals must counter this bias, if they are to be supportive, instead of adding to it.

But whatever the inclination of the professional, the significant other self-help organizations are now prepared to insist that the rights of families be respected. Belatedly, these families refuse to allow themselves and their needs to be discredited. Families must not automatically be considered patients. And though families should be expected to be supportive, significant others must not be a target for troubled family members and human service professionals. Most importantly, the efforts of besieged families to return to normalcy must not be interfered with. This means that it may be necessary to constrain troubled members legally and to compel community agents to protect the rights of the families. Strong measures may be required, but they must not be shrunk from, since the alternatives are even worse; before families can take care of others, they must be able to take care of themselves.

Families Anonymous, though it describes itself as *A KIND OF QUIET COUNTER CULTURE*, seems to shout in its brochure, as the following reveals:

> It's high time you lost your guilt feelings. . . . It's high time you realized that the drug abuser in your family must take on the responsibility for his own actions. It's high time you realized that other people's escape patterns are affecting *you*.
>
> It's time you showed your normalcy by living your own life. For the sake of yourself and the other members of your family, decide NOW to be the best sister, brother, father, mother, uncle, aunt, or grandparent you can be.
>
> Don't just sit there, getting up-tight, and ruining your own life and that of those you're concerned about. Get constructively involved. Come and talk with the rest of us who are working in this area. You'll get some new ideas of what "helping" really means.
>
> There are no fees, no community funding, no last names used.
>
> COME AND TALK IT OVER[9]

As significant others confront the blame issue full front, they are less likely to cover up and, in the idiom of some organizations, less likely to "enable" the person in his or her pathology. And as significant others change, a new environment is created within which the troubled individual may alter his or her behavior. It should never be assumed that troublesome individuals are unresponsive to their families.

RELATIONSHIP TO PROFESSIONALS

Conflicts

Assigning blame, which can masquerade as assessing the dynamics, has considerable appeal for many professionals. Too few, however, realize how seriously it undermines their effectiveness with significant others. The Yorks' comment:

> Blame can be a lot of fun and very creative. It keeps us busy with the illusion of knowing the cause of something so we really don't have to accomplish anything productive. Focusing on an illusion is a sure-fire way not to solve the problem.[10]

Later in their book, the Yorks recall their own mistakes as professionals:

> As family therapists we were also very good at blame. Implicit in our method was blame for parents. Of course we never said that we were blaming parents, but that's exactly what we did. We sincerely hope our earliest clients survived us, but if it's any consolation to them we found ourselves in their shoes and the change of role helped us realize what we had been doing.[11]

And this is how they changed:

> The way in which we therapists blame is by thinking and acting as if the children in the family are victims of their parents' anomalies. As long as parents are accepting the rap for their offsprings' behavior their children can't change. We are now aware of the power of "victims." When an unruly youth says to us, "My mother hated me, my father never paid attention to me, my uncle exposed himself to me," regardless of whether the accusations are true or not, first we show some empathy and then we ask the question, "And how do you get revenge?"[12]

Insofar as professionals espouse the Yorks' early position rather than their later one, they will embitter significant others. One member of Families Anonymous recalled that when a professional social worker was introduced at one of their open meetings, she walked out. She could not stand being in the same room with someone who personified the humiliation she had experienced at the hands of another social worker. And yet this story was followed by another about a professional whom she held in high regard. She could not praise too much the psychiatrist who had befriended her chapter. And yet her positive attitude toward this professional did little to raise her opinion of other professionals.

Professionals seem to be concerned that parents and significant others will be encouraged by self-help organizations to walk away from their responsibilities. They think the pendulum may swing too far. Possibly, but it should be more widely recognized that members of these organizations tend to be veritable models of responsibility. Furthermore, people need to recognize that there are no Solomons to set standards against which others can be judged. Balancing the interests of the family against those of the troubled person is not scientific. The problem is further complicated by the belief held by some that the troubled person as a family member has an irrevocable right to subsistence care. For these reasons, no presumption is made that these interests can be easily reconciled. It is only presumed that it will be worse if one of the parties is not seen as having a legitimate interest.

Contributions of Professionals

Many professionals are increasingly prepared to recognize that self-help organizations can be an answer to the pressures felt by families with troubled relatives. They appreciate that these organizations have an important role to play in ameliorating stigma. A study of social workers in upper New York State, for example, showed that 49 percent felt that self-help organizations played an important role in combating stigma.[13]

Starting with similar assumptions, many professionals have helped start new chapters and have also supported chapters in public forums. The work of NAMI has been praised by E. Fuller Torrey, a prominent psychiatrist. His support, and that of other leading professionals, has led to a number of mutually beneficial arrangements. In this instance, NAMI has become one of the distributors of Torrey's valuable book.[14] But however useful professionals are as catalysts, they must be prepared to "back off soon." They simply cannot expect to be permanent mainstays or guiding forces. The growth of these significant other organizations must not be hampered by a dependence on professionals. Only by themselves can these significant others affirm their legitimate rights, uncompromised by others, whether they be disturbed family members or professionals. Thus, it should be expected that they will want to negotiate or bargain with professionals rather than automatically assent to professional initiatives, no matter how well meaning. This stance is consistent with the view that all parties in the system have distinct, though admittedly overlapping, interests. Thus, it may seem advantageous to make arrangements a matter of contract rather than informal agreement. Many of these families still boil with anger when they recall how they sought to escape blame by ingratiating themselves, and by accepting inhuman burdens, at the behest of guilt-inducing professionals and official caretakers. No more!

Notes

1. B. H. Gottlieb, "Mutual-Help Groups: Members' Views of Their Benefits and of Roles for Professionals," *Prevention in Human Services*, 1 (Spring 1982), pp. 55–67.
2. Al-Anon, *Al-Anon Faces Alcoholism* (New York: Cornwall Press, 1965); Al-Anon, *Al-Anon's Twelve Steps and Twelve Traditions* (New York: Al-Anon Family Group Headquarters, 1981); and Lois W., *Lois Remembers* (New York: Al-Anon Family Group Headquarters, 1979).
3. *NAMI Newsletter* (Washington, D.C.), 7 (February 1986), p. 6.
4. R. Moroney, *Families, Social Services, and Social Policy: The Issue of Shared Responsibility*, Publication No. [ADM] 80-846 (Washington, D.C.: U.S. Government Printing Office, 1980).
5. L. I. Stein and M. A. Test, "Community Treatment of the Young Adult Patient," in B. Pepper and H. Ryglewicz, eds., *New Directions for Mental Health Services: The Young Adult Chronic Patient*, Vol. 14 (San Francisco: Jossey-Bass, 1982), pp. 61–62.
6. P. York, D. York, and T. Wachtel, *Toughlove* (Garden City, N.Y.: Doubleday & Co., 1982), pp. 10–11.
7. Ibid., pp. 111–123.
8. *NAMI Newsletter* (Washington, D.C.), 6 (June 1985), p. 3.
9. Families Anonymous, *A KIND OF QUIET COUNTER CULTURE*, Announcement (s14) (Van Nuys, Calif.: FA, undated).
10. York, York, and Wachtel, *Toughlove*, p. 56.
11. Ibid.
12. Ibid., p. 60.
13. R. W. Toseland and L. Hacker, "Social Workers' Use of Self-Help Groups as a Resource for Clients," *Social Work*, 30 (May–June 1985), pp. 232–239.
14. E. F. Torrey, *Surviving Schizophrenia: A Family Manual* (New York: Harper & Row, 1983).

13

Physical Handicap Organizations

Physical handicap organizations represent nearly every major chronic disease or condition. Some are for people with conditions that are relatively stable, some are for conditions that are likely to get worse, and some for terminal illnesses.

A list of such organizations would include Make Today Count (for the terminally ill and their families), United Ostomy Association (for people with surgically created body openings or stomas), Emphysema Anonymous, Lost Chord Clubs (for those who have had laryngectomies), Stroke Clubs, Mended Hearts (for those who have undergone open-heart surgery), Spina Bifida Association, Lupus Foundation, Deafpride, Self-Help for Hard of Hearing People, Epilepsy Foundation, National Foundation for Ileitis and Colitis, Endometriosis Association, Cerebral Palsy Association, and Alzheimer's Disease and Related Disorders Association (ADRDA).

There are also a number of self-help organizations for such inherited blood disorders as sickle cell anemia and hemophilia. They are linked to the National Association for Sickle Cell Disease, Inc., and the National Hemophilia Foundation.

Two other diseases, herpes and AIDS, seem likely to give rise to increasingly numerous, more formally structured self-help organizations.

Table 8 (p. 233) lists the major dimensions of physical handicap organizations discussed in this chapter.

Table 8.
Properties of Physical Handicap Organizations

Exemplar Organizations
Make Today Count; United Ostomy Association; Emphysema
Anonymous; Stroke Clubs; Mended Hearts; Cerebral Palsy
Association; Lost Chord Clubs; Spina Bifida Association; Lupus
Foundation; Deafpride; Self-Help for Hard of Hearing People;
Epilepsy Foundation; National Foundation for Ileitis and Colitis;
Endometriosis Association; Emerging herpes and AIDS groups

Public Image
Fast-growing organizations
Major diseases represented
Cooperative orientation
High public acceptance
Complements medical technology
Distinctive function
Rehabilitation rather than cure
Disadvantaged underrepresented

Goals
Disease-specific, adaptational goals
Lifestyle issues related to work, travel, self-reliance, social
and sexual attractiveness
Technical issues: prostheses, appliances, diet, scientific
developments

Technology
Processes: inspiration, reinforcement, modeling, information-
communication, encouragement, behavioral monitoring
Procedures: hospital visitation, individual and group
discussion, newsletters, pen pals

Career Pattern
Long term but varying in intensity
Pay back through direct helping of others and performing
organizational roles
Tribute funds and legacies continue the payback

Normalization Potential[a]
Competent models participate in the community in spite of
handicap+
Preoccupation with handicapo

Relationship to Professionals
Complementary and distinctive
Recognizes interdependence
Cooperative and reciprocal

---

[a] +, positive; o, negative.

PUBLIC IMAGE

Context of Growth

There are many demographic and cost reasons why these organizations are growing in number and importance. The percentage of the population with chronic conditions increases as the population ages. This fact, coupled with the declining mortality rates for many chronic conditions, enlarges the pool of people eligible for these organizations. The pool is further enlarged by efforts to contain costs. Chronic conditions now account for more than half the cost of all medical care.[1] Programs to contain these costs, such as DRGs (Diagnostic Related Groups), provide further incentives to use self-help organizations as a means to limit the amount of service offered by professionals. Taken together, these factors are responsible for an exponential increase in the number of people using these self-help organizations.

Public Acceptance

Physical handicap organizations have achieved greater public acceptance than most other self-help organizations. Eligible individuals seem much less reticent to participate in these organizations—at least once the physical condition has been accepted emotionally and intellectually. Even when an allowance is made for the fact that many, perhaps even the majority, of those eligible do not affiliate, this type of self-help organization reaches more of its potential market than other types. This is partly because of the endorsement of health care providers. They not only say they like them, they also make referrals and make available substantial technical assistance. The general public, too, has a warm spot for members of these organizations. They are often selected for human interest stories and are held up as exemplars of indomitable courage and unflagging optimism. The less salubrious side is that occasionally they seem to be the text for a different lesson: Nonhandicapped people are not entitled to complain or feel unjustly treated. But whatever the reasons for this enviable level of acceptance, it would be misleading to assume that handicapped people have always been accepted or that they are now universally accepted.

The position of these organizations is enviable only in comparison with that of other types of self-help organizations. Conflict and opposition are an ever-present reality, as members and supportive health professionals can attest. Many supporters of self-help organizations still rankle from run-ins with physicians, nurses, and administrators over whether it is appropriate to form local chapters or to cooperate (listing patients' names, arranging for visiting privileges, providing office space, etc.) with established self-help organizations. Should these negative experiences not be acknowledged, those who are veterans of the struggles might be tempted to write-off this optimistic account as unredeemably naïve. But recognizing that relations have not always been smooth, one should also recognize that other types of self-help organizations have a long way to go to match these organizations in terms of their relations with professionals.[2]

Sponsorship by National Foundations

Self-help organizations for the physically handicapped are also unique in that some of them are sponsored by large health foundations. Though this relationship has occasionally been stressful for both sides, these self-help organizations have, for the most part, maintained their autonomy. At the same time, they have benefited from their sponsorship by such organizations as the American Cancer Society and the American Heart Association and by cooperative arrangements with local hospitals. These alignments, along with endorsements by the health professions, are part of the extensive involvement of professionals in the programs. And though there is often conflict over turf and hegemony, these self-help organizations by and large seem to have avoided damaging compromises. This happy arrangement is largely attributable to the clarity of professional health care roles and the capacity of the self-help system to contribute in a noncompetitive way.

Limits of Professional Care

Organizations for the physically handicapped flourish because it is generally agreed that professional-technical care can go only so far in helping people with many physical diseases and conditions. Gussow and Tracy weighed this factor heavily in their explanation of the formation of these self-help organizations:

> [They] tend to form around conditions for which there is no medical cure beyond that for acute phases (this alone may account for the fact that the major infectious diseases are not represented by any self-help group), where there is a residue of chronic impairment, where problematic medical, social and psychological effects remain, and where survival beyond the acute phase entails disability. Further, and perhaps most important, these are conditions for which a viable life style is often possible when appropriate rehabilitative procedures are followed.[3]

Price of Professional Endorsement

The restrictions that accompany professional endorsement are not without cost, and some of them may even be self-imposed. It is as if they were imposed in anticipation of any possible professional criticism. Some organizations, such as Reach to Recovery and Mended Hearts, will not make an initial visit without a physician's referral. Furthermore, members must not discuss the merits of various treatment or the qualifications of practitioners. And yet as informed people, they are not unaware of the issues surrounding the relative merits of various kinds of surgery and therapy. Other organizations, however, are more willing to take stands and to disseminate information about such matters as the proper use of inhalants in emphysema, the best brands of enterostomal appliances, or the role of cognitive approaches in cancer treatment. They, too, recognize the ever-present threat of quackery, but they seem to think that it is not necessary to avoid tension between self-help organizations and medical personnel totally. They also use a number of ways to control abuses, including humor: A cartoon that appeared in *Batting the Breeze* (Fall 1983), the newsletter of Emphysema Anonymous, depicts a doctor's waiting room, in which a large sign states the following message: "Notice to All, Patients, Please do not prescribe for each other."

Apart from possibly underestimating the amount of conflict between professional and and self-help caregivers, this analysis of their relationship must address the fact that functional analyses are inclined to support the status quo; they may encourage timidity at a time when temerity is needed. Checkoway and Blum discuss this point in their engaging paper "Self-Help in Health Care: Good, But Not Good Enough."[4] They caution that there is a danger of marrying conservative politics to self-help ideologies. The upshot may be a retreat from social responsibility and social causation. If problems have their source in the social order, they need to be addressed in that context, not by self-help. And similarly, when problems are traceable to deficient professional organizations and performance, they should be addressed in that context. Self-help organizations for the physically disabled must refuse to "cool out" patients dissatisfied with their professional caregivers. These self-help organizations, however, can serve as a forum for expressions of discontent, which can be used in a campaign to change professional practices. Self-help organizations must not surrender the right to bargain and to protest as necessary for improvement of the health care system for their various constituencies.

Minority Self-Help vs. Professional Services

Too much dependence on self-help may have negative consequences for disadvantaged members of society. Minorities in particular tend to participate even less in these self-help organizations than they do in publicly supported, professionally administered agencies. In public agencies, at least, everyone recognizes that the force of law stands behind equal entitlement to services. Hence, proposals to replace professional services with self-help, particularly when they spring from a conservative political ideology, must be rejected. To adopt them would cause the most suffering among the poor, the minorities, and the socially disadvantaged. But self-help organizations must redouble their efforts to reach beyond the "middle class," since their goals are as relevant to minorities as to nonminorities. This need was evident at the National Conference on Self-Help Groups for Genetic Blood Disorders, which took place in Washington, D.C., June 24–26, 1984. Organized by Dorothy O. Blackburn Jefferson and Kermit B. Nash and sponsored by the National Institutes of Health, this conference focused on a number of disorders, including hemophilia and Tay-Sachs disease. And because sickle cell concerns were also prominently featured, it attracted a large and enthusiastic group of black self-helpers. They, in turn, were able to help other groups think about how paid coordinators might be employed along with volunteer helpers. The main point, however, is that it demonstrated once again the potential of self-help to engage minorities, given that the proper supportive circumstances are in existence.

GOALS

Specific, Adaptive, Supportive

The disease- or condition-specific goals of self-help organizations for the physically handicapped are an important factor in the public's understanding and support. Although these organizations deal with many areas, for example, health care services, education, and leisure-time opportunities, they seek only changes related to the common disease or condition. This specificity is responsible for much of the legitimacy and acceptance enjoyed by these organizations in both the general and the health care communities.

Another aspect of these goals is that adaptation after the acute medical situation has stabilized is an important focus. The   *237* self-help organization usually enters after the condition has been diagnosed and the appropriate technical treatments have been initiated. At this point, the self-help organization becomes a major force in promoting the person's adaptation within the parameters of his or her condition or illness. These goals are fundamentally behavioral, not medical. The latter province belongs to health care professionals. Notwithstanding the earlier reservations about too much cooperation between self-help organizations and professionals, functioning is facilitated when self-help begins where professional health care leaves off.

The gradually increasing importance of self-help has little, if anything, to do with deficiencies in professional services; rather, the aims of self-helpers lie in other areas. Though it can be said professionals are not well versed in these areas, they must not be criticized for failing to perform tasks they did not agree to perform. Furthermore, if professionals regularly functioned in areas beyond their expertise, they would jeopardize their primary functions. Gastroenterological surgeons could compromise their medical effectiveness by attempting to become the patient's major source of emotional support. In any case, they have less credibility than another person who is coping with the illness and leading a meaningful life. How can such a surgeon possibly match a member of an ostomy group who put it this way: "Patients want to be reassured they will experience comfort, dependability and be sexually attractive and able to have children if that is their choice. And if they want proof, I tell them, just give me a call." This is the kind of realistic hope and emotional support that is the special province of handicapped peer helpers to provide to others with the condition.

The urgent need for their support comes through in the following passage from a pamphlet published by the International Association of Laryngectomees:

THE PSYCHOLOGICAL IMPACT

A person who is newly laryngectomized undergoes a tremendous emotional shock, as does his family. The loss of voice and possibly the means of livelihood, the altered social conditions and physical limitations may combine to cause overwhelming despair in the patient and the members of his family. Even the patient who is well prepared in advance in proper instruction and advice sustains a blow and threat to his security and balance that only can be fully understood by one who has had the experience himself. At this time the patient needs all the support, understanding, patience and help that can be given. The family needs help in understanding what has happened, and what to do in the future.[5]

Self-Concept, Lifestyle, and Self-Care

Such traumas as spinal cord injury, breast surgery, ileostomy, and laryngectomy force a reassessment of one's body image, self-concept, lifestyle, and plans for self-care. The impact of the shock is likely to change one's self-concept totally. In the aftermath, profound depression and immobilization—or often their close relation, massive denial—may appear. To reach people in these overwhelmed states, it is a tremendous advantage to have credentials that include personal experience with the trauma. With this kind of referent power, it is possible to be both caring and demanding. One can be empathic and yet insist on performance. The handicapped person's new self-concept needs to be modified to make competence compatible with his or her physical condition. And eventually, with the aid of the self-help organization, many handicapped persons will come to think of themselves as being "differently abled" individuals rather than as being disabled individuals.[6]

The choices and constraints associated with lifestyle continually challenge the handicapped. To what extent will the individual choose to be identified as handicapped? How will the individual deal with a range of challenges, from the highly observable matter of finding a job to the very private matter of achieving sexual fulfillment? How will the handicapped person deal with such issues as building accessibility, transportation difficulties, and the lack of choice on restaurant menus? These are just some of the challenges facing the handicapped that can be discussed in the forums provided by self-help organizations for the physically disabled. The self-help forum can have a preeminent role in facilitating the exchange of up-to-date detailed information about possible choices in meeting these challenges to handicapped persons.

Information, often of a technical nature, is also needed to attain self-care objectives. Though professionals establish the need for appliances and prostheses, they often encourage patients to seek the counsel of peers about the convenience, care, and cost of these devices. The need for exactly this kind of information has been cited as an important factor in the formation of a number of self-help groups, such as those for people with ileostomies.[7] Similarly, professionals may establish patients' dietary requirements, but other self-helpers may be the ones who can translate these requirements into everyday recipes and eating habits. In translating the professional prescription into a practical course of action, their assistance complements and goes beyond that offered by the professional.

TECHNOLOGY

Models and Monitoring

Modeling, which is an important component of self-help technology, promotes learning through direct, close, and sustained exposure to veteran-models who are coping successfully with similar conditions. Although it may take some time, newcomers eventually will be convinced that the models once struggled (and perhaps still do) with similar conditions. As this realization dawns, they will be inspired to emulate certain aspects of the models' behavior. This emulation can entail the selective imitation of several models. Through this method, the newcomer can learn different modes of adaptation from models who have made different choices about their lifestyles and are in different stages of adaptation (or recovery).

In this process, the learner monitors the model's behavior, or learning may result from a reversal of the modeling process, whereby the model keeps tabs on the learner's behavior. Gussow and Tracy have illustrated this process as follows:

> A considerable amount of behavior monitoring goes on in the interaction among club members—some of it highly visible and obtrusive like the open ridicule practiced by some obesity groups —but, in general, for most groups, it is discreet, low-level, watchful and protective. Members come to know something about the personality and life-styles of other members, their requirements, their habits, and their behavioral boundaries. "We don't hassle them," said one Mended Hearts member in talking about those known not to be taking proper care of themselves, "but we might kid them." At one meeting a member was observed to gently refuse another an extra cup of coffee, reminding him that he already had his quota for the day. Spouses are often in the best position to monitor the behavior of patients, which is one reason some clubs encourage their participation.[8]

Instruction

Members also learn from the direct instruction of these model-teachers. Through their own experience, organized according to the self-help ideology, these teachers have accumulated a fund of information that can be transmitted to the newcomer. And not just information is derived from experience, for it is usually accompanied by a remarkably effective instructional style. The referent power they have acquired as a result of this experience makes it possible for them to insist as well as to encourage. This generous insistence is illustrated in Gussow and Tracy's account of the drills used by veterans to teach a new member the techniques of esophageal speech. How can one resist such instruction:

> They worked with one man at his home night after night prompting him "to say the same words over and over again, encouraging him to read the newspaper out loud with us," or when he really got upset and frustrated suggested he "go into another room by himself and practice there first and then come out and try it again." Recalcitrant patients often find it much more difficult to resist the overtures of club members who may initiate the help, offer it free, and provide companionship along with it, than to break appointments with a professional therapist or to resist the help of family and friends.[9]

Other Means of Communication

One-to-one relationships and small group discussions are supplemented by other means of communication to supply information and support to members. Telephone networks are common. Pen pal relationships are available to those with limited mobility or who simply like to write. Newsletters circulated by most organizations command an avid audience, who often mark favorite pieces for later study. These newsletters tend to include healthy doses of humor and inspiration, the latter often recounting how various members have inspired one another. In a different type of article, information is presented. Some articles may be quickly scanned, whereas others may be densely packed with content and require serious study. In this latter category, an article in *Batting the Breeze* (Summer 1983) provided detailed instructions on how to control housedust and other particulate material and irritants. It included technical information about how to alter the furnace and air-conditioning system to meet the special requirements of those who suffer from emphysema. Newsletters that carry these articles are likely to become an even more substantial resource as microcomputers and inexpensive software (e.g., Page Maker, Newsroom) become ever more widely accessible. Other valuable publications—brochures, booklets, and monographs—are issued irregularly. Both types of publications do much to enrich and codify the technology of the organization.

CAREER PATTERN

Options Abound

Because of improved professional care and self-care many members can expect to live significantly longer. This longevity is a *241* major factor contributing to the relatively long tenure, the multiple options, and the many changes of career that are available to members of these self-help organizations. Over the period of their long membership, handicapped individuals can choose from a number of mini-careers. The variety is greatest in autonomous organizations, those functioning without the active involvement of professionals. This fact is supported by the results of a survey of organizations for the parents of children with cancer. The researchers found that organizations without professionals were more likely to have by-laws, officers, and, in general, a more complex program.[10] Obviously, they must recruit people for these many challenging career opportunities.

With or without professionals, however, most organizations offer many challenging tasks. The organization must keep abreast of scientific matters, and those with the requisite interest may want to track research developments for the organization. Orientation sessions for families must be conducted, and members who desire more people involvement may make heavier investments in these areas. Some members prefer to work on a one-to-one basis with the distinctive concerns of individuals; others may relish the opportunity to work on programs that address the common needs of potentially large numbers of members. Still others will want to concentrate on such external activities as public education and lobbying. They might, for example, participate in a campaign to educate the public about the risks associated with elevated blood pressure or to fund programs to screen for hypertension.

Outside activities are an opportunity for members even in some of the least advocacy-minded organizations. Mended Hearts, for example, has noted:

> Our members take [an] active part in the annual heart fund drive of the American Heart Association, which is so important to heart research.
> We cooperate with other organizations in educational and research activities pertaining to heart illness.
> In these ways, we make contributions for the ultimate benefit of heart patients.[11]

These activities, which require members to go beyond the boundaries of their own organizations, may be gateways to community work. The political dimension of this work can be invoked by efforts to change the allocation of research funds. Some organizations strive to attain what they regard as their fair share of resources. Moreover, they want a say in deciding what kinds of investigations should be undertaken. To have their say, such organizations as the National Foundation for Ileitis and Colitis, Deafpride, and the Endometriosis Association expend much energy to influence the appropriations and research-allocations process. The development and maintenance of these and other social action programs is often a huge undertaking. Numerous volunteers—many who give of themselves in a manner that could not be expected of paid workers—are required. As recompense, however, these volunteers may be carving out permanently fulfilling careers for themselves.

Changes During a Career

Members have considerable latitude in deciding to what extent and where they will be active. Typically, most members will have periods of fairly intense and then not so intense involvement. A few, however, will be consistently involved in educating and supporting others, which can be a fulfilling activity. A larger number, perhaps, will participate in the organization as long as it helps them to go through a difficult transition. They do not wish to foster distinctive competencies or to be identified as handicapped. They simply wish to find alternate ways to accomplish what the nonhandicapped person accomplishes. Their long-range goal is to become free of the self-help organization; as they move toward this goal, the presence of the physically disabled in their social networks will become less important.

Member careers seem to follow a loose pattern: Early on, members tend to be involved in intensive direct service activities. Those who continue usually add an interest in program development or pursue more specialized direct service interests. A few may step outside their organization and become involved in Centers for Independent Living. These increasingly important agencies are a relatively new outlet for handicapped persons interested in a paid self-help career. They are particularly attractive because they can combine the stability of a paid organizational structure and the inspiration that is inherent in the self-help approach. It should be understood that the centers are unlikely ever to absorb more than a small percentage of eligible handicapped.

Thus, most handicapped will remain with their own self-help organizations. But many will alternate between periods of intense involvement and temporary withdrawal from the organization. Sooner or later, however, a great many will become determined to "pay back" the organization, to leave something behind. This wish can be fulfilled even in death. Members "give" insofar as they remember the self-help organization in their wills and encourage others to make memorial contributions or to develop projects in their names. As these and other tributes are publicized, *243* they make a nice point that the organization is a network of people who are both "givers and receivers."

NORMALIZATION POTENTIAL

Self-help organizations, it might be argued, encourage preoccupation with handicaps. They may encourage members to become obsessed with their handicaps, and they may rationalize and reinforce compulsive behavior. Further, they encourage an identity based on disability and on deviance and dissimilarity, rather than on similarities with "normal" people.

What these arguments fail to consider is that the organization's goal is to minimize the disability, not accentuate it, to expand, not restrict normal social functioning. Though this goal does not guarantee its achievement, most members are encouraged to believe they can do most of what nonhandicapped people do, if they make the necessary adjustments. This ability was illustrated in a story carried in *Batting the Breeze*, the newsletter of Emphysema Anonymous (Fall 1983). The writer discovered that he could enjoy a restaurant lunch if he began to prepare for it the night before. He described a systematic and unhurried plan that had him arriving at the restaurant a few minutes before his friends so that he could catch his breath and be ready for the fun with everyone.

Those who are concerned about the possible encouragement of morbid brooding may also overlook the light touch that characterizes many self-help organizations. Just because the condition is a "bummer," one isn't encouraged to cry about it, as this bit of parody from the National Foundation for Ileitis and Colitis suggested:

> Roses are red, and violets blue,
> Crohn's is the pits, and Colitis is too.
> Yes, we know it's a problem in spring as in summer;
> Just when we feel better, it strikes: What a bummer![12]

Neither is the message a stoical "learn to live with it" or "in spite of it," but rather it is an optimistic message "learn to live with it—well." And these are not empty words for they can be illustrated with real examples of what is possible, not just despite the "disability" but perhaps because of it. These examples can make one a believer in the aphorism that the devil is responsible for a lot of good. They also show that self-pity and nagging insecurity can be transformed into a secure, meaningful lifestyle, if one takes the opportunity.

RELATIONSHIP TO PROFESSIONALS

Harmonious Cooperation

More than any other self-help type of organization, organizations for the physically disabled engage in extensive, effective collaboration with health care professionals. They have no illusions about getting along without professionals, and yet they also insist that technical-professional intervention is rarely sufficient. The outcome of technical care often depends on the performance of intricate, time-consuming, energy-demanding self-care procedures. And to perform well, patients must be helped to deal with their stress constructively, a task in which self-help organizations can play an important role.[13]

Recognizing their interdependence with self-help organizations, some professionals have tried different ways of fostering this relationship. At one medical center, the social work department created a psychosocial task force to interface with self-help groups. This task force, made up of self-helpers along with a variety of hospital personnel, was charged with facilitating such relationships with self-help organizations as interaction between hospital treatment groups and self-help organizations, between outside self-help organizations and groups of eligible patients, and between advocacy organizations and interested patients and staff.[14]

Exceptions and Undercurrents

There are, however, numerous and highly publicized exceptions to the general pattern of harmony between self-help organizations and professionals. The Endometriosis Association (for women who suffer great pain because of the abnormal growth of uterine tissue) has been sharply critical of mistreatment by doctors.[15] Their outrage over the incompetence and insensitivity of professionals has found expression in public education programs and in campaigns to establish special clinics.

More often, criticism is not readily apparent on the surface, but detectable only as an undercurrent. Yet it cannot be ignored in collaborative relationships between self-helpers and professionals. Even in the health area, relationships between self-help organizations and professionals will be affected by complex cross-currents created by status striving, span of control, and personality considerations. Successful collaborators will always be looking ahead for the best line through the rapids and into calmer waters.

Overall Perspective

The exceptions notwithstanding, the health care setting already supports a good deal of interaction between self-helpers and health care providers. In their study of hospital social workers, Black and Drachman found the level of support higher in the medical services than in the psychiatric services.[16] Furthermore, more than 60 percent of the social workers were already making occasional or frequent referrals to these groups, and a sizable number of social workers consulted with or served on the advisory bodies of self-help groups. And the bottom line is that more than 79 percent of the social workers making referrals felt that the groups were helpful.

Chesler and Yoak developed a useful conceptual model in their studies of groups for parents of children with cancer, a model that can be generalized to other diseases and conditions.[16] They noted that self-help organizations can ameliorate stress in five different categories: intellectual, instrumental, interpersonal, emotional, and existential. They provide intellectual help by furnishing technical information. They provide instrumental help by helping patients complete newly emerged, concrete tasks. They provide interpersonal help by promoting interaction and meaningful relationships. They provide affective help through comforting interactions. And last, they provide existential help by facing, with the patient, the ultimate question: "Why me?" In short, these might be considered among the most important reasons professionals might want to engage in collaborative projects with self-helpers.

Notes

1. R. N. Butler et al., "Self-Care, Self-Help, and the Elderly," *International Journal of Aging and Human Development*, 10, No. 1 (1979), pp. 95–119.
2. T. J. Powell and G. P. Miller, "Self-Help Groups as a Source of Support for the Chronically Mentally Ill," in H. Fishman, ed., *Creativity and Innovation* (Davis, Calif.: Pyramid Systems, 1982), pp. 243–254.
3. Z. Gussow and G. S. Tracy, "The Role of Self-Help Clubs in Adaptation to Chronic Illness and Disability," *Social Science and Medicine*, 10 (July–August 1976), pp. 407–408.
4. B. Checkoway and S. Blum, "Self-Help in Health Care: Good, But Not Good Enough," *Citizen Participation*, 3 (January–February 1982), pp. 17–19.
5. *Rehabilitating Laryngectomees*, 60-6R-50M-12/71-NO.4506-PS (New York: International Association of Laryngectomees, undated), p. 4.

6. Some feel the term "handicapper" rather than "handicapped person" has more postiive, potentially less stigmatizing overtones. Local use should be attuned to prevailing connotations. In many situations the author prefers the term "handicapper."

7. E. Lenneberg and J. L. Rowbotham, *The Ileostomy Patient* (Springfield, Ill.: Charles C Thomas, Publisher, 1970).

8. Gussow and Tracy, "The Role of Self-Help Clubs in Adapting to Chronic Illness and Disability," p. 411.

9. Ibid.

10. M. Chesler, O. Barbarin, and J. Sebo-Stein, "Patterns of Participation in a Self-Help Group for Parents of Children with Cancer," *Journal of Psychosocial Oncology,* 2 (Fall–Winter 1984), pp. 41–64.

11. Mended Hearts, *Heart To Heart* (Boston: Mended Hearts, undated).

12. "Prose from John Wengraf," *National Foundation for Ileitis and Colitis Newsletter* (New York, N.Y.), (January 1985), p. 4.

13. C. A. Roy and E. Atcherson, "Peer Support for Renal Patients: The Patient Visitor Program," *Health and Social Work,* 8 (Winter 1983), pp. 52–56.

14. A. Lurie and L. Shulman, "The Professional Connection with Self-Help Groups in Health Care Settings," *Social Work in Health Care,* 8 (Summer 1983), pp. 69–77. Thus, in general, it can be said that health care professionals recognize the importance of self-help organizations as a complementary resource.

15. "Victims Band Together," *Newsweek,* July 15, 1985, p. 62.

16. R. B. Black and D. Drachman, "Hospital Social Workers and Self-Help Groups," *Health and Social Work,* 10 (Spring 1985), pp. 95–103.

17. M. A. Chesler and M. Yoak, "Self-Help Groups as Social Experiments: The Case of Families of Children with Cancer," *In Search of the Rules of the New Games* (Holte, Denmark: Scandinavian Seminar College, 1984), pp. 104–115.

PART FIVE

Professional Relationships with Self-Help Organizations

Few topics evoke as many differences of opinion as relationships between self-help organizations and professionals. The truths of one side are contradicted by the other side. It is not surprising that neither side is keen about empirical evaluation, as is evident by such questions as "Why evaluate when, in the long run, and by definition, self-help groups can only perpetuate a negative identity?" and "How can our program be evaluated by anyone except those of us who have experienced its benefits?" A few self-help leaders go further in opposing any cooperation with professionals: Subversion and co-optation of the self-help movement are the only possible outcomes of such cooperation. Other self-help leaders claim that self-help organizations can thrive only with the full cooperation of professionals and that the shortcomings of self-helpers are largely the result of a lack of professional support.

Self-help leaders, however, are not the only extremists.[1] Scoffing professionals insist that self-help activities are unpredictable and dangerous, and they involve themselves only to warn their clients and the general public about the dangers of self-help. The irony is that these extremists overlook the fact that members of self-help organizations use professional services more often than do nonmembers.[2] Though members more often become clients, they do not use professional services for as long a period as those who are not members—presumably because of the support of their self-help organizations.[3]

At the other extreme are professionals who romanticize the value of self-help activities, seeing them as a panacea for all problems. In suggesting that the main job of professionals is to link people with self-help modalities, such professionals sometimes seem to be reluctant to engage in close relationships. Speculation aside, however, extremist self-helpers do a disservice to prospective clients of professionals by depreciating professional help. Unfortunately, the extremists are responsible for mischief beyond both their numbers and the merits of their arguments. They have held back self-help members who otherwise would have sought complementary professional help. Members who sought such help anyway have been made to feel disloyal, and they often think less of their own self-help organization as a result. "Badmouthing" by either side damages both the self-help and the professional counseling experiences of the help-seeker. It also affects self-help leaders and professionals, who are discouraged from recommending these complementary resources to their clients and peers because they fear their colleagues' disapproval.

EMPIRICAL STUDIES

In view of the harm of such extreme opinions, it is important to examine the empirical studies of the nature and effects of these relationships, *251* on which the discussion of relationships between professionals and self-help organizations depends. Thus, the last three chapters of the book cover referral, consultation, and organizational development activities.

Founding Self-Help Organizations

To begin, it may be useful to discuss a study that examined the role of professionals in the founding of self-help organizations. The anthropologist Borman began by assuming that large official associations, including human service and health care agencies, are not up to their task. To what extent, therefore, have professionals recognized this insufficiency and tried to compensate by establishing voluntary self-help associations?[4] To explore this question, he examined the role of professionals during the formative years of ten of the most important self-help organizations. In six of the ten studied (Recovery, Inc., Integrity Groups, GROW, The Compassionate Friends, Parents Anonymous, and Epilepsy Self-Help), Borman observed that professionals had a "key" role in their founding. In the remaining four (AA, Mended Hearts, NAIM, and Synanon), he observed that professionals had an "instrumental" role in the early developmental stages of these organizations. In every instance, then, professionals were influential during the formative years of the organization, helping to sustain these groups by their encouragement and advice. They also helped their fledgling organizations obtain public acceptance. These activities, however, took on an increasingly behind-the-scenes character as the organization matured, though the professionals continued their efforts to marshal the support of various professional groups. Public support, a highly valued function, continues to be offered by contemporary professionals.

Data from Self-Helpers

Focusing on a more recent period, Toseland and Hacker conducted a telephone survey of self-help leaders in upper New York State.[5] Their study is of particular interest because, unlike the majority of studies, self-helpers were the source of data. In these other studies of frequency of contact with, professional attitudes toward, and styles of interaction with self-help organizations, the findings were from the professionals' point of view. Hence, their findings may be misleading because evidence suggests that there are significant differences in the way self-help leaders and professionals perceive each other.[6]

The groups studied by Toseland and Hacker ranged from local chapters of well-established, large self-help organizations to small, detached support groups with no regional or national connections. Many of the latter groups will probably disappear after the original members depart. Nonetheless, the pattern of professional involvement seemed similar to what Borman found in his study of the major self-help organizations. In the upper New York State area, professionals were involved in the formation of 24 of the 43 groups (56 percent). In four groups, a team of two professionals were involved in the start-up phase. Consequently, a total of 28 professionals were involved in 43 units. In New Jersey, Madara and Grish found a comparable situation; professionals had helped start 31 of the 67 groups studied.[7] In terms of participation by different professional groups, Toseland and Hacker found that social workers (eight) were most highly involved, followed by clergy (five), teachers (five), nurses (four), psychologists (three), and physicians (three).

Data from Professionals

Since the formative period of a group is relatively brief and since the number and kind of professionals (probably more unconventional professionals) involved are limited, in terms of current impact, it is even more important to ask how rank-and-file human service professionals relate to contemporary self-help organizations. Levy pursued this question, using a mailed questionnaire to collect data from a national sample of community mental health professionals on their attitudes toward and involvement with self-help organizations.[8] Overall, the data showed that positive attitudes exist, but in the abstract. Attitudes were not expressed in action, and the discrepancies between attitude and action were striking: Some 84 percent of the respondents believed that the self-help organizations with which they were familiar—the average was between six and eight—were of at least average effectiveness. Some 47 percent of these professionals felt that self-help organizations could play an "important or very important potential role" in improving community mental health. Yet a majority never made (52 percent) or received (70 percent) referrals from self-help organizations. Moreover, 70 percent of the respondents rated the probability of integration between community mental health and self-help as either uncertain or low.

Consistent with the lack of involvement, the average community mental health professional had sufficient information to comment on only one-third of the 20 major self-help organizations listed, which may be attributable in part to the absence of chapters in their local communities. But even when positive attitudes and information were reported, they did not ensure collaboration. Information alone does not ensure that professionals will actively collaborate with local chapters. This discrepancy also is a reminder that the attention given to self-help organizations in the professional literature must not be interpreted as an indication of the availability of such services. The situation is similar to the widespread attention counseling receives in the popular and professional literature, even though access to these services is not widespread.

Five years after Levy's study, Miller's study of 296 social workers from Michigan supported the hypothesis that self-help organizations are being increasingly used.[9] Although his sample was from a single profession and a single state, as contrasted with Levy's multiprofessional national sample, he found among social workers a high level of interaction with self-help organizations. In some fields, social workers made heavy use of self-help organizations as part of their overall treatment program. Some 78 percent of all social workers made referrals to self-help organizations; in the areas of substance abuse and physical health, the percentage was even higher. This finding is consistent with the finding from the Black and Drachman study that 63 percent of hospital social workers made "frequent or occasional referrals to self-help organizations."[10] In Miller's study, only 1 percent of the respondents said they knew "nothing" about self-help organizations—a finding that is consistent with the findings of a later Toseland and Hacker study that reported that in northeastern New York State, 86 percent of social workers could name at least one self-help group in their area and 46 percent could name at least five groups.[11]

The Canadian Scene

Substantial use of self-help organizations was also found among Todres's multiprofessional sample from the Toronto area,[12] though, as Bender suggested, self-help organizations may always have been more prominent in Canada.[13] Todres's 308 respondents recognized an average of 16 self-help organizations from a list of 51. In Todres's study, which replicated the findings of Toseland and Hacker's 1982 study, social workers recognized more self-help organizations (21) than did other professional groups; nurses were almost as high (20), followed by psychiatrists (16.5), psychologists (13.8), and physicians (11.5).[14] Ninety percent of these professionals indicated that they made referrals to self-help organizations, but mainly to a handful of the most widely known ones. A surprisingly large percentage (43) of the respondents had been involved as speakers or consultants to self-help organizations. The Todres and the Madara and Grish data indicated that professionals are more commonly involved as speakers than as consultants or permanent resource persons.[15] Toseland and Hacker, in 1985, found these activities to be about equally ranked.[16] If the studies are combined, the data indicate that virtually all the professionals held favorable attitudes toward self-help organizations, a slightly smaller number made referrals, and considerably fewer were involved as speakers or consultants. These findings suggest that efforts to improve utilization must focus on action, since favorable attitudes are not enough to ensure utilization.

Limitations

These studies do not provide information about the quantity and quality of contacts; yet these dimensions are as important as, or even more important than, the percentage of professionals making an occasional referral or engaging in some loosely defined collaborative activity. The impact of the large number of professionals with marginal contact might easily be exceeded by a smaller number with more frequent, more intense, and higher-quality contacts. Thus, more attention must be paid to what is being done and how much and how well it is being done, not simply to how many are doing it. It also suggests that a subset of those professionals who have made a special investment in collaborative work with self-help organizations should be studied to develop information that would then be disseminated to the majority of professionals, who are only occasionally involved. This would build a body of knowledge about exemplary interactions with self-help organizations. Also, it may be necessary to rely increasingly on specialists because self-helpers may be less tolerant of unprepared professionals than was heretofore thought.

Dissatisfying Interactions

Studies also have suggested that self-help leaders perceive more problems in self-help–professional interactions than do professionals, and this problem may grow at least as fast as the number of professionals involved in self-help. Kurtz investigated this not-very-visible level of dissatisfaction among self-helpers.[17] She asked self-help leaders, by way of questionnaires and interviews, about their attitudes toward and interactions with professionals and compared their responses with the professionals with whom they were in contact. These responses of AA members and substance abuse professionals in several Georgia communities revealed that the professionals misjudged the satisfaction of AA members with their interactions. The AA members complained of infrequent contact, a lack of understanding about AA policies with respect to professionals, and the use of disapproved interventions in substance abuse programs, for example, medication. These responses contrasted sharply with the professionals' claim of good relations. On the positive side, the complaints by AA members suggested a desire for more effective collaborative relationships on the part of the professionals.

Toseland and Hacker's 1982 study suggested that the level of satisfaction may have been somewhat higher among self-help leaders in upstate New York, though a number of these leaders were also unhappy about the shortcomings and the inappropriate behavior of some professionals.[18] The difference in geography may be an artifact, however. Better established self-help organizations, such as the AA chapters in Kurtz's study, may expect more than organizations that are still trying to win community acceptance. In any event, the leaders of 72 percent of the self-help organizations considered one or more professionals a member or a regular participant. These leaders, including even the small number who opposed direct participation by professionals, all wanted referrals from professionals. And the self-help organization leaders who wanted contact with professionals judged most of them to be sincerely interested and willing to enter into less traditional, more egalitarian relationships. Yet tension was evident in Toseland and Hacker's extensive telephone interviews with self-help leaders. There were a number of complaints about professionals' disruptive visits and premature discontinuation of contact. Self-help leaders also criticized professionals for not familiarizing themselves with the workings of the group before assuming active roles in the group.

These findings suggest that professionals may be uneasy in their roles as learners, particularly with nonprofessionals. Perhaps familiarizing oneself with self-help operations and developing relationships with *255* members before taking action is thought to be inconsistent with the professional role. Self-help members did not see it that way, and they felt that professionals could benefit from more experience with the self-help setting, which would be more broadening than the counseling setting.

Surprising Positive Interactions

Most self-help organizations, however, even those most critical of human service organizations, do maintain some contact with professionals. Unconventional professionals have been chosen as confidants by some of the most militantly antiprofessional self-help organizations. This writer has observed cordial and effective relationships between carefully selected professionals and mental patient liberation groups, and a similar pattern has been observed between professionals and members of activist gay organizations. Thus, notwithstanding the validity of their criticism and their stridency in public, self-help organizations do work with professionals. Some self-help leaders who are highly critical of professionals in public will suggest, privately, that their members consider professional services, which demonstrates that they will work with professionals who are not put off by valid criticism. They do insist that professional assistance can, in some situations, critically affect a member's well-being.

Thus, there is firm ground on which programs of collaboration can be built, despite occasional misconceptions and tactlessness. Yet it must be understood that although favorable attitudes are necessary, they do not ensure contact, and that although contact is necessary for effective linkage, the two are not equivalent.

BENEFITS OF COLLABORATION

The benefits of collaboration can be conceptualized in terms of the organizational, reference group, social network, and social learning processes (Chapters Three through Six). Through collaboration, these processes can be both strengthened and made available to more people. Collaboration is also predicated on the assumption that the benefits of self-help organizations are in some measure distinct from those available from the informal support system and the professional psychotherapy system (Chapters Seven and Eight). It is further assumed that the benefits of the self-help organization can be lost through ill-considered actions of professionals. And last, benefits are assumed to vary, since they depend on specific circumstances and relationships. Thus, they can be degraded or enhanced by professional interventions.

Enhancement of the benefits of the self-help system is closely related to the system's integrity. The vulnerability of the self-help system is a primary consideration. The next three chapters assume that collaboration can enhance the integrity of the self-help system but also mandate careful assessments of the effects rather than the intentions of collaboration. Lest the risks appear one-sided, however, it should be noted that the powers of a self-help organization can atrophy through disuse. However, if the collaboration creates new capabilities, they are likely to be sustained after the departure of the professional. The self-help organization will incorporate them as part of its repertoire.

Each collaborative approach to be addressed in Part Five has a distinctive focus. Referrals, consultation about cases and programs, and organizational development and technical assistance services are discussed.

CONCERNS ABOUT TONE AND DIRECTION

Before discussing referrals, however, a possible misunderstanding should be anticipated. The stress on mutuality in dealing with self-help organizations may seem to contradict a tone that seems more aristocratic than democratic, and the proposed strategies may seem more unilateral than reciprocal. If it seems this way, it is an artifact of the writing process. Ideas and propositions lend themselves to linear presentation, whereas actual behavior is interactive and evolutionary. It is next to impossible to represent the countless transactions involved in mutual and reciprocal collaboration. Whichever side one begins on, it is difficult to describe the microtransactions that lead to a state of constructive interdependence. It can also be said that real-world examples of collaboration will seem less contrived and less full of themselves.

Notes

1. R. W. Toseland and L. Hacker, "Social Workers' Use of Self-Help Groups as a Resource for Clients," *Social Work*, 30 (May–June 1985), p. 232.
2. T. J. Powell, "Comparisons Between Self-Help Groups and Professional Services," *Social Casework: The Journal of Contemporary Social Work*, 60 (November 1979), pp. 562–564; N. R. Raiff, "Self-Help Participation and Quality of Life: A Study of the Staff of Recovery, Inc.," *Prevention in Human Services*, 1 (Spring 1982), pp. 79–89; M. A. Lieberman and G. A. Bond, "Women's Consciousness Raising as an Alternative to Psychotherapy," pp. 150–163, and E. A. Bankoff, "Widow Groups as an Alternative to Informal Social Support," pp. 189–193, in Lieberman and L. D. Borman, eds., *Self-Help Groups for Coping with Crisis: Origins, Members, Processes, and Impact* (San Francisco: Jossey-Bass, 1979).
3. Ibid.
4. L. D. Borman, "Characteristics of Development and Growth," in Lieberman and Borman, eds., *Self-Help Groups for Coping with Crisis*, pp. 13–42.
5. R. W. Toseland and L. Hacker, "Self-Help Groups and Professional Involvement," *Social Work*, 27 (July 1982), pp. 341–347.
6. L. F. Kurtz, "Linking Treatment Centers with Alcoholics Anonymous," *Social Work in Health Care*, 9 (Spring 1984), pp. 85–94.
7. E. J. Madara and C. Grish, "Finding Out More about How Self-Help Groups Help," *Network* (New Jersey Self-Help Clearinghouse), 1 (August–September 1981), p. 2.

8. L. H. Levy, "Self-Help Groups Viewed by Mental Health Professionals: A Survey and Comments," *American Journal of Community Psychology*, 6 (August 1978), pp. 305–313.

9. G. P. Miller, "Professionals' Knowledge of, Referrals to, Utilization of, Linkages with, and Attitudes Toward Self-Help Groups." Unpublished Ph.D. thesis, University of Michigan, 1983.

10. R. B. Black and D. Drachman, "Hospital Social Workers and Self-Help Groups," *Health and Social Work*, 10 (Spring 1985), pp. 95–103.

11. Toseland and Hacker, "Social Workers' Use of Self-Help Groups as a Resource for Clients," p. 234.

12. R. Todres, "Professional Attitudes, Awareness, and Use of Self-Help Groups," *Prevention in Human Services*, 1 (Spring 1982), pp. 91–98.

13. E. I. Bender, personal communication, Los Angeles, Calif., November 1985.

14. Todres, "Professional Attitudes, Awareness, and Use of Self-Help Groups"; and Toseland and Hacker, "Self-Help Groups and Professional Involvement."

15. Madara and Grish, "Finding Out More about How Self-Help Groups Help," p. 2.

16. Toseland and Hacker, "Social Workers' Use of Self-Help Groups as a Resource for Clients."

17. L. F. Kurtz, "Cooperation and Rivalry Between Helping Professionals and Members of AA," *Health and Social Work*, 10 (Spring 1985), pp. 104–112.

18. Toseland and Hacker, "Self-Help Groups and Professional Involvement," pp. 344–345.

14

Exchanging Referrals

Lest what follows suggests that self-help organizations have less opportunity to initiate interaction between themselves and professionals, it should be understood that the order in which the intervention principles and action strategies are discussed could be reversed. Instead of having described the professional as the initiator, the author could have so described the self-help leader as using similar principles and strategies to initiate interactions with professionals and professional organizations. Indeed, the reader is encouraged to pause and reflect on how these ideas might be applied in reverse, that is, how they could be adapted for use by self-help leaders. There are differences, however, so a section toward the end of the chapter will address the distinctive concerns of the self-help leader.

Another possible misunderstanding may be related to the term *professional*. Self-helpers are seen as holding professional positions, frequently positions that are more prestigious than those held by human service workers. Yet in their capacity as self-help members or leaders, they do not claim or rely on professional authority, but rather on the knowledge gained from their own and others' experiences. Their authority and knowledge are based on personal experience as interpreted through the constructs of the self-help organization, not professional study. It is this distinction, not work or prestige, that is the reference in discussions about the differences between professionals and self-help leaders. Unless this point is made abundantly clear, professionals will appear (and may be) intolerably ignorant and arrogant, and thus erect barriers to joint efforts. Assuming constant vigilance against these misunderstandings, one can now turn to a task that involves both the self-help leader and the professional. Both the self-help leader and the professional need to identify a set of relevant organizations with which they can explore the possibilities for collaboration.

IDENTIFYING RELEVANT ORGANIZATIONS

Family and Mental Health Agencies

Depending on their fields of practice, professionals will find some self-help organizations more relevant than others. Traditional family agencies and mental health clinics, for example, are apt to seek out self-help organizations that address the personal and family difficulties commonly encountered in such agencies. They have a natural affinity for such organizations as Parents Without Partners, Al-Anon, Parents Anonymous, and Families Anonymous. Mental health agencies offering service to clients with major affective disorders (recurrent depressive and manic-depressive episodes), to clients with chronic and disabling anxiety, or to clients impaired as the result of earlier psychotic episodes have a number of choices. They will want to consider the possible relevance of Recovery, Inc., Emotions Anonymous, and GROW, as well as numerous other smaller consumer/advocacy groups. Moreover, these service agencies have another important resource in organizations aimed at the general population, because these organizations can offer relevant and valuable "mainstream" experience to their clients. Organizations such as AA, Al-Anon, OA, and even PA help some of their members by shifting attention to more manageable problems—from a mysterious, all-encompassing problem to one that is more limited in scope and amenable to being understood. Best of all, this latter problem is one that the person can control as well, or as poorly, as anyone else. Focusing attention on such common problems tends to destigmatize the individual: "Now I'm just like everyone else struggling to lose weight." The mystery has been removed because the answers, or at least the essential ones, are in the "big book" and will be revealed "as I work the program." "Now I have as much chance to lick this thing as anyone else." Those who work with the relatives of long-term clients of the mental health system will find that many of them can benefit from family support groups or significant other organizations, a growing number of which are affiliated with the National Alliance for the Mentally Ill.

Chemical Dependency and Health

Agencies concerned with chemical dependency problems have a natural interface with a number of organizations: AA, Women for Sobriety, Narcotics Anonymous, Pills Anonymous, Alateen, and so forth. Because the use of self-help organizations is further along in substance abuse agencies, precedents have been established that other agencies and self-help organizations can build on. Alcoholics Anonymous and professional agencies have pioneered practices that have been adapted and used by other self-help organizations working with professional agencies. They were the first to hold self-help meetings on agency premises. They demonstrated that self-help members could be incorporated into the volunteer and paid staff of the agencies. They also demonstrated how the self-help perspective could contribute to the work of governing and advisory boards.

In the general health field, numerous organizations address specific physical conditions or diseases. Moreover, many habit disturbance organizations are relevant to people with health conditions. Many physical disorders are made worse by smoking or by eating and drinking problems. Emphysema Anonymous and TOPS exemplify such organizations. Oncology workers will profit from becoming familiar with Lost Chord Clubs, Reach to Recovery, and Make Today Count or with such grief-oriented organizations as The Compassionate Friends and Candlelighters. Workers might also consider starting local chapters of these organizations when they are not already present in the community. Gerontology workers can choose from a number of relevant organizations—some of which enroll the elderly themselves (Gray Panthers) and some the elderly's adult daughters and sons. Among the latter, a great upsurge in self-help activity has occurred among families of Alzheimer disease victims.

COMPLEMENTARITY OF SELF-HELP AND PROFESSIONAL RESOURCES

By design, both self-help and professional personal assistance systems focus on some things and not on others. Thus, quite aside from inevitable lapses in performance, some designs render these systems insufficient. Moreover, the general strengths and limitations of the systems may have little to do with how the systems are experienced by certain individuals. Consequently, even if it is possible to say that some forms of assistance are well suited to one type of person, they are not necessarily well suited   *261* to another type of person. Thus, for many people, then, the optimum approach will be a thoughtful combination of resources from all systems, including the informal caregiver system. This combination is recommended only because it is often imprudent to rely on only one system for assistance. Moreover, it needs to be more widely and fully understood that every organization, whether professional or self-help, cannot solve all the aspects of most problems. This limitation has often been recognized by self-help organization leaders. It is also germane to note, however, after Borman, who makes the point as part of his anthropological framework, that self-help organizations are themselves a response to insufficiencies within professional organizations.[1]

Sequencing Considerations

Participation in self-help organizations can come at different points in the help-seeking sequence. Concurrent participation in self-help and professional services will often be the optimum pattern, since the combination may be synergistic. The self-helper will be better for the concurrent therapy, which will be helped by the working through that goes on in the self-help organization. In some situations, however, it will be desirable for self-help to come before or after professional service. When it comes after, it may signify the client's improved level of functioning, though the support from a mutual-aid network may still be desirable. The pattern can also be misused, providing both the self-help leader and the therapist with an excuse to avoid working through termination feelings and concerns. Thus, as long as an apparent replacement is in the offing, the therapist and the client can tacitly conspire to avoid dealing with ending their relationship. Worse yet, therapists may be tempted to use self-help organizations as a means to slough off undesirable clients. In this case, a referral to self-help can be an antitherapeutic way of dealing with unresolved countertransference problems. In promoting self-help organizations, there is the danger that some professionals will use referral to a self-help organization as a ploy to reject their clients.

When the self-help member is seeking professional counseling in addition to or as a follow-up to self-help participation different considerations apply. This plan is often encouraged by self-help leaders when they feel a member is ready for therapy. The self-help experience may have modified an earlier hostility to professional assistance, or professional assistance may be less intimidating after a period of self-help experience. Again, professional services may be seen as a means "to move to a new level" or to concentrate on different issues. In all these permutations, participation in the self-help program may or may not continue in addition to therapy. And just as therapy can be terminated and self-help initiated for the wrong reasons, so too can therapy disrupt a coherent self-help experience and thus be undertaken unwisely. Professionals may need to counsel against terminating the self-help experience if that is the only condition under which therapy can begin. More typically, however, professionals will be able to provide a valuable service by helping their new clients reconcile their expectations of both helping systems.

The way in which this reconciliation might be done will vary, depending on whether the person is already a self-help participant or is thinking about becoming one. When the person is coming from a self-help experience, the benefits of professional assistance should be discussed in a vocabulary familiar to members of that particular self-help organization. When the person is "moving on," and not simply supplementing the self-help experience, there is an additional issue in that the professional must also address separation, loss, or graduation (the metaphor should best fit the client's life and self-help experience). In so doing, it will be necessary to strike a balance between images related to promotion and graduation and images related to termination and loss. In general, psychotherapeutic terminology should be used sparingly, except when the client is exploring the possibilities of self-help after an extensive period of psychotherapy.

Initiating Contact

Having considered how and at what point self-help organizations might be helpful to clients, one can pose the question: What means are available to professionals who wish to develop direct contacts with self-help organizations? An efficient way to begin is to ask colleagues about their contacts with self-help organizations. Despite incredulous looks, some positive contacts suitable for follow-up may surface. With these leads, the process will move faster because it is often easier to build on a contact than to seek a new one. In any case, the professional should not proceed without determining whether previous contacts were made and whether they were negative or led to misleading expectations. But even if earlier contacts were positive, it will be necessary to clarify the differences between past and present approaches. The timing and tone of the clarification must also convey proper respect for the earlier relationship. And when previous contacts were negative, emergency maneuvers may be required. There is often little leeway in timing; sooner or later the grievances of   *263* previous experiences will surface, and if allowed to follow their own course, they will often emerge at the most inconvenient times. Thus, it is well to anticipate them or to give some thought as to how they can be constructively dealt with when they do come up.

Another approach open to professionals who desire to initiate contact is to ask clients about their experiences with self-help organizations. (These are clients who, independent of the professional who now wishes to make contact, have become participants in self-help.) The suggestion to ask clients about these experiences should not be confused with the questionable practice of using clients to facilitate such contacts. It is inappropriate to ask a client to become an advance agent or stalking horse so that the professional can learn more about self-help organizations. But it would seem unduly scrupulous not to ask a client about self-help who has been, or perhaps even now is, a member of a self-help organization. Unless such questions are likely to be misinterpreted or to rouse incapacitating anxiety, clients can be asked about their experiences, including, if appropriate, the names of contact people. In fact, as long as the professional is candid about the purpose of the questions, this is a legitimate way to improve the client-therapist relationship.

Beyond Clients and Colleagues

Sometimes clients and co-workers with self-help experiences are not available. There are, however, some simple but valuable sources of information. Annual meetings sponsored by such professional and policy-development organizations as the National Council of Community Mental Health Centers, the American Orthopsychiatric Association, and the National Association of Social Workers usually attract several self-help organizations as exhibitors. To be sure, discussions with these exhibitors will be limited by the setting and the small number of self-help organizations represented. Yet they can be a surprisingly useful resource for learning about the beliefs, organizational arrangements, and practices of self-help organizations. Moreover, they may lead to unexpected results. One exhibitor, for example, graciously escorted the author to an open AA meeting in a city in which the author had no self-help contacts. Or often, exhibitors can identify contacts and provide printed materials that will be useful in the home community.

On return home, additional sources of information can be consulted. Telephone directories often list these organizations.

Many self-help organizations now provide—thanks to answering machines and "call forwarding" services—information and assistance on a 24-hour, seven-day-a-week basis. Newspapers publish "community calendar" sections that summarize the purpose and activities of local self-help organizations and indicate how they can be contacted or where they meet. Some human service organizations keep useful information about contact people and schedules of events for local self-help units on file. Self-help clearinghouses collect and disseminate information in a small but growing number of communities. They also offer technical assistance to self-help organizations and professionals, a topic that will be taken up in Chapter Sixteen. In most communities, however, there are less specialized coordinating and information-disseminating agencies, such as the United Way, information and referral agencies, and a Voluntary Action agency; these are good sources of information about the self-help network. Local community mental health and family agencies are also assuming more responsibility for this function.

Still another way to get started, especially if a particular self-help organization does not have a local chapter, is to consult the publications of such organizations as the National Self-Help Clearinghouse and the New Jersey Self-Help Clearinghouse for descriptions and addresses of the national offices of various self-help organizations.[2] When an immediate response or elaboration of printed information is required, national information centers can be contacted at the addresses and telephone numbers listed in Appendix Two.

CONVERTING CONTACTS INTO RELATIONSHIPS

Generous People

The local people who turn up as contact people usually prove to be deeply committed to making their organizations available to more people. How else can one account for their generous response of time and information? How else can one interpret their willingness to cooperate with professionals? Time and again, professionals have had to stand up and take notice as self-help members take time off from work, pay for child care, and make other sacrifices to proclaim the good news about their self-help organizations. This commitment is also evident in their responsiveness to requests for appointments, to telephone calls, and to requests for literature about their organizations. Given their high level of commitment, they are often quite willing to meet the professional on his or her turf. However, one should not take advantage of this willingness without considering the alternative. Professionals can show themselves to be more genuinely interested in mutuality if they make a sincere offer to meet on the self-helpers' home ground—except, of course, when that would be awkward for the self-helper.

A Possible Agenda

Once contact has been made, a way to share information and develop a relationship must be found. One way is to "mentally walk through" the experiences a new member is likely to encounter in his or her introduction to the self-help organization. The walk should be thought of as a leisurely, purposefully digressing conversation about who the new member is apt to meet and what is expected of the new member. The self-help contact person might also be encouraged to talk about some typical experiences of a new member. This conversation—if it goes well—might lead to a request that the contact person become the professional's mentor, since the professional will need continuing information about which program components are best suited to newcomers, and why. It is hoped, too, that the "walk through" will become one of those shared experiences that lead to a meaningful relationship.

FORMALIZING AND BROADENING RELATIONSHIPS

Even as preliminary "walk through" discussions are being held, it will be necessary to consider broadening the base of these contacts and obtaining formal sanction for ongoing relationships. Often this means involving other professionals, including those in decision-making roles, in the transactions. Parenthetically, a parallel initiative for self-help leaders who wish to develop relationships with professionals would be to involve other leaders in the local chapter or meeting. Careful attention should be given to the usual practices for sanctioning new initiatives. As the process unfolds, the sequence may lead from individual meetings between self-help leaders and staff members to more formal presentations by self-helpers to professionals. (The self-help counterpart might be to have the professional speak at a meeting, or if this would violate an important norm or tradition, to a few members informally.) A natural sequel to these activities might be the inclusion of self-help leaders on program committees or in staff development programs. This takes a "money-where-your-mouth-is" approach to demonstrate the willingness of professionals to learn from self-help leaders.

This initiative should not stop at agency walls. As workshops are conducted in the community, professionals should consider asking self-help leaders to assume significant training roles. The public nature of this activity points up the value of self-help organizations, especially when other professionals are being trained. In all these initiatives, the message will be seen as credible if the self-help role is a formal, substantial one. More formal meetings provide a forum to deliberate about important details of the partnership between professional and self-help leader.

"Give and Take"

Despite a successful start, or perhaps because of it, the professional must be prepared for a certain amount of playful teasing from self-help leaders. Though some put-downs may arise from their annoyance with present and past contacts with professionals, the dominant wish of the self-helpers may be to signal a new level of acceptance. This will be especially true when the "kidding" replaces false politeness. About now, self-help leaders may find it especially good fun to tease professionals about fees; they may "joke" about parity and announce they are considering charging for their expertise. The banter may go as far as playfully ridiculing the professional's lack of knowledge in an area. This tactic has often been developed to a high art with some professors. Aggressive lectures pour forth wherever ignorance has been detected. These jabs, though they may signal acceptance, also serve another useful purpose. Their sting is mild enough to be friendly but strong enough to remind the professional of the separate interests and goals of self-help members. Box 1 (p. 268) reviews the approaches a professional might take in learning more about self-help organizations.

LINKING CLIENTS TO SELF-HELP ORGANIZATIONS

Firsthand Familiarity

Like anyone contemplating a change, the client needs reassurance that the referral is appropriate. If the counselor can explain how the aims and practices of the self-help organization fit the needs and circumstances of the client, and if the counselor dis-

---

Box 1.

*Strategies for Professionals to Develop
Contacts with Self-Helpers*

1. Confer with colleagues.
2. Discuss the experiences of clients who have had prior contact with self-help organizations.
3. Consult the literature about self-help and professional collaboration, especially the brochures and reports produced by self-help organizations.
4. Review national directories of self-help organizations.
5. Consult local community calendars and listings of self-help organizations.
6. Seek out and confer with self-help leaders who work in similar areas to one's practice.
7. Invite self-help leaders to meet other professionals and make presentations in staff meetings.
8. Invite self-help leaders to serve on agency committees.
9. Invite self-helpers to share leadership roles in workshops with professionals.
10. Develop a "give and take" approach that allows for informality, playful teasing, and the appropriate expression of annoyance.

---

plays firsthand knowledge about the concrete details of the program, the client will most likely be reassured. This reassurance should be presented in such a way as to encourage the client to reflect on some precontact apprehensions and to help him or her determine what he or she wishes to learn from a first contact with the self-help organization.

The device of a "mental walk through" can also be useful for a client. The "walk through" presumes that a guide will be useful in the help-seeker's early encounters within a self-help organization. Newcomers face a multicomponent program, and even if it were desirable to participate in all the components, time requirements would make such participation physically impossible for most people. Hence, new members need information about which components it might be best to try first. This information will also minimize the risk associated with participation.

Newcomers need to be helped to determine their own personal benefit/risk ratio for the activities of the organization. Moreover, though the individual's ratio for particular components may be highly idiosyncratic, there may be a pattern in that certain kinds of stress may be associated with some components and not with others. A knowledge of these patterns may be especially important for newcomers, since prospective members are likely to be especially vulnerable. The risk is further heightened by their not knowing what is normative behavior in these circumstances. Aware of the different potentials of these components, many organizations advise new members to participate selectively. Parents Without Partners, for example, encourages newcomers to give priority to the discussion meetings (more to the Amigo than the Speak Easy series) before becoming heavily involved in the General Meetings and the Afterglow dances that follow them. They also recommend that family activities, designed for parents and their children, be given priority over exclusively adult activities. Whether or not the client decides to affiliate with self-help, this process can be a useful exercise in decision making. The emphasis on collecting information and evaluating it before a decision is made can illustrate a process that should carry over into other spheres as well.

Ongoing Discussion

The plan as jointly formulated by the professional and the client may require that the client observe specific but limited self-help activities. Most assuredly, it should include a discussion of why these activities were chosen over others. Following a discussion of the initial experiences, the plan might be elaborated, to sample more experiences. After detailed reflections on these experiences, a decision could be made about affiliation. Negative impression should be given particular attention. The idea is not to talk clients out of their opinions, but rather to understand the basis of these opinions. Sometimes it may be the result of an out-of-the-ordinary incident or misinformation. Additional information, then, may correct the impression. But whatever the final decision, the most important goal will be to ensure that the client "owns" the decision. It would be unfortunate indeed if the client ends up nursing a grievance that he or she simply acquiesced in the counselor's wish.

From another point of view—whatever the outcome—the process can be considered constructive insofar as the client has a better understanding of what helps and what does not help. When the client understands what helps, he or she can assume   *269*

Box 2.

Strategies for Professionals to Make Effective Referrals to Self-Help Organizations

1. Confer with contact persons in self-help.
2. Discuss the rationale for the recommendation with the client.
3. Make self-help literature and brochures available to the client.
4. Discuss the principle of selective participation in program activities.
5. Develop a joint plan with the client to explore the self-help organization.
6. Discuss the client's first contacts and later experiences with the self-help organization.

---

more responsibility for managing his or her own helping experiences in the natural environment. This also means that the client can become increasingly independent of formally structured help from professionals and from peers. The entire process can also be viewed as an oblique commentary on the state of the therapeutic relationship, since the latter must also be consonant with the client's concept of help. Some carefully measured, nonthreatening discussion of parallels can help enlarge the client's concept of what might be helpful. This aim will be advanced insofar as help-seeking can be discussed in nontechnical psychotherapeutic or self-help terms. It is another way to help the client reconceptualize the task of obtaining social support, so that it can be obtained in less specialized, more natural settings. Such a discussion should identify alternative sources of support, in addition to formal self-help and psychotherapy programs. Thus, the process can be therapeutic even if the client or the counselor has strong doubts that the outcome will be affiliation with a group or organization.

If the client does move toward affiliation, it is important to make formal provisions to discuss the client's experiences regularly. By staying abreast of the self-help experience, the professional can be assured of grist for the therapeutic mill.

To sum up, making a proper referral requires that professionals have current information about and contacts with self-help organizations. (See Box 2.) They need to update their resources periodically. This is the minimal obligation of professionals, if access to and guidance in the use of self-help are to be available as a regular part of professional service programs. The low frequency of this pattern should be considered presumptive evidence that these minimal conditions have not been met.

SELF-HELP LEADERS AS INITIATORS

The discussion thus far should not imply that the professional is the sole initiator of collaboration. Nonreciprocal patterns are neither desirable nor representative of actual collaborative relationships. Consonant with this reality and the egalitarianism inherent in collaboration, the perspective shifts to consider reciprocal initiatives, that is, initiatives from self-help leaders desirous of developing relationships with professionals. Again, however, the reader will recall that much of the preceding discussion about professionals can also be applied to self-helpers. With only minor adaptations, the term *self-help leader* can be substituted for *professional*. With this in mind, attention can be turned to the distinctive tasks and opportunities facing the self-help leader.

Goals of Contact

INCREASING AWARENESS AND RESOURCES: The major goal of the self-help leader is as ambitious as it is straightforward: to increase professional responsiveness to the problem to which his or her self-help program is addressed. This often entails educating professionals about self-help's focal concerns. Concretely, it means that the self-help leader must show how such problems as child abuse, gambling, and the lack of support for the single parent lifestyle tend in some combination to be ignored, misunderstood, or inadequately responded to. Such problems as compulsive gambling frequently go undetected by professionals who are unfamiliar with the culture in which they occur. And even if they are recognized, the remedial approach may not be suited to the culture in which the problem or the predicament occurs. To say this, and to retain the goodwill of professionals, self-help leaders may have to be very diplomatic.

Self-help leaders may also aim to increase the amount of available resources. More and better trained professionals are needed. The National Alliance for the Mentally Ill exemplifies this thrust. During the eighties, they opposed the Reagan administration's plan to dismantle the clinical training program of the National Institute of Mental Health. In the area of services, they took an even stronger position to oppose administration plans   *271* to scuttle the community support program. They have a crucial stake in this program, which mobilizes and coordinates the basic necessities of shelter, food, health care, and recreation for the chronically mentally ill. The efforts of NAMI at the national level were paralleled by lobbying at the state and local level. These efforts were factors in keeping the NIMH training and community-support programs alive and increased the attention given to the chronically mentally ill at all levels of government. Many other self-help organizations seek a degree of influence similar to what NAMI has achieved.

COUNSELORS: As they tell their stories, self-help leaders may also want to size up professionals as possible counselors to whom they can entrust members. The situation is ironic; while self-helpers are lambasting professionals for their failures, particularly those related to failure to appreciate the role of self-help organizations, they are looking to them for assistance. They must depend on professionals for specialized assistance outside the self-help organization. This apparent contradiction should not immobilize either professionals or self-help leaders any more than they are immobilized by the myriad other contradictions they face.

And if this motive were not enough, many self-help leaders wishing to influence professionals can offer useful incentives. They have the power to advocate for improved budgets; they also can refer members to those professionals who understand the goals and activities of the self-help organization. For reasons that need not be wholly altruistic, many professionals will want to be counted among the understanding. But appeals to self-interest are not the only incentives self-help leaders can offer. Self-help leaders can also assume that many professionals will be gratified to have been sought out. Professionals want to help; they want to make effective use of the skills that are at the core of their personal and professional identities. Like everyone else in this economy of scarce regard, human service professionals take heart when others consult them on matters relating to their speciality.

Strategies for Contacts

Some of the strategies for initiating contacts that earlier were recommended to professionals can be easily adapted for self-helpers. Self-help leaders also need to identify relevant resources, but from their point of view, these will be agencies that are, or could be, serving their membership. Self-help leaders also need to consult directories, but in their case, these would be the larger and more complete listings of human service organizations. Similarly, they should consider becoming exhibitors or presenters at conferences for professionals. The basic assumption is that both sides have valuable information to exchange. In what follows, the reader should consider how some of the strategies recommended to self-help leaders may also be adapted for professionals.

INTRODUCTIONS: Several kinds of introductions are important to self-help leaders. Introductions by community leaders, especially those who are active in the human services as board members or in other volunteer roles, can be very helpful. At the next level, professionals who are already knowledgeable and supportive can perform a significant service by introducing self-help leaders to their colleagues. Such introductions can be one of the most important ways for "friendly" professionals and community leaders to be of assistance to self-helpers. Introductions can be geared to invite self-help leaders to visit agencies and to make presentations. Often this action will utilize the available energy. But if self-help leaders believe that they need to have more opportunties to interact with community and professional resources, they could send a letter (or make a telephone call) offering to make a no-obligation visit or a presentation; this outreach probably will generate as many requests as there are time and personnel to honor them. Sometimes surprisingly little outreach can lead to many opportunities, or a single connection with a professional can put the self-helper in touch with many other professionals in the same network.

Simulation techniques can be an especially effective means for self-help organizations to develop their contacts. Panels that demonstrate the actual workings of a self-help organization can be presented. Almost invariably, professionals will get more from this concrete demonstration than from a talk that is one step removed from the actual self-help transactions. Indeed, some professionals might be inspired to consider how they might demonstrate their approach in public education efforts—perhaps using client actors in a presentation—for when their methods are intangible to begin with, a "picture" may be worth more than a thousand words. And should professionals fail to request a demonstration, one can assume that they do not know it is an option. The use of demonstrations may also avoid the necessity of having to deal with an unfamiliar or strange vocabulary. Sometimes professionals can be put off by unfamiliar words, as can self-helpers.

Keys to Cooperation

INSTRUMENTAL RESOURCES: The principle of successful cooperation requires that both parties recognize the complementary nature of their relationship. This means that each party must have some idea about what resources can be exchanged. To make good use of resources, each party must be aware of the different instrumental resources available. The professionals' expertise lies in carrying out technical procedures based, to varying degrees, on science. Also, because of professionals' greater social sanction, they have more access to back-up care. Indeed, they may be the only access to the intensive resources required in an emergency. For reasons related to cost and risk, they frequently control admissions to long-term care institutions. Sometimes referrals must be made by professionals, or else professionals are the only ones who can complete certain forms or supply the information necessary to complete an application for service.

CREDIBILITY AND RELEVANCE: Self-help expertise, in contrast, arises from an intimate knowledge of the culture in which the problem occurs. Self-helpers are fluent in the language and symbols associated with the distinctive cultural circumstances of the problem. Their knowledge of the intricacies of its development and expression is seldom matched by professionals. Self-helpers, for example, are much more adept at recognizing the subtle and sometimes paradoxical behaviors that signify progress or stagnation and regression. Many have the uncanny ability to help others who feel they are beyond help. They can help largely because they have overcome a similar despair. Neophytes often will grant credibility only to those who have, or are recovering from, similar predicaments, those who have themselves climbed up from the depths. Once a bond has been established, these veterans can be among the most effective referral agents in helping the neophyte see professionals as a credible resource.

CREATIVE INTERDEPENDENCE: The knowledge and credibility possessed by self-help organizations can be an enormous resource for professional organizations, but it is also woefully underused. Professional human service organizations can rarely optimize their appeal to their potential constituency. They cannot control their own input and need to rely on various referring publics. Perhaps the most important of these publics are self-help organizations.

Without solid ties to the experiential world of their clients, professional technologies are likely to be arid. Moreover, the professional service frequently cannot sustain its users through the long intervals of days and weeks between appointments without the assistance of self-help organizations. And finally, professionals frequently cannot provide sufficient support for their clients during the long aftercare period. Thus, whether it recognizes it or not, the professional agency depends for support on external actors and institutions. It is the task of self-helpers to bring home these facts to professionals. Self-helpers must educate professionals to understand how their services can be frustrated or complemented by the environment. And in so doing, self-help leaders can confidently assert that their organizations may be among the most important external resources for professionals.

EXEMPLARY EXCHANGES: As professionals and self-helpers ponder possibilities for exchange, they can refer to a number of different models for guidance. The health care system encourages some important reciprocal relationships between self-help and professional services. A typical pattern of cooperation between professional and self-help care might unfold as follows: When aggressive medical or major surgical procedures are under consideration, self-help organizations support the decision process. They can offer emotional support and information about second opinions or act as a sounding board to help the person understand the pros and cons of his or her options. They may also help by relating how others have prepared for, and adapted to, certain procedures. As important as these functions are, they probably will be less important than the ones that will be brought into play after the acute state subsides. It is in the postacute stage that the patient and his or her support system (an important part of which may be the self-help organization) have the most influence on the recovery and rehabilitation process.

On another plane, health care professionals have linked with self-help organizations to improve the technology of rehabilitation. Self-help organizations that are serving people whose disease or condition (for example, emphysema, laryngectomy, or ostomy) requires special aids have contributed significantly to the technology of prostheses and other appliances. Given their sustained and intimate experience with these appliances, they provide a user's point of view. And for the most part—allowing for the usual initial resistance and occasional exceptions—professionals have been open to self-helpers' contributions. With few exceptions, health care professionals have come to view both the technical and the socioemotional functions of self-help organizations as vital to their own mission.

Box 3.

Strategies for Self-Help Leaders to Develop Linkages to Professionals

1. Contact community leaders (agency board members, clergy, county supervisors, etc.).
2. Contact friendly professionals.
3. Make appointments with agency decision makers.
4. Elicit requests to make presentations.
5. Stress the organizational benefits of mutual exchanges.
6. Solicit professional assistance with a self-help–related task.

The field of substance abuse offers another set of well-established examples of the explicit and constructive interdependence between professionals and self-help organizations. To suggest some of the ways in which this interdependency is recognized, it might be useful to note how self-help meetings are used in treatment facilities and the importance of the role assigned to them in the long-term recovery program. In the child abuse field, official arrangements have been negotiated in some communities between protective service programs and PA. Many times this cooperation has worked well, but sometimes too much cooperation may endanger important distinctions between a voluntary program and a compulsory program. Care must be taken to ensure that the requirements of legal enforcement do not compromise the voluntary character of PA, and vice versa. The general goal must be to recognize the interdependence between self-help and professional organizations without eroding the distinctive advantages of each.

As the number of collaborative programs increases, it is predictable that some of them will not be exemplary. Indeed, some—and the number will increase as self-help grows—may be counterproductive. They may become less voluntary over time, they may be distorted by arcane procedures, or they may be stifled by inflexible rules. To minimize these occurrences, it will be necessary to formulate some principles and identify some models that can be used as a measure of valid self-help programs. Meanwhile, self-help leaders must become less diffident and persuade professionals that the insufficiencies of their programs can be ameliorated through better collaboration with self-help programs. To succeed in this effort, self-help leaders must be prepared to set forth the ways in which their organizations can contribute to the goals of specific professional agencies, which, in turn, raises the consciousness of professional decision makers so that they will see that cooperation can increase the acceptance, stability, and effectiveness of the professional agency. Some steps that can facilitate this end are outlined in Box 3. Through means such as these, self-help leaders can convert professionals' need for a relationship with a self-help organization into a desire, and—better still—an explicit request for such a relationship.

Notes

1. L. D. Borman, "Characteristics of Development and Growth," in M. A. Lieberman and Borman, eds., *Self-Help Groups for Coping with Crisis: Origins, Members, Processes and Impact* (San Francisco: Jossey-Bass, 1979), pp. 13–42.
2. K. Larkin, A. Meese, and E. J. Madara, *The Self-Help Group Directory, 1984–85* (Denville: New Jersey Self-Help Clearinghouse, 1985); and A. Gartner and F. Riessman, *Help: A Working Guide to Self-Help Groups* (New York: New Viewpoints/Vision Books, 1980).

15

Exchanging Case Consultation

An exchange of referrals may be a natural path to case consultation insofar as it results in a comfortable familiarity between the sender and the receiver of referrals. Proper referral practice is much more than the mention of a resource. It often entails several contacts and substantive discussions between the professional and the self-help leader. These discussions can take place before, during, and after the period in which the individual who is referred contacts either the self-help or the professional resource. These shared experiences often favorably impress the referral partner and lead to an appreciation of the contributions of other helpers. As these impressions grow, they may flower into an effective, reciprocal consultation relationship.

THE ROAD TO CONSULTATION

The sequence may unfold as follows: The need to make initial contact becomes the need to devise a plan for a series of increasingly diverse contacts with the potential consultation partner. The exchange can be an efficient means to this end, since it allows two people to develop a relationship while minimizing the risk of embarrassing personal disclosures or inadequacies. By focusing attention on the third party, the other two parties can share as much of themselves as they like without necessarily becoming the center of attention, which could heighten the uneasiness of one or the other party. Through this relatively nonthreatening interaction, the complementarity of the two parties' approaches may become evident. Both the self-help leader and the professional will realize that, through coordinated action, they can maximize their contributions to the well-being of the member/ client. This leads to a more substantial relationship between the professional and self-help caregivers, which is increasingly based on mutual respect. From here it is a short step to a consultative relationship. In terms common to the consultation literature, it might be said that the third party is the occasion for propinquity between the professional and the self-help leader. This state is often cited as a factor that facilitates consultative relationships.[1]

Some Clarifications

The term self-help leader is used loosely here to include situations in which leadership is exercised collectively or, as in many "Anonymous" organizations, on a rotating basis.

On an even more delicate point, this discussion is meant to be respectful of the formal position many Anonymous and other types of self-help organizations take against consultation. Nothing here should be misconstrued as a quarrel with any organization that prohibits official collaboration with another organization. It frequently does seem wise to bar members from representing their organization in dealings with outsiders. Yet there is a paradox: The organizations themselves speak of working with others. Alcoholics Anonymous and others publish brochures about working with professionals and cooperating with professional service programs.[2] Of course, these activities would only infrequently be called consultations. They are more likely to be called professional education, linking, or referral coordination activities. The upshot? Practitioners who work in these important ways, whether they call it a consultation or something else, must be able to tolerate paradox. Further, they must be willing to work informally and "behind the scenes." Moreover, they must know which activities are proscribed and which are encouraged. Practitioners must also realize that an activity labeled one way might have to be rejected, but if it is labeled another way, it may be greeted enthusiastically. It would be unfortunate if such subtleties and paradoxes made professionals withdraw from these important activities. It might be well to consider that professionals sometimes find that paradoxical situations increase the power of their interventions, though no easy rules of thumb are available in this complex field. And nothing can substitute for a careful study of the norms of the particular self-help organization in which one is interested or involved.

Some professionals, however, have serious reservations about consultation. Yet on closer examination, many of these reservations seem to be a bid for a different or a broader form of consultation, with a somewhat different terminology. Gottlieb, for example, has argued against consultation with lay support networks but has argued for collaboration, networking, mutual education, and organizational development.[3] These activities are subsumed under the term *consultation*, as it is used in this chapter.

Some Cautions

Referrals as a means of developing consultation relationships also raise the specter of a possible conflict between the parties interested in consultation and the person who is being referred. It is easy to imagine a situation in which the third-party (client or self-help member) interests are misinterpreted or compromised because the first two parties (professional and self-help leader) are primarily concerned with their own relationship. When such a relationship is being cultivated, clients or self-help members may be coddled at the expense of their self-reliance. Or if one is trying to fend off the relationship, the third party may experience unaccountable expressions of disinterest from one of the first two parties. If the relationship between caregivers sours completely, frank rejection may occur. Even more seriously, the client could be caught in a conflict between the professional and the self-help leader. Other less dramatic risks, however, may be even more significant. Each caregiver may contemplate moves with one eye on his or her counterpart. Bold but sound interventions may be withheld because the initiator fears that the interventions may be misunderstood or disapproved of by the other party. A single accommodation along these lines might not be so serious, but the cumulative effect could seriously harm the self-help experience or the professional counseling experience for the individual.

It should not be assumed that the effect of a developing consultation relationship will be negative. The prospect of a future consultation relationship might well be an incentive to care for the third party at an even higher level. The third party (client or self-help member) may receive more aid because the caregivers are motivated to maintain contact and to demonstrate their helpfulness. In short, both caregivers may try harder and longer because the significance of the "case" increases if it is seen as a means to facilitate a mutually beneficial consultation exchange concerning an individual.

THE THREAT IN CONSULTATIVE RELATIONSHIPS

A transition to a consultative relationship heightens the potential threat to both parties, since the transactions now center on the immediate caregiver-consultee rather than on the remote third party. Though the focus should be on the consultee's work problem, and not on his or her personal problem, it is difficult to ponder these problems without some anxiety about personal coping patterns. The role of the consultee, in contrast to that of the referral agent, requires a more extensive, more revealing communication about the self.[4] In disclosing concerns about the case and how it has been handled, the consultee would be less than human not to be concerned about exposing personal inadequacies. The threat will loom all the larger if personal disclosures somehow seem called for. In short, what seems to be an apparently simple presentation of a work problem requires a significant amount of trust in the other person.

Compared to referral work, consultation raises doubts about larger components of the self-concept. In a referral, jeopardy is limited to the part of the self involved in that particular case. In consultation, the jeopardy may be broader and include patterns of interaction that characterize the caregiver's dealings with several clients rather than a single client. Feeling of competency in a broad range of situations may be at stake. Though the magnitude of these threats can be exaggerated, there is an element of personal and professional threat inherent in consultation. Moreover, the level of threat can be raised or lowered according to the sensitivity of the intervention; it can be elevated by too bold a consultation initiative.

Problems in Earlier Consultation Programs

Many early community mental health programs were flawed by too precipitous a move toward formal consultation. Mannino has written an insightful analysis of one of these projects.[5] This federally funded project aimed to demonstrate that the referral stage could be bypassed in order to move directly into consultant relationships with community caregivers. Community caregivers, however, objected. They expected mental health professionals to provide basic clinical services before adding other activities. Thus, they declined to enter into consultation arrangements despite the efforts of professionals. These caregivers seemed to feel that it was necessary to build trust through less risky referral experiences.

The problems might also be conceptualized as the failure of the would-be consultants to express their dependence on community caregivers. In wanting to develop an instant market for professional consultative services, they did not consider the dependency of professionals on informal caregivers and formally organized self-help programs. They might have fared better if they had acknowledged the amount of care provided by these helping agents and the unique acceptability they enjoyed among some populations. Also, they might have considered that without referrals from community caregivers, fewer professionals would be able to practice their craft. And without the willingness of caregivers to take up where professionals leave off, professional practice would be less specialized. This situation reflects the amount of aftercare and concurrent care such caregivers provide. The failure to express professional dependence on caregivers and self-help organizations is resented, and the level of collaboration is lowered. Consequently, some self-help leaders, one of the subgroups of caregiver, insist that professionals acknowledge their insufficiency and demonstrate their willingness to enter into egalitarian, interdependent relationships. For many self-help consultees, this shows that statements about reciprocal consultation relationships can be believed in.

The lesson is clear: Without real reciprocity, the tensions between professionals and self-help leaders will impede collaborative relationships. Many self-help leaders will continue to resent professional consultants, and some few will be openly antagonistic. In the absence of a detailed, widely accepted model of interdependency, self-help leaders will continue to be polarized. Some will self-righteously maintain that professionals, as experts, are solely responsible for the problems within their domain. Others will hold the opposite view, arguing that professionals have little specialized expertise and that their interest in consultation is a transparent effort to control an ever-larger territory.

Fostering Interdependency

The importance of values that favor interdependency and reciprocity raises a question about what kind of professionals are most likely to be effective consultants to self-help organizations. Lenrow and Burch have suggested that the most effective consultants, or, in their terms, *linking agents*, will be clinicians who can express their dependence on clients.[6] This is an appealing formulation because it recognizes that both clinicians and consultants must be able to express their dependence on their role partners. But since consultants need to be drawn from a wide net, a clinical test cannot be used to predict which professionals can express their dependence on consultees. A good start, however, would be to ask prospective consultants to state their concept of the optimum level of interdependency between the self-help and the professional systems. For if this potential is not really recognized, the prospective consultant will need, at the very least, to be indoctrinated into the mutual benefits of a vital interdependency; unless both sides learn to cultivate interdependency, professionals and self-help leaders will both continue to offer underdeveloped services.

But this happy interdependency will take more than agreeable words and noble propositions to effect. Otherwise the attempt to turn self-help leaders into consultees will seem more a hollow attempt to manipulate them. Self-help leaders, at some level, are not unaware of the budgetary, power, and self-aggrandizement factors that motivate offers of consultation. If the offer is to be regarded as genuine and acceptable, the consultant will have to demonstrate a willingness to overturn many of the traditions of consultation.

DEVELOPING CONSULTATION EXCHANGES

Narrow to Broad, Ad Hoc to Scheduled

Consultation may begin with a simple request for information, an apparently uncomplicated question about the availability of a substance abuse outpatient program for teenagers or a self-help organization for teenage substance abusers. If a level of comfort has been established through earlier referrals or some other means, the process of consultation may be initiated by exploring the needs that prompted the request. Thus an interest in broad problems can be expressed. The objective is to lay the groundwork for future transactions around this issue and indicate that discussion of other "cases" and a wider range of issues would be welcome. In this way, the consultant transforms the informal ad hoc transactions into more formal scheduled transactions; at the same time, he or she will be looking for an opportunity to turn the tables—to request consultation from the self-helper for one of his or her own problems. As steps are taken along these lines, a commitment to a broader consultation will develop.

It must not be expected that this process will proceed in a straight line. It is two steps forward, one step backward, and a process of skipping from topic to topic. A flexibly responsive orientation is essential. Nonetheless, progress can be made toward a more stable relationship if the consultant does not try to rush. It is important not to leave one's partner with second thoughts about earlier disclosures or uneasy promises to follow up on some action. For example, the consultant may decide to respond to a series of specific questions about public assistance for Gamblers Anonymous families before guiding the discussion toward some more general issues involved in making effective referrals. Similarly, though the aim is to include marital and parent-child issues rather than restrict the agenda to financial problems and concrete services, this must be done gradually. Movement from narrowly conceived to broader issues by the self-helper and the professional is a measure of the progress toward a significant consultative exchange.

Regularly Scheduled Conferences

Simultaneously, the strategy should be to move toward more regularly scheduled formal arrangements for the consultation. This means moving from relatively informal contacts to more formal ones. Usually, this move will be marked by more involvement of the key figures. For example, the executives of a substance abuse organization could invite Narcotics Anonymous to hold open meetings in its facilities. This action might also signal a willingness to formalize exchanges with this and, perhaps, other self-help organizations. Other signs of commitment may be observed in better planned meetings scheduled at more regular intervals and held in open community-meeting places.

The willingness of agency executives and self-help leaders (for example, from a state department of mental health and NAMI) to cooperate publicly would indicate a strong commitment to consultation exchanges, though it must be remembered that some self-help organizations will not wish to make such arrangements. Some self-helpers, particularly the members of the Anonymous organizations, would consider these arrangements inappropriate. But even here, accommodation is possible. Some members of Narcotics Anonymous, for example, might be willing to give a media interview along with agency executives, provided their identities were concealed and that it was clear that they were offering only their own views and not those of NA. A higher level of commitment might be indicated by the incorporation of self-helpers as volunteers or paid staff in relevant professional organizations. Again, the affiliation of the Anonymous organization members would not be mentioned. Similarly, members of Women

Table 9. *Patterns of Commitment in Consultative Relations*

Scope/ Formality	Narrow	Broad
Ad hoc, informal	1. Low commitment: informal, narrow	2. Intermediate commitment: informal, broad
Regular: formal	3. Intermediate commitment formal, narrow	4. High commitment: formal, broad

for Sobriety, PA, or Federation of Parents and Friends of Lesbians and Gays could be appointed to board and advisory committees or to formal consulting positions within professional organizations, analogous to the position of "counsel" in law firms. These arrangements would establish meaningful ties without obligating either organization to burdensome day-to-day coordination tasks. Some self-help organizations (Mended Hearts, Reach to Recovery, and the National Alliance for the Mentally Ill) have dealt with the ad hoc issue by requesting regular reports from professionals with whom they commonly interact.

Mutual but Formal Approaches

An actual consultation can occur in a variety of settings, such as staff and leadership development workshops sponsored by the self-help and the professional organizations. More frequently, however, it will occur as a simple conversation about a variety of issues. Later it could involve the exchange of written comments, which indicates a deepening level of commitment. A still more formal initiative might entail creating a joint task force to resolve some issues that affect both the self-help and the professional organizations or the joint sponsorship of a council with a broad representation from the areas of interest, such as child abuse and substance abuse. This sample of initiatives shows some mutual but formal approaches to a vigorous program of consultation exchange.

Table 9 shows combinations of scope (narrow versus broad) and sanction (ad hoc and informal versus regular and formal) associated with consultation exchanges. Each combination has a different level of commitment and potential influence. Of the four combinations, point 1 is the least influential form of consultation, since it involves informal arrangements and addresses specific issues. The highest level of commitment, and potentially the most influential, is point 4, in which arrangements are formal and issues are broad. The mixed cases, points 2 and 3, fall somewhere in the middle. Abstractly, it is impossible to say whether formal arrangements or broad agendas contribute more to the potential consultation exchange. But specifically, it may be clear which combination is most effective. Sometimes it will be more feasible or more profitable to consolidate the process through more formal arrangements rather than expanding the agenda. Other times, the reverse is true and the process will advance by demonstrating the usefulness of consultation. In mixed cases, the circumstances of each situation must be looked to for clues as how to proceed.

CONSULTATION DEVELOPMENT SCENARIOS

Formal Arrangements

The first scenario illustrates how the consultation can be made more formal: Following a successful consultation transaction focused on a single individual, the professional might ask the consultee (the self-helpers) if the chapter would be interested in further discussion about parent-child relationships, perhaps on the topic of distinguishing necessary firmness from unnecessary harshness. A favorable reply will lead to an opportunity for a formal meeting with the chapter. The consultation may also emanate from the self-help organization. The professional discussing eating disorders with a self-help leader might allude to other workers who have clients with the same problems. He might discuss the perplexing nature of these difficulties and the bewildering array of approaches to deal with them. This could be considered an invitation to schedule a formal meeting, and here the self-help leader would consult with the staff of the professional agency. Each response discussed illustrates a move toward making consultation more formal; the professional's allusion to the bewildering approaches suggests, in addition, interest in broadening the scope of the consultation.

This next scenario illustrates how the self-help leader acting as a consultant to a professional might build on informal specific discussions to develop a greater commitment to consultation. In the course of an informal consultation transaction, the professional might volunteer:

> Our agency probably misses a number of situations in which compulsive gambling contributes to debt problems. Though we

suspect that some of the financial distress we see may be due to gambling, we're not really sure how to find out or what to do when we find out. In short, we need to know more about spotting gambling problems and more about what can be done for a person who is strung out on gambling.

To stimulate a discussion among the consultees as well as to demonstrate some of the principles and procedures of GA, the self-help leader might explain some of the remedial methods used in Budget and Pressure Groups, stressing that the compulsive gambler must demonstrate a commitment to GA before he or she is given the opportunity to draw on the experience of more senior members. Otherwise the process might degenerate into just another "bail out." The readiness of the newcomer will be assessed as he learns that radical and often humbling changes are likely to be required of him. These are not arbitrary requirements, but rather actions made necessary by the problems associated with massive gambling debts, too little income, pending legal charges, and the pressuring of bookies and loan sharks. After such a presentation, the professional will have a much more vivid and detailed idea of what is involved in recovery. Moreover, the professional may learn how to incorporate some of these practices and beliefs into his or her approach to the client. But perhaps the most realistic benefit is that hereafter the professional can offer clients a more detailed, more credible description of the assistance available from GA.

In this last scenario, the point of view is reversed again to show how a professional might offer significant assistance to the self-help organization. The example condenses several discussions with a group of mentally restored individuals and mental health consumers. A courageous, but still tentative, member stated:

Our [self-help] group is changing. Several of the new people are so angry they always end up disrupting our meetings. They frighten other members. They are driving out the strongest and most loyal members. We're concerned that these backbone members will stop coming.

After the professional acting as the consultant in this case carefully explored the problem, the members of the self-help organization who were the consultees volunteered that "we should have regular times to discuss administrative problems." This was a crucial encounter in developing an emotional commitment to a broader form of supportive consultation. To be sure, the problem was not "solved," even though some adjustments were possible. But it was possible to commend the members for their efforts "to hang in there" and to discuss how similar problems had *287* appeared and reappeared. After several discussions, the members could accept the appreciation of others who admired their resolve to stick with a situation that would deter the less committed.

OPPORTUNISM, FALSE GLAMOUR, AND MEANS VS. ENDS

Without qualification, the preceding discussion might seem to be a pitch to develop opportunistic consultation relationships without regard to their ethics or ultimate effectiveness. It might further suggest a lack of concern for the all-too-prevalent tendency to want to become a consultant because of its "glamour" (not realizing that it is also a term for professionals out of work). Therefore, it should be said that this false glamour can spawn a host of expectations about the deference due a consultant. Were it not for the useful literature that has grown up under the heading of consultation, terms such as *collaboration, technical assistance,* and *organizational development* might have been used to avoid dysfunctional connotations. These alternative terms are useful. They are more descriptive and less mysterious, more pragmatic and less grandiose, and more egalitarian and less arrogant.

Consultants can easily become overly concerned about the self. When this happens, their judgment is impaired and they may confuse means with ends and contacts with meaningful consultations. Thus, the foregoing relationship development strategies should not be confused with, nor necessarily assumed to lead to, effective consultations. It is possible to progress from informal, narrowly based interactions to formal, broadly based ones without effective consultation or problem solving ever having occurred. These strategies merely structure a consultation; they do not assure that it will be effective. The above strategies should not be interpreted as encouragement to downplay ethical issues. Many consultants may be tempted to slight the requirements of full disclosure and full consent. That they are tempted is evident from Rosenblatt's review of a book by one of the foremost exponents of mental health consultation, Caplan.

> More impressive than the theory is the author's practical advice to consultants. The book is filled with useful hints and shrewd advice about how to get a foot in the door of a prospective customer. In this instance the customer is an agency that needs convincing about the benefits of mental health consultation. More hints follow: how to move quickly once inside the door,

how to draw up a contract, what to include in reports, and how to divest oneself of new friends within an organization who subsequently prove to be liabilities.

The author has a fine feel for techniques that will insure a consultant's acceptance within an organization, as follows:

> . . .the consultant must also ensure that significant figures of power and influence higher up in the [institutional] system . . .or in positions of influence in the community, are continually kept informed of his operations and are stimulated to support him . . .he should seize an appropriate opportunity to send them a copy of a short report about the consultation program or to visit them for an informal chat about his work, so that they may keep abreast of his progress and have a chance to make explicit their support . . .the consultant should ensure that he has visited him sufficiently recently and has kept him well enough informed of the developments in his program that the superintendent feels quite confident . . .and does not need to check up on the program immediately. . . [Quoted from Caplan.]

> Small are the risks that come from the muted tooting of one's horn or from efforts to make friends with "significant figures of power and influence.". . .

> In short, this book's primary value is that of a manual on how to succeed as a mental health consultant. This troubling thought arises in considering its uses: since the value of theme interference reduction is not proved, a consultant who reads this book may learn more about helping himself than about helping his consultees or their clients.[7]

These wonderfully sardonic comments, even if they are a bit exaggerated, should do more than amuse. They should be memorable reminders of the dehumanizing temptations that await the overanxious or unprincipled consultant. Hidden agendas, self-promotion, and opportunistic tactics will destroy the basis for meaningful consultation exchanges between self-help organizations and professionals. The principles of consultation development outlined in Box 4 (p. 290) must be understood in this context if they are not to be judged as opportunistic, ethically questionable strategies that confuse means with ends—to promote consultants, but not necessarily consultation. They should also be understood as "going with the flow," lest they seem stiff and affected.

BENEFITS OF CONSULTATION EXCHANGE

Although the different perspectives of the partners accounts for some of the benefits of consultation, the rationale for consulta- *289*

Box 4.
Principles of Consultation Development

1. Extend discussions and promote additional contacts in relation to referral cases.
2. Utilize opportunities to invite informal discussion of cases other than those explicitly referred.
3. Once consultation has begun, broaden its base by introducing new issues and related cases into the sessions.
4. Stabilize the consultation by moving toward regularly scheduled meetings with advance planning of the agenda, if feasible.
5. Secure the sanction of both organizations. Increase the number of personnel, including leaders, from both organizations who are active in the consultation project.
6. Consider the occasional use of task forces to develop and coordinate the plan of consultation, including its goals and the means by which those goals will be sought.

---

tion should not depend on this difference. In such a conceptual exposition, it would be easy to oversimplify and overrationalize the actual consultation. People, including consultants, do not interact on the basis of a single experiential dimension. What they offer reflects the whole range of their life experience, not just experiences with problems (whether from an experiential or a professional point of view). These other experiences are also implicated in the benefits of consultation (see Box 5). Isolated professional and self-help consultees may find this enough justification to enter into a consultation arrangement, since without a partner they may have too few opportunities to hear themselves talk and to obtain feedback. Though these ideas are hardly surprising, they are not trivial. This is also a good time to point out that human interactions are invariably more complicated than any systematic analysis can suggest.

Self-help leaders and professionals complement each others' problem-solving capacity in patterned ways. These patterns are rooted in their different kinds of knowledge. Starting with personal experiences, members of self-help organizations draw on the ideology of the organization to code, augment, and interpret

---

Box 5.
Distinctive Benefits of Professional Consultation

1. Comprehensive information about resources.
2. Systematic assessment and treatment approaches.
3. Integration of self-help techniques into an overall plan for the member.
4. Availability of a more complete value framework to inform interventions.
5. Scientific knowledge in selected areas.
6. Discussion of the client's first contacts and later experiences with the self-help organization.

Distinctive Benefits of Self-Help Consultation

1. Personal knowledge of the course of recovery and relapse.
2. Intimate knowledge of the social settings, cultural symbols, and specialized vocabulary associated with the problem.
3. Extraordinarily incisive intervention techniques.
4. Exposure to diverse models of successful recovery who are in different stages of their struggle.
5. Knowledge of the pitfalls that may be created by the well-intentioned advice of lay helpers.

---

their own experience. The experiential knowledge that results is an intimate knowledge of the phenomenology of the problem, including its sensory, cognitive, affective, behavioral, and cultural correlates.[8]

This knowledge also differs from what is available to other lay helpers who constitute the informal, natural network of community caregivers.[9] Sometimes the differences are such that members of the self-help organization must counteract the bad advice given by well-intentioned family members and community caregivers. For example, well-meaning relatives might say, "Every child deserves to be spanked once in a while." Or "There's no harm in betting in the office football pool." But those who have intimate knowledge of these problems know how destructive such advice is for the child abuser or the compulsive gambler. *291*

These self-helpers disapprove of practices that might start a run of self-destructive behavior, based on an insider's appreciation of the values, symbols, and special vocabulary that make up the culture surrounding the problem.

Benefits to Professionals

Given this unique knowledge, self-help leaders can inject meaning into a situation that otherwise would be misread or unread by professionals. For example, members of PA can explain the different meanings of spanking and how they can encourage or sanction abusive episodes. They can also clarify how protective service workers are viewed by persons suspected of child abuse. Parents Anonymous members can relate not only how well-intentioned and caring actions tend to be misinterpreted, they can also suggest how these misinterpretations can be anticipated. At the same time, they may startle professionals by recounting their appreciation of professionals who, in a caring way, firmly uphold reasonable standards of care.

For another example of how professionals might obtain assistance from self-help organizations, consider the benefits of consulting with members of GA. Many professionals are baffled by the unresponsiveness of people who are "in action," seen in one of its most classic forms with the compulsive gambler. Is it possible to get their attention, to break through the preoccupation with gambling and tap some concern about its consequences? Or to consider how other organizations, for example, those concerned with the chemically dependent, might help professionals, one might ask if there are different ways to regard relapses. Can relapses have a positive function? Is a relapse ever a constructive event? What are some of the common reactions to a relapse, and how can they be construed as the beginning of the recovery phase?

Or take the situation of the newly separated and divorced. Members of Parents Without Partners have much to tell professionals about the disruption and distress they felt during the process of divorce. Moreover, they can share important information about what helped them restore a sense of order and competence to their lives. Since these issues are repeatedly discussed within the local chapter, the information they offer may be more reliable than that available from many other sources. Indeed, for just these reasons, self-help organizations often use discussion guides to encourage sound discussions of such concerns.

There are other ways professionals can use members of self-help organizations to enlarge their understanding. Many professionals need to know more about the norms for sexual activity within different lifestyle groups. Are the values of single heterosexual adults, for example, different from those of married heterosexuals? How do they differ from the values of homosexuals? Do the values of a gay man differ from those of a lesbian? What meanings are attached to brief sexual encounters in these subgroups? And to what extent is there only random variation— that is, to what extent is it an individual matter? The information available from self-help organizations spans an enormous range. Or consider how members of Make Today Count can help professionals understand what it is like to have a terminal illness or to have a terminally ill loved one. Those who are left behind and join The Compassionate Friends can help professionals better understand how, and in what sense, it is possible to speak of completing bereavement.

Benefits to Self-Help Leaders

Here the question is how the professional can be useful to self-help organizations and their leaders. This may involve a consideration of the distinctive capabilities of professional assistance and the insufficiencies of experientially based assistance, which suggests how they might complement one another. Professionals often have a comprehensive knowledge of resources. And though self-help leaders may be well informed about distant, specialized resources—a residential treatment facility for drug abusers, for example—they may be at a loss when it comes to general local resources. Of course, some of this may reflect local agencies' lack of relevance. However, self-helpers may not be familiar with the standard services available from local family agencies and clinics or whether their members are eligible for welfare assistance.

Many self-helpers can call on an especially salient repertoire of intervention techniques, but they may find it difficult to integrate them with a comprehensive assessment of an individual's personal and social functioning. Hence these splendid techniques may be used in a somewhat isolated or haphazard manner. Self-helpers may need help in adjusting the techniques to the help seeker's readiness or capacity, precisely because self-help leaders have not been trained in systematic assessment and treatment procedures. Thus, the self-helper may benefit from working with a professional to select and tailor the techniques of the professional to the individual's developmental experiences and present capacities. The professional, for example, can help the self-helper determine which approach might be most suitable for people who were emotionally impaired before abusing substances, as con-   *293* trasted with those with no preexisting emotional impairment.

With no pretense that all is well in their own value education, professionals might be able to help self-helpers become less judgmental and more supportive of the self-determination rights of members of their organization. This is important, even when it is acknowledged that, in some situations, self-help leaders are much more artful in infusing their interventions with these values. The self-help leader, for example, may have a fine way of insisting that only the individual can decide to take responsibility for his or her gambling yet insisting that when it comes to restitution, a particular method should be followed. In the face of these situations, the professional will often need to take the long view, opting to teach more by example than by instruction.

In some areas, professionals will have a special capability because of the close ties between their approach and scientific findings, as in the interplay of nature and nurture in the development of schizophrenia. In such an area, professionals may offer important information or clarification. They must be mindful, however, that self-helpers also may read the scientific literature and, furthermore, that different conclusions can be drawn from the same data. Nonetheless, professionals should not back away from their obligation to provide scientifically based information on such topics as the effects of neuroleptic medication and the risk of suicide among the elderly. The task, however, requires great delicacy. The professional must interpret the studies sensitive to both the integrity of the data and the integrity of the boundaries of self-help organizations.

Notes

1. See, for example: A. R. Beisser with R. Green, *Mental Health Consultation and Education* (Los Angeles, Calif.: Institute Press, 1972); R. R. Blake and J. S. Mouton, *Consultation* (Reading, Mass.: Addison Wesley Publishing Co., 1976); G. Caplan, *The Theory and Practice of Mental Health Consultation* (New York: Basic Books, 1970); S. Cooper and W. F. Hodges, eds., *The Mental Health Consultation Field*, Vol. 11 (New York: Human Sciences Press, 1983); and F. V. Mannino and M. Shore, "The Effects of Consultation: A Review of the Empirical Studies," *American Journal of Community Psychology*, 3 (February 1975), pp. 1–21.

2. Alcoholics Anonymous, *CPC Workbook: Cooperation with the Professional Community* (New York: A.A. General Service Office, 1982); and Alcoholics Anonymous, *If You Are a Professional: A. A. Wants to Work with You* (New York: A. A. World Services, 1972).

3. B. H. Gottlieb, "Opportunities for Collaboration with Informal Sup-

port Systems," in Cooper and Hodges, eds., *The Mental Health Consultation Field*, pp. 181–203.

4. J. C. Glidewell, "The Entry Problem in Consultation," *Journal of Social Issues*, 15, No. 2 (1959), pp. 51–59.

5. F. V. Mannino, "Developing Consultation Relationships with Community Agents," *Mental Hygiene*, 48 (July 1964), pp. 356–362.

6. P. B. Lenrow and R. W. Burch, "Mutual Aid and Professional Service: Opposing or Complementary?" in B. H. Gottlieb, ed., *Social Networks and Social Support* (Beverly Hills, Calif.: Sage Publications, 1981).

7. A. Rosenblatt, book review of G. Caplan's book, *The Theory and Practice of Mental Health Consultation* (New York: Basic Books, 1970), in *Social Work*, 16 (April 1971), pp. 117–118.

8. T. S. Borkman, "Experiential Knowledge: A New Concept for the Analysis of Self-Help Groups," *Social Service Review*, 50 (September 1976), pp. 445–456.

9. T. S. Borkman, "Mutual Self-Help Groups: Strengthening the Selectively Unsupportive Personal and Community Networks of Their Members," in A. Gartner and F. Riessman, eds., *The Self-Help Revolution* (New York: Human Sciences Press, 1984), pp. 205–216.

16

Exchanging Organizational Development Services

The use of a vignette to illustrate organizational development exchanges risks the danger that it may suggest too narrow a range of exchanges. But a discussion removed from concrete events risks even more; it may seem empty rather than simply narrow. Thus, this vignette should be regarded as only one of a potential myriad of organizational development exchanges.

Consider a club of mental health consumers whose name might evoke such associations as the Intrepid Club or simply the Intrepids. There were over 120 members in this developing organization, but only about one-third of them might have been considered core members, participating in one or more activities per week. Moreover, the participation of individuals fluctuated. Members active in one season might be into something else the next; a certain amount of drifting in and out was common and acceptable.

As several Intrepids put it, "We need a lot of things." And one of these things was a natural focus for organizational development activity. To begin with, the Intrepids needed better meeting room arrangements for their weekly discussion meeting. Sometimes the community center in which they met would shift them from their regular meeting room with no advance notice. Other times they would arrive to find the door of the meeting room locked. This meant hunting down the manager, all the while worried that some members might show up and leave, not having found anyone there. At the least, the room problems did little to

give members the feeling that they belonged to an important

club. Thus, club members were eager to devise a plan to deal with these problems. Once in the room, their discussions were frustratingly repetitive, which suggested that some outside inputs might be useful. One of the issues they wanted to work on related to their excessive consumption of cigarettes, soda, and candy. Beyond jeopardizing their health, they knew that poor nutrition and fitness sapped their energy, while the extra pounds weighed down their self-esteem. Moreover, the money spent on these items often left them short of funds at the end of the month. One member suggested a nutrition and fitness program. After an enthusiastic discussion of diets and exercises, the members decided to obtain some outside help. "Who might be available, how do we get them, and how do we tell them what we want?"

The regular weekly program included volleyball and swimming sessions, but these sessions were also frustrating. Various members might slip up in making reservations, in getting information out to the members, in arranging car pools, or in finding instructors or referees. This resulted in much complaining and frequent cries for better planning.

Money to develop club activities was an ever-present problem. "Should we do a bake sale or a car wash?" "Whom can we get to help us?" "How will we divide up the responsibilities?" "If only we could get our bylaws in shape we could apply for nonprofit status. Then sources of financial support would be open to us."

The public mental health system itself was another concern: "We need to get people to go to the state hospital to visit patients about to be discharged and tell them about the Intrepids. What arrangements do we need to make? In particular how do we get around Mr. _____, who is a bottleneck?" And on a different aspect of the mental health system, "Shouldn't we have something to say about the Recipient Rights policy? Let's get someone down from the central office and talk to that person." The salience of these ever-present concerns about resources, leadership, and organizational purposes intensified at certain times. The mental health department, for example, might offer a subsidy to participate in a statewide meeting of consumer-run organizations. "Whom shall we send? What do we want that person to say? How will we divide up the money?"

These issues suggest some of the focuses for organizational development efforts. And though only one or two issues could be worked on at a time, even a little progress raised morale and spilled over into other areas of the club's functioning.

Turning the situation around, self-help organizations have a great deal to offer professional organizations. The state hospital and the local community mental health center were both having their problems in areas in which the Intrepids could provide assistance. Many patients were leaving the hospital without adequate plans having been made for them. The Intrepids had some good ideas about managing needs related to shelter, food, clothing, social activities, and employment. Moreover, they were eager to participate in a program to discuss these issues with their peers. The aftercare program run by the community mental health center was losing clients. The Intrepids felt the drop-in schedule should be changed because many of their people did not get up that early in the morning. They also felt that there would be fewer losses if the clinic developed a more effective way of soliciting and handling patients' complaints. They thought a clinic suggestion box would help. They also felt that confidentiality was being misused. Sometimes it seemed as if staff was using it as an excuse for doing nothing. The Intrepids were especially put off when "confidentiality" prevented them from getting immediate assistance for one of their members who was getting "spacy again." Some members were also willing to help out in patient education programs when the topics included managing with or without family and the pros and cons of medication. As before, there were too many issues to work on. However, a loosely connected but heated discussion of confidentiality with a clinic representative at a club meeting was followed by an improvement in club attitude toward the clinic. It was not a result one would have predicted, hearing some of the angry charges in the meeting. No doubt it was facilitated by some changes in the way the clinic interpreted confidentiality requirements.

The foregoing not only suggests how reciprocal organizational development activities can be beneficial, it should also suggest how misunderstandings can grow when there are no activities. Internal operations of both organizations can be handicapped by the lack of contacts and information when they do not recognize that their vitality depends on the quality of their external linkages. In this respect, self-help and professional organizations resemble one another, because both tend to relate to their complementary counterparts in a tenuous, fragmentary manner. This chapter shows how both types of organizations can benefit from reciprocal organizational development strategies with their natural partners in the corresponding self-help or professional system.

WHAT IS ORGANIZATIONAL DEVELOPMENT?

Hall defines the objectives and methods of organizational development (OD) by elaborating on an earlier definition by French:

"Organizational development refers to a long-range effort to improve an organization's problem-solving capabilities and its ability to cope with changes in its external environment with the help of external or internal behavior-scientist consultants or change agents, as they are sometimes called." . . . It works from the perceptions of the problems by key groups in the organization. The emphasis in OD is on units within organizations rather than on individuals, with the objective being units whose members relate to and understand each other and the objectives of their unit and the total organization.[1]

Thus the benefits available through the exchange of OD assistance with an external partner are focused on. Through these exchanges, organizations can develop and make better use of their distinctive capabilities. Consider, for example, how high school counselors might incorporate Alateen, Women for Sobriety, or the Adult Children of Alcoholics in their program. In a less public context, consider how both parties might benefit if regular interactions between high school counselors and the Federation of Parents and Friends of Lesbians and Gays occurred. Through such exchanges, both groups could better understand those functions for which they are unusually well suited, as against those that can be performed more effectively by the complementary, external organization.

Another positive feature of OD is its leverage. Even modest OD interventions, such as speaking to a related external unit, can produce benefits that will be felt throughout the organization for some time. Such collaborative activities may also lead to more appreciation of the paradox that both organizations become stronger if they recognize and actuate their potential interdependence.

Another function of collaboration on organizational development is to correct an overemphasis on clinical collaboration. Too much clinical consultation may lead to dependency and slow leadership development unless it is part of a larger plan. People who depend on consultation may feel less like leaders and be less likely to implement a progressive leadership training program. Still another hazard is that too much emphasis on common clinical problems may cause people to neglect their distinctive attributes, encouraging an inadvertent tendency to give priority to their lowest common denominator. If similarity is emphasized, it may appear to downplay the technical expertise or legal authority of the professional agency. With the self-help organization, it may downplay the importance of other goals, such as those related to lifestyle support, social reform, and prevention. As distinctive competencies are seen as less important, the financially stronger organization (often the professional organization) is the more likely to survive and to dominate. Thus, exclusive reliance on clinical collaboration may interfere with growth and differentiation within organizations and thus undermine organizations' ability to perform their highest functions, the functions for which they are best suited and for which they have the most to offer.

CHALLENGES

Both clinical and organizationally oriented consultative programs are difficult to start and sustain; but of the two, OD is the more difficult. Many of the reasons cited in Chapter Fifteen concerning a natural reluctance to become a clinical "consultee" also apply to becoming an organizational "consultee." In both the clinical and the OD situations, the role of the consultee may be perceived as implying a deficiency that puts the consultee in a "one-down" position. The threat may be even greater when the perceived deficiencies are located in the organizational sphere. Though it takes courage to ask for consultation on a clinical matter, it probably takes even more courage to reveal organizational problems to an outsider who may then be invited to work on these deficiencies within the organization. This process makes people in both types of organizations—self-help and professional— feel vulnerable. Moreover, the threat is not diminished by arguments about the necessity of developing complementary resources and gaining knowledge.

Reciprocity

The best protection against this threat, the possible exploitation of the consultee's vulnerability, may be the reciprocal nature of the consulting relationship. Each party will have an opportunity to intervene. This can be reassuring, particularly if it adds to the reassurance derived from previous experiences with less threatening interactions related to referral and clinical consultation. If OD does not have this base to build on, or if previous experiences have been less than reassuring, the pace of OD will have to be slowed accordingly. Here again, the best reassurance may be that today's consultee will be tomorrow's consultant, and vice versa. The trick will be a setup in which both parties can have short trials as providers as well as receivers of OD. Thus, both are challenged to be effective recipients. As they ponder their own reactions, they will also be better OD providers.

300   Some of these concerns and factors have a positive side. The favorable leverage of OD means that it can institute positive changes that persist long after the original interveners have departed. The persistence of these benefits beyond the OD consultant's active involvement may be a partial answer to concerns about long-term dependency relations. Once the problem-solving mechanisms are in place, the host or consultee is no longer dependent on the external consultant. Yet it is not completely reassuring; it is not enough to eliminate the threat that accompanies the risk of a potential disaster in a poorly conceived or executed OD transaction. The magnitude of the risk is often much greater than the risk that can result from a mishandled referral or an insensitive case consultation. Any problems resulting from these latter situations usually permit a more prompt and thorough recovery than is possible from a poorly conceived structural OD change. It will be easier, for example, to repair the damage resulting from an inappropriate clinical confrontation than it will be to redirect a committee embarked on an errant course. The sensitivity of OD arrangements should eliminate any embarrassment either party might have in asking for an explicit review of preceding referral and clinical consultation experiences before entering an OD relationship. This is a prudent action that should be shared before moving toward a potentially more rewarding, but also a more risky, OD relationship.

Dislike of Formality

Another challenge in OD work springs from the personal styles of the actors themselves. The initiators of collaborative projects are often inclined to behave entrepreneurially. The reward is not money but rather the satisfaction of initiating new projects. To the extent this is true, initiators may be disinclined to become involved in consolidating their gains through formal arrangements. Yet without some formal agreement, the gains are endangered. To maintain and augment gains, initiators must undertake what they often regard as an unpleasant chore. They need to involve more and different kinds of people, including those who are formal decision makers. In all except the smallest of self-help and professional organizations, this may entail establishing committees, negotiating agreements, and developing written policies. Many of these tasks may be put off by the entrepreneur. Rather than trying to override their dislike, entrepreneurs should consider bringing more organizationally minded people into the OD project. These would be people who enjoy maintaining and building a project without having to own or originate it.

Respect for both founders and builders must be maintained *301* by avoiding language that suggests status. Too often there is the temptation to tag the initiator-originator as offbeat or to damn the organization builder with the faint praise of being a "good bureaucrat." Organizational development needs both kinds of people, people who can initiate pilot projects and people who can transform these pilots into substantial, stable programs. Because good intentions are not the same as good results, it is not surprising that good starts cannot be expected to end up in the right place without continuing guidance. Organizational development can be thought of as a continued effort to see that good intentions are realized through the systematic, mutual efforts of the self-help and the professional organizations.

But does OD favor the big and the complex? The big is viewed as beautiful; the small and less complicated as underdeveloped. This is true insofar as the small group limps along in isolation, with a weak, inconsistent program. It is also true insofar as formality is responsible for the success of such organizations as AA, Recovery, Inc., PWP, and NAMI.

However, it must also be acknowledged that small can be beautiful when these conditions are not present—especially when the comparison is with OD carried out sporadically and unenthusiastically, when it becomes counterproductive or less beneficial than a sustained exchange of cases and clinical consultations. Thus, it is only generally true that the exchange of referrals progresses to the exchange of clinical consultation and finally to OD. Similarly, it is only generally true that clinical consultation will improve the referral process and that OD will improve clinical consultation by encouraging the organization to maintain a proper balance. Thus, the general propositions set forth here are subject to the qualifications and exceptions mandated by the concrete world of practice. Effective practice requires selective and qualified use of the principles derived from these propositions. An absolute and invariant adherence to these propositions is sure to mock them. In the long run, OD propositions should be treated as important questions. In the short run, they direct attention to important factors and encourage reflection about how the proposition applies—if it does—to this particular situation.

METHODS AND AIMS OF ORGANIZATIONAL DEVELOPMENT

The methods of organizational level exchanges may be direct insofar as their goal is a specific effect on outcome. They are indirect insofar as their goal is to effect the processes whereby decisions are reached. By themselves, they do not favor changes in outcome. The idea is that the former works toward a specific decision or outcome while the latter focuses on improved decision making. Neither type is inherently superior, though they may be differentially linked to such variables as the acceptability and long-term viability of the collaboration, depending on the status of the OD provider. Much of the time, professionals should emphasize the less directive, outcome-related methods. Self-help leaders, however, may have more latitude to propose a variety of modifications in the program or outcome insofar as they pose less threat to the professional organization. But there are exceptions; AA may be perceived to threaten the integrity of professional organizations in some communities.

Familiarity of the methods used is another factor to be considered in the probable acceptability and success of collaboration. Familiarity may be reassuring, whereas the lack of familiarity may be disquieting. The former is exemplified by the use of ordinary presentation-discussion methods by members of Narcotics Anonymous to inform professionals about the culture of drug addicts. The latter might be exemplified by the use of action research methods to poll the membership of a self-help organization about possible social action objectives or how the organization might cooperate with a community institution. Though these may be powerful methods, they must also be recognized as entailing a certain risk. They may distract the organization from its central purpose or distort self-help operations through misuse. As a general principle, the stronger organization should use familiar methods in order not to give even the appearance of threatening the integrity of the weaker organization.

Direct Interventions

Self-help organizations may have a direct and beneficial influence on the outcomes of professional services by enhancing the professionals' understanding of the culture in which specific problems develop and are subsequently maintained and resolved. Moreover, they know the telltale signs of these sometimes hidden problems. In GA, for example, members are well aware of the role compulsive gambling plays in family discord, personal debt, and various frauds. No doubt many welfare workers, family therapists, and probation officers fail to detect the part of compulsive gambling in these problems. Through contact with GA, they could become more skilled at such detection and could also learn how to guide affected individuals to appropriate remedial facilities. Members of GA can also offer advice about when an aggressive approach should be taken and when it should not. They will point out that unless the gambling problem is recognized, the professional will be perceived to be naive. Such discussions are also likely to make professionals feel more confident about the conditions under which their treatment methods are more likely to succeed and about how the self-help and professional modalities are complementary. This information will be more vivid than the professional's previous knowledge and may contain some ideas that might not have been evident from previous professional experience: for example, the preference for "outside" jobs or "self-employment" among compulsive gamblers. Such knowledge can directly affect outcome.

Self-helpers may also have a direct effect on outcome in using methods seldom available to professionals. The veteran handicapped have contributed important information to professionals about their experiences with various prostheses and appliances. People with ostomies, with hearing and visual impairments, or with any of a broad spectrum of other handicaps have helped professionals better understand the performance, care, and cosmetic considerations related to a variety of devices. This information has enhanced the effectiveness of professionals, particularly with patients in the early stages of adapting to their handicap who are not psychologically ready to use self-help organizations for assistance.

Indirect Process Interventions

In trying to assist self-help organizations, the professional agency should favor process goals rather than attempt to affect outcome directly. For example, simple questionnaires can be used to poll members, not about what should be done, but rather about how it should be done. Members might be asked to develop mechanisms to collect information on the effectiveness of various recruitment strategies (for example, media contacts as against agency visits) or about proposed changes in policy (for example, the role of family members). Process assistance might take the form of a plan to discuss value conflicts (for example, the importance of protecting the organization against misuse or being open to all comers), or it might address the desire for better meetings (that is, fewer interruptions and digressions) as against allowing everyone to have a say. Other examples of process assistance from the professional might be developing alternative plans to improve the committee structure or to revise the bylaws of self-help organizations. All these examples illustrate the improvement of process rather than of outcome. It is an approach that deliberately avoids specifying the direction of outcome change, and thus it may be more acceptable and valid for the outsider professional.

On occasion, however, direct, outcome-related assistance will be both sought and needed from professionals. They may be asked to consult with self-help organizations, for example, about how to obtain better foster care or hospitalization services for self-helpers. They may also be asked to provide information about the effects of medication or to intervene by requesting information about court hearing procedures or eligibility for benefits. There is still a risk, however, that these interventions will be seen as an imposition of the professional's opinion on the organization. Since they involve the professional in controversial areas, he or she may be viewed as wishing to control the self-help organization outcomes. Thus, when there is a choice, it may be wise for the professional to rely more on interventions aiming at process rather than at outcome—at least at first.

Dominant Organizations: Less Directive Methods

The general principle is that the stronger organization must be leery of working directly on outcome issues so as not to threaten the integrity of the less dominant organization. Insofar as self-help organizations tend to be less threatening because of their modest financial resources and unofficial standing, self-help leaders may have more latitude to engage in outcome interventions. It may be acceptable, for example, for self-helpers to recommend specific changes in the intake procedures of a protective services agency or in the options to be offered a parent involved in a recurrence of child abuse. A powerful organization like AA, however, should caution its members about speaking to professionals. For even when they speak as individuals, AA members may be seen as trying to dictate the basic program of the professional agency unless they are quite circumspect.

Nonetheless, self-help leaders will usually have more opportunities than professionals to offer assistance that directly bears on the outcome or proposed resolution of the problem. For example, it might be considered appropriate for self-help leaders to speak directly on the "do's and don't's" of working with clients who are still substance abusers. But if professionals issued a similar list of "do's and don't's," it might be viewed as out of place. Thus, professionals might find it more valuable and acceptable to work on such process tasks as raising the level of knowledge about the organization in the wider community. The natural affinities hypothesized between the two types of OD (process and out- *305* come) and the self-help or professional status of the consultant is intended only to exemplify the importance of clarifying the respective strengths of these two types of OD consultants or agents.

The measure of success, in any event, will be whether OD exchanges increase the legitimacy of both organizations. Members of self-help organizations are apt to feel more confident about their participation knowing that professionals may have contributed, and perhaps still are contributing, to the program. Furthermore, ongoing referrals from professionals will be taken as a further endorsement of the self-help program. Similarly, nonmember clients of professionals may be reassured to know that well-known self-help organizations actively collaborate with the agency. And at another level, these transactions should help both organizations develop more robust helping programs.

PRINCIPLES OF BUILDING SUPPORTIVE STRUCTURAL ARRANGEMENTS

Respect Structure

Since OD projects often have consequences for the entire organization, it is important that they be integrated into the overall structures of both organizations. The usual structural arrangements (linkage, authority, responsibility, etc.) need to be even more rigorously adhered to than they were in less consequential clinical exchanges (unless, of course, the intent is to upset them). Ordinarily, executives should be involved from the beginning to help develop policy about these structural arrangements, as well as to lend official sanction to the project. Joint committees and task forces can be important structural means to support and guide OD.

Involve People

These structural arrangements also have the advantage in that they tend to involve more people, which enhances the stability of the project by lessening dependence on a few actors. For unless a broad group of people feel they have a stake in the OD project, it will be seriously jeopardized as people leave or as personal alignments and loyalties shift within the agency.

Develop Resources

As arrangements are made, the OD project can increasingly draw on the total resources of both organizations. It is through these arrangements that the pooled human and material resources of both organizations are made available. Accordingly, these projects often can orchestrate a rich diversity of resources on behalf of their approved goals. Approval by their own parent organizations will later leave both organizations in the OD project in a favorable position to have their own recommendations approved. Thus, they will be able to institutionalize their own policy recommendations, that is, to incorporate their recommendations in the everyday operation of both organizations.

A Case Study

Some of these principles can be seen in collaboration between a local chapter of Make Today Count (MTC) and a university research team.[2] This analysis is based on a detailed report of the consultation procedures, a type of report that is found too infrequently in the literature. This fine report provides important insights related to the OD process with a self-help organization. The project began with the researchers asking to observe the meetings of a particular MTC chapter. The request stemmed from their participation in a research program to investigate the procedures and processes used by self-help organizations.[3] After receiving the chapter's permission, the researchers were alert for opportunities to offer assistance to the chapter, consolidate their entry, and foster a more mutual relationship. They decided to offer OD after several meetings in which they made the following observations:

> In spite of [their] assets, our observers agreed that numerous signs reflected weaknesses. For one thing, a low percentage (about 20%) of the group were cancer patients. From members' comments, we concluded the group had little success in recruiting new members. Meetings lacked a cohesive format. Organizational questions, such as the group's target population, were frequently discussed, but not resolved. There was little discussion of adjustment difficulties. Ominously, the frequency of meetings had been reduced from twice to once per month. These observations led us to believe the group was not fully meeting the members' needs.[4]

As part of their study, the consultants were able to attend the national convention of Make Today Count. There they discovered that many chapters had had difficulties similar to those of the local chapter. Furthermore, a number of the methods used by these chapters to resolve their problems were potentially relevant to the local chapter. When they returned, they shared their impressions with one of the founders. She responded en- *307* thusiastically and arranged for the research team to make a presentation to the chapter. After this report on the problem-solving methods used by other affiliates, the members discussed what might be applicable to their particular situation. The outcome was a formal request asking the team to explore and report back on possible OD strategies.

Over the next several months, the research team held many discussions with the members. Summaries of these discussions and the information collected outside were prepared. And, as the chapter had requested, the OD group produced a document containing information about how "to enhance group organization and facilitate personal discussion." These activities culminated in the presentation of a series of detailed guidelines for improving chapter meetings, including a description of procedures to facilitate group discussion. The success of this project owes much to the straightforward style and flexible procedures used by the OD consultants:

> The way in which the guidelines were presented should be mentioned. We stressed that they were not the only lines for reorganization but might be considered useful alternatives. We also recognized the group's final responsibility for implementing the guidelines. Within this context, our presentation was received enthusiastically.[5]

CRITIQUE: Although this collaboration was mutually beneficial, it departed in significant ways from the principles set forth here. The relationship remained asymmetric, according to the MTC consultees. They never quite accepted the idea that their contribution to the research project was adequate compensation for the assistance they received from the team. They could hardly feel otherwise, given the passive form of their payback; it would have been better if they could have played a more active role in the plan for and the execution of the research. But, however it might have been done, they needed to feel that they were involved in active reciprocal changes. Not having this feeling, they felt that their interviews and the observations of their activities they permitted constituted an unequal exchange with the consultants who were actively helping them.

Furthermore, the strategy of the OD consultants did not follow the recommended sequence: Organizational development did not come after clinical exchange. To be sure, this was primarily a research team, not a typical OD team, if there is such a thing. One would have a hard time knowing, given the paucity of the published material, about OD practice. But the main point is that it is hard to quarrel with what works. Theoretically oriented prescriptions must be subordinated to the injunction: Do what works. It should be considered axiomatic that the world of collaboration is seldom as simple as the concepts that purport to explain it. Thus, allowance will have to be made for numerous exceptions and adjustments if theoretically oriented principles are to be useful. It is in this sense that the project is a good example of a theoretically guided organizational development project initiated by professionals. Another project with The Compassionate Friends highlights the professional's role as an intermediary between the organization and the community.[6] Through this means the professional also helps the organization articulate its own ideology.

A Self-Help Coalition

Opportunities for initiatives from the self-help side are suggested by the activities of a Toronto-based coalition of self-help organizations that pursued a multipronged effort to change certain professional practices. Gottlieb and Schroter catalogued the coalition activities as follows: They contributed to the basic educational programs of professionals, they conducted workshops and other continuing education programs for professionals, and they participated in the staff development programs of professional agencies and clinics. The wide range of their work might well inspire self-help organizations in other communities. Additional details about their impressive "pedagogical services to health professionals" are as follows:

> In Toronto, Ontario, Community Self-Help Inc., an umbrella organization of representatives from over 30 self-help groups, has presented the work of its affiliates at numerous mental health agencies and at business and government management workshops. They have also had an impact on the training of future health care professionals. They have added to the behavioral science curriculum of freshmen medical students at the University of Toronto by offering seminars on the doctor-patient communication process and on the self-help group as an adjunct treatment resource.[7]

THE WORK OF SELF-HELP CLEARINGHOUSES

A different tack, a broker-consultant approach, has been taken by various clearinghouses listed in Appendix Two. The work of the New Jersey Self-Help Clearinghouse will be used to exemplify   *309* some of what is possible.[8] The Clearinghouse works "both sides of the street" to foster contact between self-help units and professional organizations. The result has been that agencies have developed more comprehensive ties to self-help organizations and organizations have used the Clearinghouse's OD assistance to enrich programs, in addition to the help they received in forming and strengthening ties to professional agencies.

One of the most important Clearinghouse activities involved connecting people to self-help organizations. Computerized files with up-to-date information about the location, schedules, and contact persons for a huge number of self-help organizations are maintained. Usually this is sufficient to connect callers to self-help organizations. Occasionally, it may be necessary to maintain contact with certain individuals until there are enough of them to start their own self-help group. Thus, they can become a resource for this computer-created network. (The software, MASHnet, used to maintain this network, may be purchased from the New Jersey Clearinghouse.) Sometimes it will be necessary to form, with assistance from the Clearinghouse if desired, a new chapter of an existing organization within a community. These activities are supported by a very useful published directory[9] (backed up by easily updated computer files) that lists addresses, telephone numbers, and contact persons of local chapters of self-help organizations. One of the directory's most useful features is a description of the model programs of national organizations, along with telephone numbers and addresses of the national offices. The directory also indicates if there are start-up kits, as there often are, from the "national," which can be requested by those who want to form a local chapter. A separate source book provides information about more than 450 organizations with collectively thousands of chapters throughout the country.[10] This publication will be of value to help-seekers everywhere.

Sometimes this information can be complemented by information available from a different kind of directory, one that allows self-help organizations to speak for themselves through their own brochures and publications. Gartner and Riessman's directory reproduces the brochures of major self-help organizations.[11] This is a convenient way to become acquainted with the philosophy and methods of many organizations.

However, the preference given to existing organizations by both the Clearinghouse and Gartner and Riessman's monograph is not absolute. New groups are needed when no suitable models are available. For this reason, *Help*[12] devotes a specific section to this topic, and the stance of the Clearinghouse is evident in the following letter addressed to the director of the agency:

I recently contacted the N.J. Self-Help Clearinghouse for a support group for me to attend with other parents of handicapped children. There wasn't any in many miles. So after making a few more phone calls to other mothers in the same situation, I decided to start my own group. When I called back and spoke to _____, I was encouraged, enlightened, and given much needed advice to start my support group. [She] listened to my side, as a parent, and I listened to her, as a consultant. I feel I would have never really started my group if it were not for _____.

A Clearinghouse Organizational Development Program

The ambitious organizational development goals of the New Jersey Self-Help Clearinghouse come through in the following announcement (September 21, 1982), which offered various consultation services.

Through the MENTAL HEALTH MUTUAL HELP PROJECT, consultation services will be offered at the location of selected agencies to

* assist in identifying potential group members and leaders.

* educate and train staff regarding the concepts and dynamics of self-help groups.

* meet with each group to assist in identifying needs and interests, and in setting up objectives and an organizational plan.

* assist program staff, clients, and families in utilizing the expertise of representatives of other successful groups.

* serve as a liaison between agencies, staff, groups, and individuals interested in forming and maintaining groups throughout the State.

Although this OD initiative was undertaken by a clearinghouse, similar initiatives are within the capability of other community-oriented organizations. Network development projects could be initiated by local family and mental health agencies in conjunction with local leaders of one or two of the major self-help organizations. Such an initiative might be sponsored by a community coordinating or planning agency. Additional links to the United Way or a comprehensive governmental human service agency might help the coalition remain active. The advantages of maintaining contact among self-help organizations is evident in the way certain self-help organizations have been founded.   *311*

Though not as representatives of their organization, members of AA founded Gamblers Anonymous and Overeaters Anonymous. Similarly, members of Al-Anon helped found Families Anonymous.

The members of these "parent," or predecessor, organizations used to advantage their knowledge of an approach that was built on certain minimum formal policies and procedures (steps and traditions). These proved highly adaptable to the needs of people with other troublesome conditions. And though the successful transfer of this model has been attributed to the compulsive personalities that are presumed to be common to people with these conditions, it may be that more of the explanation lies in the basic vitality of the model. The Twelve Steps and Traditions form the vital core of these organizations. These Steps and Traditions are repeatedly brought alive and infused with new energy in various chapter meetings and the publications of the National Service Office. Even more immediately, their vitality is felt in sponsorship arrangements at the local level. Because it reached its present development only after years of cautious experimentation, it is no surprise that it receives serious consideration in the search for models that might be suitable for other problematic conditions.

NEW CHAPTERS VS. NEW ORGANIZATIONS

Starting a new self-help organization is a very different matter from starting a chapter of an existing organization. Though the idea has a certain appeal when one considers how many lives have been altered for the better by some of the major self-help organizations, one must also look at how they got there and how many fell along the way. Some might also be sobered when they consider the difficult times most of the major self-help organizations went through in their development. None emerged from the minds of their founders as full-blown, successful programs. Instead, they typically started as weak, unstable groups that somehow muddled through long periods of little notice, disappointing participation, internal conflict, and underdeveloped program methods. If observers had been asked about the future of these organizations in their early years, few would have predicted such splendid results. As a matter of fact, the safest prediction for most fledgling self-help groups is that they will die after struggling for a period. The well-known organizations discussed here are rare exceptions.

Box 6.

Principles of Organizational Development

1. Begin by initiating diverse clinical consultation arrangements.
2. Next identify organizational level problems such as:
   a. insufficient information about the cultural context of the difficulty or low acceptance of the program among potential clients.
   b. insufficient information about scientific developments or alternative organizational arrangements among self-help members.
3. Explore mutual needs and possible joint projects.
4. Formulate specific alternative problem-solving strategies.
5. Solicit the preferences of the potential organization regarding these alternatives.
6. Implement and build on a low-risk pilot project.
7. Create and energize numerous formal feedback mechanisms.
8. Evaluate results.

Starting a New Chapter

This suggests that starting a new group or organization should be considered only as a last resort, and only then if the would-be founders are prepared for a long struggle to survive. And then, too, only if they appreciate that survival itself is no guarantee of effectiveness. Considering the unfavorable odds, it usually is preferable to form a chapter of an existing organization or to beef up one that already exists. The national offices of these organizations are an important resource in these endeavors. They often make informal consultation available, and some may facilitate seeding a new group with senior "on loan" members from another chapter. Most can make start-up materials available to interested persons, though these materials vary widely in the amount of guidance offered. At one end of the spectrum are the highly sophisticated aids such as the *Chapter Development Manual* of Parents Anonymous.[13] (See also Box 6.) This beautifully conceived and executed manual could be recommended to anyone contem-   *313* plating the formation of a task group, whether self-help or not. At the other end, only a modest, but still important, word of encouragement may be available. Such was contained in the following form letter received in the Spring of 1983 from Divorce Anonymous:

> We are sorry if there has been a delay in acknowledging your inquiry. D. A. is strictly an all volunteer, non-profit, non-funded, non-staffed, loosely-knit association of "people helping people."
>
> P.S. We do not have an affiliated group in your area at the present time. Why not start one? The work is most rewarding. It only takes a nucleus of 3 or more people who are willing to listen with empathy and understanding (not giving advice).
>
> In our efforts to help others, we learn, grow, and find answers for ourselves.

This modest assistance, however, is not necessarily a reliable indicator of long-term viability. Divorce Anonymous continues despite Lieberman and Borman's fear (1979) that "Divorce Anonymous, despite its long history, [is] a disintegrating group."[14] If experienced observers of self-help organizations such as these have trouble predicting which underdeveloped self-help organizations will survive, it would seem rash to write off organizations that have attractive features.

Starting from Scratch

For the ambitious, but, one hopes, not for the inordinately so, the option remains to start a self-help organization from scratch. This action can be justified only if serious consideration has been given to the advantages of starting a local chapter of an existing self-help organization as against starting the original chapter of a new self-help organization. In the former case, one can make use of both the written and oral experience of others who have passed that way before. Explorers, however, have no maps; they have only a general knowledge of the countryside through which they must pass and the hazards that must be avoided. To help them on their way, however, there are a number of guides for starting new self-help groups.[15] Yet it should be understood that the necessity of pitching such guides at a general level renders them less valuable than the aforementioned start-up kits targeted to the needs of a particular group. Moreover, these guides may also pose a danger by encouraging excessive entrepreneurial activity and thus add to the further proliferation of isolated self-help groups without ties to a supportive network made up of a national coordinating office and other chapters.

As an alternative to starting a new group, one might also consider working with the many unnetworked and underdeveloped groups already functioning in local communities. These groups have an advantage in that they have attracted people with a demonstrated commitment to self-help. Moreover, they may be hungry to work with people who can help them create robust autonomous organizations. But should none of these arguments for building on existing organizations apply, the would-be founders might well consider the "model designs" of major self-help organizations such as AA, Recovery, Inc., and The Compassionate Friends. These designs may be more suitable than the informal, undifferentiated arrangements of support groups. The self-help organizations accommodate more diverse interests and talents and are associated with a richer overall program. The suggestion is not to start by trying to fill out one of these complex designs, but rather to be prepared to move in one of these directions as the group develops. On another aspect of design, the founders of new groups might consider that the earlier founders of surviving and successful organizations did not permit themselves to become dependent on outside approval or funding.

A LAST WORD

This book, it can now be admitted, should even now be revised to accommodate greater complexity. No doubt it has shaded matters on the side of optimism and simplicity. This was inevitable, given the tremendous scope and variation inherent in the self-help field. To make sense of it, at least initially, it was necessary to deal with simple patterns and positive features before dealing with more mixed and complex ones. Thus, the reader should be on the alert to identify instances in which complexity has been glossed over; in which systematic processes have been posited but only random ones exist; and in which positive features have been highlighted while negative ones have been left in the shadows.

Another point recalls a major theme of this book: self-help organizations and minorities. The ultimate relevance of self-help organizations depends on how well they serve minorities. In many places, minorities are the numerical majority. Though people from all walks of life, from every occupation, race, and ethnic group, are members of self-help organizations, it is, nonetheless, a fact that ethnic minorities do not have equal access to self-help organizations. Other people are disadvantaged by sex. Some organizations probably enroll too few women, e.g., Narcotics Anonymous and Gamblers Anonymous, whereas many more enroll too few men, e.g., Al-Anon, Parents Anonymous, and NAMI.   *315*

In terms of these deficiencies in the analysis and in the social instrument itself, the reader is encouraged to take corrective action. As far as the analyses are concerned, more probing empirical studies and more sophisticated conceptualizations must be focused on self-help organizations. As far as the instrument goes, self-help organizations must assume more of their rightful responsibility for ethnic minorities and other disadvantaged people. They need to be more aware of their responsibility for social justice.

Notes

1. R. H. Hall, *Organizations: Structure and Process* (2nd ed.; Englewood Cliffs, N.J.: Prentice-Hall, 1977), p. 229, quoting W. French, "Organization Development: Objectives, Assumptions and Strategies," *California Management Review,* 12 (Winter 1969), p. 23.
2. R. W. Wollert, B. Knight, and L. H. Levy, "Make Today Count; A Collaborative Model for Professionals and Self-Help Groups," *Professional Psychology,* 11 (February 1980), pp. 130–138.
3. L. H. Levy, "Self-Help Groups: Types and Psychological Processes," *Journal of Applied Behavioral Science,* 12 (July–August–September 1976), pp. 310–322.
4. Wollert, Knight, and Levy, "Make Today Count," pp. 132–133.
5. Ibid., p. 133.
6. D. Klass, "Self-Help Groups for the Bereaved: Theory, Theology, and Practice," *Journal of Religion and Health,* 21 (Winter 1982), pp. 317–323.
7. B. H. Gottlieb and C. Schroter, "Collaboration and Resource Exchange Between Professionals and Natural Support Systems," *Professional Psychology,* 9 (November 1978), pp. 614–622.
8. E. J. Madara, "The Self-Help Clearinghouse Operation: Tapping the Resource Development Potential of I & R Services," *Information and Referral: The Journal of the Alliance of Information and Referral Systems,* 7 (Summer 1985), pp. 42–58; and Madara, "A Comprehensive Systems Approach to Promoting Mutual Aid Self-Help Groups: The New Jersey Self-Help Clearinghouse Model," *Journal of Voluntary Action Research,* 15 (April–June 1986), pp. 57–63.
9. K. Larkin, A. Meese, and E. J. Madara, *The Self-Help Group Directory, 1984–85* (Denville: New Jersey Self-Help Clearinghouse, 1985).
10. E. J. Madara and A. Meese, *The Self-Help Sourcebook: Finding and Forming Mutual Aid Self-Help Groups* (Denville: New Jersey Self-Help Clearinghouse, 1986).
11. A. Gartner and F. Riessman, *Help: A Working Guide to Self-Help Groups* (New York: New Viewpoints/Vision Books, 1980).
12. Ibid., pp. 162–167.
13. M. Fritz, *Chapter Development Manual* (rev. ed.; Redondo Beach, Calif.: Parents Anonymous, 1982).

14. M. A. Lieberman and L. D. Borman, eds., *Self-Help Groups for Coping with Crisis: Origins, Members, Processes, and Impact* (San Francisco: Jossey-Bass, 1979), p. 419.

15. A. Humm, *How to Organize a Self-Help Group* (New York: Self-Help Clearinghouse, City University of New York, 1979); P. R. Silverman, *Mutual Help Groups: Organization and Development* (Beverly Hills, Calif.: Sage Publications, 1980); L. E. Borck and E. Aronowitz, "The Role of a Self-Help Clearinghouse," *Prevention in Human Services,* 1 (Spring 1982), pp. 121–129; E. Bowles, *Self-Help Groups: An Instructional Guide for Developing Self-Help Groups* (New York: Center for Advanced Study in Education, City University of New York, 1978); and National Institute on Drug Abuse, *Manual for Setting Up Self-Help Groups of Ex-Narcotic Addicts,* DHHS Publication No. (ADM) 81-1087 (Washington, D.C.: Department of Health & Human Services, 1981).

Appendix I

Table A.1. Composite of the Properties of Various Types of Self-Help Organizations

Habit Disturbance

Exemplar Organizations
Alcoholics Anonymous; Women for Sobriety; Gamblers Anonymous; Narcotics Anonymous; TOPS (Take Off Pounds Sensibly); Overeaters Anonymous; I Can Quit; Weight Watchers; Smokestoppers

Public Image
  Widely recognized; large, well accepted
  Easy to understand
  Autonomous organizations
  Some commercial forms

Goals
  From a new member's point of view: Single-minded in purpose
  Specific, narrowly focused
  Concrete

Technology
  "Behavior" first
  Standardized approaches
  Reference group and fellowship processes
  Additional resources available through expanded networks
  Role development through leadership opportunities
  Printed information available

Career Pattern
  Slips common
  Repeat members
  Experience may be short and intensive for smoking
    and overeating habits
  Leadership roles formally structured

Normalization Potential[a]
  Universalizes +
  Accepts relapses
  Preoccupation with recovering°

Relationship to Professionals
  Mutual respect
  Indirect, behind the scenes
  Printed information often discussed in professional journals

[a] +, positive; o, negative.

319

Table A.1. Continued

General Purpose

Exemplar Organizations
Parents Anonymous; GROW; Emotions Anonymous; Recovery, Inc.;
The Compassionate Friends

Public Image
Distinguished by distinctive methods and
the charismatic personality of founder(s)
Size of meetings small
Number of meetings (chapters) may be large
Remedial or problem-solving approach
may have a quaint or marginal quality

Goals
General and abstract
Require personal, concrete interpretation

Technology
Cognitive-expressive techniques
Reference group processes
Identification building
Resembles psychotherapy; uses mentors
and models

Career Pattern
Long term
Intensity intermittent
Involved in multiple life spheres

Normalization Potential[a]
"Graduate" groups +
Open-ended
Entrapping o

Relationship to Professionals
Professional founders
Professional backup
Susceptible to professional domination
Potentially competitive

---

[a] +, positive; o, negative.

Table A.1. Continued

Lifestyle

Exemplar Organizations
Widow-to-widow programs; Parents Without Partners and singles
groups; La Leche League; Little People; CUB (Concerned United
Birthparents); ALMA (Adoptees' Liberty Movement Association);
Parents/FLAG (Parents and Friends of Lesbians and Gays); National
Gay and Lesbian Task Force

Public Image
    Some may be viewed with suspicion,
            e.g., gay and patient liberation organizations
    Many larger ones, e.g., singles and
            widow organizations, pose fewer challenges
            to society and are better accepted

Goals
    Advocacy and social support
    Strengthen salience of reference group
    Obtain more support from reference group

Technology
    Companionship
    Network development
    Community mobilization
    Political campaigns
    Legal initiatives

Career Pattern
    Lifelong
    Affects broad sectors of members' lives

Normalization Potential[a]
    Society is abnormal[+]
    Exaggerates and exposes "deviancy"[o]

Relationship to Professionals
    Professionals are symbols of society's oppression
    Public relationships tend to be antagonistic
            but behind the scenes cooperation is
            not uncommon

[a] +, positive; o, negative.

Table A.1. Continued

Significant Other

Exemplar Organizations
National Alliance for the Mentally Ill; Families Anonymous;
Toughlove; Al-Anon; Gam-Anon

Public Image
Advocates for the mentally ill
Restores rights to families
Balances rights of family with deviants
Public is sympathetic with goals
Fits with the conservative 1980s
Growing fast

Goals
Provides relief to families
Protects and prevents problems in families
Reform-minded

Technology
Uses network and organizational
building strategies
Social support
Education
Advocacy
Policy development

Career Pattern
Medium-term memberships
Moderate commitment
Potential conflict between advocacy
and support interests

Normalization Potential[a]
Patient, not family +
Family vs. patient[o]
Professional, not family[o]
Professional vs. family[o]

Relationship to Professionals
Bargaining
Contractual

[a] +, positive; o, negative.

Table A.1. Continued

Physical Handicap

Exemplar Organizations
Make Today Count; United Ostomy Association; Emphysema
Anonymous; Stroke Clubs; Mended Hearts; Cerebral Palsy
Association; Lost Chord Clubs; Spina Bifida Association; Lupus
Foundation; Deafpride; Self-Help for Hard of Hearing People; The
Epilepsy Foundation; National Foundation for Ileitis and Colitis;
Endometriosis Association; Emerging herpes and AIDS groups

Public Image
Fast-growing organizations
Major diseases represented
Cooperative orientation
High public acceptance
Complements medical technology
Distinctive function
Rehabilitation rather than cure
Disadvantaged underrepresented

Goals
Disease-specific, adaptational goals
Lifestyle issues related to work, travel, self-reliance, social
and sexual attractiveness
Technical issues: prostheses, appliances, diet, scientific
developments

Technology
Processes: inspiration, reinforcement, modeling, information-
communication, encouragement, behavioral monitoring
Procedures: hospital visitation, individual and group
discussion, newsletters, pen pals

Career Pattern
Long term but varying in intensity
Pay back through direct helping of others and performing
organizational roles
Tribute funds and legacies continue the payback

Normalization Potential[a]
Competent models participate in the community in spite of
handicap[+]
Preoccupation with handicap[o]

Relationship to Professionals
Complementary and distinctive
Recognizes interdependence
Cooperative and reciprocal

[a] +, positive; o, negative.

Appendix II

Self-Help Clearinghouses

NATIONAL SELF-HELP
CLEARINGHOUSE
City University of New York
Graduate Center, Room 1227
33 West 42nd Street
New York, NY 10036
(212) 840-1258 or 840-1259

CALIFORNIA SELF-HELP CENTER
UCLA, 2349 Franz Hall
405 Hilgard Avenue
Los Angeles, CA 90024
(213) 825-1799

SUPPORT GROUP CLEARINGHOUSE
OF MERCED COUNTY
Mental Health Association
P.O. Box 343
Merced, CA 95341
(209) 723-5111

SACRAMENTO SELF-HELP
CLEARINGHOUSE
Mental Health Association
5370 Elvas Avenue, Suite B
Sacramento, CA 95819

SAN DIEGO SELF-HELP
CLEARINGHOUSE
P.O. Box 86246
San Diego, CA 92138–6246
(619) 275-2344

BAY AREA SELF-HELP
CLEARINGHOUSE
c/o Mental Health Association
2398 Pine Street
San Francisco, CA 94115
(415) 921-4401

CONNECTICUT SELF-HELP/
MUTUAL SUPPORT NETWORK
The Consultation Center
19 Howe Street
New Haven, CT 06511
(203) 789-7645

SELF-HELP CENTER
1600 Dodge Avenue, Suite 2–122
Evanston, IL 60201
(312) 328-0470

SELF-HELP CENTER OF KANSAS
3428 East Central
Witchita, KS 67208
(316) 686-1205

CENTER FOR SELF-HELP
Riverwood Community Mental
Health Center
512 Ship Street, Suite 8
St. Joseph, MI 49085
(616) 983-0343

MINNESOTA MUTUAL HELP
RESOURCE CENTER
Wilder Foundation Community Care Unit
919 Lafond Avenue
St. Paul, MN 55104
(612) 642-4060

SUPPORT GROUP CLEARINGHOUSE
Kansas City Association for
Mental Health
1001 East 63rd Street
Kansas City, MO 64110
(816) 361-5007

SELF-HELP INFORMATION SERVICE
1601 Euclid Street
Lincoln, NE 68502
(402) 476-9668

NEW JERSEY SELF-HELP
CLEARINGHOUSE
St. Clare's–Riverside Medical Center
Pocono Road
Denville, NJ 07834
800-FOR-MASH

BROOKLYN SELF-HELP
CLEARINGHOUSE
30 Third Avenue
Brooklyn, NY 11217
(718) 834-7341 or 834-7332

CATTARAUGUS COUNTY SELF-HELP
CLEARINGHOUSE—CROSSTIES
American Red Cross—Olean Branch
130 South Union Street
Olean, NY 14760
(716) 372-5800

DUTCHESS COUNTY SELF-HELP
CLEARINGHOUSE
United Way of Dutchess County, Inc.
P.O. Box 832
75 Market Street
Poughkeepsie, NY 12601
(914) 473-1500

ERIE COUNTY SELF-HELP
CLEARINGHOUSE
Mental Health Association of Erie County
1237 Delaware Avenue
Buffalo NY 14209
(716) 886-1242

FULTON COUNTY SELF-HELP
CLEARINGHOUSE
Family Counseling Center
33 Bleecker Street
Gloversville, NY 12078
(518) 725-4310

CAPC SELF-HELP CLEARINGHOUSE
Community Action Planning Council of
Jefferson County
28 The Arcade Balcony
P.O. Box 899
Watertown, NY 13601
(315) 788-8471
(Jefferson and Lewis Counties)

LONG ISLAND SELF-HELP
CLEARINGHOUSE
New York Institute of Technology
Central Islip, NY 11722
(516) 348-3030

MONROE COUNTY SELF-HELP
CLEARINGHOUSE
Mental Health Chapter of
Rochester/Monroe
973 East Avenue
Rochester, NY 14607
(716) 271-3540

MONTGOMERY COUNTY ENABLERS
ADVOCATING FOR NEW SUPPORT
(MEANS)
St. Mary's Hospital
427 Guy Park Avenue
Amsterdam, NY 12010
(518) 842-1900 Ext. 328

NIAGARA COUNTY SELF-HELP
CLEARINGHOUSE
Mental Health Association in
Niagara County, Inc.
151 East Avenue
Lockport, NY 14094
(716) 433-3780

NEW YORK CITY SELF-HELP
CLEARINGHOUSE, INC.
1012 Eighth Avenue
Brooklyn, NY 11215
(718) 788-8787

ONONDAGA COUNTY SELF-HELP
CLEARINGHOUSE
The Volunteer Center, Inc.
115 East Jefferson Street, Suite 300
Syracuse, NY 13202
(315) 474-7011

TRI-COUNTY SELF-HELP
CLEARINGHOUSE
Mental Health Association in
Orange County, Inc.
255 Greenwich Avenue
Goshen, NY 10924
(914) 294-5661
(Orange, Sullivan, and Ulster Counties)

OSWEGO COUNTY SELF-HELP
CLEARINGHOUSE
Family Life Education–North
81 East Albany Street
Oswego, NY 13126
(315) 342-1463

ROCKLAND COUNTY SELF-HELP
CLEARINGHOUSE AND INFORMATION
CENTER
Mental Health Association of Rockland
Sanatorium Road, Building J
Pomona, NY 10970
(914) 354-0200 Ext. 3601

ST LAWRENCE COUNTY SELF-HELP
CLEARINGHOUSE
Reachout of St. Lawrence County, Inc.
203 Sisson Hall, Potsdam College
Potsdam, NY 13676
(315) 265-2422

SCHENECTADY COUNTY SELF-HELP
CLEARINGHOUSE
Human Services Planning Council of
Schenectady County, Inc.
432 State Street, Room 220
Schenectady, NY 12305
(518) 372-3395

SCHUYLER/CHEMUNG COUNTIES
SELF-HELP CLEARINGHOUSE
Economic Opportunity Program, Inc.
207 South Catherine Street
Montour Falls, NY 14865
(800) 348-0448

TOMPKINS COUNTY SUPPORT GROUP
CLEARINGHOUSE
Tompkins County Mental Health
Association
313 North Aurora Street
Ithaca, NY 14850
(607) 273-9250

WESTCHESTER SELF-HELP
CLEARINGHOUSE
Westchester Community College/AAB
75 Grasslands Road
Valhalla, NY 10595
(914) 347-3620

HAITIAN SELF-HELP GROUP PROGRAM
Haitian Centers Council, Inc.
50 Court Street, Suite 605
Brooklyn, NY 11201
(718) 855-7275
(Serves New York City and Rockland
County)

NEW YORK STATE SELF-HELP
CLEARINGHOUSE
New York Council on
Children and Families
Major Erastus Corning 2nd
Tower Building, 28th Floor
Empire State Plaza
Albany, NY 12223
(518) 474-6293

NORTHWEST REGIONAL SELF-HELP
CLEARINGHOUSE
718 West Burnside Street
Portland, OR 97209
(503) 222-5555

SELF HELP GROUP NETWORK OF
THE PITTSBURGH AREA
710½ South Avenue
Pittsburgh, PA 15221
(412) 247-5400

SELF-HELP INFORMATION AND
NETWORKING EXCHANGE (SHINE)
Voluntary Action Center of
Northeastern Pennsylvania
225 North Washington Avenue
Scranton, PA 18503
(717) 961-1234

DALLAS SELF-HELP CLEARINGHOUSE
Mental Health Association of
Dallas County
2500 Maple Avenue
Dallas, TX 75201–1998
(214) 871-2420

SELF-HELP CLEARINGHOUSE
Mental Health Association of
Tarrant County
3136 West Fourth Street
Forth Worth, TX 76107
(817) 335-5405

GREATER WASHINGTON SELF-HELP
COALITION
Mental Health Association of
Northern Virginia
100 North Washington Street, Suite 232
Falls Church, VA 22046
(703) 536-4100

INTERNATIONAL INFORMATION
CENTRE ON SELF-HELP AND HEALTH
(A project of the Division for Medical
Sociology of the Katholieke Universiteit
Leuven, in collaboration with the World
Health Organization, Unit for Health
Education of the Regional Office for
Europe, and the Flemish Ministry for
the Family and Welfare)
E. van Evenstraat 2C
B–3000, Leuven, Belgium

Bibliography

Ablon, J. "Dwarfism and Social Identity: Self-Help Group Participation," *Social Science and Medicine*, 15B (January 1981), pp. 25–30.

Abrahams, R. B., and Patterson, R. D. "Psychological Distress among the Community Elderly: Prevalence, Characteristics, and Implications for Service," *International Journal of Aging and Human Development*, 9 (1979), pp. 1–7.

Action Committee to Implement the Mental Health Recommendations of the 1981 White House Conference on Aging. *Mental Health Services for the Elderly: Report on a Survey of Community Mental Health Centers*, Vols. 1 and 2. Washington, D.C.: House Conference on Aging, November 1984.

Al-Anon. *Al-Anon Faces Alcoholism*. New York: Cornwall Press, 1965.

————. *Al-Anon's Twelve Steps and Twelve Traditions*. New York: Al-Anon Family Group Headquarters, 1981.

————. *Living with an Alcoholic*. 6th rev. ed. New York: Al-Anon Family Group Headquarters, 1975.

Albert-Olson, V. "La Leche League at 25: The Quiet Revolution," *Family Journal* (July 1981), pp. 23–27.

Alcoholics Anonymous. *Alcoholics Anonymous*. New York: A. A. World Services, 1955.

————. *Analysis of the 1980 Survey of the Membership of A. A.* New York: A. A. General Service Office.

————. *CPC Workbook: Cooperation with the Professional Community*. New York: A. A. General Service Office, 1982.

————. *Eastern U.S. Alcoholics Anonymous Directory*. New York: A. A. World Services, 1984.

————. *If You Are a Professional, A. A. Wants to Work with You*. New York: A. A. World Services, 1972.

————. *A Member's-Eye View of Alcoholics Anonymous*. New York: A. A. World Services, 1970.

————. *Twelve Steps and Twelve Traditions*. New York: A. A. World Services, 1952.

Almond, R. *The Healing Community: Dynamics of the Therapeutic Milieu.* New York: Jason Aronson, 1974.

American Psychiatric Association. "Position Statement on the Chronic Mental Patient," *American Journal of Psychiatry,* 136 (May 1979), pp. 748–753.

Angrosino, M. V. "Community Resources for Alcoholism Therapy: An Anthropological Overview," in R. T. Trotter II and J. Antonio Chavira, eds., *El Uso de Alcohol: A Resource Book for Spanish-Speaking Communities.* Atlanta, Ga.: Southern Area Alcohol Education and Training Program, 1977.

Anonymous. "The Compulsive Gambler," *International Journal of Offender Therapy and Comparative Criminology,* 25, No. 1 (1981), pp. 90–92.

Antze, P. "Role of Ideologies in Peer Psychotherapy Groups," in M. A. Lieberman and L. D. Borman, eds., *Self-Help Groups for Coping with Crisis: Origins, Members, Processes, and Impact.* San Francisco: Jossey-Bass, 1979.

B., Bill. *Compulsive Overeater.* Minneapolis, Minn.: CompCare, 1981.

Bachrach, L. L. "Model Programs for Chronic Mental Patients," *American Journal of Psychiatry,* 137 (September 1980), pp. 1023–1031.

Baekeland, F., and Lundwall, L. "Dropping Out of Treatment: A Critical Review," *Psychological Bulletin,* 82 (September 1975), pp. 738–783.

Baekeland, F.; Lundwall, L.; and Kissin, B. "Methods for the Treatment of Chronic Alcoholism: A Critical Appraisal," in R. J. Gibbins et al., eds., *Research Advances in Alcohol and Drug Problems.* Vol. 2. New York: John Wiley & Sons, 1975.

Bailey, M. B. "Al-Anon Family Groups as an Aid to Wives of Alcoholics," *Social Work,* 10 (January 1965), pp. 68–74.

Baker, E. K. "The Relationship Between Locus of Control and Psychotherapy: A Review of the Literature," *Psychotherapy: Theory, Research and Practice,* 16 (1979), pp. 351–362.

Baker, F. "Effects of Value Systems on Service Delivery," in H. C. Schulberg and M. Killilea, eds., *The Modern Practice of Community Mental Health.* San Francisco: Jossey-Bass, 1982.

———. "The Interface Between Professional and Natural Support Systems," *Clinical Social Work Journal,* 5 (Summer 1977), pp. 139–148.

Bakker, B.; Karel, M.; and Sewandono, I. *Vehicles in Welfare Achievement: Self-Help, Self-Care and Public Care, Three Working Papers.* Amsterdam, Netherlands: Inst. v. Wetenschapder Andragogie [Institute for the Science of Andragogy], University of Amsterdam, 1980.

Bales, R. F. "The Therapeutic Role of Alcoholics Anonymous as Seen by a Sociologist," in D. J. Pittmand and C. R. Snyder, eds., *Society, Culture, and Drinking Patterns.* New York: John Wiley & Sons, 1962.

Bandura, A. *Social Learning Theory.* Englewood Cliffs, N.J.: Prentice-Hall, 1977.

Bankoff, E. A. "Widow Groups as an Alternative to Informal Social Support," in M. A. Lieberman and L. D. Borman, eds., *Self-Help Groups for Coping with Crisis: Origins, Members, Processes, and Impact.* San Francisco: Jossey-Bass, 1979.

Barnes, J. A. "Class and Community in a Norwegian Island Parish," *Human Relations,* 7 (February 1954), pp. 39–58.

———. *Social Networks.* Module 26. Reading, Mass.: Addison-Wesley Publishing Co., 1972.

Bassuk, E. L., and Gerson, S. "Deinstitutionalization and Mental Health Services," *Scientific American,* 238 (February 1978), pp. 46–53.

Bean, M. "Alcoholics Anonymous," Parts I and II, *Psychiatric Annals,* 5 (February and March 1975), pp. 7–60, 7–61, respectively.

Beaubrun, M. H. "Alcoholism Treatment in Trinidad," in R. J. Catanzaro, ed., *Alcoholism: The Total Treatment Approach.* Springfield, Ill.: Charles C Thomas, Publisher, 1968.

Bebbington, P. E. "The Efficacy of Alcoholics Anonymous: The Elusiveness of Hard Data," *British Journal of Psychiatry,* 128 (June 1976), pp. 572–580.

Beigel, D. E.; Shore, B. K.; and Gordon, E. *Building Support Networks for the Elderly.* Beverly Hills, Calif.: Sage Publications, 1984.

Beisser, A. R., with Green, R. *Mental Health Consultation and Education.* Los Angeles, Calif.: Institute Press, 1972.

Bergin, A. E., and Lambert M. "The Evaluation of Therapeutic Outcomes," in S. L. Garfield and Bergin, eds., *Handbook of Psychotherapy and Behavior Change: An Empirical Analysis.* 2nd ed. New York: John Wiley & Sons, 1978.

Berkman, L. F., and Syme, S. L. "Social Networks, Host Resistance and Mortality: A Nine-Year Follow-Up Study of Alameda County Residents," *American Journal of Epidemiology,* 109 (February 1979), pp. 186–204.

Biegel, D. E., and Naparstek, A. J. *Community Support Systems and Mental Health.* New York: Springer Publishing Co., 1982.

Biegel, D. E.; Naparstek, A. J.; and Khan, M. "Social Support and Mental Health in Urban Ethnic Neighborhoods," in B. H. Gottlieb, ed., *Social Support Strategies.* Beverly Hills, Calif.: Sage Publications, 1983.

Black, R. B., and Drachman, D. "Hospital Social Workers and Self-Help Groups," *Health and Social Work,* 10 (Spring 1985), pp. 95–103.

Blake, R. R., and Mouton, J. S. *Consultation.* Reading, Mass.: Addison-Wesley Publishing Co., 1976.

Bliwise, N. G., and Lieberman, M. "From Professional Help to Self-Help: An Evaluation of Therapeutic Groups for the Elderly," in A. Gartner and F. Riessman, eds., *The Self-Help Revolution.* New York: Human Sciences Press, 1984.

Bloom, M. (special issue ed.). "Single-System Research Designs," *Journal of Social Service Research,* 3 (Fall 1979), entire issue.

Boissevain, J., and Mitchell, J. C. (eds.). *Network Analysis: Studies in Human Interaction.* The Hague, Netherlands: Mouton, 1973.

Bond, G. R., et al. "Growth of a Medical Self-Help Group," in M. A. Lieberman and L. D. Borman, eds., *Self-Help Groups for Coping with Crisis: Origins, Members, Processes, and Impact.* San Francisco: Jossey-Bass, 1979.

Borck, L. E., and Aronowitz, E. "The Role of a Self-Help Clearinghouse," *Prevention in Human Services,* 1 (Spring 1982), pp. 121–129.

Bordow, S., and Porritt, D. "An Experimental Evaluation of Crisis Intervention," *Social Science and Medicine,* 13A (May 1979), pp. 251–256.

Borkman, T.S. "Experiential Knowledge: A New Concept for the Analysis of Self-Help Groups," *Social Service Review,* 50 (September 1976).

———. "Mutual Self-Help Groups: Strengthening the Selectively Unsupportive Personal and Community Networks of Their Members," in A. Gartner and F. Riessman, eds., *The Self-Help Revolution.* New York: Human Sciences Press, 1984.

———. "Participation Patterns and Benefits of Membership in a Self-Help Organization of Stutterers," in A. H. Katz and E. I. Bender, eds., *The Strength in Us.* New York. New Viewpoints, 1976.

———. "Pathfinders and CLARE: Social Model Alcoholism Programs," *Citizen Participation,* 3 (January–February 1982), p. 16.

———. *A Social-Experiential Model in Programs for Alcoholism Recovery: A Research Report on a New Treatment Design.* DHHS Publication No. (ADM) 83-1259. Washington, D.C.: U.S. Department of Health & Human Services, 1983.

———. "Where Are Older Persons in Mutual Self-Help Groups?" in A. Kolker and P. Ahmed, eds., *Aging.* New York: Elsevier Biomedical, 1982.

Borkman, T. S., et al. "The Survivability of Self-Help Groups for Persons Who Stutter: A Discriminant Analysis." Unpublished manuscript, George Mason University, Fairfax, Va., 1985.

Borman, L. D. "Characteristics of Development and Growth," in M. A. Lieberman and Borman, eds., *Self-Help Groups for Coping with Crisis: Origins, Members, Processes, and Impact.* San Francisco: Jossey-Bass, 1979.

Bott, E. *Family and Social Network.* 2nd ed. New York: Free Press, 1971.

Bowles, E. *Self-Help Groups: An Instructional Guide for Developing Self-Help Groups.* New York: Center for Advanced Study in Education, City University of New York, 1978.

Branckaerts, J. "A Case Study in the Collaboration Between Professionals and Lays in a Self-Help Group: The Belgian Huntington League," in S. Hatch and I. Kickbush, eds., *Self-Help and Health.* Copenhagen, Denmark: World Health Organization, 1982.

———. "Self-Help and Research," in S. Hatch and I. Kickbush, eds., *Self-Help and Health*. Copenhagen, Denmark: World Health Organization, 1982.

Brim, J. A. "Social Network Correlates of Avowed Happiness, "*Journal of Nervous and Mental Diseases*, 158 (June 1974), pp. 432–439.

Bry, A. *EST: 60 Hours That Transform Your Life*. New York: Harper & Row, 1976.

Budson, R. D. *The Psychiatric Halfway House: A Handbook of Theory and Practice*. Pittsburgh, Pa.: University of Pittsburgh Press, 1978.

Butler, R. N., et al. "Self-Care, Self-Help, and the Elderly," *International Journal of Aging and Human Development*, 10 (1979), pp. 95–114.

Cambell, D. T., and Stanley, J. C. *Experimental and Quasi-Experimental Designs for Research*. Chicago: Rand McNally & Co., 1963.

Capildeo, R.; Court, C.; and Rose, F. C. "Social Network Diagram," *British Medical Journal*, 1 (January 1976), pp. 143–144.

Caplan, G. "Spontaneous or Natural Support Systems," in A. H. Katz and E. I. Bender, eds., *The Strength in Us: Self-Help Groups in the Modern World*. New York: New Viewpoints, 1976.

———. *The Theory and Practice of Mental Health Consultation*. New York: Basic Books, 1970.

Cassel, J. "The Contribution of the Social Environment to Host Resistance," *American Journal of Epidemiology*, 104 (August 1976), pp. 107–123.

Chamberlain, J. *On Our Own: Patient Controlled Alternatives to the Mental Health System*. New York: Hawthorn Books, 1978.

Checkoway, B., and Blum, S. "Self-Help in Health Care: Good, But Not Good Enough," *Citizen Participation*, 3 (January–February 1982), pp. 17–19.

Chesler, M.; Barbarin, O.; and Sebo-Stein, J. "Patterns of Participation in a Self-Help Group for Parents of Children with Cancer," *Journal of Psychosocial Oncology*, 2 (Fall–Winter 1984), pp. 41–64.

Chesler, M. A., and Yoak, M. "Self-Help Groups as Social Experiments: The Case of Families of Children with Cancer," *In Search of the Rules of the New Games*. Holte, Denmark: Scandinavian Seminar College, 1984. Distributed by The Danish Institute.

Chodoff, P., et al. "Stress, Defenses, and Coping Behavior: Observations on Parents of Children with Malignant Disease," *American Journal of Psychiatry*, 150 (August 1964), pp. 743–749.

Citizens Committee for New York City. *The Older Persons Handbook and New York Self-Help Handbook*. New York: Citizens Committee for New York City, 1978.

Claflin, B. "Mutual Support Groups in a Suburban Setting: The Opportunities, the Challenges," in A. Gartner and F. Riessman, eds., *The Self-Help Revolution*. New York: Human Sciences Press, 1984.

333

Cochran, M. M., and Brassard, J. A. "Child Development and Personal Social Networks," *Child Development,* 50 (1979), pp. 601–616.

Cohen, C. I. "Clinical Use of Network Analysis for Psychiatric and Aged Populations," *Community Mental Health Journal,* 15 (1979), pp. 203–213.

Cohen, C. I.; Adler, A. G.; and Mintz, J. E. "Network Interventions on the Margin," in D. L. Pancoast, P. Parker, and C. Froland, eds., *Rediscovering Self-Help.* Beverly Hills, Calif.: Sage Publications, 1983.

Cohen, C. I., and Sokolovsky, J. "Schizophrenia and Social Networks: Expatients in the Inner City," *Schizophrenia Bulletin,* 4 (1978), pp. 546–560.

Cohn, A. H. "Effective Treatment of Child Abuse and Neglect," *Social Work,* 24 (November 1979), pp. 513–519.

Colletta, N. C. "Support Systems after Divorce: Incidence and Impact," *Journal of Marriage and the Family,* 41 (1979), pp. 837–846.

Colletta, N. C., and Gregg, C. H. "Adolescent Mothers' Vulnerability to Stress," *Journal of Nervous and Mental Disease,* 169 (1981), pp. 50–54.

Collins, A. H., and Pancoast, D. L. *Natural Helping Networks.* Washington, D. C.: National Association of Social Workers, 1976.

Compassionate Friends Newsletter (Oak Brook, Ill.), 6 (Spring 1983).

Comstock, C. M. "Preventive Processes in Self-Help Groups: Parents Anonymous," *Prevention in Human Services,* 1 (Spring 1982), pp. 47–54.

Cook, T. D., and Campbell, D. T. *Quasi-Experimentation.* Chicago: Rand McNally & Co., 1979.

Cooper S., and Hodges, W. F. (eds.). *The Mental Health Consultation Field.* New York: Human Sciences Press, 1983.

Coplon, J., and Strull, J. "Roles of the Professional in Mutual Aid Groups," *Social Casework: The Journal of Contemporary Social Work,* 64 (May 1983), pp. 259–266.

Craven, P., and Wellman, B. "The Network City," *Sociological Inquiry,* 43 (1973), pp. 57–88.

Crogg, S. H.; Lipson, A.; and Levine, S. "Help Patterns in Severe Illness: The Roles of Kin Network, Non-Family Resources, and Institutions," *Journal of Marriage and the Family,* 34 (February 1972), pp. 32–41.

Custer, R. L. "An Overview of Compulsive Gambling," in P. A. Carone et al., eds., *Addictive Disorders Update.* New York: Human Sciences Press, 1982.

Custer, R. L., and Milt, H. *When Luck Runs Out.* New York: Facts on File, 1985.

Dain, N. "The Chronic Mental Patient in 19th-Century America," *Psychiatric Annals,* 10 (September 1980), pp. 323–327.

Dean, A.; Lin, N.; and Ensel, W. "The Epidemiological Significance of Social Support Systems in Depression," in R. Simmons, ed., *Research in Community and Mental Health.* Vol. 2. Greenwich, Conn.: JAI Press, 1981.

de Araujo, G., et al. "Life Change, Coping Ability, and Chronic Intrinsic Asthma," *Journal of Psychosomatic Research,* 17 (December 1973), pp. 359–363.

Dewar, R.; Whetten, D.; and Boje, D. "An Examination of the Reliability and Validity of the Aiken and Hage Scales of Centralization, Formalization, and Task Routineness," *Administrative Science Quarterly,* 25 (March 1980), pp. 120–128.

Drinan, R. F. "The Mentally Ill Elderly: An Unresolved National Problem," *Perspective on Aging* (November–December 1980).

Durlak, J. A. "Comparative Effectiveness of Paraprofessional and Professional Helpers," *Psychological Bulletin,* 86 (January 1979), pp. 80–92.

Eaton, W. W., et al. "The Design of the Epidemiologic Catchment Area Surveys: The Control and Measurement of Error," *Archives of General Psychiatry,* 41 (October 1984), pp. 942–948.

Edmunson, E., et al. "The Community Network Development Project: Bridging the Gap Between Professional Aftercare and Self-Help," in A. Gartner and F. Riessman, eds., *The Self-Help Revolution.* New York: Human Sciences Press, 1984.

———. "Integrating Skill Building and Peer Support in Mental Health Treatment," in A. Yaeger and R. Slotkin, eds., *Community Mental Health and Behavioral Ecology.* New York: Plenum Publishing Corp., 1982.

Edwards, W.; Guttentag, M.; and Snapper, K. "A Decision Theoretic Approach to Evaluation Research," in E. L. Struening and Guttentag, eds., *Handbook of Evaluation Research.* Beverly Hills, Calif.: Sage Publications, 1975.

Eisdorfer, C., and Cohen, D. "The Cognitively Impaired Elderly: Differential Diagnosis," in M. Storandt, I. C. Siegler, and M. F. Elias, eds., *The Clinical Psychology of Aging.* New York: Plenum Publishing Corp., 1978.

Ell, K. "Social Networks, Social Support, and Health Status: A Review," *Social Service Review,* 58 (March 1984), pp. 133–149.

Emotions Anonymous. *Guide for Forming and Conducting New and Existing Groups of Emotions Anonymous.* St. Paul, Minn.: EA, 1984.

———. *Suggested Format for EA Meetings.* Form No. 7. St. Paul, Minn.: EA, March 1977; rev. March 1983.

———. *Welcome! to this Meeting of: Emotions Anonymous,* Form No. 34. St. Paul, Minn.: EA, January 1984.

———. *Why Is This a Step Meeting?* St. Paul, Minn.: EA, May 1985.

Erickson, C. D. "The Concept of Personal Network in Clinical Practice," *Family Process,* 14 (December 1975), pp. 487–498.

Etzioni, A. *A Comparative Analysis of Complex Organizations.* Rev. ed. New York: Free Press, 1975.

———. *Modern Organizations.* Englewood Cliffs, N.J.: Prentice-Hall, 1964.

Evans, G. *The Family Circle Guide to Self-Help.* New York: Ballantine Books, 1979.

Fabian, E., and Jacobs, M. "Help Is Just Around the Corner—Self-Help, That Is," *Self-Helper: The California Self-Help Quarterly,* 1 (Summer 1985), pp. 3–4.

Fairweather, G. (ed.). *The Fairweather Lodge: A 25-Year Prospective.* San Francisco: Jossey-Bass, 1980.

Families Anonymous. *A KIND OF QUIET COUNTER CULTURE.* Announcement (S14). Van Nuys, Calif.: FA, undated.

Farris-Kurtz, L. "Time in Residential Care and Participation in Alcoholics Anonymous as Predictors of Continued Sobriety," *Psychological Reports,* 48 (1981), pp. 633–634.

Feld, S., and Radin, N. L. *Social Psychology for Social Work and the Mental Health Professions.* New York: Columbia University Press, 1982.

Festinger, L. *A Theory of Cognitive Dissonance.* Stanford, Calif.: Stanford University Press, 1957.

Fields, S. "Senior Actualization and Growth Exploration (SAGE)," in R. Gross, B. Gross, and S. Seidman, eds., *The New Old: Struggling for Decent Aging.* New York: Doubleday & Co., 1978.

Fine, P. "Family Networks and Child Psychiatry in a Community Health Project," *Journal of the American Academy of Child Psychiatry,* 12 (1973), pp. 675–689.

Finlayson, A. "Social Networks as Coping Resources: Lay Help and Consultation Patterns Used by Women in Husband's Post-Infarction Career," *Social Science and Medicine,* 10 (February 1976), pp. 97–103.

Fischer, C. S. *To Dwell among Friends.* Chicago: University of Chicago Press, 1982.

Fischer, C. S., et al. *Networks and Places: Social Relations in the Urban Setting.* New York: Free Press, 1977.

Freedman, D. X. "Psychiatric Epidemiology Counts," *Archives of General Psychiatry,* 41 (1984), pp. 931–933.

French, J. R. P., Jr., and Raven, B. "The Bases of Social Power," in D. Cartwright, ed., *Studies in Social Power.* Ann Arbor: University of Michigan Press, 1959.

Fritz, M. *Chapter Development Manual.* Rev. ed. Redondo Beach, Calif.: Parents Anonymous, 1982.

————. *The Parents Anonymous Chairperson—Sponsor Manual.* Rev. ed. Torrance, Calif.: Parents Anonymous, 1982.

Froland, C. "Formal and Informal Care: Discontinuities in a Continuum," *Social Service Review,* 54 (December 1980), pp. 572–587.

Froland, C., et al. *Helping Networks and Human Services.* Beverly Hills, Calif.: Sage Publications, 1981.

————. "Linking Formal and Informal Support Systems," in B. Gottlieb, ed., *Social Networks and Social Support.* Beverly Hills, Calif.: Sage Publications, 1981.

————. "Social Support and Social Adjustment: Implications for Mental Health Professionals," *Community Mental Health Journal,* 15 (Summer 1979), pp. 82–93.

Gamblers Anonymous. *Sharing Recovery Through Gamblers Anonymous.* Los Angeles, Calif.: GA Publishing, 1984.

Gambrill, E. D. *Casework: A Competency-Based Approach.* Englewood Cliffs, N.J.: Prentice-Hall, 1983.

Gambrill, E. D., and Barth, R. P. "Single-Case Study Designs Revisited," *Social Work Research and Abstracts,* 16 (Fall 1980), pp. 15–20.

Garb, J. R., and Stunkard, A. "Effectiveness of a Self-Help Group in Obesity Control—Further Assessment," *Archives of Internal Medicine,* 134 (October 1974), pp. 716–726.

Garbarino, J. "Social Support Networks: Rx for the Helping Professional," in J. K. Whittaker and Garbarino, eds., *Social Support Networks: Informational Helping in the Human Services.* Hawthorne, N.Y.: Aldine Publishing Co., 1983.

Garfield, S. L. "Research on Client Variables in Psychotherapy," in Garfield and A. E. Bergin, eds., *Handbook of Psychotherapy and Behavior Change: An Empirical Analysis.* 2nd ed. New York: John Wiley & Sons, 1978.

Garrison, J.; Kulp, C.; and Rosen, S. "Community Mental Health Nursing: A Social Network Approach," *Journal of Psychiatric Nursing,* 15 (January 1977), pp. 32–36.

Garrison, V. "Support Systems of Schizophrenic and Non-Schizophrenic Puerto Rican Migrant Women in New York City," *Schizophrenia Bulletin,* 4 (1978), pp. 561–596.

Gartner, A. "A Typology of Women's Self-Help Groups," *Social Policy,* 15 (Winter 1985), pp. 25–30.

Gartner, A., and Riessman, F. *Help: A Working Guide to Self-Help Groups.* New York: New Viewpoints/Vision Books, 1980.

————. *Self-Help in the Human Services.* San Francisco: Jossey-Bass, 1977.

————. "Self-Help and Mental Health," *Hospital and Community Psychiatry,* 33 (August 1982), pp. 631–635.

————. (eds.). *The Self-Help Revolution.* New York: Human Sciences Press, 1984.

Gerard, D. L. "The Abstinent Alcoholic," *Archives of General Psychiatry,* 112 (December 1955), pp. 460–464.

Glasgow, R. E., and Rosen, G. M. "Self-Help Behavior Therapy Manuals: Recent Developments and Clinical Usage," *Clinical Behavior Therapy Review,* 1 (Spring 1979), pp. 1–20.

Glidewell, J. C. "The Entry Problem in Consultation," *Journal of Social Issues,* 15, No. 2 (1959), pp. 51–59.

Goffman, E. *Stigma.* Englewood Cliffs, N.J.: Prentice-Hall, 1963.

Goldman, H. H.; Adams, N. H.; and Taube, C. A. "Deinstitutionalization: The Data Demythologized," *Hospital and Community Psychiatry,* 34 (February 1983), pp. 129–134.

Goldner, V. "Overeaters Anonymous," in A. Gartner and F. Riessman, eds., *The Self-Help Revolution.* New York: Human Sciences Press, 1984.

Goldstein, A. P., and Simonson, N. R. "Social Psychological Approaches to Psychotherapy Research," in A. E. Bergin and S. L. Garfield, eds., *Handbook of Psychotherapy and Behavior Change: An Empirical Analysis.* New York: John Wiley & Sons, 1971.

Gordon, A. J. "The Cultural Context of Drinking and Indigenous Therapy for Alcohol Problems in Three Migrant Hispanic Cultures: An Ethnographic Report," *Journal of Studies on Alcohol,* 9, Supp. No. 9 (January 1981), pp. 217–240.

Gordon, R. D.; Kapostins, E. E.; and Gordon, K. K. "Factors in Postpartum Emotional Adjustment," *Obstetrical Gynecology,* 25 (February 1965), pp. 156–166.

Gordon, R. E., et al. "Reducing Rehospitalization of State Mental Patients: Peer Management and Support, in A. Yaeger and R. Slotkin, eds., *Community Mental Health.* New York: Plenum Publishing Corp., 1982.

Gore, S. "The Effects of Social Support in Moderating the Health Consequences of Unemployment," *Journal of Health and Social Behavior,* 19 (June 1978), pp. 157–165.

Gottlieb, B. H. "The Contribution of Natural Support Systems of Primary Prevention Among Four Subgroups of Adolescent Males," *Adolescence,* 10 (Summer 1975), pp. 207–220.

————. "Mutual-Help Groups: Members' Views of Their Benefits and of Roles for Professionals," *Prevention,* 1 (Spring 1982), pp. 55–67.

————. "Opportunities for Collaboration with Informal Support Systems," in S. Cooper and W. F. Hodges, eds., *The Mental Health Consultation Field.* New York: Human Sciences Press, 1983.

————. *Social Networks and Social Support.* Beverly Hills, Calif.: Sage Publications, 1981.

————. *Social Support Strategies*. Beverly Hills, Calif.: Sage Publications, 1983.

Gottlieb, B. H., and Schroter, C. "Collaboration and Resource Exchange Between Professionals and Natural Support Systems," *Professional Psychology*, 9 (November 1978), pp. 614–622.

Gourash, N. "Help Seeking: A Review of the Literature," *American Journal of Community Psychology*, 6 (October 1978), pp. 413–425.

Granovetter, M. "The Strength of Weak Ties," *American Journal of Sociology*, 78 (May 1973), pp. 1360–1380.

————. "The Strength of Weak Ties: A Network Theory Revisited," in R. Collins, ed., *Sociological Theory 1983*. San Francisco: Jossey-Bass, 1983.

Gray Panthers, *Two Portraits of Old Age in America*. Philadelphia: Gray Panthers, undated.

Greenson, R. R. "The Working Alliance and the Transference Neurosis," *Psychoanalytic Quarterly*, 34 (April 1965), pp. 155–181.

Grimso, A.; Helgesen, G.; and Borchgreuink, C. "Short-Term and Long-Term Effects of Lay Groups on Weight Reduction," *British Medical Journal*, 283 (October 1981), pp. 1093–1095.

Grosz, H. *Recovery, Inc., Survey*. Chicago: Recovery, Inc., 1973.

GROW, Inc. *Organizer's Training Manual*. Sydney, Australia: GROW Publications, 1981.

————. *The Program of Growth to Maturity*. Sydney, Australia: GROW Publications, 1981.

Gruenberg, E., and Archer, J. "Abandonment of Responsibility for the Seriously Mentally Ill," *Milbank Memorial Fund Quarterly/Health and Society*, 57 (Fall 1979), pp. 485–506.

Gussow, Z., and Tracy, G. S. "The Role of Self-Help Clubs in Adaptation to Chronic Illness and Disability," *Social Science and Medicine*, 10 (July–August 1976), pp. 407–414.

Hage, J., and Aiken, M. "Routine Technology, Social Structure and Organization Goals," *Administrative Science Quarterly*, 14 (September 1969), pp. 366–375.

Hall, D. *The Politics of Schizophrenia: Psychiatric Oppression in the U. S.* Lanham, Md.: University Press of America, 1983.

Hall, R. H. "The Concept of Bureaucracy: An Empirical Assessment," *American Journal of Sociology*, 69 (1963), pp. 32–40.

————. *Organizations: Structure and Process*. 3rd ed. Englewood Cliffs, N.J.: Prentice-Hall, 1982.

Hammer, M. "Influence of Small Social Networks as Factors in Mental Hospital Admission," *Human Organization*, 22 (1963), pp. 243–251.

————. "Predictability of Social Connections Over Time," *Social Networks*. 2 (1980), pp. 165–180.

―――. "Social Supports, Social Networks, and Schizophrenia," *Schizophrenia Bulletin*, 7, No. 1 (1981), pp. 45–56.

Hammer, M.; Makiesky-Barrow, S.; and Gutwirth, L. "Social Networks and Schizophrenia," *Schizophrenia Bulletin*, 4 (1978), pp. 522–545.

Hansell, N. *The Person-in-Distress: On the Biosocial Dynamics of Adaptation.* New York: Behavioral Publications, 1976.

Hansell, N., and Willis, G. L. "Outpatient Treatment of Schizophrenia," *American Journal of Psychiatry*, 134 (October 1977), pp. 1082–1086.

Harris, E. T. "Parents Without Partners, Inc.: A Resource for Clients," *Social Work*, 11 (April 1966), pp. 92–98.

Hasenfeld, Y. *Human Service Organizations.* Englewood Cliffs, N.J.: Prentice-Hall, 1983.

Hasenfeld, Y., and English, R. A. *Human Service Organizations: A Book of Readings.* Ann Arbor: University of Michigan Press, 1974.

Hatfield, A. B. "Help-Seeking Behavior in Families of Schizophrenics," *American Journal of Community Psychology*, 7 (1979), pp. 563–569.

―――. "Psychological Costs of Schizophrenia to the Family," *Social Work*, 23 (September 1978), pp. 355–359.

―――. "Self-Help Groups for Families of the Mentally Ill," *Social Work*, 26 (September 1981), pp. 408–413.

Hausknecht, M. *The Joiners.* New York: Bedminster Press, 1962.

Henderson, S., et al. "Social Relationships, Adversity, and Neurosis: A Study of Associations in a General Population Sample," *British Journal of Psychiatry*, 136 (1980), pp. 574–583.

Henry, S., and Robinson, D. "Understanding Alcoholics Anonymous," *Lancet*, 1 (8060) (1978), pp. 372–375.

Herman, J. L. *Father-Daughter Incest.* Cambridge, Mass.: Harvard University Press, 1981.

Hersen, M., and Barlow, D. H. *Single Case Experimental Designs: Strategies for Studying Behavior Change.* New York: Pergamon Press, 1979.

Hess, B. B., and Bond, K. (eds.). *Leading Edges: Recent Research on Psychosocial Aging.* Washington, D. C.: U. S. Government Printing Office, 1981.

Hill, K., *Helping You Helps Me.* Ottawa, Ont.: Canadian Council on Social Development, 1984.

Hinrichsen, G. A.; Revenson, T. A.; and Shinn, M. "Does Self-Help Help? An Empirical Investigation of Scoliosis Peer Support Groups," *Journal of Social Issues*, 41, No. 1 (1985), pp. 65–87.

Hirsch, B. J. "Natural Support Systems and Coping with Major Life Changes." *American Journal of Community Psychology*, 8 (April 1980), pp. 159–172.

―――. "Psychological Dimensions of Social Networks: A Multimethod

Analysis," *American Journal of Community Psychology*, 7 (June 1979), pp. 263–277.

———. "Social Networks and the Coping Process," in B. Gottlieb, ed., *Social Networks and Social Support*. Beverly Hills, Calif.: Sage Publications, 1981.

Holmes, S. "Parents Anonymous: A Treatment Method for Child Abuse," *Social Work*, 23 (May 1978), pp. 245–247.

Holmes, S., et al. "Working with the Parent in Child-Abuse Cases," *Social Casework*, 56 (January 1975), pp. 3–12.

Holmes, T., and Rahe, R. "The Social Readjustment Rating Scale," *Journal of Psychosomatic Research*, 11 (August 1967), pp. 213–218.

Hooyman, N. "Social Support Networks in Services to the Elderly," in J. K. Whittaker and J. Garbarino, eds., *Social Support Networks: Informal Helping in the Human Services*. Hawthorne, N.Y.: Aldine Publishing Co., 1983.

Horowitz, A. "Social Networks and Pathways to Psychiatric Treatment, *Social Forces*, 56 (1977), pp. 86–105.

Huey, K. "Developing Effective Links Between Human Service Providers and the Self-Help System," *Hospital and Community Psychiatry*, 28 (August 1977), pp. 767–770.

Humm, A. "The Changing Nature of Lesbian and Gay Self-Help Groups," in A. Gartner and F. Riessman, eds., *The Self-Help Revolution*. New York: Human Sciences Press, 1984.

———. *How to Organize a Self-Help Group*. New York: Self-Help Clearinghouse, City University of New York, 1979.

Hurvitz, N. "Peer Self-Help Psychotherapy Groups: Psychotherapy Without Psychotherapists," in P. Roman and H. M. Trice, eds., *The Sociology of Psychotherapy*. New York: Jason Aronson, 1974.

Hyman, H. H., and Singer, E. *Readings in Reference Group Theory and Research*. New York: Free Press, 1968.

Hyman, H. H., and Wright, C. R. "Trends in Voluntary Association Memberships of American Adults: Replication Based on Secondary Analysis of National Sample Surveys," *American Sociological Review*, 36 (April 1971), pp. 191–206.

Institute for Social Research, University of Michigan. "Black Americans Surveyed," *ISR Newsletter* (Spring–Summer 1983), pp. 3 and 7.

International Association of Laryngectomees. *Rehabilitating Laryngectomies*. 60-6R-50M-12/71-NO.4506-PS. New York: International Association of Laryngectomees.

Jackson, J. H., and Morgan, C. P. *Organization Theory*, 2nd ed. Englewood Cliffs, N. J.: Prentice-Hall, 1982.

Janis, I. L. "The Role of Social Support in Adherence to Stressful Decisions," *American Psychologist*, 83 (February 1983), pp. 143–160.

Jayaratne, S., and Levy, R. L. (eds.). *Empirical Clinical Practice*. New York: Columbia University Press, 1979.

Jeger, A. M.; Slotnick, R. S.; and Schure, M. "Toward a Self-Help/Professional Collaborative Perspective in Mental Health," in B. H. Gottlieb, ed., *Social Support Strategies.* Beverly Hills, Calif.: Sage Publications, 1983.

Jertson, J. M. "Self-Help Groups," *Social Work,* 20 (March 1975), pp. 144–145.

Jilek-Aall, L. "Acculturation, Alcoholism, and Indian-Style Alcoholics Anonymous," *Journal of Studies on Alcohol,* 9, Supp. No. 9 (January 1981), pp. 143–158.

Jones, L. "The Absence of the Black Professional and Semi-Professional in the Membership of Alcoholics Anonymous," in *Proceedings, Association of Labor-Management Administrators and Consultants on Alcoholism, Eighth Annual Meeting.* Arlington, Va.: Association of Labor-Management Administrators and Consultants on Alcoholism, 1980.

Jonqinans, D. J. "Politics on the Village Level," in J. Boissevain and J. C. Mitchell, eds., *Network Analysis: Studies in Human Interaction.* The Hague, Netherlands: Mouton, 1973.

Juel-Nielsen, N. "Epidemiology," in J. G. Howells, ed., *Modern Perspectives in the Psychiatry of Old Age.* New York: Brunner/Mazel, 1975.

Kagey, J. R.; Vivace, J.; and Lutz, W. "Mental Health Primary Prevention: The Role of Parent Mutual Support Groups," *American Journal of Public Health,* 71 (February 1981), pp. 166–167.

Kanzler, M.; Jaffe, J. H.; and Zeidenberg, P. "Long- and Short-Term Effectiveness of a Large-Scale Proprietary Smoking Cessation Program: A Four-Year Followup of Smokenders Participants," *Journal of Clinical Psychology,* 32, No. 13 (1976), pp. 661–669.

Katz, A. H. "Application of Self-Help Concepts in Current Social Welfare," *Social Work,* 10 (July 1965), pp. 68–74.

———. "Self-Help Groups: An International Perspective," in A. Gartner and F. Riessman, eds., *The Self-Help Revolution.* New York: Human Sciences Press, 1984.

———. "Self-Help and Human Services," *Citizen Participation,* 3 (January–February 1982), pp. 18–19.

———. "Self-Help and Mutual Aid, *Annual Review of Sociology,* 7 (1981), pp. 129–155.

———. "Self-Help Organizations and Volunteer Participation in Social Welfare," *Social Work,* 15 (January 1970), pp. 51–60.

Katz, A. H., and Bender, E. I. *The Strength in Us: Self-Help Groups in the Modern World.* New York: New Viewpoints, 1976; Oakland, Calif.: Third Party Associates, forthcoming, 1987.

Katz, D., and Kahn, R. L. *The Social Psychology of Organizations.* 2nd ed. New York: John Wiley & Sons, 1978.

Kaufman, G. "The Meaning of Shame: Toward a Self-Affirming Identity," *Journal of Counseling Psychology,* 21 (November 1974), pp. 568–574.

Kelly, O., and Murray, W. C. *Make Today Count.* New York: Delacorte Press, 1975.

Kiesler, D. J. "Some Myths of Psychotherapy Research and the Search for a Paradigm," *Psychological Bulletin,* 65 (February 1966), pp. 110–136.

Killilea, M. "Interaction of Crisis Theory, Coping Strategies, and Social Support Systems," in H. C. Schulberg and Killilea, eds., *The Modern Practice of Community Mental Health.* San Francisco: Jossey-Bass, 1982.

———. "Mutual Help Organizations: Interpretations in the Literature," in G. Caplan and Killilea, eds., *Support Systems and Mutual Help: Multidisciplinary Explorations.* New York: Grune & Stratton, 1976.

Killworth, P., and Bernard, H. "Informant Accuracy in Social Network Data," *Human Communication Research,* 4 (Fall 1977), pp. 3–18.

Kirkpatrick, J. *Turnabout: Help for a New Life.* Garden City, N.Y.: Doubleday & Co., 1977.

Klass, D. "Self-Help Groups for the Bereaved: Theory, Theology, and Practice," *Journal of Religion and Health,* 21 (Winter 1982), pp. 317–323.

Kleiman, M.; Mantell, J.; and Alexander, E. "Collaboration and Its Discontent," *Journal of Applied Behavioral Sciences,* 12 (July–August–September 1976), pp. 403–409.

Klerman, G. L. "Better But Not Well: Social and Ethical Issues in the Deinstitutionalization of the Mentally Ill," *Schizophrenia Bulletin,* 3, No. 4 (1977), pp. 617–631.

Knight, B., et al. "Self Help Groups: The Members' Perspectives," *American Journal of Community Psychology,* 8 (February 1980), pp. 53–65.

Korte, C., and Milgram, S. "Acquaintance Networks between Racial Groups: Application of the Small World Method," *Journal of Personality and Social Psychology,* 15 (1970), pp. 101–116.

Kratochwill, T. R. *Single Subject Research.* New York: Academic Press, 1982.

Kropotkin, P. *Mutual Aid.* Boston: Porter Sargent, 1902.

Kurtz, E. *Not-God: A History of Alcoholics Anonymous.* Center City, Minn.: Hazelden Foundation, 1979.

———. *Shame and Guilt: Characteristics of the Dependency Cycle.* Center City, Minn.: Hazelden Foundation, 1981.

Kurtz, L. F. "Cooperation and Rivalry Between Helping Professionals and Members of AA," *Health and Social Work,* 10 (Spring 1985), pp. 104–112.

———. "Ideological Differences Between Professionals and A. A. Members," *Alcoholism Treatment Quarterly,* 1 (Summer 1984), pp. 73–85.

———. "Linking Treatment Centers with Alcoholics Anonymous," *Social Work in Health Care,* 9 (Spring 1984), pp. 85–94.

343

Ladas, A. K. "Information and Social Support in the Outcome of Breast-feeding," *Journal of Applied Behavioral Science*, 8, No. 1 (1972), pp. 110–114.

Lamb, H. R., et al. *Community Survival for Long-Term Patients*. San Francisco: Jossey-Bass, 1976.

Larkin, K., and Madara, E. J. *The Self-Help Group Sourcebook 1983*. Denville: New Jersey Self-Help Clearinghouse, 1983.

Larkin, K.; Meese, A.; and Madara, E. J. *The Self-Help Group Directory, 1984–85*. Denville: New Jersey Self-Help Clearinghouse, 1985.

Lauman, E. O. *Bonds of Pluralism: The Form and Substance of Urban Social Networks*. New York: John Wiley & Sons, 1973.

Lavoie, F. "Action Research: A New Model of Interaction Between the Professional and Self-Help Groups," in A. Gartner and F. Riessman, eds., *The Self-Help Revolution*. New York: Human Sciences Press, 1984.

Leach, B. "Does Alcoholics Anonymous Really Work?" in P. G. Bourne and R. Fox, eds., *Alcoholism: Progress in Research and Treatment*. New York: Academic Press, 1973.

Leach, B., and Norris, J. L. "Factors in the Development of Alcoholics Anonymous (AA)," in B. Kissin and H. Begleiter, eds., *Treatment and Rehabilitation of the Chronic Alcoholic*. New York: Plenum Publishing Corp., 1977.

Leinhardt, S. (ed.). *Social Networks*. New York: Academic Press, 1977.

Lennenberg, E., and Rowbotham, J. L. *The Ileostomy Patient*. Springfield, Ill.: Charles C Thomas, Publisher, 1970.

Lenrow, P. B., and Burch, R. W. "Mutual Aid and Professional Service: Opposing or Complementary?" in B. H. Gottlieb, ed., *Social Networks and Social Support*. Beverly Hills, Calif.: Sage Publications, 1981.

Lerman, P. *Deinstitutionalization*. New Brunswick, N.J.: Rutgers University Press, 1982.

Leutz, W. "The Informal Community Caregiver: A Link Between the Health Care System and Local Residents," *American Journal of Orthopsychiatry*, 46 (October 1976), pp. 678–688.

Levens, H. "Organizational Affiliation and Powerlessness: A Case Study of the Welfare Poor," *Social Problems*, 16 (October 1968), pp. 18–32.

Levin, L. S.; Katz, A. H.; and Holst, E. *Self-Care: Lay Initiatives in Health*. New York: Prodist, 1976.

Levinson, H. "Diagnosis and Intervention in Organizational Settings," in H. C. Schulberg and M. Killilea, eds., *The Modern Practice of Community Mental Health*. San Francisco: Jossey-Bass, 1982.

———. *Organizational Diagnosis*. Cambridge, Mass.: Harvard University Press, 1972.

Levitz, L. S., and Stunkard, A. "A Therapeutic Coalition for Obesity:

Behavior Modification and Patient Self-Help," *American Journal of Psychiatry*, 131 (April 1974), pp. 423–427.

Levy, J. E., and Kunitz, S. J. *Indian Drinking: Navajo Practices and Anglo-American Theories*. New York: John Wiley & Sons, 1974.

Levy, L. "The National Schizophrenia Fellowship: A British Self-Help Group," *Social Psychiatry*, 16 (July 1981), pp. 129–135.

Levy, L. H. "Issues in Research and Evaluation," in A. Gartner and F. Riessman, eds., *The Self-Help Revolution*. New York: Human Sciences Press, 1984.

———. "Self-Help Groups: Types and Psychological Processes," *Journal of Behavioral Science*, 12 (July–August–September 1976), pp. 310–322.

———. "Self-Help Groups Viewed by Mental Health Professionals: A Survey and Comments," *American Journal of Community Psychology*, 6 (August 1978), pp. 305–313.

Lieber, L. L. "Parents Anonymous: The Use of Self-Help in the Treatment and Prevention of Family Violence," in A. Gartner and F. Riessman, eds., *The Self-Help Revolution*. New York: Human Sciences Press, 1984.

Lieberman, M. A., and Bond, G. A. "Self-Help Groups: Problems of Measuring Outcomes," *Small Group Behavior*, 9, No. 2 (1978), pp. 221–241.

———. "Women's Consciousness Raising as an Alternative to Psychotherapy," in Lieberman and L. D. Borman, eds., *Self-Help Groups for Coping with Crisis: Origins, Members, Processes, and Impact*. San Francisco: Jossey-Bass, 1979.

Lieberman, M. A., and Borman, L. D. "The Impact of Self-Help Groups on Widows' Mental Health," *National Reporter*, 4 (1981), pp. 2–6.

———. *Self-Help Groups for Coping with Crisis: Origins, Members, Processes, and Impact*. San Francisco: Jossey-Bass, 1979.

Lieberman, M. A., and Gourash, N. "Effects of Change Groups on the Elderly," in Lieberman and L. D. Borman, eds., *Self-Help Groups for Coping with Crisis: Origins, Members, Processes, and Impact*. San Francisco: Jossey-Bass, 1979.

Lieberman, M. A., and Mullan, J. "Does Help Help? The Adaptive Consequences of Obtaining Help from Professionals and Social Networks," *American Journal of Community Psychology*, 6 (October 1978), pp. 499–517.

Lieberman, M. A., and Videka-Sherman, L. "The Impact of Self-Help Groups on the Mental Health of Widows and Widowers," *American Journal of Orthopsychiatry*, 56 (July 1986), pp. 435–449.

Lifton, R. J. *Home from the War*. New York: Simon & Schuster, 1973.

Lin, N., et al. "Social Support, Stressful Life Events, and Illness: A Model and an Empirical Test," *Journal of Health and Social Behavior*, 20 (1979), pp. 108–109.

Lippit, G. L. *Organizational Renewal*. New York: Appleton-Century-Crofts, 1969.

Litwak, E., and Szelenyi, I. "Primary Group Structures and Their Functions: Kin, Neighbors, and Friends," *American Sociological Review,* 34 (August 1969), pp. 465–481.

Lofland, J. F., and LeJeune, R. A. "Initial Interaction of Newcomers in Alcoholics Anonymous: A Field Experiment in Class Symbols and Socialization," *Social Problems,* 8 (Fall 1960), pp. 102–111.

Lott, A. J., and Lott, B. E. "Group Cohesiveness as Interpersonal Attraction: A Review of Relationships with Antecedent and Consequent Variables," *Psychological Bulletin,* 54 (October 1965), pp. 259–309.

Low, A. *Mental Health Through Will Training.* Winnetka, Ill.: Willet Publishing Co., 1950.

Lowenthal, M. F., and Robinson, B. "Social Networks and Isolation," in R. Binstock and E. Shanas, eds., *Handbook of Aging and the Social Sciences.* New York: D. Van Nostrand Co., 1976.

Lowenthal, M. F., et al. *Aging and Mental Disorder in San Francisco: A Social Psychiatric Study.* San Francisco: Jossey-Bass, 1967.

Lurie, A., and Shulman, L. "The Professional Connection with Self-Help Groups in Health Care Settings," *Social Work in Health Care,* 8 (Summer 1983), pp. 69–77.

Lusky, R. A., and Ingman, S. R. "The Pros, Cons and Pitfalls of 'Self-Help' Rehabilitation Programs," *Behavior Science and Medicine,* 13A (January 1979), pp. 113–121.

Lynd, H. M. *On Shame and the Search for Identity.* New York: Science Editions, 1961.

Madara, E. J. "A Comprehensive Systems Approach to Promoting Mutual Aid Self-Help Groups: The New Jersey Self-Help Clearinghouse Model," *Journal of Voluntary Action Research,* 15 (April–June 1986), pp. 57–63.

———. "The Self-Help Clearinghouse Operation: Tapping the Resource Development Potential of I & R Services," *Information and Referral: The Journal of the Alliance of Information and Referral Systems,* 7 (Summer 1985), pp. 42–58.

Madara, E. J., and Grish, C. "Finding Out More about How Self-Help Groups Help," *Network* (New Jersey Self-Help Clearinghouse), 1 (August–September 1981), p. 2.

Madara, E. J., and Meese, A. *The Self-Help Sourcebook: Finding and Forming Mutual and Self-Help Groups.* Denville: New Jersey Self-Help Clearinghouse, 1986.

Maguire, L. "The Interface of Social Workers with Personal Networks," *Social Work with Groups,* 3 (Fall 1980), pp. 39–49.

———. "Natural Helping Networks and Self-Help Groups," in M. Nobel, ed., *Primary Prevention in Mental Health and Social Work.* New York: Council on Social Work Education, 1981.

———. *Understanding Social Networks.* Beverly Hills, Calif.: Sage Publications, 1983.

Mallory, L. *Leading Self-Help Groups.* New York: Family Service America, 1984.

Mannino, F. V. "Developing Consultation Relationships with Community Agents," *Mental Hygiene,* 48 (July 1964), pp. 356–362.

Mannino, F. V., and Shore, M. "The Effects of Consultation: A Review of the Empirical Studies," *American Journal of Community Psychology,* 3 (February 1975), pp. 1–21.

Marieskind, H. I. "Women's Self-Help Groups," in A. Gartner and F. Riessman, eds., *The Self-Help Revolution.* New York: Human Sciences Press, 1984.

Martin, G., and Pear, J. *Behavior Modification: What It Is and How to Do It.* 2nd ed. Englewood Cliffs, N.J.: Prentice-Hall, 1983.

Maxwell, M. A. "Alcoholics Anonymous: An Interpretation," in D. J. Pittman and C. R. Snyder, eds., *Society, Culture, and Drinking Patterns.* New York: John Wiley & Sons, 1962.

———. "Contemporary Utilization of Professional Help by Members of Alcoholics Anonymous," *Annals of the New York Academy of Science,* 273 (1976), pp. 436–441.

McKinlay, J. B. "Social Networks, Lay Consultation, and Help-Seeking Behavior," *Social Forces,* 5 (December 1973), pp. 275–292.

McLanahan, S. S.; Wedemeyer, N. V.; and Adelberg, T. "Network Structure, Social Support, and Psychological Well-Being in the Single-Parent Family," *Journal of Marriage and the Family,* 43 (August 1981), pp. 601–612.

Medvene, L. J. "An Organizational Theory of Self-Help Groups," *Social Policy,* 15 (Winter 1985), pp. 35–37.

———. "Self-Help and Professional Collaboration," *Social Policy,* 15 (Winter 1985), pp. 15–18.

Meichenbaum, D. *Cognitive Behavior Modification: An Integrative Approach.* New York: Plenum Publishing Corp., 1977.

Mellor, M. J.; Rzetelny, H.; and Hudis, I. "Self-Help Groups for Caregivers of the Aged," in *Strengthening Informal Supports for the Aging: Theory, Practice and Policy Implications.* New York: Natural Supports Program, Community Service Society, 1981.

Mended Hearts. *Heart to Heart.* Boston: Mended Hearts, undated.

Merton, R. K., and Rossi, A. K. "Contributions to the Theory of Reference Group Behavior," in H. H. Hyman and E. Singer, eds., *Readings in Reference Group Theory and Research.* New York: Free Press, 1968.

Miller, G. P. "Professionals' Knowledge of, Referrals to, Utilization of, Linkages with, and Attitudes Toward Self-Help Groups." Unpublished Ph.D. thesis, University of Michigan, 1983.

Miller, L. K. *Principles of Everyday Behavior Analysis.* 2nd. ed. Monterey, Calif.: Brooks/Cole, 1979.

Miller, P., and Ingham, J. "Friends, Confidants and Symptoms," *Social Psychiatry,* 11 (April 1976), pp. 51–58.

Miller, W. C. *The Addictive Behaviors: Alcoholism, Drug Abuse, Smoking, and Obesity*. Oxford, England: Pergamon Press, 1980.

Minde, K., et al. "Self-Help Groups in a Premature Nursery—Evaluation." *Journal of Pediatrics*, 96, No. 5 (1980), pp. 933–940.

Mindel, C. H., and Wright, R., Jr. "The Use of Social Services by Black and White Elderly: The Role of Social Support Systems," *Journal of Gerontological Social Work*, 4 (Spring–Summer 1982), pp. 107–125.

Mischel, W. "A Cognitive-Social Learning Approach to Assessment," in T. V. Merluzzi, C. R. Glass, and M. Genest, eds., *Cognitive Assessment*. New York: Guilford Press, 1981.

Mitchell, J. C. (ed.). *Social Networks in Urban Situations*. Manchester, England: University of Manchester Press, 1969.

Mitchell, R., and Hurley, D. "Collaboration with Natural Helping Networks," *Community Mental Health Journal*, 16 (1980), pp. 277–298.

Mitchell, R. E., and Trickett, E. J. "Task Force Report: Social Networks as Mediators of Social Support," *Community Mental Health Journal*, 16 (Spring 1980), pp. 27–44.

Moroney, R. *Families, Social Services, and Social Policy: The Issue of Shared Responsibility*, Publication No. [ADM] 80-846. Washington, D. C.: U. S. Government Printing Office, 1980

Mowrer, O. H. "The Mental Health Professions and Mutual Help Programs: Co-optation or Cooperation," in A. Gartner and F. Riessman, eds., *The Self-Help Revolution*. New York: Human Sciences Press, 1984.

Mowrer, O. H., and Vattano, A. J. "Integrity Groups: A Context for Growth in Honesty, Responsibility, and Involvement," *Journal of Applied Behavioral Science*, 12 (July–August–September 1976), pp. 419–431.

Mueller, D. "Social Networks: A Promising Direction for Research on the Relationship of the Social Environment to Psychiatric Disorder," *Social Science and Medicine*, 14A (March 1980), pp. 147–161.

Munoz, R. F., et al. *Social and Psychological Research in Community Settings: Designing and Conducting Programs for Social and Personal Well-Being*. San Francisco: Jossey-Bass, 1979.

Naparstek, A.; Biegel, D.; and Spiro, H. *Neighborhood Networks for Humane Mental Health Care*. New York: Plenum Publishing Corp., 1982.

Narcotics Anonymous. *Group*. I.P. No. 2. Van Nuys, Calif.: NA World Service, 1976.

———. *Misconceptions*. Van Nuys, Calif.: NA World Service, undated.

———. *White Book*. Van Nuys, Calif.: NA World Service, 1976.

National Alliance for the Mentally Ill (Washington, D.C.). *NAMI Newsletter*, 6 and 7 (1985 and 1986), pp. 3 and 6, respectively.

National Foundation for Ileitis and Colitis (New York, N.Y.). "Prose from John Wengraf," *Newsletter* (January 1985).

National Gay Task Force. *Twenty Questions about Homosexuality.* New York: National Gay Task Force, undated. (Now National Gay and Lesbian Task Force, Washington, D.C.)

National Institute on Aging. *Toward an Independent Old Age: A National Plan for Research on Aging.* Washington, D.C.: U.S. Government Printing Office, 1982.

National Institute on Alcohol Abuse and Alcoholism. "Growth of AA, Treatment Cited Over Past 15 Years." *NIAA Information and Feature Service,* IFS 104 (February 1, 1983), p. 2.

National Institute on Drug Abuse. *Manual for Setting Up Self-Help Groups of Ex-Narcotic Addicts.* DHHS Publication No. [ADM] 81-1087. Washington, D.C.: Department of Health & Human Services, 1981.

"National Plan for the Chronically Mentally Ill." Final Draft Report to the Secretary of Health and Human Services. Washington, D.C.: U.S. Government Printing Office, 1980.

Newsome, M. "Neighborhood Service Centers in the Black Community," *Social Work,* 18 (March 1973), pp. 50–54.

Nuckolls, K. B.; Cassel, J. C.; and Kaplan, B. H. "Psychosocial Assets, Life Crisis, and the Prognosis of Pregnancy," *American Journal of Epidemiology,* 95 (November 1972), pp. 431–441.

Nurco, D. N., and Mahofsky, A. "The Self-Help Movement and Narcotic Adults," *American Journal of Drug and Alcohol Abuse,* 8, No. 2 (1981), pp. 139–151.

Ogborne, A. C., and Claser, F. B. "Characteristics of Affiliates of Alcoholics Anonymous: A Review of the Literature," *Journal of Studies on Alcohol,* 42 (July 1981), pp. 661–675.

Oldham, D. "Compulsive Gamblers," *Sociological Review,* 26 (1978), pp. 327–371.

O'Leary, M., et al. "Differential Alcohol Use Patterns and Personality Traits among Three Alcoholics Anonymous Attendance Level Groups: Further Considerations of the Affiliation Profile," *U.S. Journal of Drug and Alcohol Dependence,* 5 (1980), pp. 135–144.

Omark, R. C. "The Dilemma of Membership in Recovery, Inc., A Self-Help Ex-Mental Patients' Organization," *Psychological Reports,* 44 (June 1979), pp. 1119–1125.

Pancoast, D. L., and Chapman, N. J. "Roles for Informal Helpers in the Delivery of Human Services," in B. H. Gottlieb, ed., *Social Support Strategies.* Beverly Hills, Calif.: Sage Publications, 1983.

Pancoast, D. L.; Parker, P.; and Froland, C. (eds.). *Rediscovering Self-Help.* Beverly Hills, Calif.: Sage Publications, 1983.

Parents Anonymous. *Chapter Development Manual.* Redondo Beach, Calif.: Parents Anonymous, 1974.

Parents Without Partners. *The Single Parent.* Washington, D. C.: PWP, 1967.

Pattison, E. M. "Clinical Social Systems Intervention," *Psychiatry Digest*, 38 (April 1977), pp. 25–33.

Pattison, E. M., et al. "Social Network Mediation of Anxiety," *Psychiatric Annals*, 9 (September 1979), pp. 56–67.

Peharik, G., "Follow-Up Adjustment of Outpatient Dropouts," *American Journal of Orthopsychiatry*, 53 (July 1983), pp. 501–511.

Percy, W. *Lost in the Cosmos: The Last Self-Help Book*. New York: Farrar, Straus & Giroux, 1983.

Perlman, H. H. "Intake and Some Role Considerations," *Social Casework*, 41 (April 1960), pp. 171–177.

Perrow, C. *Organizational Analysis: A Sociological View*. Belmont, Calif.: Wadsworth Publishing Co., 1970.

Perrucci, R., and Targ, D. *Mental Patients and Social Networks*. Boston: Auburn House, 1982.

Pettigrew, T. F. "Social Evaluation Theory: Convergences and Applications," in D. Levine, ed., *Proceedings: Nebraska Symposium on Motivation*, Vol. 15, Lincoln: University of Nebraska Press, 1967.

Pilsuk, M., and Froland, C. "Kinship, Social Networks, Social Support and Health," *Social Science and Medicine*, 12B (October 1978), pp. 213–228.

Pilsuk, M., and Minkler, M. "Supportive Networks: Life Ties for the Elderly," *Journal of Social Issues*, 36, No. 2 (1980), pp. 95–116.

Pilsuk, M., and Parks, S. H. "The Place of Network Analysis in the Study of Supportive Social Associations, *Basic and Applied Social Psychology*, 2 (April–May–June 1981), pp. 121–135.

———. "Structural Dimensions of Social Support Groups," *Journal of Psychology*, 106 (November 1980), pp. 121–135.

Pittman, D. J., and Snyder, C. R. "Responsive Movements and Systems of Control," in Pittman and Snyder, eds., *Society, Culture and Drinking Patterns*. New York: John Wiley & Sons, 1962.

Platman, S. R. "The Chronically Mentally Ill: Sharing the Burden with the Community," in B. H. Gottlieb, ed., *Social Support Strategies*. Beverly Hills, Calif.: Sage Publications, 1983.

Plog, S. C., and Ahmed, P. I. (eds.). *Principles and Techniques of Mental Health Consultation*. New York: Plenum Publishing Corp., 1977.

Polich, J. M.; Armor, D. J.; and Braiker, H. B. *The Course of Alcoholism: Four Years After Treatment*. Santa Monica, Calif.: Rand Corp., 1980.

Politser, P. E., and Pattison, E. M. "Mental Health Functions of Community Groups," *Group*, 10 (1979), pp. 19–26.

———. "Social Climates in Community Groups: Toward a Taxonomy," *Community Mental Health Journal*, 16 (Fall 1980), pp. 187–200.

Powell, T. J. "Comparisons Between Self-Help Groups and Professional Services," *Social Casework: The Journal of Contemporary Social Work*, 60 (November 1979), pp. 561–565.

———. "Constructive 'Action' in the Treatment of Compulsive Gamblers," *National Council on Compulsive Gambling Newsletter*, 1 (December 1982), p. 5.

———. "Impact of Social Networks on Help-Seeking Behavior," *Social Work*, 26 (July 1981), pp. 335–337.

———. "Improving the Effectiveness of Self-Help," *Social Policy*, 16 (Fall 1985), pp. 22–29.

———. "Interpreting Parents Anonymous as a Source of Help for Those with Child Abuse Problems," *Child Welfare*, 58 (February 1979).

———. "The Use of Self-Help Groups as Supportive Reference Communities," *American Journal of Orthopsychiatry*, 45 (October 1975), pp. 756–764.

Powell, T. J., and Miller, G. P. "Self-Help Groups as a Source of Support for the Chronically Mentally Ill," in H. Fishman, ed., *Creativity and Innovation*. Davis, Calif.: Pyramid Systems, 1982.

Premack, D. "Reinforcement Theory," in D. Levine, ed., *Proceedings: Nebraska Symposium on Motivation, 1965*. Vol. 13. Lincoln: University of Nebraska Press, 1965.

"Presentation by Three Compulsive Gamblers," in P. A. Carone et al., eds., *Addictive Disorders Update*. New York: Human Sciences Press, 1982.

President's Commission on Mental Health. *Report to the President*. Vol 1. Washington, D.C.: U.S. Government Printing Office, 1978.

———. "Task Panel on Community Support Systems." *Report to the President*. Vol. 2. (Appendix.) Washington, D.C.: U.S. Government Printing Office, 1978.

R., R. "All at Sea." *A. A. Grapevine* (New York), October 1980.

Rafael, B. "Preventive Intervention with the Recently Bereaved," *Archives of General Psychiatry*, 34 (December 1977), pp. 1450–1452.

Raiff, N. R. "Self-Help Participation and Quality of Life: A Study of the Staff of Recovery, Inc." *Prevention in Human Services*, 1 (Spring 1982), pp. 79–89.

Rappaport, J., et al. "Collaborative Research with a Mutual-Help Organization," *Social Policy*, 15 (Winter 1985), pp. 12–24.

Regier, D. A.; Goldberg, I. D.; and Taube, C. A. "The De Facto US Mental Health Services System," *Archives of General Psychiatry*, 35 (June 1978), pp. 685–693.

Regier, D. A., et al. "The NIMH Epidemiologic Catchment Area Program," *Archives of General Psychiatry*, 41 (October 1984), pp. 934–941.

"Returning the Mentally Disabled to the Community: Government Needs to Do More." Report to the Congress by the Comptroller General of the United States. Washington, D.C.: U.S. Government Printing Office, 1977.

Richardson, A., and Goodman, M. *Self-Help and Social Care.* London, England: Policy Studies, 1983.

Riessman, F. "The 'Helper' Therapy Principle," *Social Work,* 10 (April 1965), pp. 27–32.

———. "New Dimensions in Self-Help," *Social Policy,* 15 (Winter 1985), pp. 2–4.

———. "The Self-Help Ethos," *Social Policy,* 13 (Summer 1982), p. 1.

Robins, L. N., et al. "Lifetime Prevalence of Specific Psychiatric Disorders in Three Sites," *Archives of General Psychiatry,* 41 (October 1984), pp. 949–958.

Robinson, D. *Talking Out of Alcoholism: The Self-Help Process of Alcoholics Anonymous.* London, England: Croom Helm, 1979.

Robinson, D., and Henry, S. *Self-Help and Health: Mutual Aid for Modern Problems.* London, England: Martin Robinson, 1977.

Robinson, D., and Robinson, Y. *From Self-Help to Health.* London, England: Concord Books, 1979.

Rodolfa, E., and Hungerford, L. "Self-Help Groups: A Referral Source for Professional Therapists," *Professional Psychology,* 13 (1982), pp. 345–353.

Rosen, A. "Psychotherapy and Alcoholics Anonymous: Can They Be Coordinated?" *Bulletin of the Menninger Clinic,* 45 (May 1981), pp. 229–246.

Rosengren, W. "Structure, Policy, and Style: Strategies of Organizational Control," *Administrative Science Quarterly,* 12 (March 1967), pp. 140–164.

Rosenthal, R. "Assessing the Statistical and Social Importance of the Effects of Psychotherapy," *Journal of Consulting and Clinical Psychology,* 51 (1983), pp. 4–13.

Roy, C. A., and Atcherson, E. "Peer Support for Renal Patients: The Patient Visitor Program," *Health and Social Work,* 8 (Winter 1983), pp. 52–56.

Sagarin, E. *Odd Man In: Societies of Deviants in America.* New York: Quadrangle, 1969.

Sakber, E. J.; Beery, W. L.; and Jackson, E. J. R. "The Role of the Health Facilitator in Community Health Education," *Journal of Community Health,* 2 (1976), pp. 5–20.

Sanders, D. H. "Innovative Environments in the Community: A Life for Chronic Patients," *Schizophrenia Bulletin,* 6 (1972), pp. 49–59.

Sauerman, T. *Coming Out to Your Parents.* Los Angeles, Calif.: Parents and Friends of Lesbians and Gays, 1984.

Schachter, S. "Don't Sell Habit Breakers Short," *Psychology Today,* August 1982.

———. *The Psychology of Affiliation.* Stanford, Calif.: Stanford University Press, 1959.

————. "Recidivism and Self-Care of Obesity and Smoking," *American Psychologist,* 37 (April 1982), pp. 436–444.

Schmidt, R.; Scanlon, J. W.; and Bell, J. B. *Evaluability Assessment: Making Public Progams Work Better.* Washington, D.C.: Urban Institute, 1978.

Schofield, W. *Psychotherapy: The Purchase of Friendship.* Englewood Cliffs, N.J.: Prentice-Hall, 1964.

Schuckit, M. A. "Geriatric Alcoholism and Drug Abuse," *Gerontologist,* 17 (April 1977), pp. 168–174.

Schulberg, H. C. "Community Support Programs: Program Evaluation and Public Policy," *American Journal of Psychiatry,* 136 (November 1979), pp. 1433–1437.

Schulberg, H. C., and Bromet, E. "Strategies for Evaluating the Outcome of Community Services for the Chronically Mentally Ill," *American Journal of Psychiatry,* 138 (July 1981), pp. 930–935.

Schulberg, H. C., and Killilea, M. "Community Mental Health in Transition," in Schulberg and Killilea, eds., *The Modern Practice of Community Mental Health.* San Francisco: Jossey-Bass, 1982.

Seashore, S. E., et al. (eds.) *Assessing Organizational Change: A Guide to Methods, Measures, and Practices.* New York: John Wiley & Sons, 1983.

Sehnert, K. W. "A Course for Activated Patients," *Social Policy,* 8 (November 1977), pp. 40–46.

Sevitz, L. S., and Stunkard, A. "A Therapeutic Coalition for Obesity: Behavior Modification and Patient Self-Help," *American Journal of Psychiatry,* 131, No. 4 (1974), pp. 423–427.

Shapiro, D. A., and Shapiro, D. "Comparative Therapy Outcome Research: Methodological Implications of Meta-analysis," *Journal of Consulting and Clinical Psychology,* 51 (February 1983), pp. 42–53.

Shapiro, J. H. *Communities of the Alone: Working with Single Room Occupants in the City.* New York: Association Press, 1971.

————. "Dominant Leaders among Slum Hotel Residents," *American Journal of Orthopsychiatry,* 39 (July 1969), pp. 644–650.

Sheldon, D. M. "Self-Help in Mental Health?" *Journal of the Maine Medical Association,* 69 (July 1978).

Shimkin, D. B.; Shimkin, E. M.; and Frate, D. A. *The Extended Family in Black Societies.* The Hague, Netherlands: Mouton, 1978.

Silbert, M. H. "Delancey Street Foundation: A Process of Mutual Restitution," in A. Gartner and F. Riessman, eds., *The Self-Help Revolution.* New York: Human Sciences Press, 1984.

Silverman, P. R. "The Mental Health Consultant as a Linking Agent," in B. H. Gottlieb, ed., *Social Support Strategies.* Beverly Hills, Calif.: Sage Publications, 1983.

————. *Mutual Help Groups: A Guide for Mental Health Workers.* Rockville, Md.: National Institute of Mental Health, 1978.

———. *Mutual Help Groups: Organization and Development.* Beverly Hills, Calif.: Sage Publications, 1980.

———. "People Helping People: Beyond the Professional Model," in H. Schulberg and M. Killilea, eds., *The Modern Practice of Community Mental Health.* San Francisco: Jossey-Bass, 1982.

———. "Services for the Widowed During the Period of Bereavement," in *Social Work Practice.* New York: Columbia University Press, 1966.

———. "Services to the Widowed: First Steps in a Program of Preventive Intervention," *Community Mental Health Journal,* 1 (1967), pp. 37–44.

———. "The Widow as a Caregiver in a Program of Preventive Intervention with Other Widows," *Mental Hygiene,* 54 (1970), pp. 540–545.

Silverman, P. R., and Smith, D. " 'Helping' in Mutual Help Groups for the Physically Disabled," in A. Gartner and F. Riessman, eds., *The Self-Help Revolution.* New York: Human Sciences Press, 1984.

Smiles, S. *Self-Help, with Illustrations of Character, Conduct and Perseverance.* St. Louis, Mo.: Crawford & Co., undated.

Smith, J. C.; Glass, G. V.; and Miller, T. I. *The Benefits of Psychotherapy.* Baltimore, Md.: Johns Hopkins University Press, 1980.

Smyer, M. A. "The Differential Usage of Services by Impaired Elderly," *Journal of Gerontology,* 35 (March 1980), pp. 249–255.

Snow, D., and Gordon, J. "Social Network Analysis and Intervention with the Elderly," *Gerontologist,* 20 (August 1980), pp. 463–467.

Snowdon, J. "Self-Help Groups and Schizophrenia," *Australian and New Zealand Journal of Psychiatry,* 14 (1980), pp. 265–268.

Sokolovsky, J., and Cohen, C. "Toward a Resolution of Methodological Dilemmas in Network Mapping," *Schizophrenia Bulletin,* 7 (1981), pp. 109–116.

Sokolovsky, J., et al. "Personal Networks of Ex-mental Patients in a Manhattan SRO Hotel," *Human Organization,* 37 (1978), pp. 5–15.

Spiegel, D. "Self-Help and Mutual-Support Groups: A Synthesis of the Recent Literature," in D. E. Biegel and A. J. Naparstek, eds., *Community Support Systems and Mental Health.* New York: Springer Publishing Co., 1982.

Stein, L. I., and Test, M. A. "Community Treatment of the Young Adult Patient," in B. Pepper and H. Ryglewicz, eds., *New Directions for Mental Health Services: The Young Adult Chronic Patient.* Vol. 14. San Francisco: Jossey-Bass, 1982.

———. (eds.). *Alternatives to Mental Hospital Treatment.* New York: Plenum Publishing Corp., 1978.

Steinman, R., and Traunstein, D. "Redefining Deviance: The Self-Help Challenge in the Human Services," *Journal of Applied Behavioral Sciences,* 12 (July–August–September 1976), pp. 410–418.

Stevens, S. M. "Alcohol and World View: A Study of Passamaquoddy

Alcohol Use," *Journal of Studies on Alcohol*, 9, Supp. No. 9 (January 1981), pp. 122–142.

Stokes, B. "Self-Help in the Eighties," *Citizen Participation*, 3 (January–February 1982), pp. 5–6.

Strupp, H. H., and Hadley, S. W. "A Tripartite Model of Mental Health and Therapeutic Outcomes," *American Psychologist*, 32 (March 1977), pp. 187–196.

Stunkard, A. J. "The Success of TOPS, a Self-Help Group," *Postgraduate Medicine*, 18 (May 1972), pp. 143–147.

Stunkard, A. J., and Penick, S. "Behavior Modification in the Treatment of Obesity: The Problem of Maintaining Weight Loss," *Archives of General Psychiatry*, 36 (1979), pp. 801–806.

Swenson, C. "Social Networks, Mutual Aid, and the Life Model of Practice," in C. Germain, ed., *Social Work Practice: People and Environments*. New York: Columbia University Press, 1979.

Talbott, J. A. (ed.). *The Chronic Mentally Ill: Treatment, Programs, Systems*. New York: Human Sciences Press, 1981.

———. (ed.). *The Chronic Mental Patient*. Washington, D.C.: American Psychiatric Association, 1978.

———. (ed.). *The Chronic Mental Patient: Five Years Later*. New York: Grune & Stratton, 1984.

Tax, S. "Self-Help Groups: Thoughts on Public Policy," *Journal of Applied Behavioral Science*, 12 (July–August–September 1976), pp. 448–454.

Taylor, M. C. "Alcoholics Anonymous: How It Works, Recovery Processes in a Self-Help Group," *Dissertation Abstracts International*, 39 (1977), 7532A.

Tedeschi, J. T., and Lindskold, S. *Social Psychology: Interdependence, Interaction, and Influence*. New York: John Wiley & Sons, 1976.

Test, M. A., and Stein, L. I. "Practical Guidelines for the Community Treatment of Markedly Impaired Patients," *Community Mental Health Journal*, 12 (April 1976), pp. 72–82.

———. "Training in Community Living: A Follow-Up Look at a Gold-Award Program," *Hospital and Community Psychiatry*, 27 (March 1976), pp. 193–194.

Thomas, E. J. "Research and Service in Single-Case Experimentation: Conflicts and Choices," *Social Work Research and Abstracts*, 14 (Winter 1978), pp. 20–31.

Thompson, J. D. *Organizations in Action*. New York: McGraw-Hill Book Co., 1967.

Tietjen, A. M. "Integrating Formal and Informal Support Systems: The Swedish Experience," in J. Garbarino and S. H. Stocking, eds., *Protecting Children from Abuse and Neglect*. San Francisco: Jossey-Bass, 1980.

Toch, H. *The Social Psychology of Social Movements.* Indianapolis, Ind.: Bobbs-Merrill Co., 1965.

Todres, R. "Professional Attitudes, Awareness, and Use of Self-Help Groups," *Prevention in Human Services,* 1 (Spring 1982), pp. 91–98.

———. *Self-Help Groups: An Annotated Bibliography 1970–1982.* New York: National Self-Help Clearinghouse.

Tolsdorf, C. C. "Social Networks, Support, and Coping: An Explanatory Study," *Family Process,* 15 (1976), pp. 407–417.

Torrey, E. F. *Surviving Schizophrenia: A Family Manual.* New York: Harper & Row, 1983.

Toseland, R. W., and Hacker, L. "Self-Help Groups and Professional Involvement," *Social Work,* 27 (July 1982), pp. 341–347.

———. "Social Workers' Use of Self-Help Groups as a Resource for Clients," *Social Work,* 30 (May–June 1985), pp. 232–239.

Traunstein, D. M. "From Mutual-Aid Self-Help to Professional Service," *Social Casework: The Journal of Contemporary Social Work,* 65 (December 1984), pp. 622–627.

Trice, H. M., and Roman, P. M. "Delabeling, Relabeling, and Alcoholics Anonymous," *Social Problems,* 17 (June 1970), pp. 538–546.

———. "Sociopsychological Predictors of Affiliation with Alcoholics Anonymous," *Social Psychiatry,* 5 (January 1970), pp. 51–59.

Trimble, D. A. "A Guide to Network Therapies," *Connections,* 3 (1980), pp. 9–21.

Tripodi, T., and Harrington, J. "Uses of Time-Series Designs for Formative Program Evaluation," *Journal of Social Service Research,* 3 (Fall 1979), pp. 67–78.

Tuckman, B. W. "Developmental Sequence in Small Groups," *Psychological Bulletin,* 63, No. 6 (1965), pp. 655–664.

Turkat, D. "Social Networks: Theory and Practice," *Journal of Community Psychology,* 8 (April 1980), pp. 99–109.

Turkington, C. "Recovery, Inc., Joins the Mainstream," *APA Monitor* (March 1982).

Turner, J., and Ten Hoor, W. "The NIMH Community Support Program: Pilot Approach to a Needed Social Reform," *Schizophrenia Bulletin,* 4 (1978), pp. 319–348.

Vachon, M. L. S., et al. "A Controlled Study of Self-Help Intervention for Widows," *American Journal of Psychiatry,* 137 (November 1980), pp. 1380–1384.

Vallance, T. R., and D'Augelli, A. R. "The Professional as Developer of Natural Helping Systems: Conceptual, Organizational and Pragmatic Considerations," in B. H. Gottlieb, ed., *Social Support Strategies.* Beverly Hills, Calif.: Sage Publications, 1983.

Valle, R., and Mendoza, L. *The Elder Latino.* San Diego, Calif.: Campanile Press, 1978.

Valle, R., and Vega, W. (eds.). *Hispanic Natural Networks: Mental Health Promotion Perspectives.* Sacramento: State of California, 1980.

Vattano, A. J. "Power to the People: Self-Help Groups," *Social Work*, 17 (July 1972), pp. 7–15.

Veroff, J.; Kulka, R.; and Douvan, E. *Mental Health in America: Patterns in Help Seeking from 1957 to 1966.* New York: Basic Books, 1981.

Videka, L. "Psychosocial Adaptation in a Medical Self-Help Group," in M. A. Lieberman and L. D. Borman, eds., *Self-Help Groups for Coping with Crisis: Origins, Members, Processes, and Impact.* San Francisco: Jossey-Bass, 1979.

Videka-Sherman, L. "Coping with the Death of a Child: A Study Over Time," *American Journal of Orthopsychiatry*, 52 (October 1982), pp. 688–698.

———. "Effects of Participation in a Self-Help Group for Bereaved Parents: Compassionate Friends," *Prevention in Human Services*, 1 (1982), pp. 69–78.

Videka-Sherman, L., and Lieberman, M. "The Effects of Self-Help and Psychotherapy Intervention on Child Loss: The Limits of Recovery," *American Journal of Orthopsychiatry*, 55 (January 1985), pp. 70–82.

Vinokur-Kaplan, D. "The Relevance of Self-Help Groups to Social Work Education," *Contemporary Social Work Education*, 2, No. 2 (1978), pp. 79–86.

Volkman, R., and Cressey, D. "Differential Association and the Rehabilitation of Drug Addicts," *American Journal of Sociology*, 69 (1963), pp. 129–142.

W., G. "A. A. Friends Make Hard Times a Whole Lot Easier," *A. A. Grapevine* (New York, N.Y.), February 1984.

W., Lois. *Lois Remembers.* New York: Al-Anon Family Group Headquarters, 1979.

Wachtel, P. L. *Psychoanalysis and Behavior Therapy.* New York: Basic Books, 1977.

Walker, K. N.; MacBride, A.; and Vachon, M. H. S. "Social Support Networks and the Crisis of Bereavement," *Social Science and Medicine*, 11 (January 1977), pp. 35–41.

Wasow, M. *Coping with Schizophrenia.* Palo Alto, Calif.: Science & Behavior Books, 1982.

Weber, G. H., and Cohen, L. M. *Beliefs and Self-Help.* New York: Human Sciences Press, 1982.

Wechsler, H. "The Self-Help Organization in the Mental Health Field: Recovery, Inc., A Case Study," *Journal of Nervous and Mental Disease*, 130 (April 1960), pp. 297–314.

Weight Watchers International. *Promises.* Manhasset, N.Y.: Weight Watchers International, 1978.

Weiss, R. S. "Parents Without Partners as a Supplementary Community," *Marital Separation.* New York: Basic Books, 1975.

Wellman, B. "Applying Network Analysis to the Study of Support," in B. H. Gottlieb, ed., *Social Networks and Social Support.* Beverly Hills, Calif.: Sage Publications, 1981).

———. "Network Analysis: Some Basic Principles," in R. Collins, ed., *Sociological Theory 1983.* San Francisco: Jossey-Bass, 1983.

Wellman, B., and Leighton, B. "Networks, Neighborhoods, and Communities," *Urban Affairs Quarterly,* 15 (March 1979), pp. 363–390.

Wheat, P. *Hope for the Children: A Personal History of Parents Anonymous.* Minneapolis, Minn.: Winston Press, 1980.

Whitely, O. R. "Life with Alcoholics Anonymous: The Methodist Class Meeting as a Paradigm," *Journal of Studies on Alcohol,* 38 (May 1977), pp. 831–848.

Whittaker, J. K., and Garbarino, J. "Mutual Helping in Human Service Practice," in Whittaker and Garbarino, eds., *Social Support Networks: Informal Helping in the Human Services.* Hawthorne, N.Y.: Aldine Publishing Co., 1983.

Willen, M. L. "Parents Anonymous: The Professional's Role as Sponsor," in A. Gartner and F. Riessman, eds., *The Self-Help Revolution.* New York: Human Sciences Press, 1984.

Wilson, G. T. "Weight Control Treatments," in J. D. Matarazzo et al., eds., *Behavioral Health.* New York: John Wiley & Sons, 1984.

Withorn, A. "Help Ourselves: The Limits and Potential of Self-Help," *Social Policy,* 11, No. 3 (1980).

Wollert, R. W.; Barron, N.; and M., Bob. "Parents United of Oregon: A Self-Help Group for Sexually Abusive Families," *Prevention in Human Services,* 1 (Spring 1982), pp. 99–109.

Wollert, R. W.; Knight, B.; and Levy, L. H. "Make Today Count: A Collaborative Model for Professionals and Self-Help Groups," *Professional Psychology,* 1 (February 1980), pp. 130–138.

Wollert, R. W.; Levy, L. H.; and Knight, B. G. "Help-Giving in Behavioral Control and Stress Coping Self-Help Groups," *Small Group Behavior,* 13 (May 1982), pp. 204–218.

Yalom, I. *The Theory and Practice of Group Psychotherapy.* 2nd ed. New York: Basic Books, 1975.

Yoak, M., and Chesler, M. "Alternative Professional Roles in Health Care Delivery: Leadership Patterns in Self-Help Groups," *Journal of Applied Behavioral Science,* 21 (October–November–December 1985), pp. 427–444.

York, P.; York, D.; and Wachtel, T. *Toughlove.* Garden City, N.Y.: Doubleday & Co., 1982.

Zajonc, R. B. "Social Facilitation," in D. Cartwright and A. Zander, eds., *Group Dynamics.* 3rd ed. New York: Harper & Row, 1968.

Index